Skagen
Frederikshavn
Grenå
Aarhus
Helsingør
Frederiksværk
Hillerød
Hørsholm
Frederikssund
Holbæk
COPENHAGEN
Kalundborg
Roskilde
NORTHWESTERN ZEALAND
Sorø
Køge
Ringsted
Odense
Slagelse
Nyborg
FUNEN
Næstved
Faaborg
Svendborg
SOUTHERN ZEALAND AND THE ISLANDS
Stege
Rudkøbing
Nakskov
Nykøbing F.
Gedser
BORNHOLM
Denmark
BORNHOLM

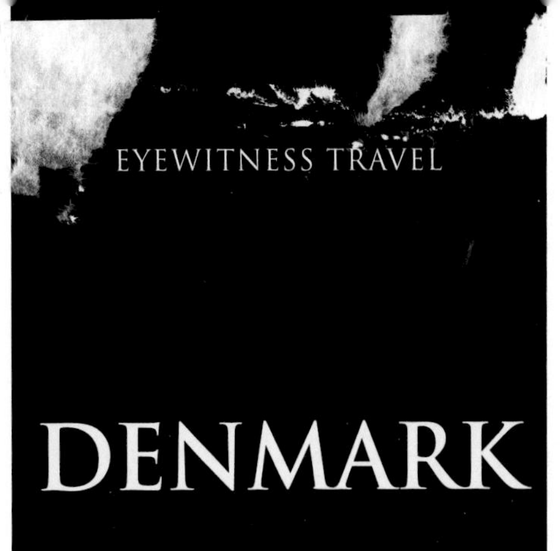
EYEWITNESS TRAVEL
DENMARK

EYEWITNESS TRAVEL
DENMARK
Main Contributors
Monika Witkowska and Joanna Hald
DK

LONDON, NEW YORK,
MELBOURNE, MUNICH AND DELHI
www.dk.com

Produced by Wydawnictwo Wiedza i Życie, Warsaw

Senior Graphic Designer Paweł Pasternak
Editors Maria Betlejewska, Joanna Egert-Romanowska
Authors Joanna Hald, Marek Pernal, Jakub Sito, Barbara Sudnik-Wójcikowska, Monika Witkowska

Cartographers Magdalena Polak, Olaf Rodowald, Jarosław Talacha
Photographers Dorota and Mariusz Jarymowiczowie
Illustrators Michał Burkiewicz, Paweł Marcza
Graphic Design Paweł Pasternak
DTP Elżbieta Dudzińska

For Dorling Kindersley
Translator Magda Hannay
Editor Matthew Tanner
Senior Dtp Designer Jason Little
Production Controller Rita Sinha

Printed in China

First published in the UK in 2005
by Dorling Kindersley Limited, 80 Strand, London WC2R 0RL, UK

15 16 17 18 10 9 8 7 6 5 4 3 2 1

Reprinted with revisions 2008, 2010, 2013, 2015

A CIP catalogue record is available from the British Library.

ISBN: 978-1-40937-056-7

Floors are referred to throughout in accordance with european usage; ie the "first floor" is the floor above ground level.

Front cover main image: Beach hut on the foreshore of Marstal in Ærø island, Funen

◀ Glim Kirke, a church near Roskilde set amongst fields of wildflowers

Contents

Altar from Vor Frelsers Kirke, Copenhagen

Introducing Denmark

Nytorv, a colourful and bustling square in central Copenhagen

Copenhagen Area by Area

The Little Dancer by Edgar Degas, housed at Ny Carlsberg Glyptotek, Copenhagen

Denmark Region by Region

Svaneke's yacht marina

Travellers' Needs

Survival Guide

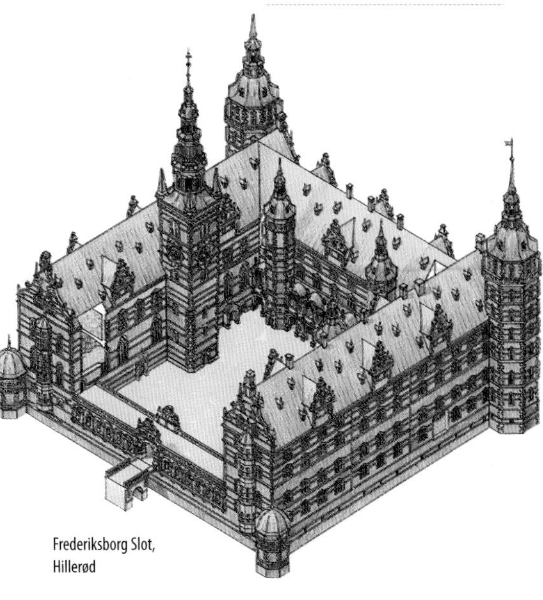

Frederiksborg Slot, Hillerød

HOW TO USE THIS GUIDE

This guide will help you get the most out of a visit to Denmark. The first section, *Introducing Denmark,* provides information about the country's geographic location, its history and culture. The sections devoted to the capital and other large cities, as well as to individual regions, describe the major sights and visitor attractions. Information on accommodation and restaurants can be found in the *Travellers' Needs* section. The *Survival Guide* provides practical tips on everything a visitor may need to know, from money and language to getting around and seeking medical care.

Copenhagen

This section has been divided into three parts, each devoted to a separate part of the city. Sights outside the capital's centre are described in the *Further Afield* section. All sights are numbered and plotted on the area map. Detailed information for each sight is given in numerical order.

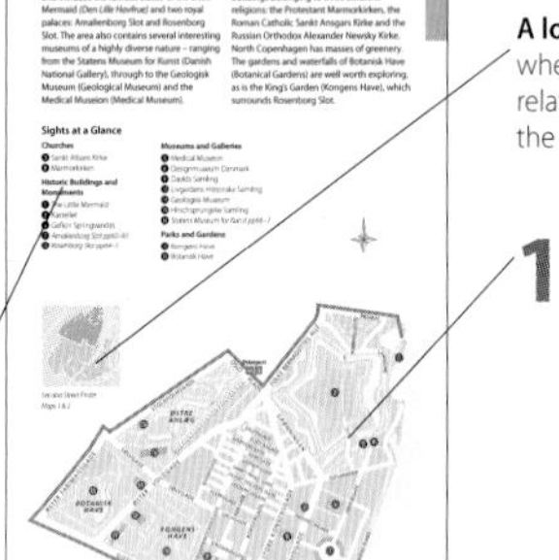

Pages referring to Copenhagen are marked in red.

A locator map shows where visitors are in relation to other areas of the city.

1 Area Map
For easy reference the sights are numbered and plotted on the area map, as well as on the main map of Copenhagen *(see pp112–15).*

Sights at a Glance lists the sights in an area by category: churches, museums and art galleries; streets and squares; parks and gardens.

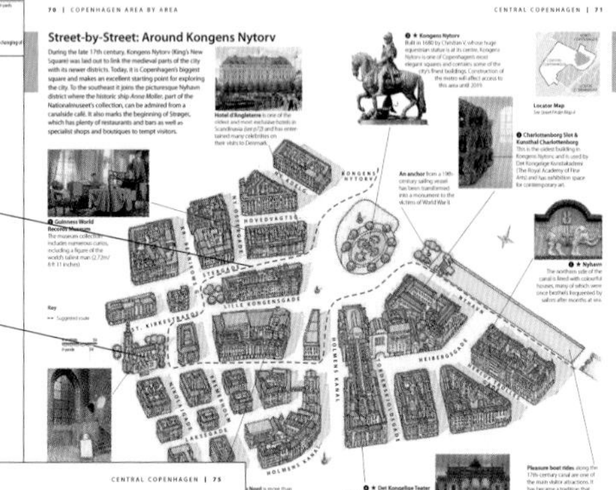

A suggested route for sightseeing is indicated by a dotted red line.

2 Street-by-Street Map
Provides a bird's-eye view of the town centre described in the section.

Star Sights indicate parts of buildings, historic sights, exhibits and monuments that no visitor should miss.

3 Detailed Information
All the major sights of Copenhagen are described individually. Practical information includes addresses, telephone numbers, the most convenient buses and trains, and opening hours.

Denmark Region by Region

In this guide Denmark is divided into seven regions, each of which has a separate section devoted to it. The most interesting cities, towns, villages and sights worth visiting are marked on each regional map.

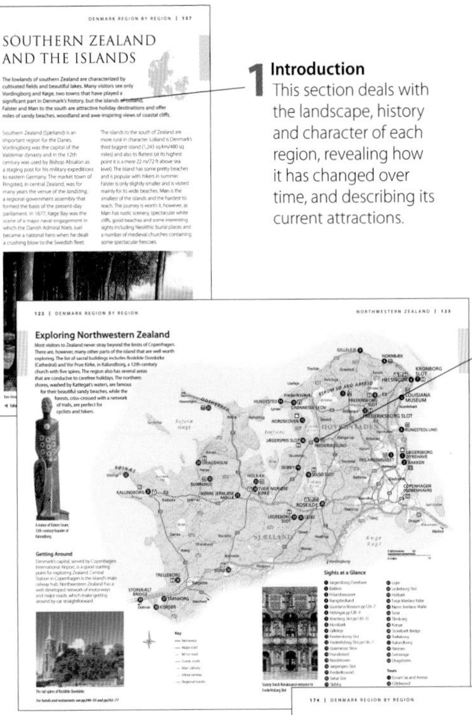

1 Introduction
This section deals with the landscape, history and character of each region, revealing how it has changed over time, and describing its current attractions.

2 Regional Map
The regional map shows the main road network and the overall topography of the region. All sights are numbered, and there is also information on public transport and getting around.

Boxes highlight interesting aspects or people associated with a sight.

Each region of Denmark can be found by using the colour code. The colours are explained on the inside front cover.

3 Detailed Information
Towns, villages and major tourist attractions are listed in numerical order, corresponding with the area map. Each entry contains information on important sights.

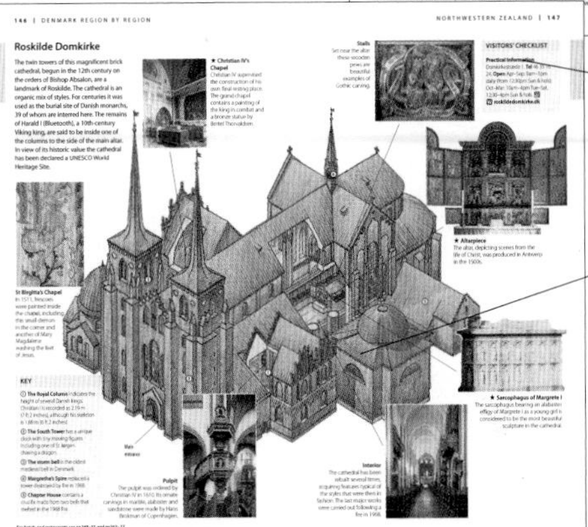

The Visitors' Checklist provides practical information to help plan your visit.

4 Major Sights
At least two pages are devoted to each major sight. Historic buildings are dissected to reveal their interiors. Major towns and town centres have street maps with the principal sights marked on them.

INTRODUCING DENMARK

DISCOVERING DENMARK

The following itineraries have been designed to take in as many of Denmark's sights as possible, without exhausting the visitor. First is a two-day tour of Copenhagen, Denmark's capital, with ideas to extend the stay with trips to *Roskilde* or Helsingør. There is a three-day tour of Bornholm, the "sunshine island" with its own distinct character and history in the Baltic Sea. For those able to extend their visit to Copenhagen and travel further afield, there are suggestions for a week-long gourmet tasting tour of Zealand and its regional specialities; and ideas for making the most of three days in Jutland enjoying the region's rich artistic heritage. Finally, a one-week itinerary is designed to best explore the unique northerly landscapes of the Faroe Islands and Greenland. Choose one or two to follow, or simply take inspiration in combining your favourite aspects of all the tours.

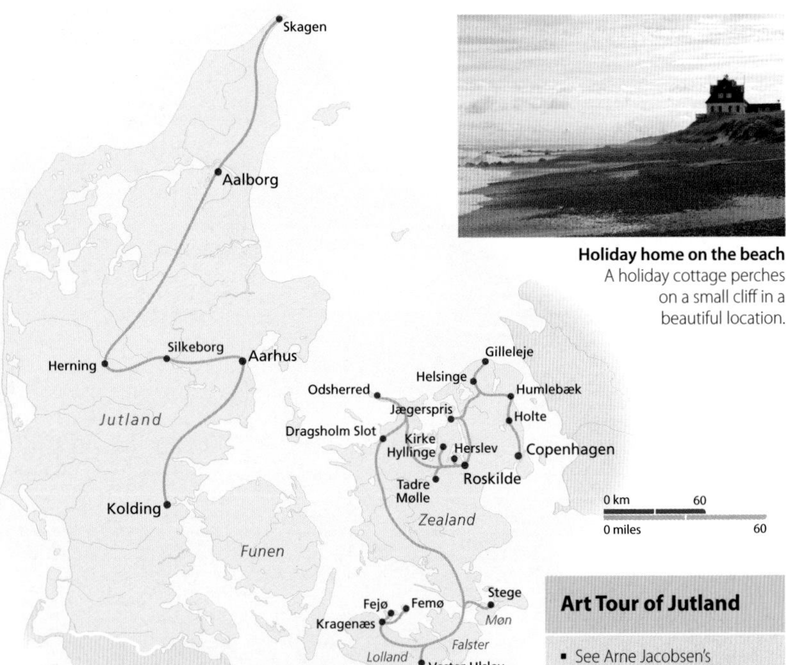

Holiday home on the beach
A holiday cottage perches on a small cliff in a beautiful location.

Gourmet Tour of Zealand, Lolland and Møn

- Sample the culinary treats of Copenhagen's gourmet marketplace, TorvehallerneKBH.
- Enjoy dining in the idyllic setting of Søllerød Kro, one of Denmark's top restaurants.
- Take a guided tour of ice cream maker Hansens Is near Jægerspris.
- Try modern-day Viking food at Restaurant Snekken, next door to the Vikingeskibsmuseet.
- Sample freshly smoked fish from the Arne Jacobsen-designed smokehouse in Havnebyen on the Odsherred peninsula.
- Taste regional specialities *bidesild* (pickled herrings) and wheat cakes on the island of Møn.

Art Tour of Jutland

- See Arne Jacobsen's groundbreaking Kubeflex summerhouse outside Trapholt museum, Kolding.
- Stimulate your senses on the skywalk "Your Rainbow Panorama" at ARoS Kunstmuseum in Aarhus.
- Visit the Museum Jorn in Silkeborg to see works by Denmark's *enfant terrible*, Asger Jorn.
- Get inside the fantastic imaginations of CoBrA artists at HEART Herning Museum of Contemporary Art.
- Appreciate the unique quality of light in Skagen.

◀ A street scene as depicted by an oil painter from the Danish School

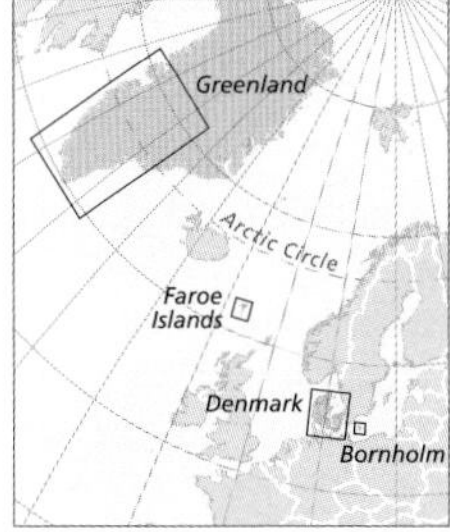

Locator Map

Cruise boat, Greenland
A boat trip is an essential part of a trip to Greenland. Trips can include wildlife-watching, including puffin colonies and whales, and also take in Greenland's monumental icebergs.

Key

- Art tour of Jutland
- Gourmet tour of Zealand, Lolland and Møn
- A Week in Greenland and the Faroes
- Three Days on Bornholm

Faroe Islands

Saksun
Eysturoy
Mykines
Sørvágur
Tórshavn
Sandoy
Atlantic Ocean
0 km 20
0 miles 20
Suðuroy

A Week in Greenland and the Faroes

- Sample puffin, musk ox and other regional specialities in one of Tørshavn's innovative gourmet restaurants.
- Enjoy the breathtaking views from atop Slættaratindur peak on Eysturoy, the highest point on the Faroes.
- Take a sailing trip to Mykines island to watch the puffins.
- Visit the Norse church ruins on Hvalsey Fjord, south Greenland.
- Cross the Arctic Circle and witness climate changes first-hand on the edge of the Greenland Ice Cap.
- Experience huge whales and monumental icebergs in Disko Bay.

Three Days on Bornholm

- Enjoy a herring lunch fresh from the smokehouse in Hasle.
- Explore the ruins of Hammerhus Slot.
- Visit the picturesque villages of Gudjem and Svaneke, on Bornholm's east coast.
- Visit Bornholm's biggest round church in Østerlars – and its smallest, in Nyker.
- Enjoy a pub lunch (or dinner) on the main square in Bornholm's award-winning brewery, Svaneke Bryghus.

Bornholm

Hammershus Slot
Sandvig
Allinge
Gudhjem
Hasle
Østerlars Kirke
Svaneke
Nyker
Rønne
Bornholm
Aakirkeby
Nexø
0 km 4
0 miles 4

Herring smokehouse at a museum in Hasle, Bornholm
Diners enjoying produce from the Silderøgerierne Museum smokehouse with its distinctive white chimneys.

Two Days in Copenhagen

Denmark's capital combines old-fashioned charm with modern design and efficient transport networks.

- **Arriving** Kastrup Airport is 8 km (5 miles) southeast of the city on the island of Amager. Both the Metro and regional trains travel to the city centre in 15 minutes.

Day 1

Morning Follow in the footsteps of Peter the Great by racing up the unique spiral walkway of the **Rundetårn** *(p75)* and be rewarded with great views over the city. Then take a leisurely stroll through the Latin Quarter to the **Nationalmuseet** *(pp88–9)*; with limited time, focus perhaps on the prehistoric finds. Afterwards, cross Frederiksholms Kanal onto Slotsholmen, an island that's packed with museums, to check out **Christiansborg Slot** *(pp90–91)* current seat of Parliament with the remains of four other castles beneath. Highlights include the Great Hall and its royal tapestries and the Throne Room.

Afternoon If visiting between April and early September or in the month preceding Christmas, spend an afternoon enjoying the cafés and entertainment of **Tivoli Gardens** *(pp80–81)*; if your trip is out of season, then **Ny Carlsberg Glyptotek** *(pp82–3)* makes a worthy alternative.

The Royal Room of Christian IV's Rosenborg Slot, Copenhagen

The atmospheric ruins of Hammershus Slot, Bornholm

Day 2

Morning Begin day two by visiting **Rosenborg Slot** *(pp64–5)*, a magnificent Renaissance palace that guards the country's crown jewels in its basement. Stroll through the palace's green grounds, Kongens Have, into the elegant Frederiksstaden district, passing the Baroque dome of the **Marmorkirken** *(p62)* before reaching the grand **Amalienborg Palace** complex *(pp60–61)*; the museum is located in Christian VIII's palace. If time allows, walk up Amaliegade to **Kastellet** *(p58)*; the town's citadel is a pleasant park, and there are plenty of great cafés in the vicinity.

Afternoon After recharging over lunch, hit the shops on Europe's longest pedestrian street, Strøget, which opens out into Kongens Nytorv, a busy square with the pleasant canalside street, **Nyhavn** *(p72)* at the opposite side. Then give your feet a well-earned rest by taking a boat tour of the city's canals, including the chance to see the famous **Little Mermaid** statue *(p58)*. End your trip with an evening meal overlooking the canal in either Nyhavn or **Christianshavn** *(p92)*.

To extend your trip...

Spend a day in **Helsingør** *(pp128–9)*, the best location for **Kronborg Slot** *(pp130–31)* and **M/S Museet for Søfart** (the Danish Maritime Museum) or **Roskilde** *(pp144–7)*, with its Domkirke and Vikingeskibsmuseet.

Three Days on Bornholm

The island of Bornholm, out in the Baltic, has long been a popular holiday destination for Danes. Known for its round churches and traditional smokehouses, the northern coast has a rocky coastline while the southern end offers sandy beaches. Bornholm is great for touring by car, bus or bike.

- **Arriving** Take the train to Ystad in Sweden from Copenhagen's Central Train Station, then ferry to Rønne (travel time about 3 hours).
- **Transport** Bornholm has a good bus network, though a car is more practical. The more active could cycle.
- **Booking Ahead** Not necessary, though DSB sell combined tickets.

Day 1: Rønne to Allinge

Start the tour in **Rønne**, Bornholm's biggest town *(p226)*: Allow 1–2 hours to stroll around its squares and streets, including a visit to Bornholm Museum to brush up on local history before moving on to **Nyker** *(p226)*, and Bornholm's smallest round church. Enjoy a *sild* lunch in the old smokehouse in **Hasle** *(p226)*, a town centred around herring. Spend the afternoon in the north of the island exploring **Hammershus Slot** *(p224)*, 13th-century castle ruins perched precariously on a cliff.

For practical information on travelling around Denmark, *see pp296–305*

Spend the evening in **Allinge** and **Sandvig** *(p224)*, two pleasant seaside towns that merge into one. If time allows, check out Madsebakke Helleristninger, the bronze age rock paintings on the outskirts of Allinge; they are thought to be 4,000 years old.

Day 2: Gudhjem to Svaneke
Leave Allinge along the coastal road towards **Gudhjem** *(p230)*, stopping along the way to visit **Bornholms Museum** *(p226)*, showcasing local art in a modern building. Take an hour or two to explore the picturesque fishing village of Gudhjem, including the **Oluf Høst Museet** *(p230)*, eating lunch in one of the town's numerous cafés. Then, head a few miles inland to view Bornholm's largest round church, **Østerlars Kirke** *(p230)*, and the medieval exhibits and demonstrations at recreated medieval village **Middelaldercenter** *(p230)*. Round off the day in **Svaneke** *(p227)*, 14 km (9 miles) down the coast. This picturesque town offers many dining options, including Røgeriet *(p275)*, a casual smokehouse eatery.

Day 3: Nexø and Aakirkeby
On the final day of the tour explore the island's southern end, with the morning spent exploring Nexø, a busy working town where you can visit the town museum. After lunch, head west to **Aakirkeby** *(p227)*, and spend at least two hours at **NaturBornholm**, a state-of-the-art natural history museum on Aakirkeby's southern outskirts.

Anna Ancher Returning From Flower Picking (1902) by Michael Peter Ancher

Art Tour of Jutland

Jutland's artistic heritage is as rich and varied as its landscape. In the late 1800s, an artists' colony was formed around a fishing village at Denmark's northernmost tip; while in the 20th century, the artist Asger Jorn pushed artistic limits from his base in Silkeborg.

- **Duration** Three day tour; allow an extra day at the end to return home from Skagen.
- **Airports** Billund Airport is centrally located in the middle of Jutland.
- **Transport** This itinerary can be made by train, with direct rail connections to all destinations, or with a hire car.

Day 1: Modern Art and Design
Start in **Kolding** *(p201)*, checking out **Trapholt** *(p201)*, an excellent modern art and design museum that includes a large collection of Richard Mortensen works, a sculpture park and Arne Jacobsen's innovative Kubeflex summerhouse. From here, it's 98 km (60 miles) to **Aarhus** *(pp192–3)* north along Jutland's east coast. (The train takes 75 minutes). A 10-minute walk from the train station, the city's modern art museum, **ARoS** *(p192)*, is one of Europe's largest.

Day 2: The CoBrA Movement
After an early breakfast, make the one-hour journey to **Silkeborg** *(p191)* to learn more about the avant-garde CoBrA movement. South of the town centre, **Museum Jorn** *(p191)* houses Asger Jorn's collection, acquired from 1953–73.

Herning *(p191)*, some 37 km (22 miles) west of Silkeborg, is about 45 minutes away. On the eastern outskirts of town is Birk Centerpark, location of the fascinating **HEART Herning Museum of Contemporary Art** *(p191)* with work by artists of the CoBrA movement.

Day 3: The Skagen Painters
Start the day in Aalborg with a whistle-stop tour of **Kusten Museum of Modern Art Aalborg** *(p213)* before travelling the two-hour journey to the northernmost point of Denmark, Skagen to fully appreciate the "unique quality of light" that transformed this small fishing village into a major artists' colony in the late 1800s. At **Skagens Museum** *(p209)*, you can visit the studios of Michael Ancher and P.S. Krøyer and view many important works from the period.

Olafur Eliasson's *Your Rainbow Panorama* at ARoS Kunstmuseum, Aarhus

Gourmet Tour of Zealand, Lolland and Møn

Denmark is increasingly gaining a reputation for an organic, seasonal and healthy kitchen, and this tour kicks off in the markets and delis of Copenhagen before heading out to the region's farms and fishing villages.

- **Duration** One week.
- **Airports** Copenhagen Airport.
- **Booking ahead** Some of the restaurants, such as Søllerød Kro, definitely require reserving in advance, as do any guided tours.

Day 1: Copenhagen
Begin the tour in **TorvehallerneKBH** *(p104)*, a gourmet marketplace built as a replacement for the original green market that once stood on Israels Plads. If nothing takes your fancy, grab lunch on the go from the Økologiske Pølsemand – an organic hot dog stand next to Rundetaarn, then breathe in the exciting atmosphere in Kødbyen, the city's old meat-packing district that buzzes with trendy eateries. Round off the day in Nørrebro, with dinner in the restaurant of micro-brewery Nørrebro Bryghus or in one of the eateries on Jægersborggade.

Day 2: Humlebæk and Holte
Travel up the coast from Copenhagen to Krogerup Avlsgaard farm in **Humlebæk** *(pp123)*, where you can visit the farm shop of Aarstiderne, a supplier of organic fruit and vegetables to many Copenhagen residents. Browse, buy or simply enjoy the peaceful natural surroundings (open Fri–Sun only). The farm shop is located 200 m (125 miles) north of **Louisiana Museum** *(pp126–7)*, at Krogerupvej 3. Break for lunch in the art museum café. Afterwards, return southwards to Holte, for evening dining in one of Denmark's best restaurants, Søllerød Kro (advance booking is essential).

Day 3: Helsinge and Jægerspris
If you've timed it right, visit Fuglebjerggaard near Helsinge, an organic farm that opens on Saturdays. If you have time – or the farm is closed – visit the harbour at **Gilleleje** *(p132)*, an excellent place to sample fresh fish. Next, travel westwards to **Jægerspris** *(p139)* to visit Hornsherred Mejeri, home of Hansens Flødeis, an ice cream manufacturer that still uses traditional methods. The dairy arranges guided tours in summer; pre-booking is necessary.

Day 4: Roskilde and Lejre
Visit the harbour at **Roskilde** *(p144–5)*, home to the **Vikingeskibsmuseet** *(p145)* and the adjacent Restaurant Snekken, where the exhibits are brought to life with a modern interpretation of Viking food. After a hearty lunch, travel to the villages of Herslev and Kirke Hyllinge, home to the Herslev and Hornbeer micro-breweries respectively. Part of **Roskilde Museum** *(p144)*, the old water mill Tadre Mølle near Kirke Hvalsø produces flour using traditional methods.

Day 5: Odsherred
Head to Sjællands Odde on the **Odsherred** peninsula *(p155)* to see the smokehouse in Havnebyen, designed by Arne Jacobsen. The shop is open in the summer holidays. If you have already booked table, enjoy a veritable banquet in the stately surroundings of **Dragsholm Slot** *(p154)*.

Smørrebrød – a hearty Danish open sandwich on rye bread

Day 6: The Smålandshavet Archipelago
The two islands of **Fejø** and **Femø** *(p158)* are the largest islands in the Smålandshavet Archipelago; reached by ferry from Kragenæs on Lolland, just north of Bandholm. The boat takes 50 minutes to Femø, but stops at Fejø first. Both islands are famed for their fruit trees.

Day 7: Møn and Lolland
Stege *(p173)*, the largest town on the island of Møn is a great place for trying regional specialities such as *bidesild* (herring bites) and wheat cakes coated in cheese. A good lunch spot to find these delicacies is Kaj Kok in Landsled (on Klintevej between Stege and Elmelunde). Finally, head south through **Falster** *(pp170–71)*, and into **Lolland** *(pp163–70)*, to Vester Ulslev Vingaard, one of Denmark's few commercial vineyards, 14 km (8 miles) east of Rødby. The shop is open when the owner is home so call ahead to be sure.

TorvehallerneKBH, the modern covered market at Israels Plads, Copenhagen

For practical information on travelling around Denmark, *see pp296–305*

A Week in Greenland and the Faroes

Denmark's two northern territories have remote, harsh scenery in common, but the rocky, green terrain of the Faroes is very different in character from the unique frozen landscapes of Greenland. Combine both in a week-long tour of adventure and discovery.

- **Arriving** Several airlines make regular flights from Copenhagen to Vágur Airport on the Faroes; or take the 38-hour ferry from Hirtshals in North Jutland to Tørshavn, which runs twice weekly. Between the Faroes and Greenland, the most direct route is with a stopover in Reykjavik, Iceland: flights go to several airports in the territory.
- **Transport** A car is essential for touring the Faroes; you can take a car on the boat to Tørshavn or obtain a hire car from Vágur Airport. Travel around Greenland is more difficult, as the road network is inadequate; internal flights, public helicopters and ferries can all be used.
- **Booking ahead** Any internal flights, tours or world-renowned restaurants will need pre-booking.

Day 1: Streymoy island, Faroes

Start the tour in **Tørshavn** *(p240)*, exploring the Faroese capital, with modern areas as well as an old town. On the same island, head north to **Saksun** *(p240)*, a small settlement where the turf-roofed **Dúvugarðar Museum** *(p240)* puts island life in a historical perspective. Head back to Tørshavn for an evening meal in one of the town's innovative restaurants.

Day 2: Eysturoy Island, Faroes

Cross the bridge at Nesvik on Streymoy to tour the north-eastern section of **Eysturoy** *(p241)*, the second-largest of the Faroe Isles. Take in the views at the top of Slættaratindur peak, the highest point in the Faroes. Visit the Vermakelda natural springs south of Fuglafjørður, which are said to have healing properties; finally, be fascinated by the constant rocking motion of the two Rinkusteinar boulders, near Oyndarfjørður, which move as the sea ebbs around them.

Russell Glacier, on th edge of the Greenland Ice Cap

Day 3: Vágar and Mykines Islands, Faroes

Reach **Vágar** island *(p240)* via the sub-sea tunnel. On your way to Sørvágur, look out for the tall, pointy rock nicknamed "Trollukonufingur'" ("Troll Woman's Finger"). Leave the car behind in Sørvágur to sail to tiny **Mykines** *(p241)* to view the puffins. Overnight close to Vágar Airport for an early morning flight to Greenland.

Landed fishing boats in the harbour at Eysturoy, the Faroe Islands

Day 4: Qaqortoq, Greenland

Start your exploration of Greenland in the south of the territory in **Qaqortoq** *(p236)*, formerly Julianehåb, by choosing between visits to the Norse church ruins on Hvalsey Fjord, Uunartoq hot springs and the Upernaviarsuk agricultural research centre.

Day 5: Nuuk, Greenland

Spend a less exhausting day exploring Greenland's lively capital, **Nuuk** *(p236)*. Post a letter to Father Christmas at Nuuk Post Office, and learn more about Greenland's history in the **National Museum** on Hans Egedesvej *(p236)*.

Day 6: Kangerlussuaq, Greenland

Hit **Kangerlussuaq** *(p236)* and you've crossed over the Arctic Circle and into an icy, polar landscape. Take an excursion to Russell Glacier, on the edge of the Greenland Ice Cap, and/or Sugar Loaf Mountain (pre-book this via a private tour company).

Day 7: Ilulissat, Greenland

End the week in Greenland's frozen north, exploring Disko Bay, with views of immense ice-bergs and the UNESCO World Heritage site, Ilulissat Ice Fiord, where climate change becomes a tangible concept. If weather permits, take a whale-watching tour out into the bay. Check out too the house of polar explorer, Knud Rasmussen, the Museum of Hunting and Fishing or the Cold museum *(p237)*.

Putting Denmark on the Map

Denmark is situated between the North Sea to the west and the Baltic Sea to the southeast. Most of Denmark consists of Jutland, a peninsula that covers 29,766 sq km (11,493 sq miles). The rest of the country consists of some 400 islands, of which the largest are Bornholm, Funen and Zealand. Far to the north, Greenland and the Faroe Islands are self-governing overseas regions of Denmark.

Key

- Motorway
- Motorway under construction
- Major road
- Other road
- National border

Faroe Islands *(see p238)*

Streymoy
Borðoy
Eysturoy
Vágar
Tórshavn
Sandoy
Hirtshals
Suðuroy
0 km 15
0 miles 15

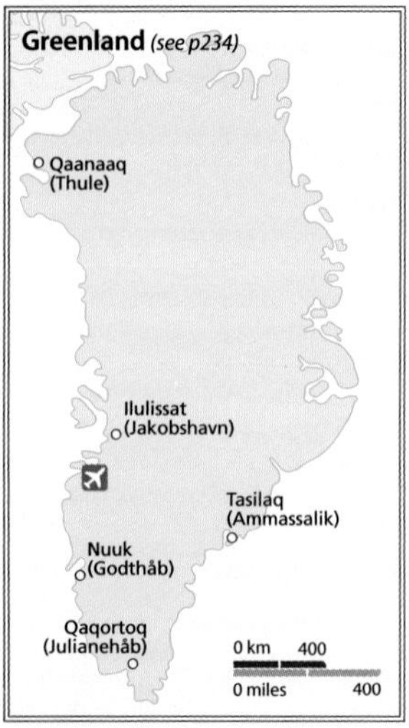

Greenland *(see p234)*

Qaanaaq (Thule)
Ilulissat (Jakobshavn)
Tasilaq (Ammassalik)
Nuuk (Godthåb)
Qaqortoq (Julianehåb)
0 km 400
0 miles 400

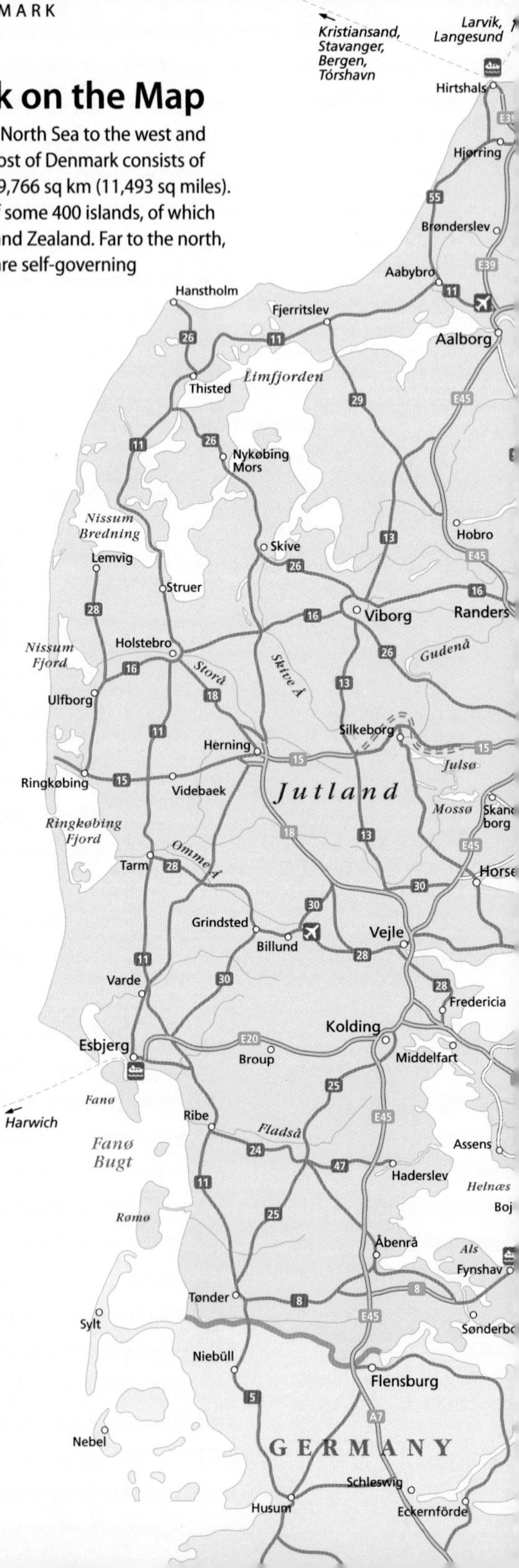

Kristiansand, Stavanger, Bergen, Tórshavn
Larvik, Langesund
Hirtshals
Hjørring
Brønderslev
Aabybro
Hanstholm
Fjerritslev
Aalborg
Thisted
Limfjorden
Nykøbing Mors
Nissum Bredning
Lemvig
Skive
Hobro
Struer
Viborg
Randers
Nissum Fjord
Holstebro
Storå
Skive Å
Gudenå
Ulfborg
Herning
Silkeborg
Julsø
Ringkøbing
Videbaek
Jutland
Ringkøbing Fjord
Mossø
Skanderborg
Omme Å
Tarm
Horsens
Grindsted
Billund
Vejle
Varde
Fredericia
Esbjerg
Kolding
Broup
Middelfart
Fanø
Harwich
Ribe
Fladså
Fanø Bugt
Assens
Haderslev
Helnæs
Rømø
Åbenrå
Als
Fynshav
Tønder
Sylt
Sønderborg
Niebüll
Flensburg
Nebel
GERMANY
Schleswig
Husum
Eckernförde

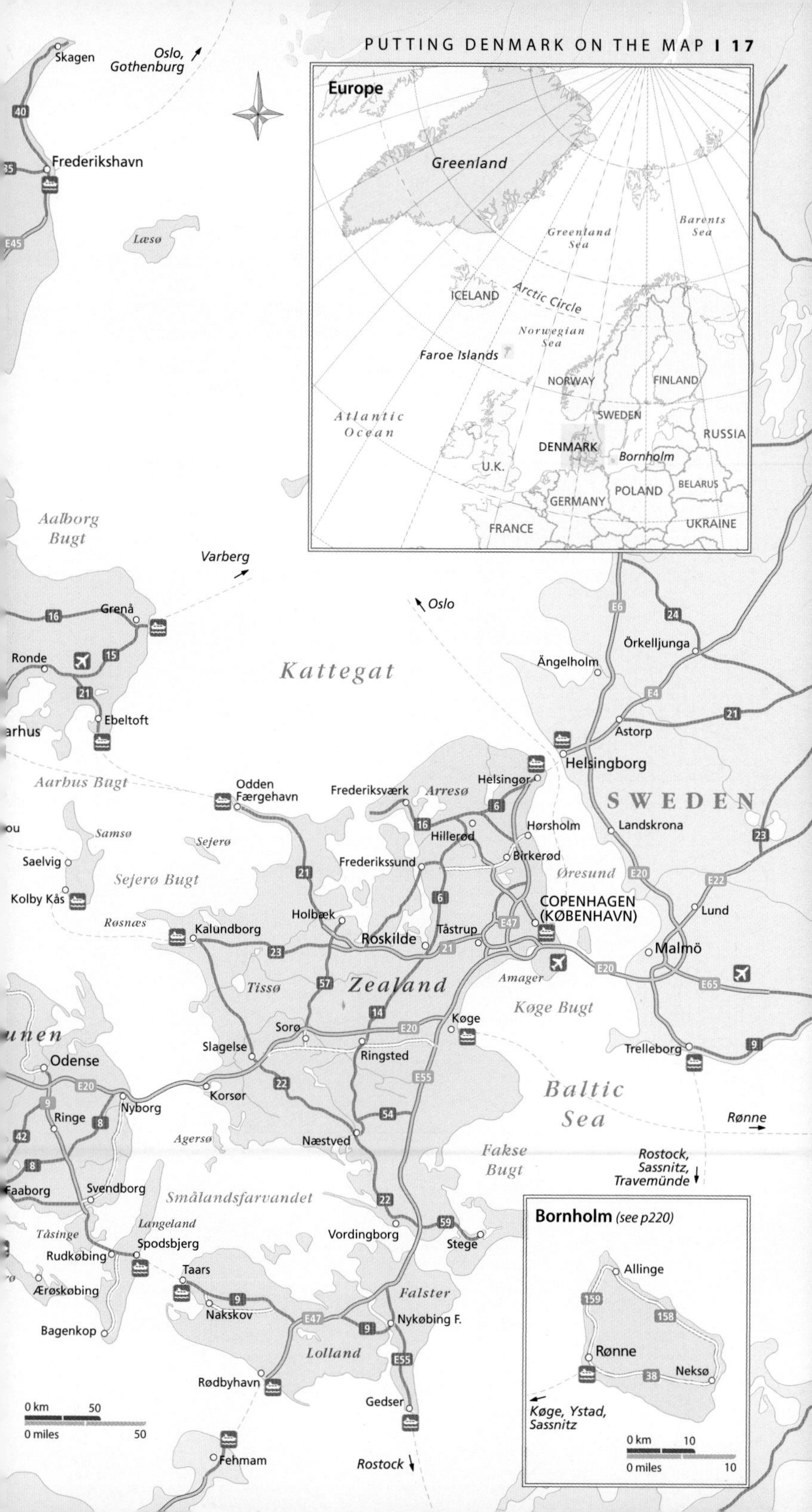
Skagen
Oslo, Gothenburg
Frederikshavn
Læsø
Europe
Greenland
Greenland Sea
Barents Sea
ICELAND
Arctic Circle
Norwegian Sea
Faroe Islands
NORWAY
FINLAND
SWEDEN
Atlantic Ocean
RUSSIA
DENMARK
Bornholm
U.K.
POLAND
BELARUS
GERMANY
FRANCE
UKRAINE
Aalborg Bugt
Varberg
Oslo
Grenå
Ronde
Örkelljunga
Ängelholm
Kattegat
Ebeltoft
Astorp
Helsingborg
Aarhus Bugt
Odden Færgehavn
Frederiksværk
Arresø
Helsingør
SWEDEN
Samsø
Sejerø
Hillerød
Hørsholm
Landskrona
Saelvig
Frederikssund
Birkerød
Øresund
Sejerø Bugt
Kolby Kås
Holbæk
COPENHAGEN (KØBENHAVN)
Lund
Røsnæs
Kalundborg
Roskilde
Tåstrup
Malmö
Amager
Tissø
Zealand
Køge Bugt
Køge
Sorø
Slagelse
Ringsted
Trelleborg
Odense
Korsør
Baltic Sea
Nyborg
Ringe
Rønne
Agersø
Næstved
Fakse Bugt
Rostock, Sassnitz, Travemünde
Svendborg
Smålandsfarvandet
Bornholm (see p220)
Langeland
Tåsinge
Vordingborg
Stege
Rudkøbing
Spodsbjerg
Allinge
Taars
Ærøskøbing
Falster
Nakskov
Nykøbing F.
Bagenkop
Lolland
Rønne
Neksø
Rødbyhavn
Gedser
Køge, Ystad, Sassnitz
0 km 50
0 miles 50
0 km 10
0 miles 10
Fehmam
Rostock

A PORTRAIT OF DENMARK

Denmark is most famous for its association with the Vikings and the writer Hans Christian Andersen. It has, of course, far more to offer visitors, including miles of sandy coastline, beautiful countryside and historic buildings. Copenhagen, the country's capital, has a rich cultural life and world-class museums.

Denmark, the southernmost and most continental of the Scandinavian countries, occupies over 480 islands, of which about 100 are inhabited. It acts as a bridge between mainland Europe and Scandinavia and is linked with the European continent by a narrow stretch of land, in the southern part of the Jutland peninsula, at the border with Germany.

Although not part of the Scandinavian peninsula, the Danes are linked with their northern neighbours by ties of common history and culture. There are also linguistic similarities and Danes can easily converse with people from Sweden or Norway.

The country has strong links with two autonomous regions: the Faroe Islands and Greenland, both of which are represented in the Danish parliament. Denmark exercises control over their banking, foreign policy and defence.

Denmark is a low-lying country with wide stretches of cornfields, moors and forests, and several national parks. In addition, it has vast sand dunes, fjords and long stretches of beach. The country's immaculate towns and villages, with colourful houses adorned with flowers, include many examples of half-timbered design.

Majestic castles, palaces and historic churches pepper the Danish landscape. There are also many Viking ruins, as well as older remains including ancient dolmens dating from the Stone Age.

Denmark is acknowledged to be a peaceful and liberal country, with a well-organized transport system and a comprehensive system of social welfare.

Picturesque houses along the bank of Nyhavn, Copenhagen

◀ Inscription and a Viking boat on a rune stone, Ringkøbing Fjord

Changing of the guards at Amalienborg Slot, Copenhagen

It has enviably low levels of crime and corruption. In rural areas it is not unusual to see stalls by the roadside on which local farmers have left their produce on sale unattended.

Traditions and Politics

The national flag – the Danneborg – is the world's oldest and the Danes demonstrate their patriotism by unfurling it during state and family celebrations. According to legend, the flag takes its origin from a banner, bearing a white cross on a red background, which was dropped from heaven to rally the Danish knights during a battle fought in present-day Estonia in the early 13th century.

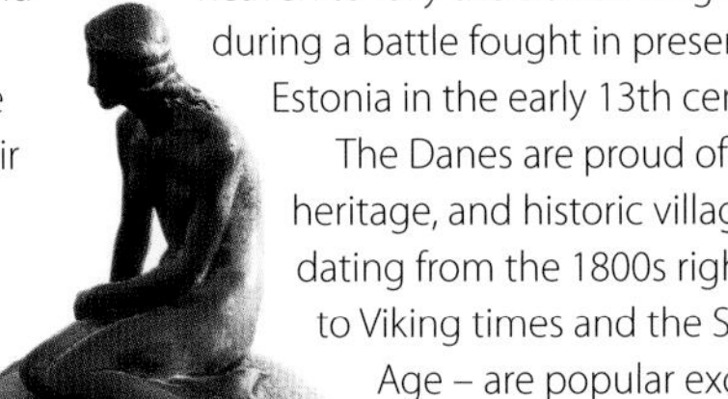

Statue of the Little Mermaid – a symbol of Copenhagen

The Danes are proud of their heritage, and historic villages – dating from the 1800s right back to Viking times and the Stone Age – are popular excursion destinations. Most Danes regard the fact that their monarchy is the oldest in the world with pride. The present queen, Margrethe II, has been on the throne since 1972 and is the first female monarch in Denmark since the 14th century. In addition to performing all ceremonial functions, this popular queen is credited with transforming the monarchy into a modern institution.

In political matters, the monarchy's influence is limited by the Danish constitution. The direction of national policy is determined in the Folketinget, the chamber in Christiansborg Slot, Copenhagen, where the country's 179 members of parliament sit. About a dozen parties are represented in parliament. Elections take place every four years and over 90 per cent of those eligible to vote turn out at election time. Most important national issues are decided by popular vote, however. Decisions made in referenda have included the Danes' approval of a constitutional amendment allowing a woman to inherit the throne in 1953 and, in 2000, the rejection of the euro.

Charming half-timbered house in Rønne, on the island of Bornholm

Society and Everyday Life

View of Gammel Estrup, Jutland, surrounded on all sides by water

Denmark is largely inhabited by ethnic Danes who are ancestors of the Teutonic tribes that once populated all of Scandinavia.

Harald I (Bluetooth), Denmark's second king, was baptised as a Catholic in 960 and Denmark remained a Catholic country until well into the 16th century, when the ideas of the German Protestant reformer Martin Luther won widespread support. Lutheranism became the official religion of Denmark with the accession of Christian III in 1534. Today, about 90 per cent of the population are Protestant, and although the churches remain fairly empty, many Danes subscribe to a tax that supports the Church and observe traditions such as christenings and confirmations.

Although Denmark is largely an ethnically homogenous country, relaxed immigration policies introduced in the 1960s helped to establish small communities of foreign nationals from outside Europe. Copenhagen is home to significant numbers of Turks and Palestinians as well as new arrivals from Iraq and Afghanistan.

When it comes to bringing up children, many parents continue with their careers after taking parental leave. The progressive welfare system enables most women to return to work, at least part time.

Denmark's famous liberalism is perhaps best illustrated by "Christiania", a hippy commune that sprang up in the borough of Christianshavn in central Copenhagen in 1971. Allowed to remain as a social experiment, it is inhabited by about 900 people seeking an alternative lifestyle.

The Danes are similarly relaxed when it comes to issues such as marriage. The country's divorce rate is one of the highest in Europe and nearly 20 per cent of couples co-habit without ever getting married. Abortion has been available "on demand" since the 1960s.

Harbour and sailing boat jetty, Maribo (Lolland)

Father and son feeding pigeons in one of Copenhagen's open squares

Economy and Ecology

The Danish economy is fairly robust and the country has the EU's highest per-capita Gross National Product and a high standard of living.

Denmark was for centuries a land of farmers and fishermen. Today less than 5 per cent of the country's population are employed in agriculture. Fishing, however, is still an important sector of the economy. The country is a major exporter of fish and is also known for its dairy and pork products. Other exports include beer, furniture and home electronics.

The Danes attach great importance to environmental issues. The country has an extensive network of alternative energy sources and the state-subsidized power-generating windmills are a common feature of the landscape. These supply over 20 per cent of the country's electricity. Major investments are also made in the use of solar power and the island of Ærø, south of Funen, has one of the world's largest solar power stations. All new building projects are scrutinized to minimize the impact on the environment. Danes take great care of their coastline, many resorts have been awarded the blue flag, denoting clean beaches. Recycling domestic waste is normal practice in Denmark, as is the use of environmentally friendly packaging (a large amount of the country's paper production comes from recycled sources).

Culture, Art and Design

Denmark's cultural events range from major music festivals to local parades and concerts. Even smallish towns consider it a point of honour to organize festivals and concerts, putting on anything from classical music to pop and rock. One of the largest events is the July rock festival in Roskilde, which attracts over 130,000 visitors to see a mix of crowd-pleasing international acts, up-and-coming bands

Seaside scenery in Allinge, Bornholm

The unmistakable silhouette of the modern Tycho Brahe Planetarium, Copenhagen

and local Scandinavian headliners. Copenhagen's July jazz festival, held every year since 1979, is one of the top events of its kind in Europe and has attracted top performers including Dizzy Gillespie, Miles Davis and Oscar Peterson.

Denmark has a wide variety of wonderful museums, including the Ny Carlsberg Glyptotek *(see pp82–3)* and the Nationalmuseet *(see pp88–9)*, both in Copenhagen, as well as the Arken and Louisiana museums, which are within easy reach of the capital. The Nationalmuseet devotes much of its space to exhibits relating to Danish culture and history, but it also has world-class collections of Greek, Roman and Egyptian artifacts. Among the Glyptotek's collection are examples of 19th-century European painting, representatives of Denmark's "Golden Age" *(see pp46–7)* and works by major international artists such as Edgar Degas, Pierre Auguste Renoir and Paul Gauguin.

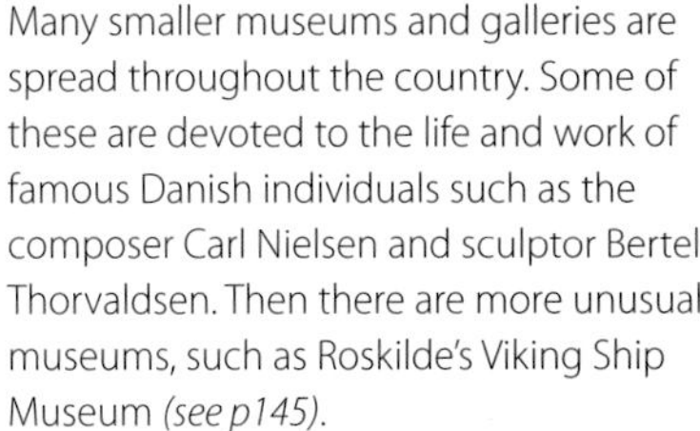

Sculpture from Holmegård

Many smaller museums and galleries are spread throughout the country. Some of these are devoted to the life and work of famous Danish individuals such as the composer Carl Nielsen and sculptor Bertel Thorvaldsen. Then there are more unusual museums, such as Roskilde's Viking Ship Museum *(see p145)*.

Among the country's best-known architects and designers are Ole Kirk Christiansen, inventor of the ever-popular LEGO®; Jørn Utzon, creator of the Sydney Opera House; and Arne Jacobsen, a pioneer of Danish modernism famous for his furniture and minimalist tableware. Prominent examples of Danish applied art include jewellery by Georg Jensen and sleek, high-end audio and visual equipment by Bang & Olufsen.

Oven-smoked fish, a popular delicacy

Danish Landscape and Flora

More than three quarters of Denmark is less than 100 m (330 ft) above sea level. Most of its landforms are of glacial origin, which adds variety to the lowland scenery. Forests, whose wholesale destruction was halted in the 19th century, occupy only a small percentage of the landscape and include commercial forests planted with spruce and fir, and natural forests dominated by beech and oak. Pastures and meadows are also distinctive features of the landscape and most of these are given over to crop cultivation and the rearing of livestock. A large portion of Denmark's highly diversified coastline consists of dunes, marshland and tidal flats.

Danish Fauna

Many mammals, including elks and bears, have disappeared in Denmark. What forests remain provide a habitat for deer, marten, wild boar and hare. Excellent nesting grounds are a haven for many birds including geese, storks, swans and sandpipers. The largest wild animal to be found in Denmark is the red deer, while polar bears can still be found in Greenland.

Zealand
The island covers an area of 7,000 sq km (2,702 sq miles), and has a diverse landscape. In its northern section, on the outskirts of Copenhagen, there are fragments of natural forests – all that remains of a vast former wilderness. Elsewhere, the island has lakes, beaches and pasture land.

Seaside Centaury *(Centaurium littorale)* is a species associated with salt flats, but can also sometimes be found growing on seaside sands.

White Helleborine *(Cephalanthera damasonium)* is an orchid with creamy-white flowers, and is often found in forests.

Helleborine *(Epipactis)* is found in several different varieties in Denmark. This orchid can be recognized by its labium, which is divided into two parts.

Bornholm
This island, largely composed of volcanic rock, has a mild climate. Its rugged granite cliffs, with stone rubble at their base, rise to over 80 m (262 ft) in height. At its northeastern end the well-preserved deciduous forests grow to the edge of the cliffs. The southern coast has long stretches of white-sand beaches.

Bird's Eye Primrose *(Primula farinosa)* is a rare peat bog species, which in Denmark is found only in isolated clusters.

Common Wintergreen *(Pyrola minor)* has a distinctive rosette of slightly leathery leaves; it grows in forests and deciduous woodlands, on acid soil.

Wild Strawberry *(Fragaria vesca)* grows on woodland glades and banks. Its small red berries are sweet and fragrant.

Five species of seal can be found on the coast of Greenland. The largest of these is the hooded seal, the male of which can weigh up to 400 kg (884 lbs). The Inuit still rely on seals for clothing and food.

The mute swan is Denmark's national bird and can be found in many parks and ponds throughout the country.

The greylag goose is one of Denmark's largest wild geese. Pairs mate for life; some 10,000 pairs are thought to be breeding in Denmark.

White storks, which winter in Africa, can be seen in summer in Denmark's marshes, meadows and pastures.

Funen

The island that separates Jutland from Zealand is famous for its scenery and is known as the "garden of Denmark" because it produces much of the country's fruit and vegetables. The terrain in the north of the island eventually levels out into marshland, while in the south it is more hilly.

Mountain Arnica *(Arnica montana)*, contrary to its name, is also found growing on lowlands, meadows, pastures and by roads. It is a valuable medicinal plant.

Sea Rocket *(Cakile maritima)* is a delicate plant associated solely with Funen's sandy coast.

Sea Holly *(Eryngium maritimum)* is a typical plant of the seaside dunes and comes in white and grey varieties.

Jutland

Lakes, which occupy about one per cent of Denmark's total area, are clustered mainly in central Jutland. Yding Skovhøj and Møllehøj, Denmark's highest peaks, can also be found here – rising a little over 170 m (560 ft) above sea level. Himmelbjerget is 147 m (482 ft) above sea level and is a famous viewpoint.

Field Fleawort *(Senecio integrifolius)* is a rare species, found in meadows, grasslands, pastures and woodlands.

Field Gentian *(Gentiana campestris)* is in danger of extinction and is legally protected in Denmark and many other European countries.

Cinquefoil *(Potentilla)* belongs to the rose family. There are several varieties growing in Denmark with yellow flowers.

Danish Architecture

Denmark's architecture includes many of the styles found elsewhere in Europe. The country's vernacular architecture includes 17th-century fortress churches and half-timbered houses. The influence of Baroque and Dutch Renaissance dominated the style of palaces built in the 17th and 18th centuries. Denmark's native character re-established itself with Neo-Classicism at the end of the 19th century and this trend has continued with contemporary landmark designs.

Dutch Renaissance Frederiksborg Slot, built mainly in the 17th century

Romanesque Architecture

The first Danish churches were built of wood, but they were quickly replaced by Norman structures that were usually constructed of granite. The 10th to 12th centuries marked the arrival of brick and stone Romanesque architecture, exemplified by the churches in Viborg and Ribe. Village churches, such as the one in Hover, Jutland, were usually built as single-aisle structures, with an apse or presbytery. The historic round churches found on Bornholm represent a very distinctive style. These medieval fortress-like buildings were built in the 12th century and were used not only for religious purposes but as places of refuge. Three-storeys high, the top two storeys were used as storage rooms and also provided shelter for the local population in times of danger.

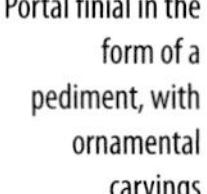

Portal finial in the form of a pediment, with ornamental carvings

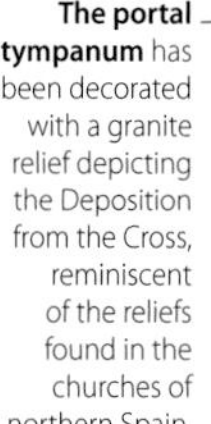

The portal tympanum has been decorated with a granite relief depicting the Deposition from the Cross, reminiscent of the reliefs found in the churches of northern Spain.

Ribe Domkirke is a prime example of a Romanesque cathedral. Built on the site of a wooden structure, this stone building was begun in 1150. One of its most notable features is the "Cat's Head" door on the south side.

Sankt Bendts Kirke, Ringsted, was built during the reign of Valdemar I (1152–82) as a tomb for his father, Canute III. Later, more royals were buried here including Valdemar I. Its rich architecture encompasses an imposing edifice with a front tower, a presbytery enclosed with an apse and a mighty transept.

Round churches were used as shelters during enemy raids.

Nylars' round church on Bornholm, built around 1150

Gothic Architecture

One of the earliest Gothic buildings in Denmark is Roskilde's Domkirke (Cathedral), founded by Bishop Absalon in 1170. The most prominent example of the mature Gothic is the cathedral church in Odense. The introduction of red brick is an important element of the Danish Gothic style. Other typical features of Gothic architecture are its severe forms, ornate decorations and a façade that features stepped peaks. Many Gothic buildings have whitewashed or polychromatic interiors.

Sankt Knuds Domkirke in Odense is a magnificent example of pure Gothic church brickwork. Most of the cathedral is 13th-century but the finely detailed gilded altar dates from the early 16th century and is the work of Claus Berg, a master craftsman from Lübeck.

Renaissance Architecture

Danish Renaissance architecture grew out of the church's practice of importing architects for major projects in the late 16th century. Dutch architects and craftsmen were employed by Frederik II, and later by Christian IV in the 17th century, to build grand palaces such as Frederiksborg Slot in Hillerød and Kronberg Slot in Helsingør.

Triton figure from the Neptune fountain at Frederiksborg, by Adrian de Vries (c.1615)

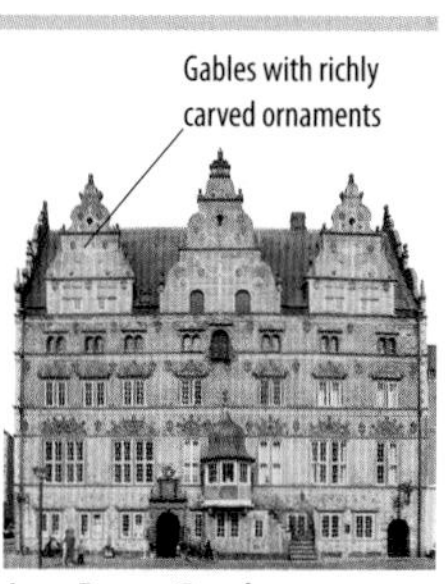

Gables with richly carved ornaments

Jens Bangs Stenhus, Aalborg, is, along with the Børsen (Stock Exchange), Copenhagen, and the quaint streets and crooked houses of Christianshavn, a fine example of town architecture from this period.

Kronborg Slot, a stately castle built in 1585 by Frederik II, and later rebuilt by Christian IV

Baroque Architecture

From the mid-17th to mid-18th centuries Baroque in Denmark left its mark mainly on residential architecture. The best examples are Copenhagen's palaces – Charlottenborg and Christiansborg – along with the grand residence in Ledreborg. The main force behind Baroque in Denmark was the architect Nicolai Eigtved. His greatest achievement was the Frederikstad district in Copenhagen, which was built in a French style and intended as a royal quarter.

Audience Room in Frederiksborg Slot with moulded decorations

Fredensborg Slot is a sumptuous early-18th-century castle and was built by Frederik IV to a design by Johann Cornelius Krieger in an Italian Baroque style.

Altar from Vor Frelsers Kirke (Our Saviour's Church), Copenhagen

20th-century Architecture

In the early part of the 20th century Danish architecture began to reflect a desire for better design in housing and everyday objects, resulting in Modernism and, subsequently, Functionalism. A major result of this trend was the creation of the Design Council at the Association of Architects, in 1907. Characteristics of modern Danish architectural practice are an honest use of materials, clean lines and an abundance of natural light.

The "Black Diamond", an extension of Det Kongelige Bibliotek (The Royal Library), Copenhagen, represents a Neo-Modernist trend that has gained favour in Denmark.

Water emphasises the visual link with a ship

Arken's Museet for Moderne Kunst (Museum of Modern Art) was designed by the then 25-year-old architect Søren Robert Lund, in metal and white concrete, and is a splendid example of Danish Deconstructivism.

Danish Design

LEGO® bricks, chairs by Arne Jacobsen, audio-visual equipment by Bang & Olufsen, jewellery by Georg Jensen: all are recognized throughout the world as examples of a Danish aesthetic. Design has a high profile in Denmark and constitutes an important source of revenue for the country, as well as being a major element of the national identity, supported by many institutions. Two good places to learn more about the traditions and history of Danish design are the Designmuseum Danmark and the Danish Design Centre, both of which are in Copenhagen.

Danish glass is admired throughout the world. The Holmegård factory was founded in the first half of the 19th century and initially employed workers brought over from Norway.

Bang & Olufsen high-fidelity products have been manufactured since 1925. The beauty of these products resides in the discreet use of the latest technology, which is coupled with audiophile performance.

Large windows blur the boundary between a room's interior and the outside.

Furniture designer Kaare Klint was fascinated by the possibility of combining ergonomics with traditional furniture design. His designs draw on many sources including pieces from 18th-century England.

The Bodum company was founded at the end of World War II by Peter Bodum. His smart and simple kitchen appliances, designed in the 1950s, are produced to this day and still enjoy great popularity.

LEGO® is the name of the toy company founded in 1932 by Ole Kirk Christiansen. Christiansen started by producing wooden toys and, in 1958, introduced the now familiar plastic building bricks. The well-known brand name is a contraction of the Danish phrase *leg godt* ("play well").

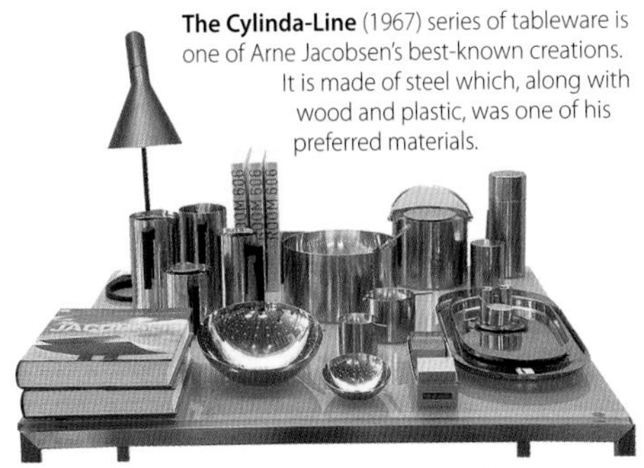

The Cylinda-Line (1967) series of tableware is one of Arne Jacobsen's best-known creations. It is made of steel which, along with wood and plastic, was one of his preferred materials.

The "Pins" stool (2002), by Hans Sandgren Jacobsen, is an example of modern design that still maintains Danish precision and aesthetics.

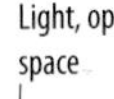

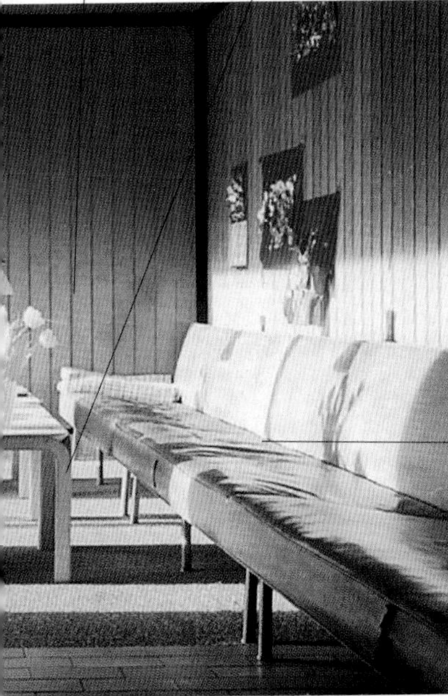

This Lamp by Poul Henningsen, from a series of lamps produced for Louis Poulsen & Co, is the result of a persistent endeavour by the designer to create lamps that give maximum natural light, while eliminating all shadows. He achieved the desired result by employing sets of curved lampshades to produce a soft, dispersed light.

Danish porcelain, particularly the *Flora Danica* dinner service (1789), is famous throughout the world. This service is decorated with floral motifs drawn by the botanist Teodor Homskjal, a pupil of Swedish botanist Linnaeus.

Design For Living

Following World War II, Danish architects began to take an interest in the architectural styles of a number of other countries, drawing on many influences to produce open-plan house designs. This trend is, perhaps, best exemplified by houses that architects have built for themselves, such as the home of Jørn Utzon in Hellebæk, erected in 1952.

Arne Jacobsen

Born in 1902, Arne Jacobsen is the unquestionable "star" of Danish design. In his youth, Jacobsen was fascinated by the work of the Swiss-born architect Le Corbusier, especially his focus on functionality. As a designer Jacobsen created many well-known pieces including the Ant (1951). This plywood chair could be stacked and was the forerunner of chairs found in schools and cafés all over the world today. The majority of Jacobsen's chair designs, including the Egg and the Swan, are still being produced. He died in 1971.

Danish Art

Both painting and sculpture have an important place in the history of Danish art. Sculpture flourished particularly during the Late Gothic and Mannerist periods, but above all, thanks to the genius of sculptor Bertel Thorvaldsen, during the so-called "Golden Age" in the early 19th century, which saw a flowering of Danish expression. Painting also flourished during this period and the formal portraiture of earlier painters such as Jens Juel began to be replaced with lively depictions of everyday life by artists such as Christoffer Wilhelm Eckersberg and his student Christen Købke.

View from the Loft of the Grain Store at the Bakery in the Citadel (1831), Christen Købke

Wounded Philoctetes (1774–75), Nicolai Abildgaard (Statens Museum for Kunst)

Old Masters

There are many well-preserved medieval works of art in Denmark, including Romanesque paintings and, in the churches of Zealand, the cycles of frescoes dating mainly from the 12th century.

The subsequent centuries were dominated by formal portraiture. Among the most outstanding, and the largest in size, are the oil paintings on display in Rosenborg Slot in Copenhagen, produced after 1615 by Dutch artists including Reinchold Timm and Rembrandt. The artists working for Christian IV, in Kronborg, included the Dutch painter Gerrit van Honthorst, who painted for the court of Denmark between 1635 and 1641. During the reign of Frederik IV the influences of French painting became more pronounced. During the Rococo period a French influence was also present and can be seen in the works of Scandinavians such as Johan Salomon Wahl and Carl Gustaf Pilo. The turning point in the development of Danish painting came with the founding of the Royal Academy of Fine Arts in 1754. Its alumni included many prominent painters from the period such as Jens Juel and Nicolai Abildgaard, who studied in Rome, from 1772 to 1776.

The "Golden Age"

The period between 1800 and 1850 saw a great surge in creativity. One of the prime movers of the "Golden Age" *(see pp46–7)* was Christoffer Wilhelm Eckersberg, who drew much of his inspiration from the native Danish landscape, as well as from scenes of everyday life. He had studied in Paris where he was taught by Jacques Louis David to see nature for what it was. Eckersberg returned to Denmark, fired with the belief that truth is beauty. He brought back the precision of Neo-Classicism and made it a dominant trait in Danish painting. Portraiture during the "Golden Age" was also of a very high standard. Among the other outstanding artists of the period are Christian Albrecht Jensen and Christen Købke.

Modern Art

After 1880 Realism and Naturalism ruled supreme in Danish painting. Their most famous exponent was the Skagen School, which placed an emphasis on natural light and its effects. Among the leading members of this school were Peder S. Krøyer and Anna and Michael Ancher. Around 1900, Danish painting came to be dominated by Symbolism. The situation changed just

Dead Drunk Danes (1960), Asger Jorn

before World War I, when new trends, such as the experiments with form by the Expressionists and Cubists, began to challenge existing traditions in art. The ranks of Danish Cubists included Jais Nielsen and Vilhelm Lundstrom. One of the most important phenomena of the 1950s was CoBrA (Copenhagen–Brussels–Amsterdam), a movement that tried to give free expression to the unconscious. One of the movement's founders was the Danish artist Asger Jorn, whose vivid abstract paintings have received international acclaim.

High altar of Roskilde Domkirke, 16th century

Sacred Art

Before turning to Protestantism Danish churches were richly decorated. In the 16th century, after the Reformation, many frescoes were painted over, as they were considered to be examples of Catholic flamboyance. Surviving to this day are a few gilded altars dating from the Romanesque period (12th–13th centuries); two of them are still found in their original locations, in Sahl and Stadil churches. Some outstanding altarpieces were created in the Late Gothic period (late 15th and early 16th centuries) by woodcarvers from Lübeck, notably Claus Berg. The work of Berg, which includes the main altar in the cathedral in Odense, is particularly striking. Filled with emotional charge and high in drama, his carving maintains a realism of detail that is typical of work found in southern Germany.

The Renaissance high altar in Roskilde Domkirke was made in Antwerp in 1560. It was originally intended for Gdansk, until it was requisitioned by Danish customs authorities.

The 17th century saw a culmination of the Reformation. At that time large sums of money were spent on building churches and chapels, notably Holmens Kirke in Copenhagen, for which Frederik III ordered a sumptuously decorated altarpiece sculpted from raw oak wood.

Sepulchral Sculpture

With the passing of the medieval era, funereal or sepulchral sculpture began to enjoy success in Denmark. Characteristic of this period are the works of the sculptor and architect Cornelius Floris of Antwerp, who designed the tomb of Christian III (d.1559) in Roskilde Domkirke (Cathedral), west of Copenhagen. It is made of multi-coloured marble and extraordinarily richly ornamented, with an open-plan colonnade that contains two statues of the monarch. This is one of Europe's largest royal tombs from this period.

Self-portrait, by Bertel Thorvaldsen

Renaissance tombs and epitaphs of the aristocracy, found in great numbers throughout Denmark, were more modest, and usually limited to a single slab of stone bearing the image of the deceased in a prostrate position, with an inscription. A new type of tombstone appeared in the 17th century. Its main creator was Thomas Quellinus of Antwerp. His marble tombs realistically depicted the deceased, and were accompanied by personified images of his or her virtues.

Tomb of Christian III in Roskilde Domkirke, by Cornelius Floris

Modern Sculpture

Prior to the 19th century sculpture was treated in Denmark solely as a means of portraying the monarchy. This art form began to be taken more seriously with the establishment of the Royal Academy, however, and among its early exponents were Johanes Wiedeweilt (d.1802) and Nicolai Dajon (d.1823). Sculpture was only elevated to a high form of art, however, by Bertel Thorvaldsen (d.1844), who created an austere variety of Classicism based on his in-depth studies of classical antiquity while in Rome. After working in southern Europe for many years, Thorvaldsen returned home to a hero's welcome in 1838. He bequeathed many of his finest works to the city of Copenhagen on condition that a museum was established in which to house them (Thorvaldsens Museum, *see p89*).

DENMARK THROUGH THE YEAR

Denmark is roughly on the same latitude as Moscow and southern Alaska but has a fairly mild climate. The coldest months are January and February, and most events and festivals are scheduled for spring and summer. The Danes like to enjoy themselves, and during the summer holiday season the whole country comes alive, with almost every town having its own festival. Denmark is not a large country yet it hosts many world-class events, including one of the oldest rock-music festivals, in Roskilde, which is attended by many major international acts. The world-famous Copenhagen jazz festival also attracts top performers. As elsewhere in Europe, religious festivals such as Christmas are widely observed and provide an opportunity for people to spend time with their families.

Royal family at the official celebrations of the Queen's 64th birthday (2004)

Spring

Spring arrives slowly in Denmark, but its advent is welcomed with great celebration around the country. The biggest of the festivals is Copenhagen's Whitsun Carnival, when the streets fill with Danes dressed in colourful costumes to mark the end of the long winter.

March

Aalborg Opera Festival *(1st half of Mar)*, Aalborg. In early March opera lovers congregate to hear some of the world's best performers.

April

Tivoli Gardens Concert Series *(mid-Apr)*, Copenhagen. The Tivoli amusement park and gardens open for the summer season. On Fridays the entrance fee includes access to the very popular late-night concerts.

Birthday of Queen Margrethe II *(16 Apr)*, Copenhagen. The Danish queen is very popular, and on this day large crowds of loyal Danes congregate outside Amalienborg Slot to sing "Happy Birthday", which is accompanied by the ceremonial changing of the Livgarden (royal guards).

Store Bededag *(4th Friday after Easter)*. Common Prayer Day or Great Prayer Day is a movable Easter feast. Following the introduction of Protestantism to Denmark in the 16th century, the church calendar was revised and several feasts were combined into one – the Store Bededag. On this day many Danes eat wheat buns – *varme hveder*.

CPH:PIX *(2nd half of Apr)*, Copenhagen. This is the biggest international film festival in Denmark. Film entries include Scandinavian producers, as well as many world-famous directors.

May

Arbejdernes Kampdag *(1 May)*. Rallies are held to mark International Workers' Day.

Pinsedag. Whitsunday.

Viking Market *(1st weekend in May)*, Ribe. Held at the Viking Museum, this annual event recreates a Viking marketplace complete with displays of Viking crafts.

Aalborg Carnival *(Whitsun weekend)*, Aalborg. A week of celebrations leading up to Whitsun, including a fireworks display and Northern Europe's biggest parade.

Ølfestival *(mid-May)*, Copenhagen. This lively three-day beer festival includes stalls, music and, more than 800 different beers from around 70 exhibitors, which include both Danish and foreign breweries.

Classic Race Aarhus *(mid- to late May)*, Aarhus. Experience an historic drive through the decades in Aarhus when around 300 historical vehicles from Denmark and abroad gather for this classic race.

Copenhagen Marathon *(late May)*, Copenhagen. This race attracts around 10,000 amateur and elite runners from many European countries.

Whitsun Carnival *(Whitsun weekend)*, Copenhagen. This three-day event includes a parade, dancing and special activities for children.

Viking Market, Ribe

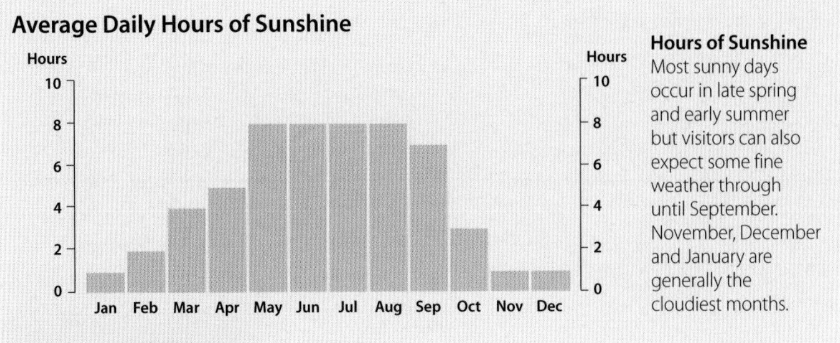

Hours of Sunshine
Most sunny days occur in late spring and early summer but visitors can also expect some fine weather through until September. November, December and January are generally the cloudiest months.

Roskilde Festival – one of Denmark's most popular events

Summer

Summer festivities begin with Sankt Hans Aften (23 June) when bonfires are lit on many beaches. Numerous attractions are scheduled for the summer holidays – from local one-day events to major festivals.

June

International Sand Sculpture Festival *(from early Jun)*, various towns. Competition to build the best sand sculptures.
International Kite Festival *(mid-Jun)*, Fanø. This four-day festival attracts over 5,000 kite-flyers.
River Boat Jazz Festival *(end Jun)*, Silkeborg. Jazz bands perform all around Silkeborg, some on boats.
Sankt Hans Eve *(23 Jun)*. Midsummer Night is celebrated around camp fires.

July

Ringridning *(Jul)*, several towns in Sønderjylland. At this colourful festival, horse riders use a lance or spear to target a series of metal rings suspended in mid-air.
Roskilde Festival *(begin Jul)*, Roskilde. This rock festival has been attracting some of the biggest names in music since 1971. Past performers include Bob Dylan, Bob Marley and David Bowie.
Copenhagen Jazz Festival *(early Jul)*, Copenhagen. For two weeks jazz, blues and fusion blast out of almost every public space in the city.
Aarhus International Jazz Festival *(mid-Jul)*, Aarhus. A second opportunity in this month to hear some top-class jazz.
Hans Christian Andersen Plays *(end Jul–early Aug)*, Odense. Each year, one of Andersen's fairy tales is performed outside in Den Fynske Landsby (Funen Village).

August

Cultural Harvest. Festivals celebrated in castles and stately homes, including exhibitions and theatre.
Kulturhavn *(early Aug)*, Copenhagen. Festivalgoers can enjoy the range of free cultural experiences on offer at this harbour-based festival. These include dance, music, children's activities, watersports, theatre and Secret Harbour Tours exploring little-known areas of the city's waterways.
Copenhagen International Fashion Fair *(early Aug)*, Copenhagen. Top Scandinavian and European fashion designers present their latest collections.
Hamlet Summer *(early to mid-Aug)*, Helsingør. Performances of Shakespeare's *Hamlet* and other works are staged in Kronborg Slot.
International Film Festival *(mid-Aug)*, Odense.
Schubertiade *(mid-Aug–early Sep)*, Roskilde. Top musicians perform a selection of the works of Franz Schubert.
Copenhagen Cooking *(end of Aug)*, Copenhagen. Ten days of cooking events, from tastings and street kitchens to special menus.
European Medieval Festival *(end of Aug)*, Horsens. For two days the city is transformed into a 15th-century market town.

Copenhagen Cooking brings street kitchens and outdoor cooking events to the city

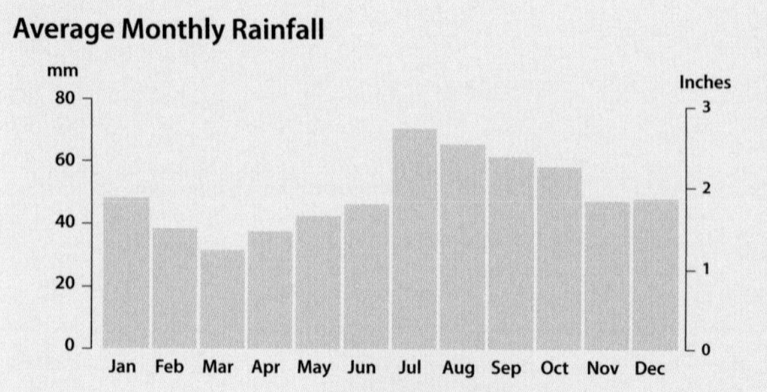

Rainfall
July is one of the warmest, but also one of the wettest, months. The best time to visit is in late spring, when it is warm and there is very little rain.

Autumn

Early autumn provides the final opportunity to stage outdoor performances of jazz and theatre. The beginning of October marks a transition between the carefree holiday season and the beginning of the new school year with months of hard work and study ahead. Theatres stage their first-night performances, and cold autumn evenings bring music-lovers into the clubs.

Israels Plads flower market, Copenhagen, in early autumn

September

Golden Days *(2 weeks in Sep)*, Copenhagen. This annual event celebrates Copenhagen's rich cultural heritage and city life through a series of exhibitions, lectures, concerts, debates and themed walks.

Around Limfjorden Race *(early or mid-Sep)*, Løgstør, Thisted, Struer, Nykøbing Mors, Fur and Skive. The biggest annual sailing event in Scandinavia is an exciting five-day race in traditional boats around the Limfjord Bay.

Father Christmas Parade during Christmas celebrations in Tønder

Tourde Gudenå *(mid-Sep)*, Skanderborg. Kayak and canoe contest attracting many participants and spectators.

October

Night of Culture *(2nd Fri in Oct)*, Copenhagen. A night when it is possible to visit many exhibitions, museums, castles, theatres and churches, including some buildings that are usually closed to visitors.

Mix Copenhagen *(1st half of Oct)*, Copenhagen. International gay, lesbian, bi-sexual and transgender film festival.

Tivoli Halloween *(2nd half of Oct)*, Copenhagen. Witches, lanterns and pumpkins.

November

Tivoli Christmas *(Nov–Dec)*, Copenhagen. Events for the young and young at heart in Tivoli as Christmas draws closer. Among the attractions are a Christmas market, ice-skating on a frozen artificial lake and the chance of spotting a Christmas pixie.

Copenhagen Irish Festival *(1st half of Nov)*, Copenhagen. Four days of celebrations and plenty of Irish music.

Feast of St Morten *(10 Nov)*. St Morten's Evening is often marked by roasting a goose.

CPH:DOX *(early to mid-Nov)*, Copenhagen. This is the largest documentary-film festival in northern Europe.

Tønder – The Christmas Town *(mid-Nov)*, Tønder. A colourful parade featuring a multitude of Father Christmases, accompanied by marching bands, passes along the main street of the town.

Street vendor roasting almonds on a Copenhagen pavement

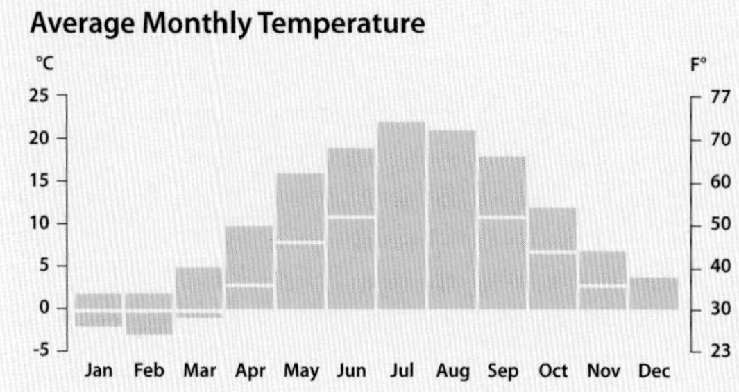

Temperature
This chart shows the average maximum and minimum temperatures for each month. Summer temperatures reach about 20° C (68° F), although temperatures can top 25° C (77° F). Winters can be cold with the temperature often dropping below zero, though severe frosts are rare.

Winter

Winter is the quietest time of the year. Little happens and the weather is not conducive to outdoor entertainment. The Christmas period abounds in concerts, however. These are often staged in churches and feature choral ensembles singing psalms and carols. Denmark's streets are beautifully decorated and illuminated at this time and Christmas fairs are held throughout the country, with plenty to eat and drink, and the occasional parade.

December

Jul *(24–26 Dec)*. The Danes celebrate Christmas in family circles. As in most of Europe, children play a central role. Danes tend to celebrate on Christmas Eve, decorating the tree the night before Christmas and often hanging it with real candles. The traditional Christmas dinner is also eaten on the 24th and usually consists of roast duck with red cabbage and potatoes. Rice pudding is eaten for dessert; whoever finds the hidden almond receives a prize.

January

Nytårsdag *(1 Jan)*. New Year's Day witnesses a boisterous welcome to the New Year in Denmark. Many towns stage firework displays, while classical concerts are performed in most major cities.

February

Wondercool *(throughout Feb)*, Copenhagen. A fusion event, mixing music, art, food, design and architecture. On Saturdays guests can join gastronomic cruises on boats that drop them off at six different restaurants. Alternatively, visitors can enjoy an after-hours dining experience in a museum.
Fastelavn *(last Sun before Lent)*. Shrovetide is a time for fun and games. The Danish tradition of "knocking a cat out of the barrel" is still practised by children in fancy-dress. Originally the barrel, hanging from a string, contained a real cat, which was held to be a symbol of evil. Today, the barrel contains sweets, toys and fruit, which eventually fall to the ground.

Symphony orchestra performing for Aalborg's New Year concert

New Year fireworks in Tivoli, Copenhagen

Public Holidays

New Year Nytår (1 Jan)
Maundy Thursday
Good Friday
Easter Day Påske
International Workers' Day Arbejdernes Kampdag (1 May)
Common Prayer Day Store Bededag (Apr/May)
Ascension Day Kristi Himmelfartsdag (May/Jun)
Whitsunday, Whitmonday Pinse (May/Jun)
Constitution Day Grundslovsdag (5 Jun)
Christmas Day (25 Dec)
Boxing Day (26 Dec)

THE HISTORY OF DENMARK

Denmark's history has long been associated with the sea. Viking raids on England and elsewhere between the 9th and 11th centuries marked the beginnings of Danish influence and by the late Middle Ages Denmark had a tight grip on trade in the Baltic. The country later lost its position as a world power, but continues to play an important role in the international arena.

The earliest evidence of human existence to be found in Denmark dates from about 12,000 BC after the first warm phase at the end of the last ice age. From 7000–3900 BC, the sea level rose so much that the northern parts of Denmark were divided into islands and deep fjords. Between 3900 and 1700 BC the first agricultural settlements began to emerge. The period is marked by the clearing of forests, the rise of small communities, and the mining of flint. Denmark's Bronze Age dates from around 1800 BC and jewellery and cult objects have been unearthed from this period. By about 500 BC iron had largely replaced bronze.

Unification

During the late Iron Age (5th and 6th centuries AD) a Nordic tribe known as Danes began to take control of the Jutland peninsula, forming a social order based around tribal structures.

As a result of the threat from the south presented by the Frankish empire under Charlemagne, these clans began to co-operate as a defensive measure. The Danish strategic position was strengthened in about AD 737 by the building of the Danevirke, a rampart that cut across the Jutland peninsula. This wall, and the forces of Godfred, king of Jutland, forced Charlemagne to recognize the local Eider River as the Franco-Danish border in AD 811.

After Godfred's death, rivalry between different clans again brought chaos. The first ruler to restore unity was Gorm the Old, the son of a Norwegian chieftain who had conquered the Jutland peninsula in the late 9th century. Gorm's son, Harald I (Bluetooth) took the throne in AD 950 and extended his power base across the rest of Denmark. Harald I's conquest enabled the widespread adoption of Christianity, which not only unified the country but also appeased Denmark's Frankish neighbours.

Increased security gave new impetus to a series of Viking *(see pp38–9)* raids on the British Isles and Ireland. These raids made it possible for Danish kings to win control of England and, for a period, an Anglo-Danish kingdom was formed under Canute I (The Great), who ruled as monarch of Denmark, England and Norway until his death in 1035. After his death, England broke away from Danish control and Denmark fell into disarray for some time.

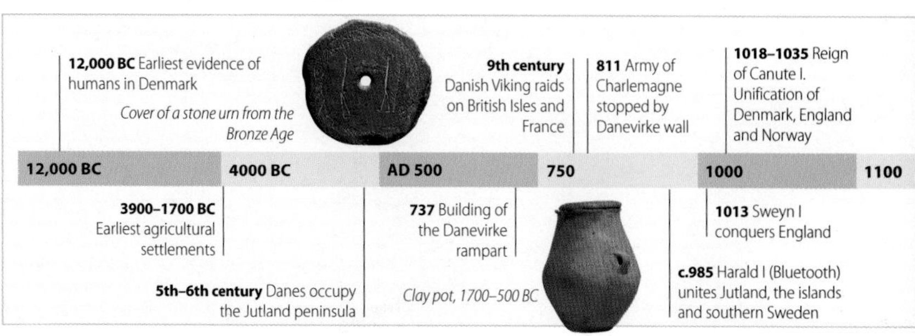

◀ **Painting featuring the Danish flag descending from heaven during Valdemar II's campaign in present-day Estonia in 1219**

The Vikings

The term Viking is generally used to refer to the Scandinavian peoples who journeyed overseas in wooden ships, between AD 800 and 1100, to raid and trade throughout the North and Irish seas and along the rivers of eastern and western Europe. Early Viking raiders targeted monasteries for their wealth and the ferocity of these lightning raids spread terror throughout Christian Europe, giving rise to the image of Vikings as plunderers and rapists. In fact these pagan people were expert sailors and ventured as far as North America where they traded in such items as tusks and pelts.

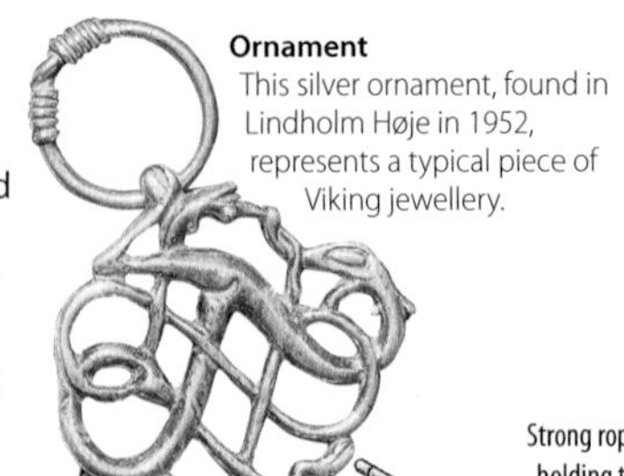

Ornament
This silver ornament, found in Lindholm Høje in 1952, represents a typical piece of Viking jewellery.

Silver Coin
The Vikings established trade routes to the East and the West. From the 9th century, silver coins, such as this one from the market place of Hedeby, were used as currency.

Viking Chieftain
In the 19th century a view of Vikings began to take hold, which saw them as barbarians. This portrait by Carl Haag is typical of the common image. Actually they were skilled craftsmen, traders, and hunters.

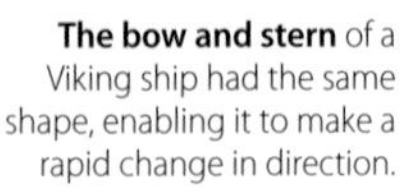

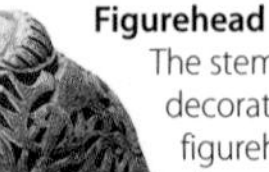

Figurehead
The stems of ships were decorated with figureheads, in the form of a snake or a dragonhead. The loss of a figurehead was believed to be a bad omen.

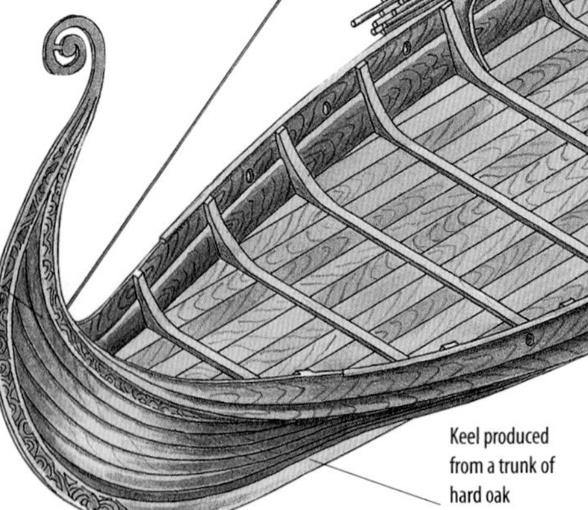

Viking Ship
Viking warships were usually about 28 m (92 ft) in length. The longest one ever found measured nearly 70 m (230 ft). Along with a 60-strong crew of oarsmen, they could carry as many as 400 people.

Key

— Viking expeditions

Woman Statuette
The independent and self-reliant Viking women ran their homes and farms for many months when their men went out to sea.

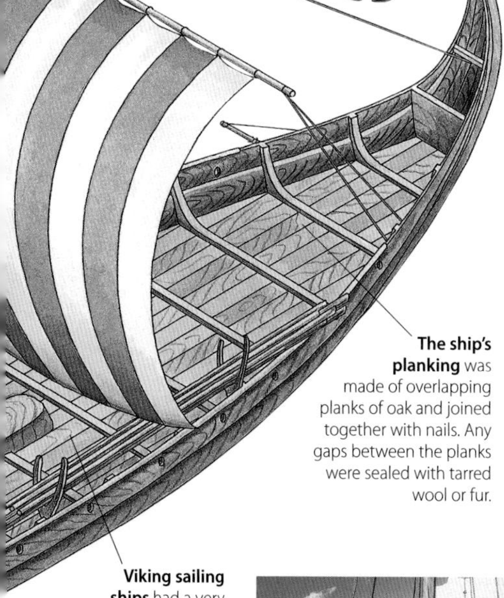

The ship's planking was made of overlapping planks of oak and joined together with nails. Any gaps between the planks were sealed with tarred wool or fur.

Viking sailing ships had a very shallow draught and could sail in waters less than 1 m (3.3 ft) deep.

Viking Raids
Early raids were carried out only during spring and summer. From about 845, Vikings began wintering at the mouths of foreign rivers, making raids possible throughout the year.

Viking Architecture

Few Viking buildings, which were built of earth, wood and stone, have survived. The best preserved are the round fortresses erected during the reign of Harald I (Bluetooth), in the late 10th century, at strategic points around Fyrkat (eastern Jutland), Aggersborg (northern Jutland), Trelleborg (Zealand) and Nonnebakken (Funen). These fortified settlements were surrounded by circular embankments 120 m (394 ft) in diameter, 12 m (39.4 ft) wide and rising to a height of 4 m (13 ft).

The Frykat fortress included 16 huge buildings containing domestic quarters, and was probably inhabited by between 800 and 1,000 people. Close to where the fortress stood, there is now a replica Viking farmstead including houses, outbuildings and traditionally clothed volunteers.

This replica longhouse, near Fyrkat, was built using authentic tools and materials, with knowledge gained from archaeological research.

Viking house doors, such as these in Frederikssund, were heavily built as a defence against intruders as well as the forces of nature.

Valdemar I removing a pagan statute on the coast of Rugia

The Middle Ages

King Canute's son Hardicanute died in 1042 and the Anglo-Danish kingdom disintegrated as the successors of Denmark's eighth monarch, Sweyn II (1047–74), began fighting each other for the throne. As royal supremacy weakened, the power of wealthy landowners and church leaders grew and this early medieval period of Denmark's history is scarred by internal strife and corruption.

This period of unrest came to an end with the succession of Valdemar I (The Great) in 1157. He reunited the country and enacted Denmark's first written laws (the Jutland Code). With help of the powerful Bishop Absalon, he made a series of successful raids against the Wends in eastern Germany. By the time of Valdemar II's succession, Denmark had won control of Meklenburg, Holstein, Lübeck and Estonia, making it one of the greatest powers in northern Europe.

Denmark's pre-eminence ended in 1227 when the country was defeated by its German vassals at the Battle of Bornhøved. Denmark was forced to give up much of its recently acquired territory and, following the death of Valdemar II in 1241, the Danish monarchy lost much of its power. Successive monarchs were forced into enacting laws which for the time were quite progressive, including the end of imprisonment without just cause (1282) and the establishment of the first supreme court in 1360.

The Kalmar Union

One of the greatest achievements of King Valdemar IV (1340–75) was to arrange the marriage of his daughter Margrete to Norway's King Haakon. Margrete succeeded in forming the Kalmar Union, an alliance uniting Denmark, Norway and Sweden under a common sovereign. The main aim of the union was to counter the dominance of the Hanseatic League, which under the influence of Germany dominated trade in the region.

Queen Margrete, regent of Denmark and the initiator of the Kalmar Union

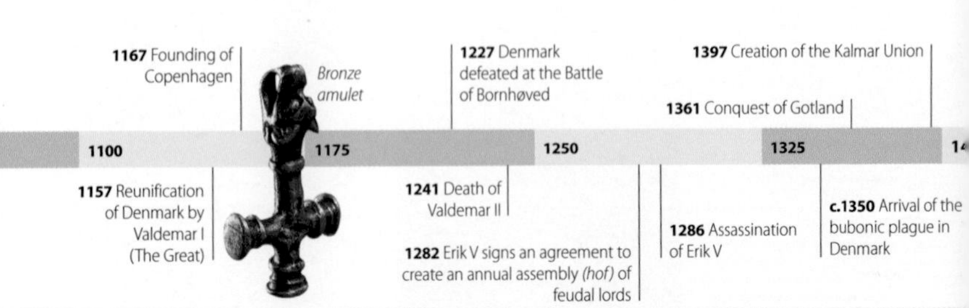

Gustav Vasa persuading Lübeck authorities to join in the attack on Christian II

While each country remained free to follow their own policies, they were obliged to fight any wars together and elect a common monarch. In 1397, Margrete's grand-nephew Erik of Pomerania was crowned king of Denmark, Norway and Sweden.

Initially, a long line of military successes, the introduction of customs duties in the Øresund (Sound) and a growing demand for Danish produce strengthened the country's position. Soon, however, Denmark's domination in the Baltic was challenged by the growing power of Sweden. In 1520 the Danish king, Christian II, ruthlessly suppressed an insurrection by what is known as the Stockholm Bloodbath. Three years later, however, Sweden elected its own king, Gustav Vasa, effectively putting an end to the union.

Wooden altar by Abel Schrøder, 1661, in Holmens Kirke, Copenhagen

Wars With Sweden

Denmark's and Sweden's aims to gain control of Øresund lead to a long series of wars between the two countries during the 16th and 17th centuries. In addition to these battles, the Thirty Years War took place (1616–48). Denmark was involved from 1625 to 1629 and suffered a disastrous defeat, while Sweden, joining in 1630, gained power and wealth. Renewed warring between the two countries ended in 1658 with Denmark losing all of its territories on the Swedish mainland. Two more wars occurred, 1675–79 and 1709–20.

Towards Absolute Monarchy

The strength of the monarchy had been increased by the introduction of Lutheranism in 1536, which placed the wealth of the Catholic church in the hands of the Crown. The king, however, was still elected by the nobility. Although political power was divided between the Crown and Council, the nobles often had the last say. After the defeats of 1658, state coffers were empty and King Fredrik III needed to take control. This led to the instatement of absolute monarchy *(see pp42–3)*.

Christian IV, King of Denmark, welcomed in Berlin by the Brandenburg Elector, 1595

The Era of Absolute Monarchy

Frederik III introduced hereditary monarchy in 1660 in an effort to curtail the power of the nobles of the Council *(see p41)*. In 1665, he took the matter further and passed the Royal Act, which declared the sovereign to be beyond the law and inferior only to God. Five years later Christian V became the first monarch to be crowned under the new system. The people seemed to prefer an almighty king to the old nobility, and kings continued to rule as absolute monarchs until 1848.

Frederik III
Crowned King of Denmark and Norway in 1648, Frederik III ruled until his death in Copenhagen castle in 1670. To this day, his grave can be found in Roskilde cathedral.

Academy of Knights
Denmark's elite schools were established by Frederik III. These academies became popular in the 17th century.

Frederiksborg Chapel
The Slotskirken (Palace Chapel) is where Danish kings were crowned from 1670 to 1840.

Copenhagen (c.1700)
Following the introduction of absolute monarchy the Danish capital's defences were strengthened.

Holmens Kirke, built in 1619 to serve the Royal Navy

Holmens Canal

The Holmens Drawbridge enabled ships to enter the canal.

The Introduction of Absolutism in Denmark

The decision by Frederik III to introduce absolute monarchy in Denmark in 1665 was met with general approval. The ceremonial meeting between the king and the parliament has been immortalized in minute detail in many paintings including examples found in Rosenborg and Frederiksborg.

Corfitz Ulfeldt
Corfitz Ulfeldt, son-in-law of Christian IV, was a typical example of the powerful nobility. After a disagreement with Frederik III, he switched sides and negotiated the Roskilde Treaty on Sweden's behalf in 1658.

Colourful burgher homes were built in the form of narrow-fronted terraced houses.

Børsen (the Stock Exchange)

Numerous inhabitants of the capital attended the celebrations marking the introduction of absolute monarchy.

Boats moored along the canal

The king's troops

Frederik VII
In 1848 Frederik VII renounced absolute power and, with a new constitution, turned Denmark into a democratic country, with guaranteed freedom of speech.

Architecture

The period of absolute monarchy brought with it many magnificent buildings. The most opulent examples of the residential architecture of this period include Charlottenborg in Kongens Nytorv, Copenhagen, which was completed in 1683 as a palace for the royal family *(see pp72–3)*. Other outstanding buildings from this period are Ledreborg, a stately home designed by the architect Lauritz de Thurah *(see p143)*, Copenhagen's Børsen (Stock Exchange) and Amalienborg Slot *(see pp60–61)*, which was designed by Nicolai Eigtved, the architect also responsible for Copenhagen's Frederiksstad district.

Vor Frelsers Kirke was built in 1696 by Lambert van Haven in Dutch Renaissance style. The spire was added by Lauritz de Thurah in 1752 *(see pp92–3)*.

Christian VII's Palace at Amalienborg has typically opulent Rococo interiors, designed by Nicolai Eigtved and the sculptor Le Clerk.

Painting by C.A. Lorentzen of the British attack on the Danish fleet, 1801

The Age of Reform

A peace treaty with Sweden signed in 1720 marked the beginning of the longest war-free period in Denmark's history. The absence of external threats encouraged economic growth and this in turn brought about a period of social change, which became more urgent as the French Revolution gathered pace. Under Frederik VI (1808–39) feudal obligations such as compulsory labour were abolished and large tracts of land were broken up and redistributed to peasants. At the same time landowners were given a role in government and compulsory education was introduced for all children under the age of 14.

The Napoleonic Wars

The outbreak of the Napoleonic Wars in 1796 eventually brought this period of peace and reform to a halt. Denmark, which derived major benefits from trade, tried to remain neutral in the face of the conflict in Europe but, in 1801, Britain accused Denmark of breaking the British trade embargo and attacked and destroyed the Danish fleet in Øresund. In 1807 the British, fearing the strengthening of a Franco-Danish alliance, struck again and bombarded Copenhagen for four days. By the end of the attack much of the city was ablaze and the naval yard was destroyed. The British then sailed away with what remained of the Danish fleet, which included 170 gunboats. In the aftermath of this assault, Denmark joined the continental alliance against Britain and Britain in turn blockaded Danish waters.

The war ended with the signing of the Kiel Peace Treaty in 1814 under which Denmark lost some 322,000 sq km (124,292 sq miles) of territory, including Norway. The new boundaries left Denmark with a mere

Peasants give thanks to Christian VII for abolishing serfdom, painting by C.W. Eckersberg

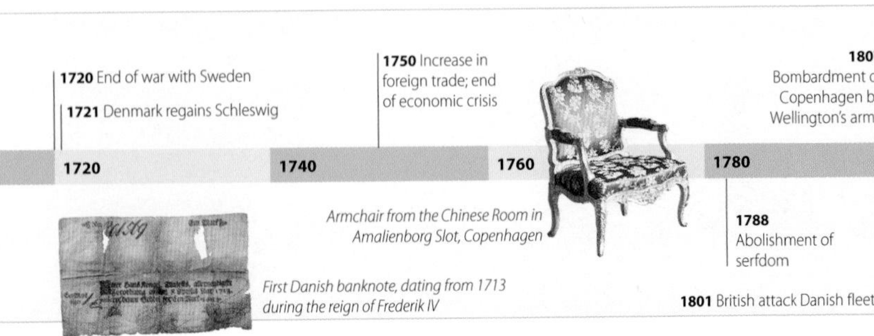

Armchair from the Chinese Room in Amalienborg Slot, Copenhagen

First Danish banknote, dating from 1713 during the reign of Frederik IV

Painting by C.W. Eckersberg depicting bombardment of Copenhagen in 1807

58,000 sq km (22,388 sq miles), which included the Duchy of Schleswig, with its Danish-German population, and the Holstein and Lauenburg dukedoms.

The Napoleonic Wars had a catastrophic effect on Denmark. The British blockade led to famine and starvation while territorial losses and wartime destruction resulted in a bankrupt state treasury. Culturally, however, this was the beginning of Denmark's Golden Age *(see pp46–7)*.

Denmark's national emblem, 1774–1820

Schleswig Conflict

Events in Europe, including the 1830 July Revolution in France, contributed to the weakening of absolute monarchy. With increasing force, demands were made for the creation of a representative government. Eventually, in 1848, pressure from liberal circles resulted in the enactment of a new constitution, ending absolute monarchy.

The new constitution included the incorporation of the duchies of Schleswig and Holstein as permanent regions of Denmark. With the support of Prussia, the armies of Schleswig and Holstein rose up against the Danish authority. War ensued and ended in 1851 with the defeat of the duchies, but failed to solve the conflict. Trouble erupted again in 1863, when the Danish parliament agreed a new joint constitution for the Kingdom of Denmark and the Duchy of Schleswig. A year later, on the pretext of defending the German populations within the duchies, Prussia and Austria declared war on Denmark. Within months Denmark was defeated and the contested duchies were lost to Prussia and Austria.

The shock of defeat led Denmark to declare its neutrality and concentrate on rebuilding the economy. Danish agriculture entered a period of rapid growth, assisted by a high demand for grain in Britain, and the railway system was extended to cover much of the country. By the end of the 19th century Denmark had a well-developed economic base that included mature shipbuilding and brewing industries.

Return of Danish soldiers to Copenhagen in 1864 depicted in a painting by Otto Bache

1813 State Treasury declared bankrupt

1814 Kiel Peace Treaty; loss of Norway

1820

1835 First edition of Hans Christian Andersen's *Fairy Tales*

1840

1843 First philosophical works by Søren Kierkegaard published

1848 End of absolute monarchy

1848–51 Civil war over the duchies of Schleswig and Holstein

Christian VIII, King of Denmark (1839–48)

1860

1864 War with Prussia and Austria

1873 Banning of child labour

1880

1884 First Social Democrats elected to parliament

Denmark's Golden Age

The period of political and economic turmoil that occurred during the Napoleonic wars, and the years immediately following them, witnessed an unprecedented flourishing of culture. The leading figures of Denmark's "Golden Age", which lasted throughout the first half of the 19th century, achieved recognition far beyond the borders of Denmark. Among the most prominent are the sculptor Bertel Thorvaldsen, the painter Christoffer Wilhelm Eckersberg and the romantic poet Adam Oehlenschläger. More famous than these, however, are the writer Hans Christian Andersen and the philosopher Søren Kierkegaard.

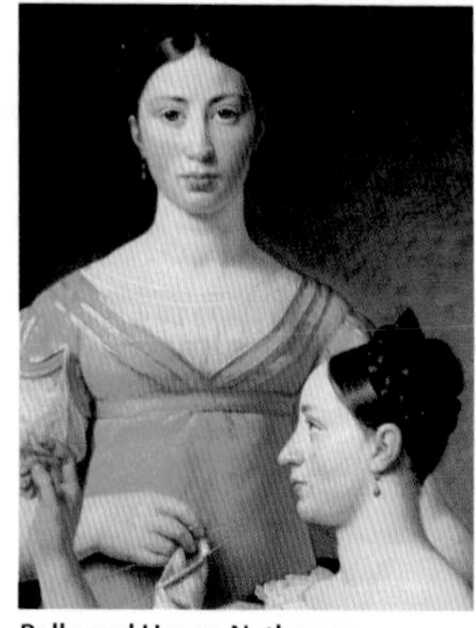

Bella and Hanna Nathansson
This portrait was painted by the "father of Danish painting" Christoffer Wilhelm Eckersberg.

Interior of a House
The drawing room of a Copenhagen merchant, portrayed in this painting by Wilhelm Marstrand, represents a typical interior of a middle-class home during the 1830s.

Bertel Thorvaldsen
This sculpture (1817) of a shepherd boy is one of many Neo-Classical statues by Bertel Thorvaldsen.

Parade
Festivals, parades and fairs coloured the lives of Copenhagen's citizens.

H.C. Andersen Telling his Stories
An illustration from one of the earliest editions of Hans Christian Andersen's tales, which are some of the most famous works of children's literature.

Wilhelm Morstrand, Albert Küchler and Dietlev Blunck on the balcony

Jørgen Sonne

Artists of the Golden Age

This painting, entitled A Group of Danish Artists Visiting Rome *was painted in 1837 by Constantin Hansen. Like many painters of this period, Hansen learnt his craft abroad and returned to Denmark with a fresh perspective.*

H.C. Andersen
Born in humble circumstances in 1805, the popular writer later socialized with the bourgeoisie and at court.

Andersen's Inkpot
As well as writing nearly 200 fairy tales, Andersen also wrote novels, librettos and other works.

Søren Kierkegaard
One of the forerunners of Existentialism, Kierkegaard (1813–55) described human life in terms of ethics, aesthetics and religion.

The Golden Age in Copenhagen

Following the ravages that befell Copenhagen at the turn of the 18th and 19th centuries, including the 1807 British bombardment *(see p44)*, the city was rebuilt in a new form. Classicism became the dominant architectural style. Christian Frederik Hansen and other Danish architects often drew their inspiration from antiquity. Office buildings, as well as the new bourgeois residences, were adorned with columns, porticoes and tympanums. The most interesting buildings include Thorvaldsens Museum, the Domhuset (Court House) in Nytorv, and the Harsdorff Hus in Kongens Nytorv.

Thorvaldsens Museum was built in 1848 and approved personally by the sculptor who had bequeathed his work to the city. This building is decorated with friezes by Jørgen Sonne *(see p89)*.

Vor Frue Kirke was designed by Christian Frederik Hansen, who took his inspiration from Classical buildings. It had an imposing façade, but no tower until Frederik VI declared that a tower was essential *(see p76)*.

Stockholm, Copenhagen and Oslo portrayed in a satirical magazine, in 1906

World War I

Before World War I Denmark had maintained good relations with both Britain and Germany and with the outbreak of war the Danish government declared its neutrality. This brought considerable benefits to the country's economy, although a third of Denmark's merchant fleet was sunk during the conflict. Also, the war drew attention to the commercial and strategic importance of Denmark's colonies in the West Indies, and the USA bought the Virgin Islands from Denmark in 1917.

Germany's defeat in 1918 revived the old Schleswig-Holstein problem. Under the Treaty of Versailles, the area was divided into two zones and, after a referendum in 1920, the northern part of the former duchy was returned to Denmark. The southern zone remained with Germany.

World War II

In September 1939, during Hitler's invasion of Poland, Denmark again confirmed its neutral status. This failed to stop the Third Reich from invading Denmark on 9 April 1940, and after a brief period of resistance by the royal guards at Amalienborg Slot Germany began a "peaceful occupation". Hoping to minimize casualties, the government in Copenhagen decided on a policy of limited co-operation. Opposition among ordinary Danes to this occupation was widespread, however, and in 1943 an increasingly strong resistance movement brought an end to the policy of collaboration. Following a wave of strikes and anti-German demonstrations, the government resigned and was replaced by a German administration.

The Nazis disarmed the Danish army and fleet and began to round up Danish Jews. Fortunately, most were spirited away at night in fishing boats by the Danish Resistance to neutral Sweden.

The final 18 months of the war saw the Danish Freedom Council, an underground movement that organized the Resistance, become increasingly active. The Danish

US State Secretary hands the Danish minister a cheque in payment for the Virgin Islands

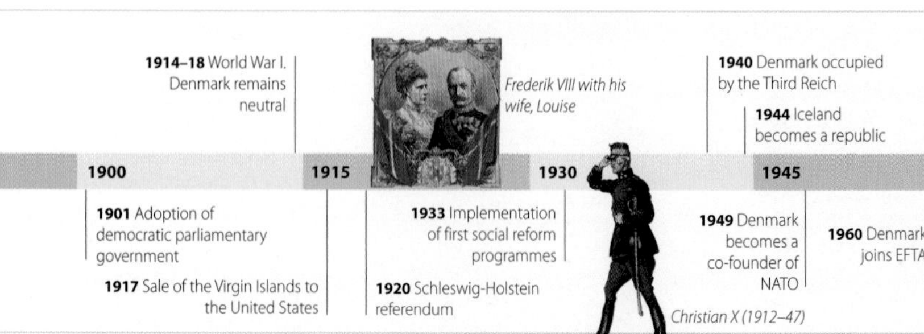

Germans on the streets of Copenhagen during World War II

Resistance, which by 1945 had some 50,000 operatives ready to assist the Allies, did all it could to hamper the German war effort, including blowing up railway lines and sabotaging German-run factories. With the German surrender in 1945, a new government composed of Resistance leaders and pre-war politicians was formed in Denmark.

Margrethe II, Queen of Denmark

Postwar Denmark

Thanks to the activities of the Resistance, Denmark was recognized as a member of the Allied Forces and joined the United Nations in 1945. In 1949 it joined the ranks of NATO. This move marked a departure from a policy of neutrality, which the country had followed since 1864. Denmark's participation in the Marshall Plan enabled the country to thoroughly modernize its industry and agriculture and laid the foundations for postwar prosperity. A new constitution, enacted in 1953, introduced a single-chamber parliament and changed the rules governing female succession to the throne. These new rules were applied in 1972 when Queen Margrethe II ascended the throne following the death of her father, Frederik IX.

Denmark did not participate in the talks which in 1957 resulted in the formation of the European Union, but in 1973, after a referendum, it became the first Scandinavian country to join the EU. Denmark's EU membership has remained a controversial subject with many Danes, however, and 87 per cent voted against the adoption of the euro. Throughout the 1960s and 1970s a series of reforms, including a generous system of social welfare and a virtual lack of censorship, bolstered the country's reputation as a liberal country. In the 1970s and 1980s Denmark entered a conservative phase with calls for curbs on immigration and tax cuts. However, it is still acknowledged as a tolerant society, with a high standard of living, a strong sense of social conscience and many positive policies towards protecting the environment. In 2009, Anders Fogh Rasmussen, the country's former prime minister, was appointed secretary general of NATO.

Anders Fogh Rasmussen, secretary general of NATO

1972 Queen Margrethe II ascends the throne of Denmark

1973 Denmark joins the European Union

1975

1990

1992 Rejection of the Maastricht Treaty, by public referendum

2000 Denmark rejects adoption of the euro

2002 Copenhagen Summit; negotiations end on the enlargement of the EU

2004 Wedding of the Crown Prince

Marriage of Prince Frederik and Mary Donaldson

2005

2005 Bi-centenary of H.C. Andersen

2009 Anders Fogh Rasmussen appointed secretary general of NATO

2014 Copenhagen hosted the 59th annual Eurovision Song Contest

2020

i'm lovin' it
REKLAMEPLADS
38 69 76 11
CITY
LG Mobile
PALACE

COPENHAGEN AREA BY AREA

Copenhagen at a Glance

Copenhagen's main attractions include its three royal palaces (Rosenborg, Amalienborg and Christiansborg), as well as numerous museums, churches and monuments, including the much-loved Little Mermaid. There is no shortage of parks. The most famous of these is Tivoli in central Copenhagen. The city centre is compact and can easily be explored on foot. Enjoyable alternatives to walking are touring the city on a bicycle or riding one of the waterbuses that run along some of the most interesting canals.

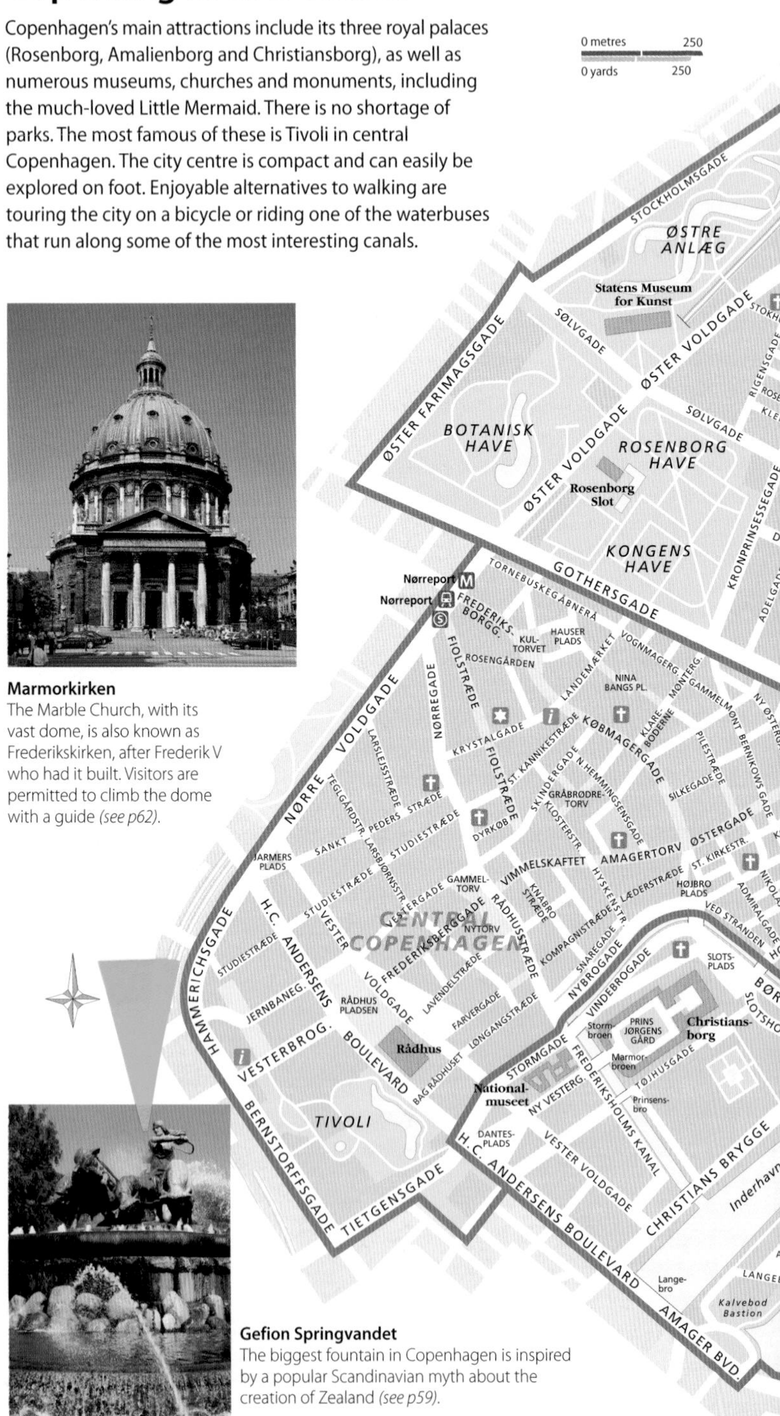

Marmorkirken
The Marble Church, with its vast dome, is also known as Frederikskirken, after Frederik V who had it built. Visitors are permitted to climb the dome with a guide *(see p62)*.

Gefion Springvandet
The biggest fountain in Copenhagen is inspired by a popular Scandinavian myth about the creation of Zealand *(see p59)*.

◀ A view of Copenhagen, the Rådhus (City Hall) and beyond

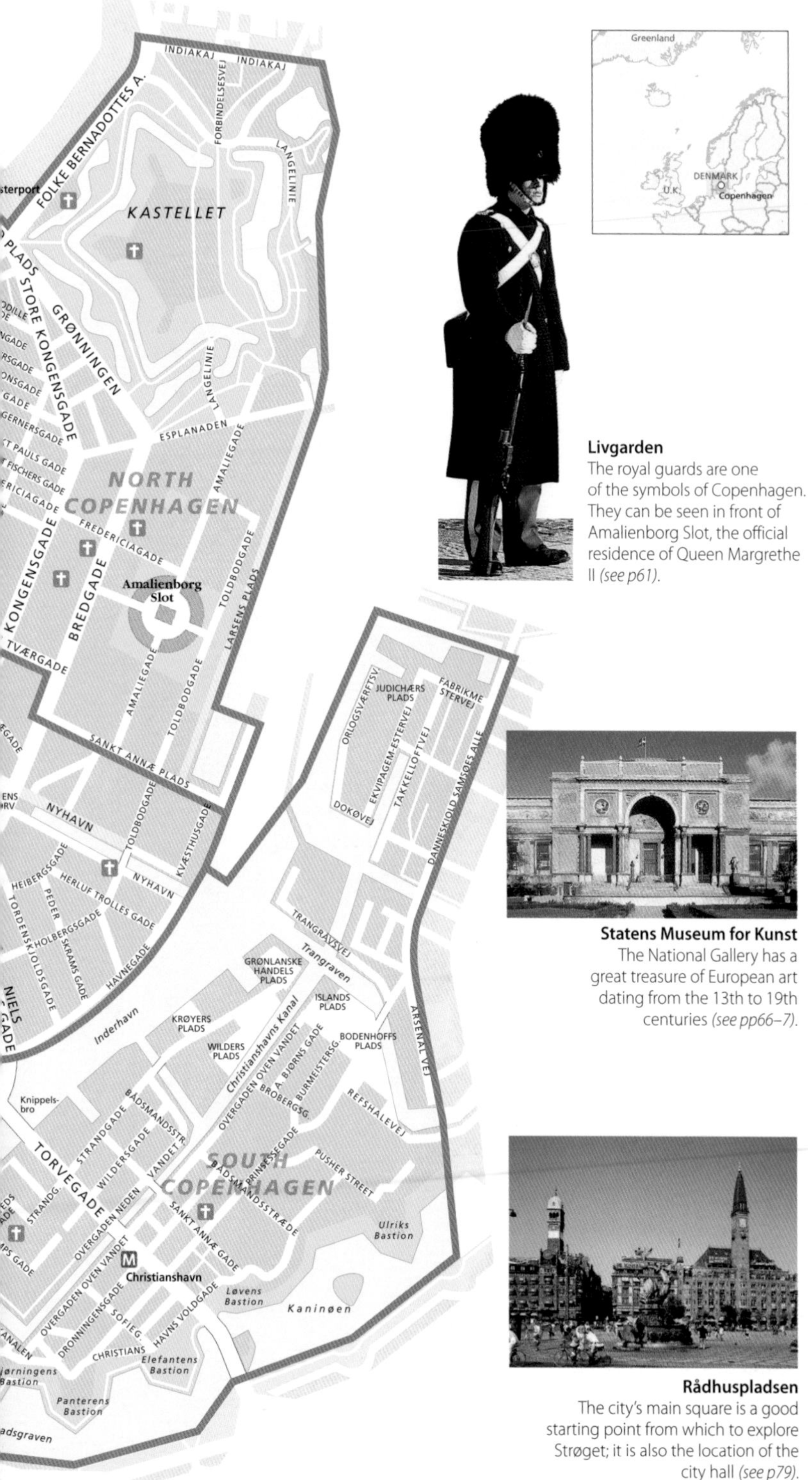

Livgarden
The royal guards are one of the symbols of Copenhagen. They can be seen in front of Amalienborg Slot, the official residence of Queen Margrethe II *(see p61)*.

Statens Museum for Kunst
The National Gallery has a great treasure of European art dating from the 13th to 19th centuries *(see pp66–7)*.

Rådhuspladsen
The city's main square is a good starting point from which to explore Strøget; it is also the location of the city hall *(see p79)*.

NORTH COPENHAGEN

The north of the city is particularly attractive and includes the famous statue of the Little Mermaid *(Den Lille Havfrue)* and two royal palaces: Amalienborg Slot and Rosenborg Slot. The area also contains several interesting museums of a highly diverse nature – ranging from the Statens Museum for Kunst (Danish National Gallery), through to the Geologisk Museum (Geological Museum) and the Medical Museion (Medical Museum).

Standing close to one another are sacred buildings belonging to three different religions: the Protestant Marmorkirken, the Roman Catholic Sankt Ansgars Kirke and the Russian Orthodox Alexander Newsky Kirke. North Copenhagen has masses of greenery. The gardens and waterfalls of Botanisk Have (Botanical Gardens) are well worth exploring, as is the King's Garden (Kongens Have), which surrounds Rosenborg Slot.

Sights at a Glance

Churches

3 Sankt Albans Kirke
8 Marmorkirken

Historic Buildings and Monuments

1 The Little Mermaid
2 Kastellet
4 Gefion Springvandet
7 *Amalienborg Slot pp60–61*
12 *Rosenborg Slot pp64–5*

Museums and Galleries

5 Medical Museion
6 Designmuseum Danmark
9 Davids Samling
11 Livgardens Historiske Samling
14 Geologisk Museum
15 Hirschsprungske Samling
16 *Statens Museum for Kunst pp66–7*

Parks and Gardens

10 Kongens Have
13 Botanisk Have

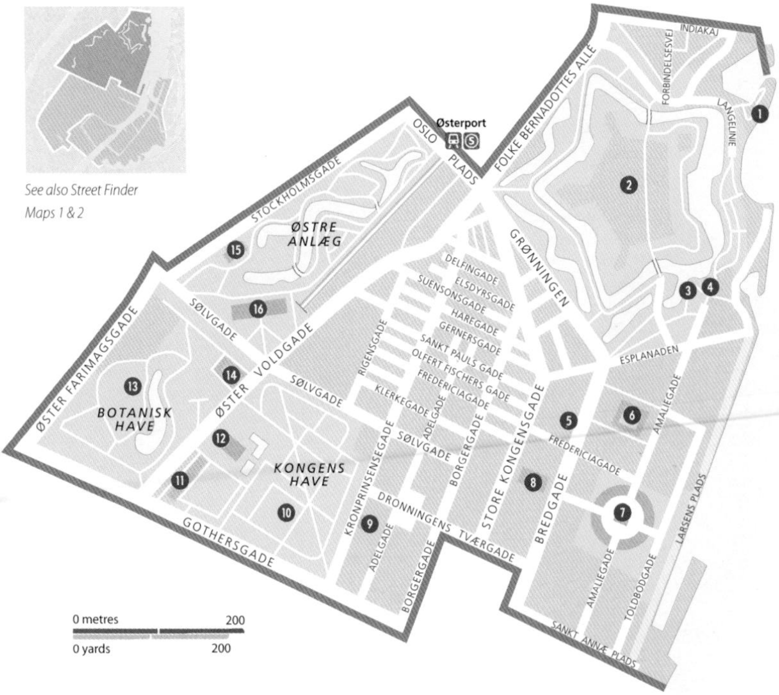

See also Street Finder Maps 1 & 2

INDIAKAJ
FORBINDELSESVEJ
LANGELINIE
FOLKE BERNADOTTES ALLE
Østerport
OSLO PLADS
STOCKHOLMSGADE
ØSTRE ANLÆG
GRØNNINGEN
DELFINGADE
ELSDYRSGADE
SUENSONSGADE
HAREGADE
GERNERSGADE
SANKT PAULS GADE
OLFERT FISCHERS GADE
FREDERICIAGADE
ESPLANADEN
SØLVGADE
ØSTER VOLDGADE
ØSTER FARIMAGSGADE
BOTANISK HAVE
RIGENSGADE
KLERKEGADE
ADELGADE
BORGERGADE
KRONPRINSENSEGADE
STORE KONGENSGADE
AMALIEGADE
KONGENS HAVE
DRONNINGENS TVÆRGADE
BREDGADE
LARSENS PLADS
TOLDBODGADE
GOTHERSGADE
SANKT ANNÆ PLADS

0 metres 200
0 yards 200

◀ The changing of the Livgarden (royal guards)

For keys to symbols *see back flap*

Street-by-Street: Around Amalienborg Slot

The main reason to come to this part of Copenhagen is to visit Amalienborg Slot, the official residence of Queen Margrethe II, which is guarded by soldiers in traditional uniforms. The best time to visit is at noon, when the daily ceremony for the changing of the guard takes place. Frederik V made Amalienborg Slot the focal point of a new, smart district, which he built to mark the 300th anniversary of the Oldenburg dynasty, celebrated in 1748. In honour of the king the district was named Frederiksstaden.

❶ Medicinsk-Historisk Museum, a medical museum, is housed in the former Danish Academy of Surgery and has on display some gruesome human remains as well as an old operating theatre.

Alexander Newsky Kirke is a Russian Orthodox church and was completed in 1883. It was a gift from Tsar Alexander III to mark his marriage to a Danish princess.

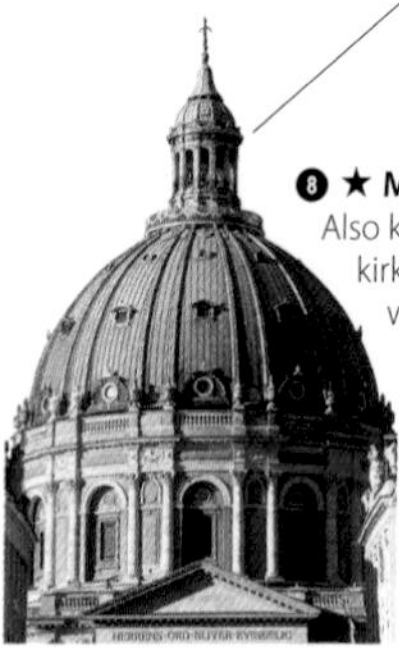

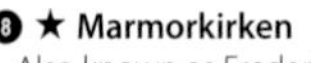

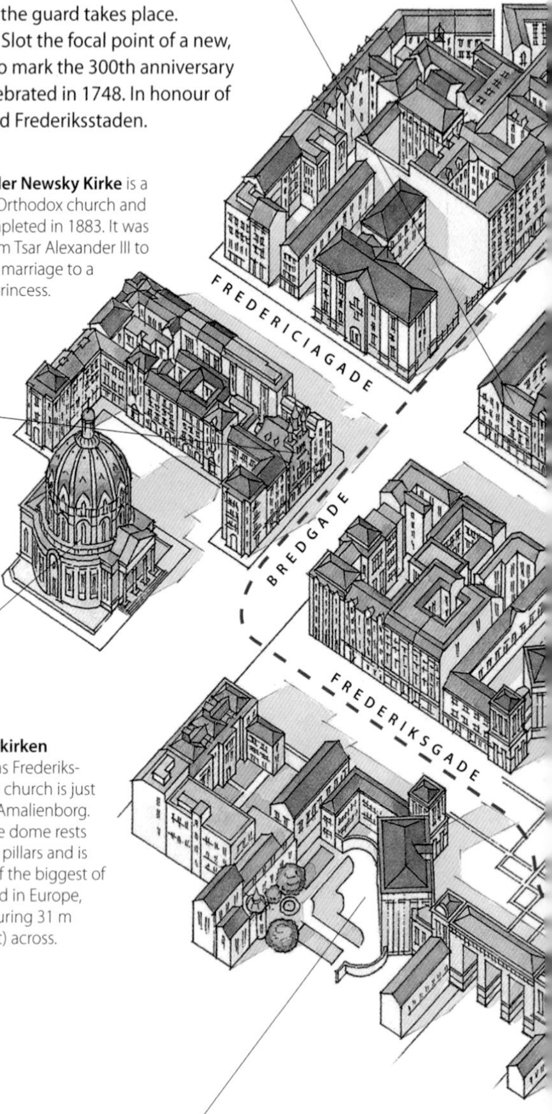

❽ ★ Marmorkirken
Also known as Frederiks-kirken, this church is just west of Amalienborg. Its huge dome rests on 12 pillars and is one of the biggest of its kind in Europe, measuring 31 m (102 ft) across.

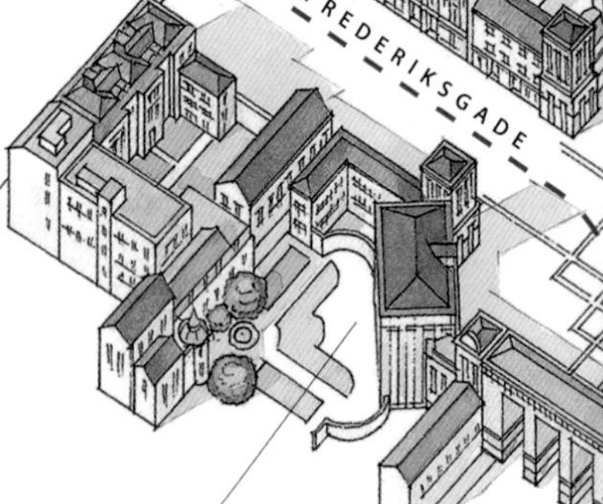

❼ ★ Amalienborg Slot
Consisting of four almost identical buildings, the palace has been the main residence of the Danish royal family since 1794.

0 metres 50
0 yards 50

Key

– – Suggested route

6 ★ Designmuseum Danmark
Before this building provided an exhibition space to showcase Danish design, it served as the city hospital in the 18th century.

Locator Map
See Street Finder Map 2

Sankt Ansgars Kirke is on the site of a Roman Catholic chapel and was once used by Copenhagen's foreign population. The present building was completed in 1842 and consecrated 23 years later.

Afstøbningssamling, or Royal Cast Collection, has over 2,000 sculpture casts, including a copy of the *Venus de Milo* and copies of statues from the Acropolis.

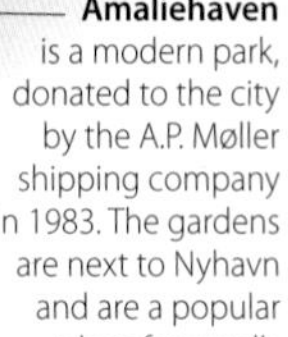

Amaliehaven is a modern park, donated to the city by the A.P. Møller shipping company in 1983. The gardens are next to Nyhavn and are a popular place for a walk.

❶ The Little Mermaid

Langelinie. **Map** 2 F3. Ⓢ Østerport. 26. **mermaidsculpture.dk**

The tiny figure of the Little Mermaid *(Den Lille Havfrue)*, sitting on a rock and gazing wistfully at the passing ships, is Denmark's best-known monument. The sculpture, commissioned by Carl Jacobsen, head of the Carlsberg brewery, was inspired by the ballet version of *The Little Mermaid*, which in turn was based on Hans Christian Andersen's tale about a mermaid who falls in love with a prince.

The sculptor, Edvard Eriksen (1876–1959), wanted to use as his model Ellen Price, a prima ballerina who had played the part of the mermaid. However, when the dancer learned where the statue was to be located she refused to continue posing and allowed only her face to be used. As a result, the body was modelled on that of the sculptor's wife.

The final bronze cast was placed at the end of the harbour promenade in 1913. Since then, the sculpture has fallen victim to vandals and pranksters on a number of occasions. In 1961 she had her hair painted red. In 1964 her head was cut off; some time later she lost both arms and in 1998 she lost her head once again. Now, moved a little further towards the sea, she enjoys more peace.

The Little Mermaid, Copenhagen's most famous landmark

One of the buildings inside the Kastellet

❷ Kastellet

Map 2 E3. **Tel** 33 11 22 33 (for tours of the grounds). Ⓢ Østerport. 1A, 15, 20E, 26. **Open** fortress grounds only. **kastellet.info**

A fortress was first built on this site in 1626 but a Swedish attack in 1658 revealed its numerous weak points and on the orders of Frederik III the defences were rebuilt. The works were completed in 1663. The final structure, known as the Kastellet (Citadel), consisted of a fort in the shape of a five-pointed star surrounded by high embankments and a deep moat. In the 19th century the fortress was partially demolished and rebuilt once more. During World War II it was taken over by the occupying German forces who used it as their headquarters. It is now used by the Danish military, although the grounds and ramparts are open to visitors.

In the 19th century Kastellet served as a prison. The prisoner's cells were built against the church so that the convicts, unseen by the public, could participate in the mass by peering through small viewing holes cut into the walls.

❸ Sankt Albans Kirke

Churchillparken. **Map** 2 E3. **Tel** 33 11 85 18. 1A, 15. **Open** summer: 10am–4pm Mon–Fri. **st-albans.dk**

This church was built in 1887 to serve the city's Anglican community and is named after Saint Alban, a 4th-century Roman soldier who converted to Christianity and suffered a martyr's death.

Churchillparken, just south of Kastellet

The Story of the Little Mermaid

The heroine of Andersen's tale is a young mermaid who lives beneath the waves with her five sisters. The little mermaid rescues a prince from a sinking ship and falls in love with him. Desperate to be with the prince, she is seduced by a wicked sea witch into giving up her beautiful voice in return for legs so that she can go ashore. The price is high, and the witch warns the mermaid that should the prince marry another she will die. For a long time the prince adores his new, mute lover but in the end he is forced into marrying a princess from another kingdom. Before the wedding is to take place on board a ship, the mermaid's sisters swim to the ship and offer the mermaid a magic knife. All she need do is stab the prince and she will be free to return to the water. The mermaid cannot bring herself to murder the prince and, as dawn breaks, she dies.

Andersen surrounded by fairytale characters

Situated not far from the Gefion fountain, along Langelinie promenade in Churchillparken, the elegant Gothic church was a gift from Edward, Prince of Wales, who at the time was vying for the hand of Princess Alexandra, the daughter of Christian IX. They married in 1863, and the prince ascended to the throne as Edward VII in 1901. The church's interior has attractive stained-glass windows and a miniature copy of Bertel Thorvaldsen's sculpture – *St John the Baptist Praying in the Desert*. Religious services are still held here in English and the congregation often includes visitors to the city.

❹ Gefion Springvandet

Map 2 F3. 🚌 1A, 15.

Built in 1908, the Gefion fountain is an impressive work by Anders Bundgaard and one of Copenhagen's largest monuments. Its main feature is a statue of the goddess Gefion – a mythical Scandinavian figure. According to legend, the king of Sweden promised to give the goddess as much land as she could plough in one night. Gefion, who took him at his word, turned her four sons into oxen and harnessed them to a plough. By the time the cock crowed she had managed to plough a sizeable chunk of Sweden. She then picked it up and threw it into the sea, and so formed the island of Zealand. The hole left behind became Lake Vänern (whose shape closely resembles that of Zealand).

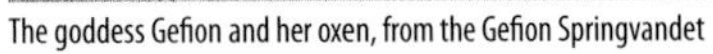

The goddess Gefion and her oxen, from the Gefion Springvandet

Visitors engaging with installations at the Medical Museion

❺ Medical Museion

Bredgade 62. **Map** 2 E4. **Tel** 35 32 39 00. Ⓢ Østerport. 🚌 1A, 15, 19. **Open** noon–4pm Wed–Fri & Sun. **museion.ku.dk**

A combined museum and research unit at the University of Copenhagen, the Medical Museion was founded on a private initiative in 1907. It marked the 50th anniversary of the Danish Medical Association with a public exhibition of historical medical artefacts. The museum remained public until 1918, when it was taken over by the university.

The museum's main exhibition and event site is situated on Bredgade in the former Royal Academy of Surgeons building, which dates from 1787, and the adjacent buildings in Frederiksstaden. This central Copenhagen neighbourhood is a candidate for inclusion in UNESCO's World Heritage List. Medical Museion has one of the biggest and richest historical collections of medical artefacts in Europe. The collections contain up to 250,000 artefacts. There is also a large image collection, a document archive, and a historical book collection. A satellite exhibition is located in the main building of the Faculty of Health and Medical Sciences on Blegdamsvej.

❻ Designmuseum Danmark

Bredgade 68. **Map** 2 E4. **Tel** 33 18 56 56. Ⓢ Østerport. Ⓜ Kongens Nytorv. 🚌 1A, 15. **Open** 11am–5pm Tue–Sun (to 9pm Wed). **designmuseum.dk**

Designed by the Danish architects Nicolai Eigtved and Lauritz de Thurah and erected in the mid-18th century, the buildings that now house the Designmuseum Danmark were originally the city hospital; it was here that the philosopher Søren Kierkegaard died in 1855. The hospital was closed in 1919 and renovated to suit the purposes of a museum. Today the museum is Denmark's largest museum for Danish and international design and a central exhibition forum for industrial design and applied arts in Scandinavia. The museum shop is an excellent source of industrial design, ceramics, glass and textiles.

Nearby, on the same side of the street, is **Sankt Ansgars Kirke**, a Roman Catholic church that has a small exhibition devoted to the history of Danish Catholicism.

❼ Amalienborg Slot

The Amalienborg Palace complex consists of four buildings around an octagonal square. They were meant as residences for four wealthy families, but when Christiansborg Slot burned down in 1794, Christian VII bought one of the four palaces and turned it into his residence. Designed by Nicolai Eigtved, Christian VII's Palace is renowned for its Great Hall, which has splendid Rococo woodcarvings and stucco decoration. Since 1885, the palace has been used mostly for royal guests and ceremonial purposes. The palace is closed for renovations during 2015.

Balustrade Statues
All the palace statues were renovated in the late 1970s by sculptor Eric Erlandsen with the help of experts from the Statens Museum for Kunst (Danish National Gallery).

Gallery
The palace gallery has a beautiful ceiling and is the work of Fossatti. The French architect Nicolas-Henri Jardin designed the furniture.

Velvet Chamber
The tiled stove in this room comes from a factory in Lübeck. The silk velvet wall hangings were presents from Ludwig XV to an important high court official named Count Moltke.

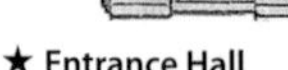

★ Entrance Hall
The entrance hall has been renovated to appear as it would have done when the palace was first built. Its decorations have been recreated according to period designs. The statue of Andromeda is a cast of the original marble sculpture.

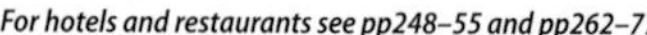

For hotels and restaurants see pp248–55 and pp262–77

★ Great Hall
This elegant room is an example of the artistry of Nicolai Eigtved and is the most beautiful Rococo chamber in Denmark.

VISITORS' CHECKLIST

Practical Information
Amalienborg Slot, Christian VII's Palace, Amalienborg Slotsplads.
Tel 33 12 21 86. **Open** May–Oct: 10am–4pm daily, Nov–Apr: 11am–4pm Tue–Sun. compulsory: 11:30am (Danish); 1pm & 2:30pm (English).
amalienborg.dk

Transport
Kongens Nytorv. Nørreport. 1A, 19, 26, 29, 650S.

The royal guards, sporting bearskin hats, stand watch, day and night, in front of the palace.

Clock
This grandfather clock is one of many objects on display in the palace.

Royal Residence

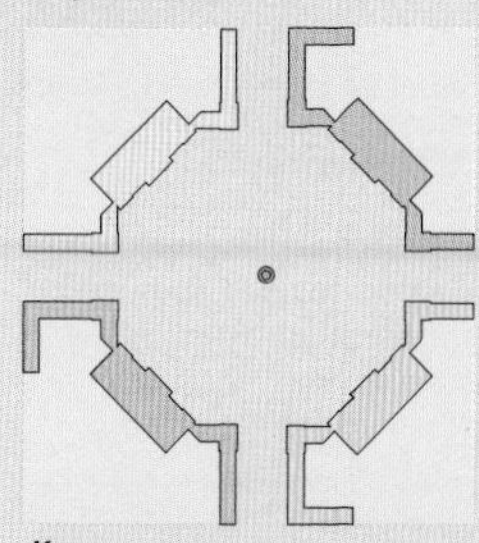

Key

- Christian IX's Palace
- Christian VII's Palace
- Christian VIII's Palace
- Frederik VIII's Palace

The name Amalienborg actually refers to an earlier palace, built in 1669 by Frederik III for his young bride Sophie Amalie. The present complex consists of four palaces grouped around a square, collectively known as Amalienborg, which is in the heart of Frederiksstaden. The equestrian statue of Frederick V in the middle of the complex is the work of French sculptor Jacques Saly who spent 30 years working on it. The statue reputedly cost as much as the entire complex.

Changing of the Guard
Every day at noon, the Livgarden (royal guards) walk from Amalienborg Palace to Rosenborg Castle for the Changing of the Guard.

❽ Marmorkirken

Frederiksgade 4. **Map** 2 D4. **Tel** 33 15 01 44. 1A, 15, 19, 26. Church: **Open** 10am–5pm Mon–Thu & Sat (to 6:30pm Wed), noon–5pm Fri & Sun. Dome: **Open** 1pm, 3pm Sat & Sun. **marmorkirken.dk**

The vast dome of the Baroque Frederikskirken, also known as Marmorkirken or the Marble Church, leads many visitors to suspect that its architect, Nikolai Eigtved, based his design on St Peter's Basilica in Rome. The church was named after Frederik V who wanted to celebrate the fact that his family had ruled Denmark for 300 years by building a new district in Copenhagen – Frederiksstaden – with the church as its focal point. When work began, in 1749, it was assumed that the church would be constructed of marble imported from Norway (hence its alternative name). However, it quickly became apparent that the cost of such a venture would exceed the financial resources of the treasury and in 1770 work was abandoned.

A century later the building was completed using local Danish marble. The most obvious feature of the church is its dome – one of the largest in Europe. Visitors can climb the 260 steps to enjoy wonderful city views from the top of the bell tower. Inside the church are frescoes by Danish artists. On the outside, the building has statues of Danish saints.

17th-century bronze vessel from India, Davids Samling

❾ Davids Samling

Kronprinsessegade 30. **Map** 2 D5. **Tel** 33 73 49 49. Ⓢ Ⓜ Nørreport. 1A, 15, 19, 26, 42, 43, 350S. **Open** 1–5pm Tue–Sun (to 9pm Wed). **davidmus.dk**

The museum's founder, Christian Ludvig David (1878–1960), was a lawyer who in 1945 established the C.L. David Foundation and Collection, which still owns and administers the museum and holdings. David's great-grandfather owned the building in Kronprinsessegade 30 from 1811 until his death in 1830. David acquired the building in 1917 – a century after his family had lived there – and made it his home until his death in 1960. To expand the museum, the foundation bought the neighboring building, at Kronprinsessegade 32, in 1986.

The museum is best known for its extensive collection of Islamic art, which includes items from Spain, Persia, India and elsewhere. Among the many treasures, some of which date as far back as the 6th century, are ceramics, silks, jewellery and ancient daggers inlaid with jewels. The museum also houses a small collection of European art, as well as examples of 18th-century English, French and German furniture. There is also a collection of Danish silver dating from the 17th and 18th centuries.

Circular grand nave of Marmorkirken, decorated with wall paintings

❿ Kongens Have

Map 1 C5. **Open** 7am–dusk daily.

The King's Garden was established by Christian IV in 1606 and is Copenhagen's oldest park, retaining most of its original layout. In the 17th century the gardens supplied the royal court with fresh fruit, vegetables and roses to adorn the royal apartments.

Today, the shady gardens, criss-crossed by paths and with numerous benches, are one of the favourite places for Copenhagen's citizens to walk and relax. Here, visitors can also find one of the capital's most famous monuments. Unveiled in 1877, it is a statue of Hans Christian Andersen enchanting a group of children with some of his fairy tales.

Leafy Kongens Have surrounding Rosenborg Slot

⓫ Livgardens Historiske Samling

Gothersgade 100. **Map** 1 B5. **Tel** 45 99 40 00. Ⓢ Ⓜ Nørreport. 5A, 6A, 14, 42, 43, 150S, 173E, 184, 185, 350S. **Open** 11:30am–3pm Sat & Sun. **forsvaret.dk/lg**

The Livgarden or royal guards, dressed in colourful uniforms and sporting furry busbies, are one of the symbols of Copenhagen. Many people come to watch them during the daily ceremony for the changing of the guard in front of Amalienborg Slot, but even their daily marches between Rosenborg and Amalienborg palaces are a popular sight. The museum is housed in a cluster of over 200-year-old barracks and contains background

Vast palm house, built in 1874, in Copenhagen's Botanisk Have

information on the guards' history. Examples of their uniforms are on display along with weapons, paintings, historical documents, and musical instruments played by the guardsmen.

⓬ Rosenborg Slot

See pp64–5.

⓭ Botanisk Have

Gothersgade 128. **Map** 1 B4. **Tel** 35 32 22 22. 5A, 6A, 14, 40, 42, 43, 150S, 173E, 184, 185, 350S. S M Nørreport. **Open** May–Sep: 8:30am–6pm daily; Oct–Apr: 8:30am–4pm Tue–Sun. W **botanik.snm.ku.dk**

The 20,000 species of plants gathered in the Botanical Gardens include native Danish plants, as well as some highly exotic ones collected from around the world. The garden was established in 1872, on the grounds of old town fortifications. Bulwarks have been turned into rockeries, and the moat that once surrounded the fortified walls is now a lake filled with water and marsh plants.

The gardens themselves have much to offer. There is a small forest, waterfalls and greenhouses, one of which contains more than 1,000 varieties of cactus. Elsewhere, it is possible to see coffee and pineapples growing. A special attraction is the roof-top walk in the steamy palmhouse. The open-air café in front of the palmhouse offers magnificent views of the garden.

⓮ Geologisk Museum

Øster Voldgade 5–7. **Map** 1 C4. **Tel** 35 32 22 22. S M Nørreport. 6A, 26, 42, 43, 184, 185. **Open** 10am–4pm Tue–Fri, 1–4pm Sat & Sun. W **geologi.snm.ku.dk**

Standing close to the eastern end of Botanisk Have, the Geological Museum opened in 1893 and occupies an Italian Renaissance-style building. Its carved stone decorations include rosettes, columns and arches.

The earliest museum exhibits are the meteorites on display in the courtyard. The biggest of these was found in Greenland in 1963 and, at 20 tonnes (17.86 tons), is the sixth largest in the world. On the ground and first floors are glass cabinets filled with minerals and fossils including the imprint of a jellyfish made over 150 million years ago. Elsewhere, there is an exhibition devoted to volcanoes, displays relating to the history of man and collections of dinosaur bones.

A separate section is devoted to oil and gas exploration and the geology of Denmark. Colourful stones and rock crystals are on sale in the museum shop.

⓯ Hirschsprungske Samling

Stockholmsgade 20. **Map** 1 C3. **Tel** 35 42 03 36. S Østerport. 6A, 14, 26, 40, 42, 43, 150S, 184, 185. **Open** 11am–4pm Tue–Sun. W **hirschsprung.dk**

This gallery, one of Copenhagen's best, owes its existence to the art patronage of Heinrich Hirschsprung (1836–1908), a Danish tobacco baron who supported many Danish artists. The Hirschsprung collection has been on public display since 1911 and is housed in a Neo-Classical building on the outskirts of Østre Anlæg park.

The collection includes works by prominent Danish artists from the 19th and 20th centuries such as Eckersberg, Købke, Bendz, Marstrand, Anna and Michael Ancher, P.S. Krøyer and Vilhelm Hammershøi. A free tour at 2pm on Sundays highlights the works of a different artist each week and lasts around 45 minutes.

One of the exhibition rooms inside the Hirschsprungske Samling

⑫ Rosenborg Slot

This royal palace is one of Copenhagen's most visited attractions and contains thousands of royal objects including paintings, trinkets, furniture and a small armoury. Most impressive of all is the underground treasury containing the crown jewels and other royal regalia. The exquisite Dutch-Renaissance brick palace was erected in 1606, on the orders of Christian IV, to serve as a summer residence. It was used by successive monarchs until the early 18th century when Frederik IV built a more spacious palace at Fredensborg. In the early 19th century Rosenborg was opened to the public as a museum.

★ Treasury
The underground treasury rooms house the royal jewels, including the Crown of Christian IV which weighs 2.89 kg (6.4 lbs).

★ Long Hall
17th-century tapestries decorate the walls of the hall, which also contains a collection of 18th-century silver furniture including three silver lions that once guarded the king's throne.

Tower Stairway
Equestrian paintings, portraits, and a series of 17th-century floral watercolours by Maria Merian are hung on the walls.

Christian IV's Winter Room
The most important of King Christian IV's private chambers has a fine collection of Dutch paintings and a speaking tube connected to the wine cellar below.

KEY

① **The spire-topped tower was converted from a bay**

② **The Main Tower** was originally shorter and was raised in the 1620s.

③ **The third floor** was completed in 1624 and was designed to provide space for the magnificent, long banqueting hall.

Marble Hall
The hall's Baroque décor was commissioned by Frederik III. The Italian decorator Francesco Bruno gave the ceilings new stuccowork and clad the walls with imitation marble.

VISITORS' CHECKLIST

Practical Information
Øster Voldgade 4A. **Map** 1 C4. **Tel** 33 15 32 86. **Open** May, Sep & Oct: 10am–4pm daily; Jun–Aug: 10am–5pm daily; Nov–Apr: 10am–2pm Tue–Sun. **Closed** 1 Jan, 22–26 & 31 Dec.
W **rosenborgcastle.dk**

Transport
S M Nørreport. 5A, 6A, 26, 150S, 173E, 184, 185

Glass Cabinet
This second-floor room, designed in 1714 and commissioned by King Frederik IV, contains his elaborately displayed collection of Venetian glass. It is the only known cabinet of its kind.

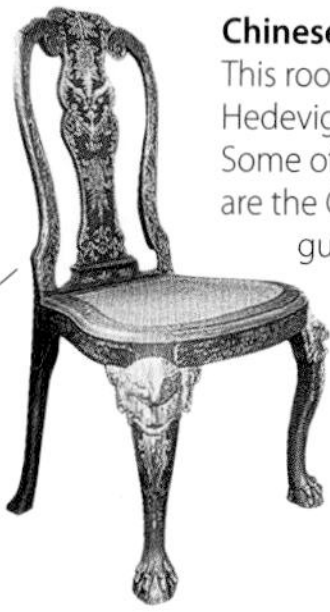

Chinese Drawing Room
This room was used by Sophie Hedevig, sister of Frederik IV. Some of its most distinctive items are the Chinese-style chairs, a guitar encrusted with ivory and tortoiseshell and bearing the princess's monogram, a 17th-century Japanese porcelain jug and an ebony table.

Royal Chamber of Frederik IV
The table standing at the centre of the room was given to Frederik IV in 1709 by the Grand Duke of Tuscany. The magnificent rock crystal chandelier was probably made in Vienna.

⑯ Statens Museum for Kunst

The Danish National Gallery houses a fascinating collection of European art. Among the Danish painters represented here are artists from the "Golden Age", such as Christoffer Wilhelm Eckersberg and Constantin Hansen, and members of the Skagen School, including Peder Severin Krøyer, and Anna and Michael Ancher. There are also works by Old Masters like Bruegel, Rubens and Rembrandt, as well as masterpieces by 20th-century giants such as Picasso, and contemporary installation art. Weekend workshops inspire children to make their own art.

1st floor

The Last Supper (1909)
Emil Nolde, a well-known representative of German Expressionism, has often pursued religious themes in his art.

A Mountain Climber (1912)
This Expressionist painting explores the relationship between humans and nature. It is one of a number of works by the Danish artist J.F. Willumsen.

★ Portrait of Madame Matisse (1905)
This portrait by Henri Matisse combines some of the most typical elements of Fauvism including simple lines and sharply contrasting colours.

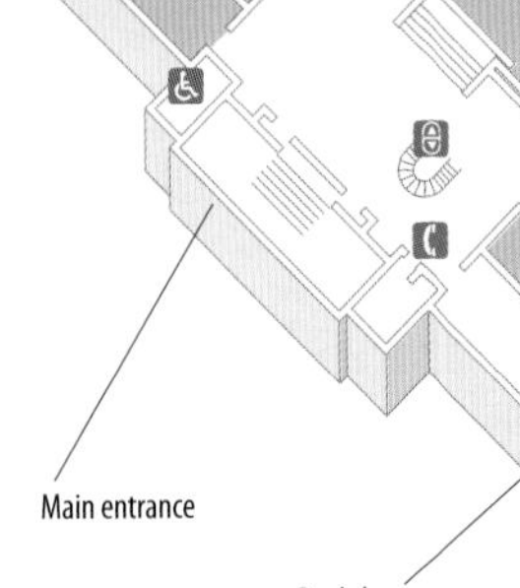

For hotels and restaurants see pp248–55 and pp262–77

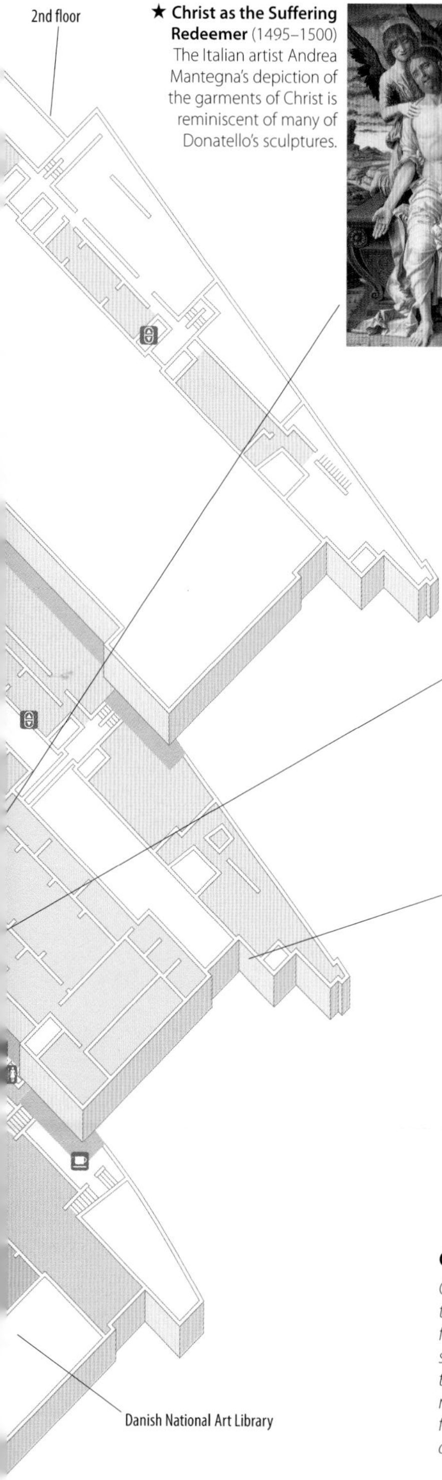

★ Christ as the Suffering Redeemer (1495–1500)
The Italian artist Andrea Mantegna's depiction of the garments of Christ is reminiscent of many of Donatello's sculptures.

VISITORS' CHECKLIST

Practical Information
Sølvgade 48–50. **Map** 1 C4.
Tel 33 74 84 94. **Open** 10am–5pm Tue–Sun (to 8pm Wed).
(for special exhibitions only).
smk.dk

Transport
Østerport, Nørreport.
Nørreport, Kongens Nytorv.
6A, 14, 26, 40, 42, 43, 150S, 173E, 184, 185, 350S.

The Strife of Lent with Shrove-Tide (1550–69)
This detail from a 16th-century Renaissance painting by Pieter Bruegel is typical of his earthy moralizing.

The New Wing, a striking Modernist structure by Anna Maria Indrio, opened in 1998 and is linked to the old building by a glass-roofed atrium.

Key

- European art, 1300–1800
- The X-Room
- Children's workshop
- Sculpture Street
- Danish and international art after 1900
- Temporary exhibitions
- Danish and Nordic art, 1750–1900

Danish National Art Library

Gallery Guide

Contemporary art exhibitions are held in the X-Room, while Sculpture Street is the venue for contemporary Danish and international sculpture. The permanent collection is on the first floor and in the New Wing. The museum also has a number of spaces reserved for temporary exhibitions on particular artists or eras.

CENTRAL COPENHAGEN

The Strøget, a chain of five pedestrianized streets, links the city's two main squares, Kongens Nytorv and Rådhuspladsen. Shops and restaurants line the promenade, which bustles with activity well into the night. Lined with café terraces and restored 18th-century houses, Nyhavn is a quayside street that is particularly lively in the summer months. Central Copenhagen's many museums include the Ny Carlsberg Glyptotek, housing one of the world's best collections of painting and sculpture, and the Guinness World Records Museum. On a fine day it is well worth visiting the famous Tivoli amusement park and gardens. The Latin Quarter, located around the old university, has some pleasant traffic-free streets, such as Fiolstræde, which is lined with second-hand bookshops. A climb up the spiral walkway of the 17th-century Rundetårn (Round Tower) is rewarded by magnificent views over the city.

Sights at a Glance

Churches

9 Helligåndskirken
15 Sankt Petri Kirke
16 Vor Frue Kirke

Museums and Galleries

5 Guinness World Records Museum
6 Post & Tele Museum
7 Nikolaj, Copenhagen Contemporary Art Centre
12 Kunstforeningen GL STRAND
18 Ripley's Believe It Or Not!
22 *Ny Carlsberg Glyptotek pp82–3*

Streets and Squares

1 Nyhavn
3 Kongens Nytorv
8 Højbro Plads
13 Gråbrødretorv
17 Nytorv
20 Rådhuspladsen

Historic Buildings

2 Charlottenborg Slot and Kunsthal Charlottenborg
11 Rundetårn
14 Universitet
19 *Rådhus pp78–9*

Gardens

21 *Tivoli pp80–81*

Theatres

4 Det Kongelige Teater
10 Skuespilhuset

See also Street Finder Maps 3 & 4

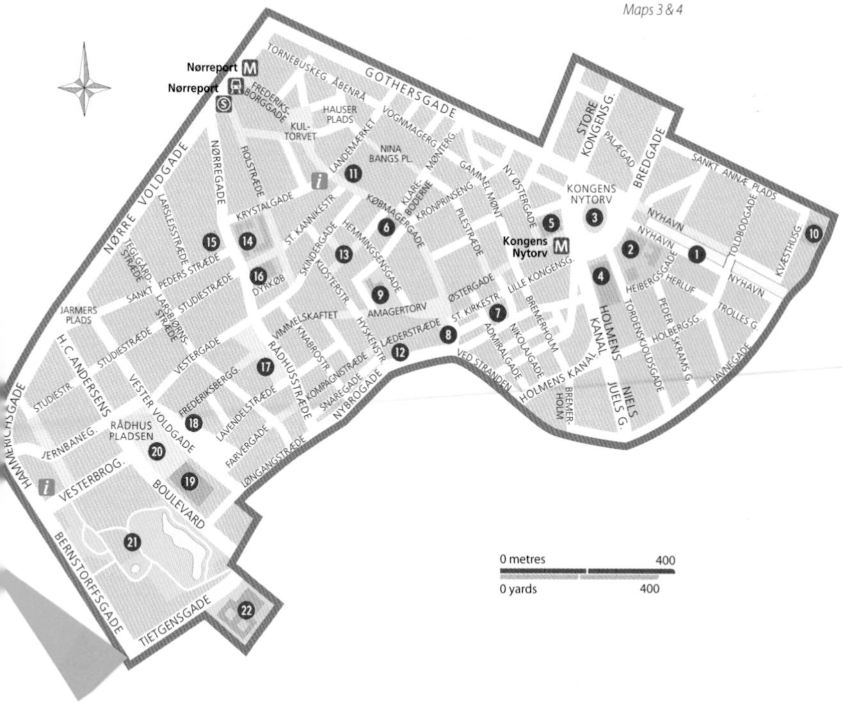

0 metres 400
0 yards 400

◀ Old and new buildings standing alongside each other in central Copenhagen

For keys to symbols *see back flap*

Street-by-Street: Around Kongens Nytorv

During the late 17th century, Kongens Nytorv (King's New Square) was laid out to link the medieval parts of the city with its newer districts. Today, it is Copenhagen's biggest square and makes an excellent starting point for exploring the city. To the southeast it joins the picturesque Nyhavn district where the historic ship *Anna Moller*, part of the Nationalmuseet's collection, can be admired from a canalside café. It also marks the beginning of Strøget, which has plenty of restaurants and bars as well as specialist shops and boutiques to tempt visitors.

Hotel d'Angleterre is one of the oldest and most exclusive hotels in Scandinavia *(see p72)* and has entertained many celebrities on their visits to Denmark.

5 Guinness World Records Museum
The museum collection includes numerous curios, including a figure of the world's tallest man (2.72m/ 8 ft 11 inches).

Key

- - Suggested route

0 metres 50
0 yards 50

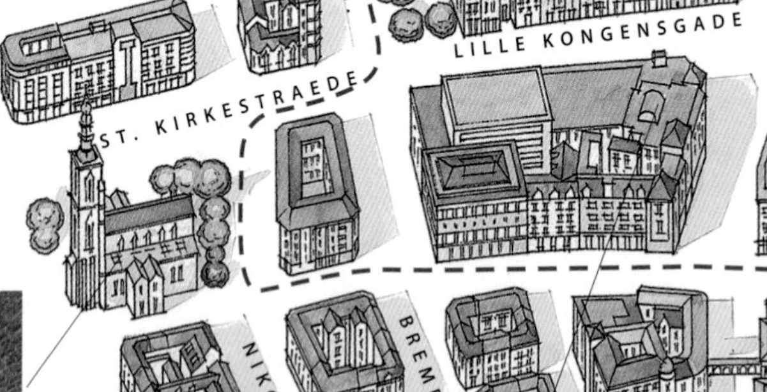

7 Nikolaj
This 13th-century former church has had a number of other purposes since the early 1800s. It was used for "happenings" in the 1960s and now houses the Copenhagen Contemporary Art Center.

Magasin du Nord is more than 100 years old and is one of the biggest and most exclusive department stores in Scandinavia.

❸ ★ Kongens Nytorv
Built in 1680 by Christian V, whose huge equestrian statue is at its centre, Kongens Nytorv is one of Copenhagen's most elegant squares and contains some of the city's finest buildings. Construction of the metro will affect access to this area until 2019.

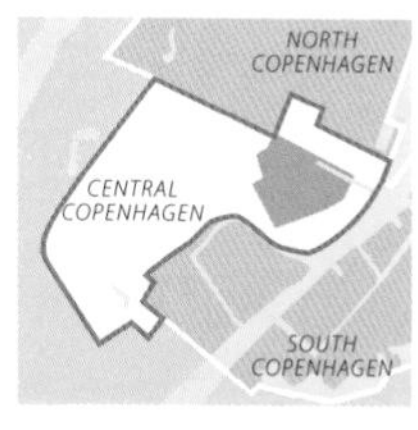

Locator Map
See Street Finder Map 4

❷ Charlottenborg Slot & Kunsthal Charlottenborg
This is the oldest building in Kongens Nytorv, and is used by Det Kongelige Kunstakademi (The Royal Academy of Fine Arts) and has exhibition space for contemporary art.

An anchor from a 19th-century sailing vessel has been transformed into a monument to the victims of World War II.

❶ ★ Nyhavn
The northern side of the canal is lined with colourful houses, many of which were once brothels frequented by sailors after months at sea.

Pleasure boat rides along the 17th-century canal are one of the main visitor attractions. It has became a tradition that each year old sailing ships arriving in Copenhagen moor alongside Nyhavn.

❹ ★ Det Kongelige Teater
This 19th-century building houses a prominent theatre, staging both drama and ballet.

Nyhavn, lined with bars, restaurants and cafés

❶ Nyhavn

Map 4 E1.

Lined on both sides with colourful houses, this 300-m (328-yard) long canal, known as the New Harbour, was dug by soldiers between 1671 and 1673 and was intended to enable ships loaded with merchandise to sail into the centre of Copenhagen. Today, stylish yachts as well as atmospheric old wooden boats are moored along many of the quays.

When Hans Christian Andersen lived here, the area north of the canal was a notorious red-light district with a seedy reputation thanks to the cheap bars, rough-and-ready hotels, tattoo parlours and numerous brothels. Since then Nyhavn has smartened up a great deal (though a few tattoo parlours still remain) and is now one of the city's best-known districts. The boozy joints packed with sailors are long gone and have been replaced with bars, cafés and restaurants targeting a more prosperous clientele. The place is especially popular on warm summer evenings, and many of the restaurants and bars can get extremely busy – particularly on the north side of the harbour. The huge anchor found at the Kongens Nytorv end of the canal once belonged to *Fyen*, a 19th-century frigate, and has been used to commemorate Danish sailors who lost their lives during World War II.

❷ Charlottenborg Slot & Kunsthal Charlottenborg

Kongens Nytorv 1. **Map** 4 D1. **Tel** 33 36 90 50. M Kongens Nytorv. 1A, 15, 19, 26, 350S. **Open** 11am–5pm Tue–Sun (to 8pm Wed).
W **kunsthalcharlottenborg.dk**

This Baroque palace was built between 1672 and 1683 for Queen Charlotte Amalie (wife of Christian V), and was named after her. In the mid-18th century King Frederik V handed over the palace to the newly created Royal Academy of Fine Arts, and it is now filled with faculty and students. An adjacent exhibition building holds both Kunsthal Charlottenborg and the Danish Art Library.

One of Charlottenborg's portals

❸ Kongens Nytorv

Map 4 D1.

King's New Square was created more than 300 years ago. This is one of Copenhagen's central points and the site of Det Kongelige Teater (The Royal Theatre) and Charlottenborg Slot. As well as marking the end of Nyhavn, it is also a good starting point for exploring Strøget, Copenhagen's famous walkway, which is lined with shops and restaurants.

At the centre of this oval square is an equestrian statue of Christian V, on whose orders the square was built. The original sculpture was made in 1688 by a French artist. Unfortunately, with time, the heavy lead monument, which depicts Christian V as a sombre Roman general, began to sink, distorting the proportions of the figure. In 1946 the monument was recast in bronze.

Each June graduates gather in the square to dance around the statue as part of a traditional matriculation ceremony.

Kongens Nytorv was once filled with elm trees, planted in the 19th century. Sadly, these

Hotel d'Angleterre's Romantic Origins

In the mid-18th century Jean Marchal, a young hairdresser and make-up artist travelling with a troupe of actors, arrived in Copenhagen. Jean decided to settle in town and took the job of valet to Count Conrad Danneskiold Laurvig. At a reception, to which he accompanied the count, he met Maria Coppy, daughter of the court chef. They married in 1755 and, exploiting the culinary talents of Maria, opened a restaurant with a handful of bedrooms for passing travellers. Unfortunately neither lived long enough to fully enjoy the fruits of their enterprise. Their small hotel has survived and thrived, having undergone a great many changes including the addition of around 100 or so rooms. It now receives some of the world's most distinguished figures.

Hotel d'Angleterre

Equestrian statue of Christian V in Kongens Nytorv

fell prey to disease in 1998 and the square has since been replanted. Construction of the metro will affect access to the square until 2019.

❹ Det Kongelige Teater

August Bournonvilles Passage, Kongens Nytorv. **Map** 4 D1. **Tel** 33 69 69 33. **kgl-teater.dk**

Anyone visiting the area around Kongens Nytorv is usually struck by the sight of the Royal Theatre, a vast Neo-Renaissance building that has been the main arts venue in Denmark since it was founded in 1748. The present building, which occupies the original site, dates from 1894. For many years, this theatre set itself apart by putting on ballet, opera and theatre in the same space. The complex includes two theatres – Gamle Scene (Old Stage) and Nye Scene (New Stage), the latter popularly known as Stærekassen and built in 1931. Since the opening of Operaen, the striking opera house across the harbour from Amalienborg Slot in 2005 *(see p93)*, the Old Stage primarily hosts ballet, while drama is staged at the Skuespilhuset *(see p75)*.

The statues at the front of the theatre celebrate two distinguished Danes who made contributions to the development of theatre and the arts. One is the playwright Ludvig Holberg, often hailed as the father of Danish theatre, the other is the poet Adam Oehlenschlager.

❺ Guinness World Records Museum

Østergade 16. **Map** 4 D1. **Tel** 33 32 31 31. Kongens Nytorv. 1A, 15, 19, 26, 350A. **Open** Jan–mid-Jun, Sep–Dec: 10am–6pm daily (to 8pm Fri & Sat); mid-Jun–Aug: 10am–10pm daily. **Closed** 1 Jan, 24–25 Dec, 31 Dec. **guinness.dk**

Visitors to the Guinness World Records Museum are welcomed at the entrance by a replica of the world's tallest man. Inside is a collection of the biggest, smallest, fastest, heaviest, longest and shortest, as well as a number of rooms in which visitors can try to beat a world record or experience how it feels to drive a car at 500 km/h (311 mph). A film showing how people from all over the world have trained for their record-breaking attempts can also be seen. In the sports gallery, visitors can test themselves as a professional racing cyclist.

❻ Post & Tele Museum

Købmagergade 37. **Map** 3 C1. **Tel** 33 41 09 00. Nørreport. Kongens Nytorv. 1A, 15, 19, 26, 350S. **Open** 10am–4pm daily. **Closed** 1 Jan, 24, 25 & 31 Dec. **ptt-museum.dk**

This museum dedicated to postal and telecommunication services grew from a core collection gathered by Jens Wilken Mørch, who started his career in the Danish Post in 1856 and eventually became head postmaster. The museum opened to the public in 1913; the exhibits relating to telecommunications were incorporated in 1931, when the museum absorbed the collection of an engineer named Hans Haller.

The permanent collection consists of three sections that give an overview of the many developments in the world of postal and telecommunication services. The highlight of The King's Post Office (1624–1848) is a full-size replica of a spherical mail coach; there are also uniforms and portraits of eminent figures within the mail service. The Age of Invention (1849–1920) focuses on maritime postal history and the early years of telegraphy and telephony. The final section looks at postal and telecommunication services after the 1920s, all the way through to the Internet age. There are also temporary exhibitions and a children's playground located inside a giant 3D stamp.

Entrance to the Guinness World Records Museum

Nikolaj, Copenhagen Contemporary Art Centre in the former Sankt Nikolaj Kirke

❼ Nikolaj, Copenhagen Contemporary Art Centre

Nikolaj Plads 10. **Map** 3 C1. **Tel** 33 18 17 80. Ⓢ Nørreport. Ⓜ Kongens Nytorv. 🚌 1A, 2A, 15, 19, 26, 350S. **Open** noon–5pm Tue–Sun (to 9pm Thu). 🎟 (free on Wed).
W kunsthallennikolaj.dk

This unique exhibition space, partly housed in the rebuilt Sankt Nikolaj Kirke, focuses on Danish and international contemporary art.

Nikolaj presents art that has not been shown before and that inspires public debate. Nikolaj Kunsthal focuses on experimental and innovative art, while also allowing a dialogue between Danish and international art, historical perspectives and the most recent trends. Nikolaj Kunsthal presents five or six exhibitions annually. Among these, one is aimed specifically at children and young people. Another, the Fokus Video Art Festival, takes place in February and premieres works by both Danish and international artists alongside artist talks and events.

The historical cultural heritage of the building is used in the institution's graphic identity and the exhibitions, with the large arched spaces often being included in the works on show.

❽ Højbro Plads

Map 3 C1.

This cobbled square is one of the most enchanting places in Copenhagen. Although at first glance it looks like a single large unit, it is in fact divided into Højbro Plads and Amagertorv.

Højbro Plads contains a vast monument to Bishop Absalon, who from his horse points out towards Christiansborg Slot on the other side of the canal. In Amagertorv, the former city market, is a 19th-century fountain with three birds about to take flight. It is named Storkespringvandet (The Stork Fountain) though the birds are actually herons.

The northern section of Amagertorv has an interesting twin-gabled house, built in 1616, in the style of the Dutch Renaissance. It is one of the city's oldest buildings and houses the Royal Copenhagen Porcelain Shop. Adjacent to it is the showroom of Georg Jensen, which specializes in upmarket silverware. A small museum is devoted to the work of Jensen and contains some of his early pieces.

Portal of Helligåndskirken – one of Copenhagen's oldest churches

❾ Helligåndskirken

Niels Hemmingsensgade 5. **Map** 3 C1. **Tel** 33 15 41 44. **Open** noon–4pm Mon–Fri; also 7–11:30pm Fri.
W helligaandskirken.dk

Dating originally from the early 15th century when it was an Augustinian monastery, the "Church of the Holy Spirit was built on an even earlier religious site, founded in 1238. The church, which is one of the oldest in Copenhagen, acquired its towers in the late 16th century and its sandstone portal, originally intended for the Børsen (Stock Exchange), early in the 17th century. The building was ravaged by one of the city's great fires in 1728, and has been largely rebuilt, although some original 14th-century walls in the right-hand wing can still be seen. Now surrounded by a park, the church still holds religious services. It is also used for art shows and exhibitions, which provide an occasion to admire its magnificent vaults.

In the churchyard is a memorial to Danish victims of the Nazi concentration camps.

Strøget

The word "Strøget" ("pedestrian street") cannot be found on any of the plates bearing street names; nevertheless, all those who know the city are familiar with it. Copenhagen's main walkway runs east to west. It is made up of five interconnected streets: Østergade, Amagertorv, Vimmelskaftet, Nygade and Frederiksberggade. Pedestrianized in 1962, it has since become one of the town's favourite strolling grounds. Shops range from exclusive boutiques to souvenir and toy shops, along with numerous cafés and restaurants. There are also some pretty churches and squares and a handful of museums. Every day (when the Queen is in residence), at about 11:45am, the Livgarden or royal guards march along Østergade, heading for Amalienborg Slot for the changing of the guards.

Tourist train running along Strøget

⑩ Skuespilhuset

Sankt Annæ Plads 36. **Map** 4 E1.
Tel 33 69 69 33.
W kglteater.dk

Throughout the 1900s, a number of venues across the city were used to house the Royal Danish Theatre's Drama Department – with varying degrees of success. Although the need for a suitable playhouse was recognized as early as the 1880s, it was not until 2001 that the government unveiled plans to build a dedicated theatre.

Skuespilhuset, the Royal Danish Playhouse, was inaugurated in 2008. The strikingly modern building offers a range of performance spaces, including the main auditorium (Main Stage) seating 650, two small stages (Portscenen) seating 200 and the Studio Stage, which has seats for 100 people. There are also several open-air spaces, such as the waterfront foyer and the footbridge terrace, which are used for children's activities and other events. In addition to its seasonal repertoire of plays, the theatre hosts ballets, public lectures, concerts and Q&As with playwrights, directors and actors. Note that all drama performed here is in Danish.

Designed by Danish architects Boje Lundgaard and Lene Tranberg, the theatre incorporates a variety of materials: the dark cladding on the external walls was created with ceramic tiles; the outside of the stage tower is covered with copper; and the footbridge linking the foyer to the harbourfront promenade is made from oak.

Rundetårn's cobbled spiral ramp winding to the top of the tower

⑪ Rundetårn

Købmagergade 52A. **Map** 3 C1.
Tel 33 73 03 73. **Open** mid-Mar–20 May & 21 Sep–mid-Oct: 10am–6pm daily; 21 May–20 Sep: 10am–8pm daily; mid-Oct–mid-Mar: 10am–6pm Tue–Sun. **W rundetaarn.dk**

The round tower, 35 m (115 ft) tall and 15 m (49 ft) in diameter, provides an excellent vantage point from which to view Copenhagen. Access to the top is via a cobbled spiral ramp, 209 m (686 ft) long, which winds seven and a half times round to the top. Over the years the Rundetårn has been damaged by several fires and part of the observatory was rebuilt in the 18th century.

Rundetårn was erected on the orders of Christian IV, and was originally intended as an observatory for the nearby university. It is still used by the university, making it the oldest working observatory of its kind in Europe.

In 1642, during the tower's opening ceremony, Christian IV is said to have ridden his horse up the spiralling pathway to the top. In 1716, the Tsar of Russia, Peter the Great, allegedly repeated this stunt during a visit to Copenhagen and was followed by his wife Tsarina Catherine I who, as legend has it, climbed to the top in a coach drawn by six horses.

The modern-day equivalent of such antics is an annual bicycle race: the winner is the person who cycles to the top and back again in the fastest time, without dismounting or falling off.

Skuespilhuset, on the Copenhagen waterfront

⑫ Kunstforeningen GL STRAND

Gammel Strand 48. **Map** 3 C1. **Tel** 33 36 02 60. M Kongens Nytorv. 1A, 2A, 6A, 15, 26, 29. **Open** 11am–5pm Tue–Sun (to 8pm Wed).
W glstrand.dk

GL STRAND was founded in 1825 by the artist and professor C.W. Eckersberg as a way to bridge the gap between the elitist art establishment and the viewing public, thereby making art more accessible. Its mission today is to focus on and support young, emerging artists. The gallery has occupied its current premises, a building on Gammel Strand designed by the 18th-century architect Philip de Lange, since 1952. GL STRAND doesn't have a permanent collection, relying instead on temporary shows spotlighting individual artists. During the course of its history, GL STRAND has hosted many fascinating exhibitions by the likes of Edvard Munch (1908), Asger Jorn (1953), the American film director and visual artist David Lynch (2010) and Louise Bourgeois (2011).

Outdoor restaurant tables in Gråbrødretorv

⓭ Gråbrødretorv

Map 3 C1. 🚌 6A.

This charming, cobblestone square is filled with music from buskers in summer when the restaurant tables spill out into the street. It is an excellent place to stop for a lunch. The square dates back to 1238, and its name refers to the so-called Grey Brothers, Franciscan monks who built the city's first monastery here. A great fire in 1728 destroyed the surrounding buildings; the present buildings date mainly from the early 18th century.

⓮ Universitet

Vor Frue Plads. **Map** 3 B1. Ⓢ Ⓜ Nørreport. 🚌 5A, 6A, 14, 42, 43, 150S, 173E, 184, 185, 350S.
W ku.dk/english

The cobbled Vor Frue Plads and its surrounding university buildings are the heart of the so-called Latin Quarter (Latin was once spoken here). Despite the fact that the university was founded by Christian I in 1479, the buildings that now stand in Vor Frue Plads date from the 19th century. They house only a handful of faculties including law; the remaining departments and staff have moved to the main campus, on the island of Amager, east of Copenhagen.

The vast, Neo-Classical university building stands opposite Vor Frue Kirke. It has an impressive entrance hall decorated with frescoes depicting scenes from Greek mythology, which are the work of Constantin Hansen. Adjacent to the university building is the 19th-century university library. On the library's main staircase is a glass cabinet containing fragments from a cannon ball that was fired during the British bombardment in 1807. The ball struck the library and ironically hit a book entitled *The Defender of Peace*. A number of second-hand bookshops are located along Fiolstræde, which runs up to the Universitet.

⓯ Sankt Petri Kirke

Larslejstræde 11. **Map** 3 B1. **Tel** 33 13 38 33. Ⓢ Ⓜ Nørreport. 🚌 5A, 6A, 14, 42, 43, 173E, 150S, 350S. **Open** Apr–Sep: 11am–3pm daily. burial chapel only. **W sankt-petri.dk**

Saint Peter's church has been the main church for Copenhagen's German community since 1586. It dates from 1450 but suffered serious damage in the course of a series of fires and the British bombardment of 1807. However, many of the bricks used in the building work are from the original structure. Particularly noteworthy is the "burial" chapel containing numerous tombs and epitaphs, mainly from the 19th century. There are also some interesting tablets commemorating the dead which can be seen on the church's outside wall.

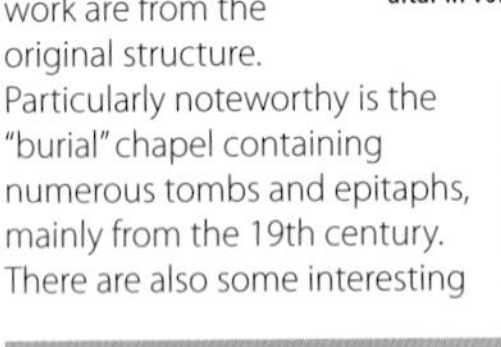

Statue of Christ from the high altar in Vor Frue Kirke

⓰ Vor Frue Kirke

Nørregade 8. **Map** 3 B1. **Tel** 33 37 65 40. Ⓢ Ⓜ Nørreport. 🚌 5A, 6A, 14, 42, 43, 150S, 173E, 184, 185, 350S.
Open 8am–5pm daily.
W koebenhavnsdomkirke.dk

Copenhagen's cathedral, Vor Frue Kirke (Church of Our Lady), has a somewhat sombre look and is the third consecutive church to be built on this site. The first, a small 12th-century Gothic church, was consumed by fire in 1728, while the next one was destroyed by British bombs in 1807 (the tower presented an excellent target for the artillery). The present structure dates from 1820 and was designed by Christian Frederik Hansen. Its interior is a veritable art gallery, full of sculptures by the prominent Danish sculptor Bertel Thorvaldsen *(see p89)*. Standing on both sides are marble statues of the 12 apostles; the central section of the altar has a kneeling angel and a vast figure of Christ – one of the artist's most famous masterpieces. Thorvaldsen is also the creator of the relief depicting St John the Baptist, seen at the entrance to the cathedral. During Sunday mass

The imposing Neo-Classical façade of the Universitet

Interior of Vor Frue Kirke, with statues by Bertel Thordvaldsen

it is sometimes possible to see Queen Margrethe II among the congregation. In the past she used to occupy a special royal box. But attitudes have changed and today, not wishing to distance herself from her subjects, the Danish monarch is to be found sitting in the pews.

⑰ Nytorv

Map 3 B1.

Although Nytorv looks like one big square, it is in fact made up of two separate areas – Gammeltorv (Old Square) and Nytorv (New Square) which are separated by the Nygade section of the Strøget walkway. To the northwest of Strøget, Gammeltorv was a busy market place in the 14th century and therefore has the longest trading tradition in Copenhagen. Today, the square is dominated by a small fruit and vegetable market along with stalls selling jewellery and all kinds of handicrafts.

Standing at the centre of the square is Caritas Springvandet (The Charity Fountain), which dates from 1609. This Renaissance treasure is the work of Statius Otto, and depicts a pregnant woman carrying one child in her arms and leading another by the hand – a symbol of charity and mercy. Water flows from the woman's breasts and also from the urinating boy at her feet (the holes were blocked with lead for reasons of decency in the 19th century). The fountain was commissioned by Christian IV to draw the public's attention to his charitable virtues. At one time it supplied the city's inhabitants with water brought along wooden pipes from a lake 5 km (3 miles) north of Copenhagen.

Nytorv was established in 1606 and for a long time was used by the authorities as a place of execution. The squares were joined together and given their present form soon after the city hall was destroyed by fire in 1795. The outline of the city hall can still be seen in Nytorv's pavement.

The striking Neo-Classical Domhuset, or Court House, with its six large columns, on the south side of Nytorv was completed in 1815 to a design by Christian Frederik Hansen, the Danish architect who worked on rebuilding the town after a fire in 1795. The materials used in the rebuilding work included those taken from the ruined Christiansborg Slot, and the resulting building is redolent of an ancient temple. The building was first used as the city hall, becoming the fifth seat of the town's authorities. In the early 20th century the city hall was moved to the Rådhus. The inscription seen on the front of the Domhuset refers to its more recent function as a court house and quotes the opening words of the Jutland Code of 1241: "With law the land shall be built".

⑱ Ripley's Believe It Or Not!

Rådhuspladsen 57. **Map** 3 B2. **Tel** 33 32 31 31. 2A, 5A, 6A, 10, 12, 14, 26, 29, 33, 67, 68, 69, 173E, 250S. **Open** Sep–mid-Jun: 10am–6pm Sun–Thu, 10am–8pm Fri–Sat; mid-Jun–Aug: 10am–10pm daily. **Closed** 1 Jan, 24, 25 & 31 Dec. **ripleys.dk**

This museum is part of an American chain that is based on an idea of Robert L. Ripley, a radio presenter, comic book writer and adventurer, who dreamt up a freakshow in the early 20th century to stun and amaze his American audience.

The museum may well prove popular with children. Many strange exhibits are on display, some of which were collected by Ripley himself. Here, visitors can marvel at a man who eats bicycles or a doll covered in 7,000 buttons, wince at a collection of medieval torture instruments and shrunken voodoo heads, and be astounded by various freaks of nature including a fish covered in fur and a two-headed cow.

Nytorv, a colourful and bustling square

⓳ Rådhus

The red-brick Rådhus (City Hall), which opened in 1905, was designed by the Danish architect Martin Nyrop (1849–1921), who was inspired by Italian buildings but also employed some elements of Danish medieval architecture. Its large main hall, sometimes used for exhibitions and official events, is decorated with statues of Nyrop as well as three other prominent Danes – Bertel Thorvaldsen, H.C. Andersen and Niels Bohr. Though it is an official building, the Rådhus is open to visitors. It is well worth climbing the 298 stairs to the top of the 105-m (344-ft) tower to reach the city's highest viewpoint.

Ceilings
The Rådhus rooms and chambers are full of details and architectural flourishes such as intricate brickwork, mosaics and decorated ceilings.

National flag of Denmark

Copenhagen's Emblem
This has changed little since the 13th century. It consists of three castle towers, symbolically drawn waves of the Øresund and images of the sun and moon.

★ Main Hall
This vast, rectangular hall on the first floor is flanked by cloisters and topped with a glazed roof. It has Italianate wall decorations and a number of sculptures.

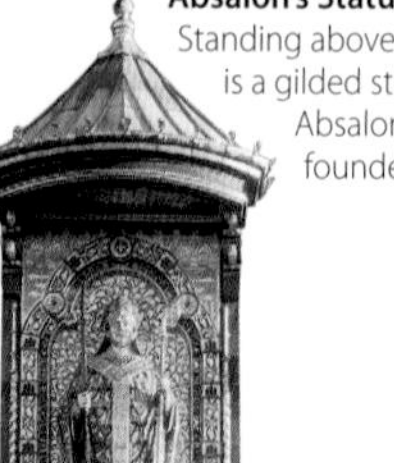

Absalon's Statue
Standing above the main entrance is a gilded statue of Bishop Absalon, the 12th-century founder of Copenhagen.

Main entrance

★ World Clock
Jens Olsen spent 27 years building this clock. Its extraordinary mechanism was set in motion in 1955. One of its many functions is to provide a calendar for the next 570,000 years.

Clock Tower
The peals from the tower's bells are heard throughout the streets of Copenhagen and are also transmitted by radio across the whole of Denmark.

VISITORS' CHECKLIST

Practical Information
Rådhuspladsen 1. **Map** 3 B2.
Tel 33 66 33 66. **Open** 9am–4pm Mon–Fri, 9:30am–1pm Sat. (in English) 3pm Mon–Fri, 10am Sat. Tower: **Open** 11am & 2pm Mon–Fri, noon Sat. World Clock: **Open** 8:30am–4:30pm Mon–Fri, 10am–1pm Sat. **kk.dk**

Transport
Central Station.
6A, 11, 26, 29, 33.

Staircase
The stately rooms on the top floors are reached by graceful stairs with marble balustrades.

⑳ Rådhuspladsen

Map 3 A2 & B2.
Central Station. 6A, 11, 26, 29, 33.

This open space is the second biggest square in the Danish capital (after Kongens Nytorv). City Hall Square was established in the second half of the 19th century, following the dismantling of the western gate that stood on this site, and the levelling of the defensive embankments. Soon afterwards it was decided to build the present city hall, providing further impetus to the development of the surrounding area. The square has been pedestrianized since 1994 and is popular with shoppers and sightseers. It is also a gathering point for revellers on New Year's Eve.

A number of monuments in Rådhuspladsen are worthy of note. Standing immediately by the entrance to the city hall is the Dragon's Leap Fountain, erected in 1923. A little to one side, by Rådhus's tower, is a tall column, unveiled in 1914, featuring two bronze figures of Vikings blowing bronze horns. Close by, in Hans Christian Andersens Boulevard, is a sitting figure of Andersen, facing Tivoli gardens. Another curiosity is an unusual barometer hanging on a building that is covered with advertisements, located at the corner of Vesterbrogade and H.C. Andersens Boulevard. It includes a figure of a girl, who in fine weather rides a bicycle. When it rains she opens her umbrella. A nearby thermometer gives a reading of the daily temperature.

The Rådhus with its red brick elevations

㉑ Tivoli

When Tivoli first opened in 1843 it had only two attractions: a carousel pulled by horses and a roller coaster. Today Tivoli is an altogether grander affair. Part amusement park, part cultural venue, part wonderland, it is one of the most famous places in Denmark and much loved by the Danes themselves, who regard it as one of their national treasures. Situated in the heart of the city, this large garden is planted with almost one thousand trees and blooms with 400,000 flowers during the summer. At night, when it is lit by myriad coloured bulbs, it is a truly breathtaking sight.

The Ferry Boat Inn
Located next to the jetty, this is one of 30 restaurants in Tivoli. It also houses a micro-brewery.

Frigate
The huge frigate *St George III*, a pirate-themed family restaurant, is moored on Tivoli's picturesque lake – the remains of a former moat.

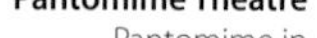

Pantomime Theatre
Pantomime in Denmark dates back to the early 19th century. The Chinese-style pavilion hosts regular performances and is the oldest building in Tivoli gardens.

Main Entrance
The main gate, in Vesterbrogade, was built in 1890.

★ Pagoda
The tower, built in the style of a Japanese or Chinese pagoda, houses a restaurant that has been here since its construction in 1900; it specializes in pan-Asian cuisine.

VISITORS' CHECKLIST

Practical Information
Vesterbrogade 3. **Map** 3 A2–B2. **Tel** 33 15 10 01. **Open** 11am–10pm daily (to midnight Fri & Sat). Summer season: mid-Apr–mid-Sep; Halloween season: last 2 wks in Oct; Christmas season: mid-Nov–end Dec. **tivoli.dk**

Transport
Central. 1A, 2A, 5A, 6A, 10, 11A, 15, 26, 30, 40, 47, 65E, 250S.

Concert Hall
Tivoli's pastel-coloured concert hall was built in 1956 and updated in 2005. Concerts range from rock to symphonies, and in the basement is Europe's longest seawater aquarium.

Amusements
Rides and other amusements, including vintage cars for smaller children, are scattered throughout the park.

Tivoli Boys Guard

A group of boys dressed in smart uniforms and marching to the beat of drums is a frequent sight when strolling along the park's avenues on weekends. According to promoters of the gardens, "the Queen has her own guards and the Tivoli has its own". Made up of about 100 boys, aged between 8 and 16, the Tivoli Boys Guard is smartly dressed in red jackets and busbies and covers some 300 km (186 miles) a year. The marching band was founded in 1844 and is one of Tivoli's four orchestras, the other three being the Symphony Orchestra, the Tivoli Big Band and the Tivoli Promenade Orchestra.

Boys Guard marching through Tivoli

★ Nimb Building
This palatial Moorish-style building houses two restaurants, a bar and a café, as well as an upmarket boutique hotel.

㉒ Ny Carlsberg Glyptotek

This world-class art museum boasts over 10,000 treasures including Ancient Egyptian art, Greek and Roman sculptures and a huge collection of Etruscan artifacts. It also exhibits a wealth of Danish paintings and sculptures from the era known as the Golden Age *(see pp46–7)* and exquisite works by French Impressionist masters such as Degas and Renoir. It has grown from the fine collection of sculptures *(glyptotek)* donated by Carl Jacobsen, founder of the New Carlsberg Brewery, and the museum now consists of three architecturally different buildings, the first one built in 1897 and the latest added in 1996.

★ Ancient Egyptian Art
The outstanding collection of Egyptian art ranges from delicate vases to monumental statues, such as this granite figure of Ramses II from the 2nd millennium BC.

Danish Sculpture
Sculptures representing the great artistic flourishing of Denmark's Golden Age include works such as Jens Adolph Jerichau's *Penelope* (1840s), as well as many pieces by H.W. Bissen.

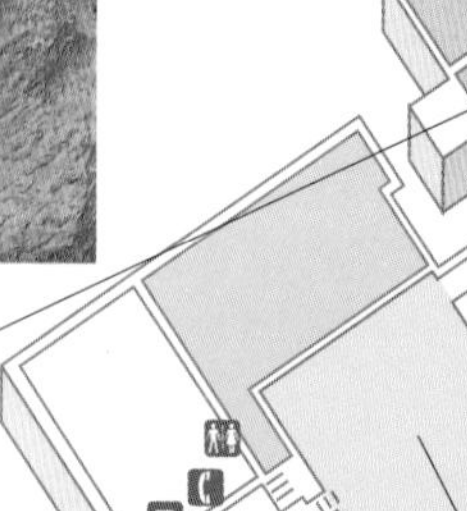

★ The Kiss
This famous pair of lovers is one of 35 works by Auguste Rodin, which constitutes the largest collection of the artist's works anywhere outside France.

Alabaster Relief
This 9th-century BC relief depicting the Assyrian King Assurnasirpal II is part of the multifaceted collection representing the Middle East.

Winter garden

For hotels and restaurants see pp248–55 and pp262–77

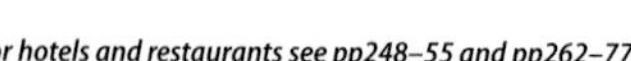

Landscape from Saint-Rémy
Along with this picture painted by Vincent van Gogh during his stay in a psychiatric hospital in 1889, the museum has numerous works by many of the Impressionists and Post-Impressionists, including Gauguin, Toulouse-Lautrec, Monet and Degas.

2nd floor

VISITORS' CHECKLIST

Practical Information
Dantes Plads 7. **Map** 3 B3. **Tel** 33 41 81 41. **Open** 11am–5pm Tue–Sun. **Closed** 1 Jan, 5 Jun, 24 & 25 Dec. (free Sun and to under-18s). **glyptoteket.dk**

Transport
5A, 12, 33

The Little Dancer
The statue of a 14-year-old dancer dates from 1880 and is one of the most famous sculptures to be produced by Edgar Degas.

★ Head of Satyr
This beautiful painted terracotta *Head of Satyr* is part of the Etruscan collection, which includes vases, bronze sculptures and stone sarcophagi dating from the 8th to the 2nd century BC.

1st floor

Gallery Guide

The horseshoe-shaped Dahlerup Building (1897) contains mainly Danish and French sculpture. Ancient artefacts from the Mediterranean and Egypt are found via the Winter Garden in the Kampmann Building (1906). The Larsen Building (1996), rising within one of the courtyards of the Kampmann Building, houses French painting.

Key

- Ancient Mediterranean
- French painting and sculpture
- Danish painting and sculpture
- Egyptian, Greek and Roman sculpture
- Temporary exhibitions
- Non-exhibition space

Ground floor

Winter Garden

This green oasis of palm trees, planted under a glass dome, was included in the original design as a way of attracting visitors who might not normally be interested in art. It has always provided a pleasant place in which to stroll during a visit. Many visitors are drawn to the *Water Mother* sculpture by Kai Nielsen. Unveiled in 1920, it depicts a naked woman reclining in a small pool, surrounded by a group of babies. The Winter Garden is also used as a concert venue.

SOUTH COPENHAGEN

Criss-crossed by canals and waterways, this part of Copenhagen contains two areas that both complement and contrast each other. The islet of Slotsholmen is dominated by Christianborg Slot, standing on the site of a fort built by Bishop Absalon in the 12th century, when there was nothing here but a tiny fishing village. The area flourished and in 1443 København, or "merchant's port", was made the Danish capital. Many historical sights are situated here.

Across the water is Christianshavn where the "free state of Christiania", an alternative community, has been in existence since the 1970s. Both Christianshavn and nearby Holmen have undergone a period of redevelopment, and the area has become one of Copenhagen's more fashionable districts. The city's striking opera house has taken centre stage with its location on Dokøen, an islet that was once used as a naval base.

Waterbus tours provide an enjoyable way of getting to know the area. Alternatively, a bicycle can be useful for exploring the many nooks and crannies of Christianshavn.

Sights at a Glance

Churches

9 Vor Frelsers Kirke

Museums

1 *Nationalmuseet pp88–9*
2 Thorvaldsens Museum
6 Tøjhusmuseet
10 Orlogsmuseet

Historic Buildings

3 Folketinget
4 *Christiansborg Slot pp90–91*
5 Børsen
7 Det Kongelige Bibliotek

Places of Interest

8 Christianshavn
11 Christiania
12 Operaen

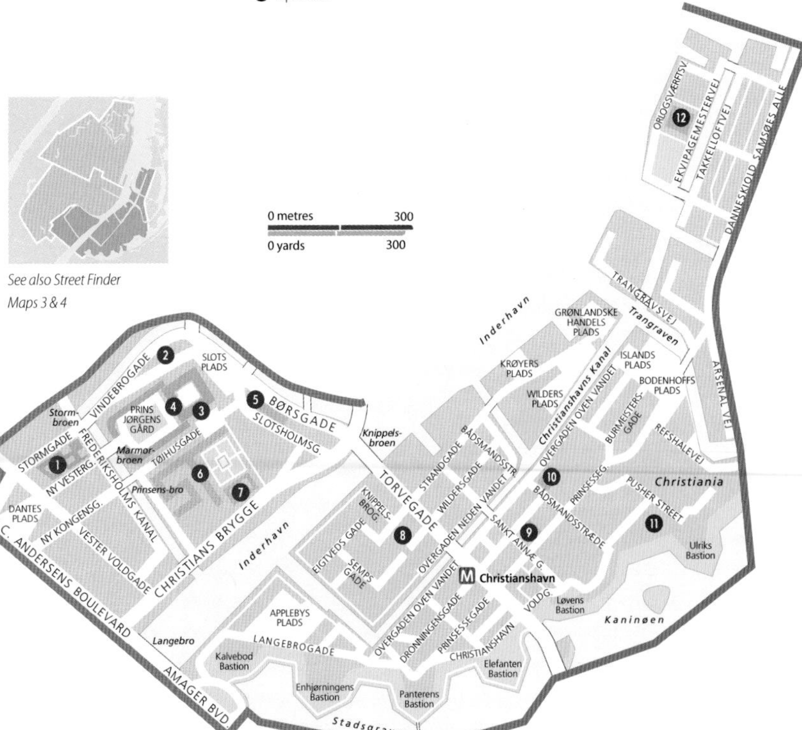

See also Street Finder Maps 3 & 4

◀ Den Sorte Diamant (the Black Diamond), an extension to the Royal Library

For keys to symbols *see back flap*

Street-by-Street: Around Christiansborg Slot

Christiansborg Slot, with its adjoining palace buildings including the palace church, former royal coach house and royal stables, as well as Tøjhusmuseet, Det Kongelige Bibliotek and Børsen, are all situated on the islet of Slotsholmen. The island derives its name from a castle that was built on this site in 1167 by Bishop Absalon. Opposite the palace, on the other side to the canal, is the Nationalmuseet, which has many exhibits relating to the history of Copenhagen and the rest of Denmark.

❷ Thordvaldsens Museum
The collection confirms the genius of the Danish sculptor, whose tomb can be found in the museum courtyard.

❶ ★ Nationalmuseet
This museum was founded in 1807, though its origins date back to 1650 when Frederik I established his own private collection.

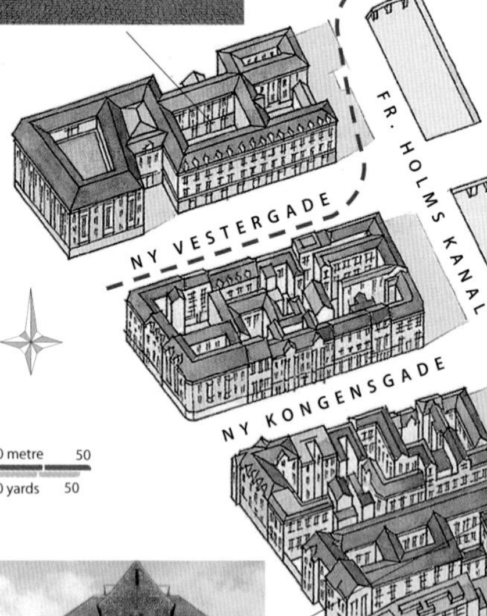

VINDEBROGADE

TOJHUSGADE

BRYGHUSGADE

CHRISTIA
BRYGG

0 metre 50
0 yards 50

❻ Tøjhusmuseet
Visitors interested in militaria will enjoy the huge array of arms and armour in this museum.

For hotels and restaurants see pp248–55 and pp262–77

❹ ★ Christiansborg Slot
Although this has not been the home of the royal family for more than 200 years, the palace rooms are still used for grand occasions, such as state banquets attended by Queen Margrethe II.

CENTRAL COPENHAGEN
SOUTH COPENHAGEN

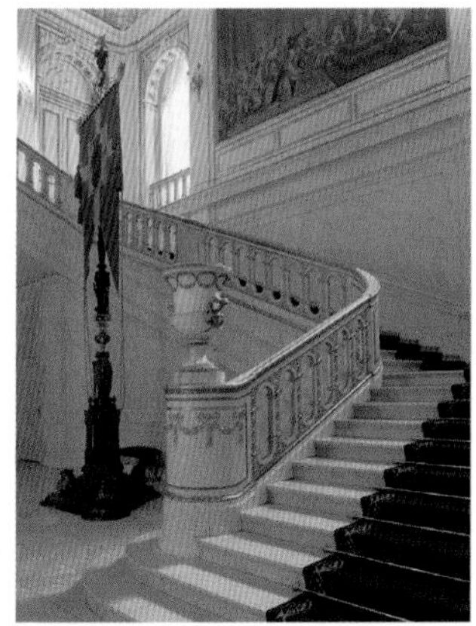

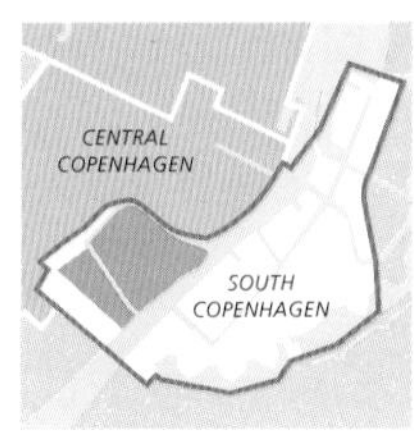

Locator Map
See Street Finder Maps 3 & 4

Key

— Suggested route

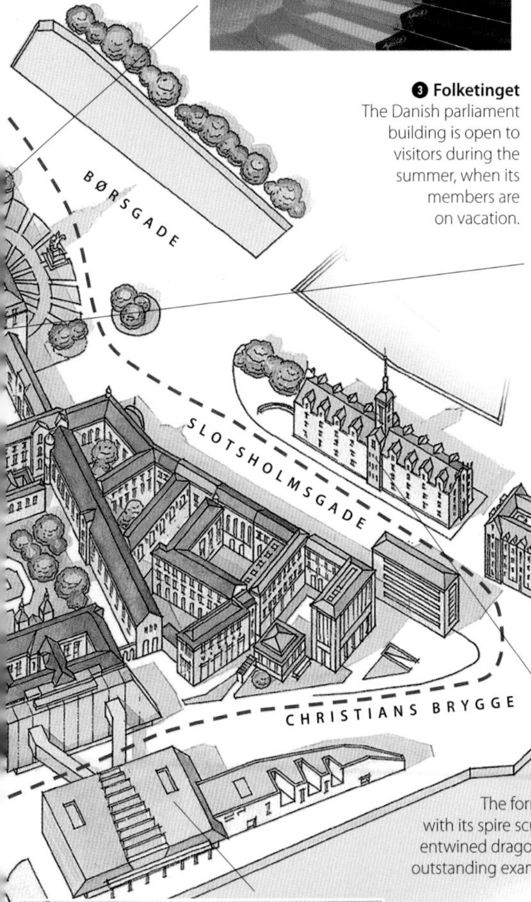

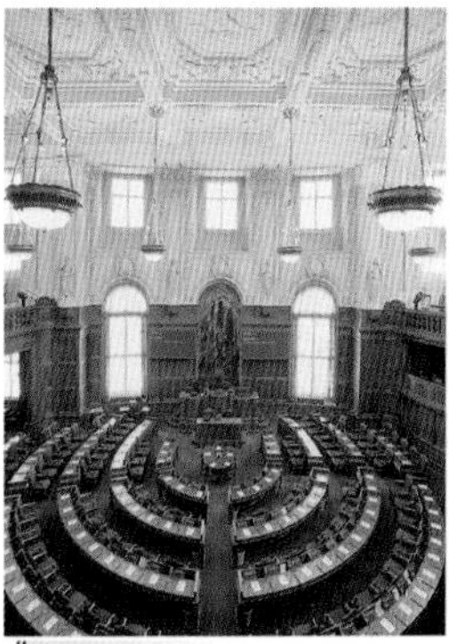

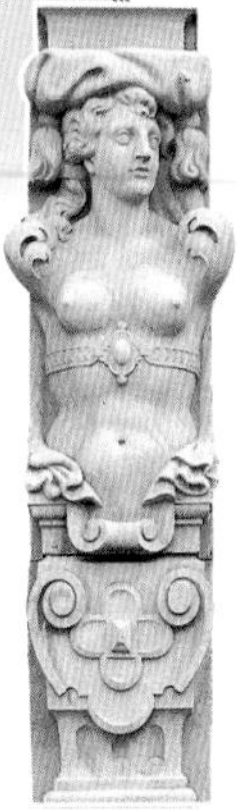

BØRSGADE
SLOTSHOLMSGADE
BØRSGADE
CHRISTIANS BRYGGE

❸ Folketinget
The Danish parliament building is open to visitors during the summer, when its members are on vacation.

❺ Børsen
The former Stock Exchange, with its spire sculpted in the form of entwined dragon tails, represents an outstanding example of 17th-century public architecture.

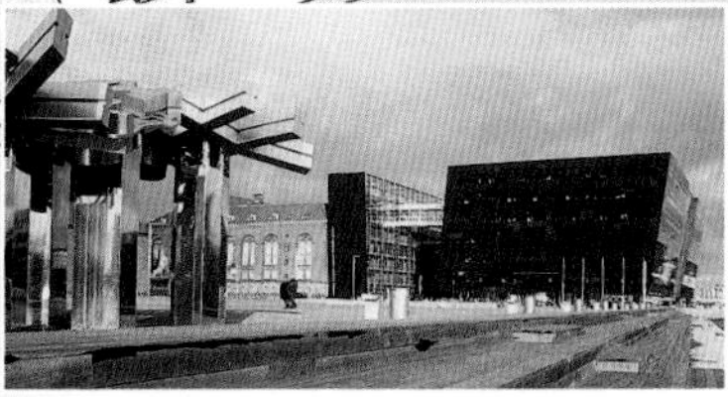

❼ Det Kongelige Bibliotek
The library's "Black Diamond" extension, utilizing black glass and granite imported from Zimbabwe, is one of the capital's most innovative buildings.

❶ Nationalmuseet

Exhibits in this prestigious museum include many items relating to Denmark's history as well as artifacts from all over the world. It is worth allocating several hours for a visit. Among the vast array on display are Inuit costumes and tools, rune stones, priceless Egyptian jewellery and medieval church interiors. There is a good children's section, where kids will enjoy trying on armour or "camping out" in a Bedouin tent. All exhibits are labelled in English.

Antiquities
Greek pottery, Etruscan jewellery and Egyptian mummies are on display in the Egyptian and Classical section.

★ Inuit Culture
Included in the ethnographic section are rooms devoted to the Inuit containing many costumes, including a suit made of bird feathers, as well as traditional kayaks and harpoons.

3rd floor

Ethnography
Items from around the world include exhibits from Africa, India and Japan. One room is devoted to world music.

1st floor

Key

- Pre-history (1300 BC–AD 1050)
- Middle Ages & Renaissance (1050–1660)
- Tales of Denmark (1660–2000)
- Ethnography
- History of the Museum
- Royal Collection of Coins
- Ethnographic Treasures
- Near East & Antiquities

Helmet
This Bronze-Age helmet, in the museum's pre-history department, dates from the 9th century BC and was found at Viksø on Zealand.

Children's Museum

Main entrance

VISITORS' CHECKLIST

Practical Information
Ny Vestergade 10. **Map** 3 B2. **Tel** 33 13 44 11. **Open** 10am–5pm Tue–Sun. **natmus.dk**

Transport
1A, 2A, 6A, 12, 15, 26, 29, 33, 650S.

Gallery Guide

The collection is spread over four floors with pre-history on the ground floor. The medieval department shares the first floor with Ethnography, which continues on the second floor with exhibits relating to the Inuit. A section designed to appeal to children aged between four and 12 is on the ground floor.

2nd floor

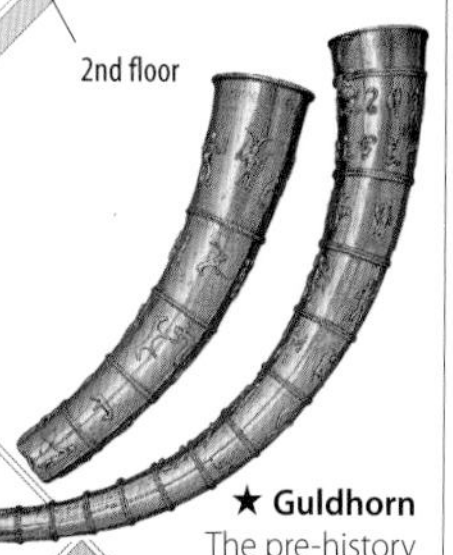

★ Guldhorn
The pre-history section contains, among other exhibits, fragments of golden horns forged around 400 BC.

Ground floor

❷ Thorvaldsens Museum

Bertel Thorvaldsens Plads 2. **Map** 3 C2. ***Tel*** 33 32 15 32. Central. Nørreport, Kongens Nytorv. 1A, 2A, 15, 26, 29. **Open** 10am–5pm Tue–Sun. thorvaldsensmuseum.dk

Located behind the palace church (Christiansborg Slotskirke), Thorvaldsens Museum was the first art museum in Denmark and opened in 1848. The Danish sculptor Bertel Thorvaldsen (1770–1844) lived and worked in Rome for more than 40 years, but towards the end of his life he bequeathed all his works and his collection of paintings to his native Copenhagen. The collection is placed in Christianborg's old Coach House. The building is worth a visit in its own right, with a frieze on the outside by Jørgen Sonne and mosaic floors within.

Despite the fact that he worked on some of his pieces for 25 years, Thorvaldsen's output is staggering and includes sculptures based on classical mythology, busts of well-known contemporaries such as the English poet, Lord Byron, monumental studies of Christ and a number of self-portraits. The museum also displays Thorvaldsen's drawings and sketches and includes items from his private collection of paintings and Egyptian and Roman artefacts.

Vaulted ceiling and decorative floor in Thorvaldsens Museum

❸ Folketinget

Christiansborg. **Map** 3 C2. Jun–Sep: daily.

The Folketinget is the Danish parliamentary chamber. Seating for the 179 members is arranged in a semi-circle with "left wing" MPs positioned on the left and "right wing" MPs on the right. The civil servants' offices occupy the largest section of the palace. Separate offices are used by Queen Margrethe II, whose duties include chairing weekly meetings of the State Council and presiding over the annual state opening of parliament in early October.

❹ Christiansborg Slot

See pp90–91.

❺ Børsen

Slotsholmsgade. **Map** 4 D2. **Closed** to visitors. borsbygningen.dk

Copenhagen's former Stock Exchange was built between 1590 and 1640 on the orders of Christian IV, to a design by Lorentz and Hans van Steenwinckel. Today, the building houses the city's Chamber of Commerce and is not open to the public, but its stunning Renaissance façade, copper roofs, numerous gables and unusual spire have made it one of Copenhagen's best-known sights. Its sleek 54-m (177-ft) spire, carved to resemble the entwined tails of four dragons, is a city landmark. Topping the spire are three crowns representing Denmark, Sweden and Norway. Trade in goods continued at Børsen until 1857, when it was purchased by a private association of wholesalers who pledged to maintain the historic building.

Dragon tails forming Børsen's tower

❹ Christiansborg Slot

On the Copenhagen Castle Island visitors can experience the magnificent Royal Reception Rooms, which are richly decorated with art, chandeliers, gold and marble. The royal family lived here until the palace burned down in 1794. The grand rooms of the present palace (completed in 1928) are used by the Queen for state dinners, banquets and receptions. In the Great Hall stunning tapestries portray the history of Denmark. There are also underground ruins of medieval castles and a tower which offers splendid views of Copenhagen.

★ Throne Room
As in every royal palace, the Throne Room is one of the grandest rooms in Christiansborg. However, Queen Margrethe II is famous for her "common touch" and has apparently never sat on this magnificent royal seat.

Velvet Room
Completed in 1924, this room is noteworthy for its grand marble portals, reliefs and luxurious velvet wall linings.

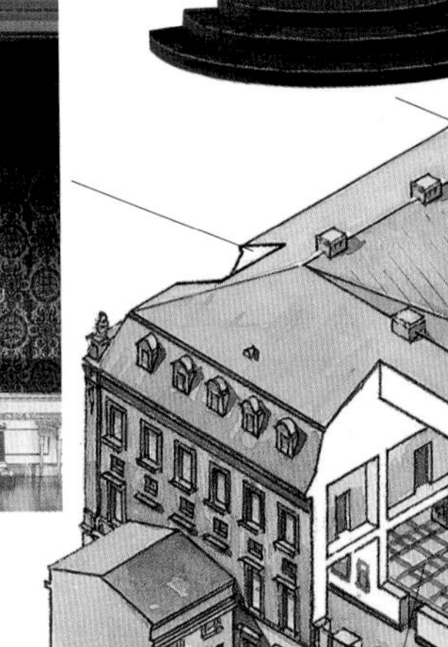

Decorative Vase
This vase can be found in the Frederick VI Room, one of the many state rooms in the palace. It was a gift to Queen Juliane Marie of Brunsvick, second wife of King Frederik V.

The Dining Hall is decorated with portraits of Danish kings and contains two crystal chandeliers.

★ Great Hall
The 17 tapestries on display here were commissioned in 1990 for Queen Margrethe II's 50th birthday and completed in 2000. Made by Bjørn Nørgaard, they depict key events in Danish history.

Tower Room
Copenhagen's tallest tower is 106 m (348 ft) high and topped with a 5-m (16-ft) crown. The tower's interior has a series of tapestries created by Joakim Skovgaard depicting scenes from Danish folk tales.

VISITORS' CHECKLIST

Practical Information
Christiansborg Slotsplads. **Map** 3 C2. **Tel** 33 92 64 92. Reception Rooms: **Open** 10am–5pm Tue–Sun (May–Sep: 10am–5pm daily). **Closed** 4, 12 & 18 Jun, 9 Jul. 11am (Danish), 3pm (English). Ruins: **Open** 10am–5pm Tue–Sun (May–Sep: 10am–5pm daily). **christiansborg.dk**

Transport
1A, 2A, 11A, 14, 26, 40, 66.

★ Castle Ruins
Under the palace are the ruins of the previous castles, including parts of Bishop Absalon's castle and the Copenhagen Castle.

Library
A small portion of the vast royal collection is housed here. The remaining volumes are kept at Amalienborg Slot *(see pp60–61)*.

Alexander Room
Bertel Thorvaldsen's frieze depicting Alexander the Great entering Babylon is displayed in this room.

6 Tøjhusmuseet

Tøjhusgade 3. **Map** 3 C2. **Tel** 33 11 60 37. 1A, 2A, 15, 26, 29. **Open** noon–4pm Tue–Sun. **thm.dk**

The Royal Danish Arsenal was built between 1598 and 1604 and was one of the earliest of Christian IV's building projects. When completed, the 163-m (535-ft) long complex was one of the largest buildings in Europe and was capable of equipping an entire army. In 1611 the building was extended to include a harbour pool, which was situated next door in what are today the Library Gardens. The building now serves as a museum. Its collection covers the history of artillery from the invention of gunpowder up to the present day (exhibits include artillery guns as well as firearms). Suits of armour and military uniforms are also on display.

Cannon from the Tøjhusmuseet collection

7 Det Kongelige Bibliotek

Christians Brygge, entrance from Søren Kierkegaards Plads 1. **Map** 4 D2. **Tel** 33 47 47 47. 9A. 991, 992. **Open** 10am–9pm Mon–Sat. **kb.dk**

The Royal Library is an excellent example of how to merge two very different architectural forms. The original library building is 19th century. The

Gate leading to the old section of Det Kongelige Bibliotek

Neo-Classical building's courtyard has been transformed into a garden and contains a statue of the Danish philosopher and theologian Søren Kierkegaard. Next to the old building is the ultra-modern library, linked by a special passage to its historic predecessor. Often referred to by its nickname, the "Black Diamond", because of its angular black glass-and-granite exterior, the extension houses library and exhibition areas, the National Photography Museum, a concert hall and a restaurant and café. It is worth stepping inside, if only to see the vast ceiling mural by Per Kirkeby.

8 Christianshavn

Map 4 D & 4 E.

This district, which is sometimes referred to as "Little Amsterdam" because of its many canals, can be explored on foot, by bicycle or by hopping aboard a waterbus. Built in the first half of the 17th century by Christian IV, Christianshavn was originally intended both as a fortified city and a naval base. The area was the site of the first boatyards established in Copenhagen, as well as the warehouses belonging to major shipping lines. It is also where most sailors and boatyard workers lived. Up until the 1980s, Christianshavn was known only as the site of the "free state of Christiania" and was considered to be unattractive, poor and neglected. Since the 1990s, however, Christianshavn, together with nearby Holmen, has blossomed thanks to a sustained programme of urban redevelopment. Run-down warehouses have been transformed into trendy restaurants, cafés, company offices and smart apartments, which are favoured by artists and young professionals.

9 Vor Frelsers Kirke

Sankt Annæ Gade 29. **Map** 4 E2. **Tel** 32 54 68 83. Christianshavn. 2A, 19, 47, 66, 350S. **Open** 11am–3:30pm daily. Tower: **Open** 10am–4pm Mon–Sat, 10:30am–3:30pm Sun & hols (late Jun–mid-Sep: open until 7:30pm daily). **Closed** in heavy rain or strong winds. **vorfrelserskirke.dk**

Our Saviour's Church is most famous for its extraordinary spire, completed in 1752, and accessible via a spiral staircase that runs around the exterior. Be warned – it takes considerable

Yachting marina and houses built out over the water, in Christianshavn

For hotels and restaurants see pp248–55 and pp262–77

stamina to climb all 400 steps, not to mention a good head for heights. The spire is Copenhagen's second-highest panoramic viewpoint and once you have caught your breath at the top you will be rewarded with a fabulous view of the city from 90 m (295 ft) up.

The spire's creator was the architect Lauritz de Thurah, who struck upon the idea of a spiral staircase while visiting the church of Sant'Ivo alla Sapienza in Rome. Legend has it that Thurah was so obsessed by his work that when it was alleged that his encircling staircase wound up the wrong way he committed suicide by leaping from the top of the tower. The truth is more prosaic, however, as the architect died in his own bed, poor and destitute, seven years after completing the tower. The tale was nevertheless made into a movie by the Danish director Nils Vest in 1997.

piral stairs of Vor lsers Kirke's tower

The church itself is also worth visiting. It was built in 1696, to a design by Lambert von Haven. Inside, a Baroque altar by the Swede Nicodemus Tessin is adorned with cherubs. The huge three-storey organ dates from 1698. It has more than 4,000 pipes and is supported by two giant elephants.

⑩ Orlogsmuseet

Overgaden oven Vandet 58. **Map** 4 E2. **Tel** 33 11 60 37. Ⓜ Christianshavn. 🚌 2A, 19, 47, 66, 350S. **Open** noon–4pm Tue–Sun.
Ⓦ **orlogsmuseet.dk**

The Royal Danish Naval Museum's building dates from 1780 and was once a sailors' hospital. Among its exhibits are navigation instruments, ships' lights, figureheads that were once fixed to the bows of windjammers, and uniforms.

Entrance to Christiania – a successful example of alternative living

A collection of over 300 model ships includes one that dates back to 1687.

⑪ Christiania

Map 4 D3 & E3. Ⓜ Christianhavn. 🚌 2A, 19, 47, 66, 350S.
Ⓦ **christiania.org**

The "free state of Christiania" has been in existence since 13 November 1971, when a group of squatters took over some deserted military barracks to the east of Christianshavn and established a commune. The local authorities initially tried to force the squatters to leave, but as the community's numbers swelled, the government decided to treat Christiania as a "social experiment". Today the community has about 900 residents.

The community has its own kindergarten, infrastructure and system of government, which are financed in part by the proceeds of its cafés and restaurants and the sale of locally made handicrafts. Christiania was initially linked with hippy drug culture, and cannabis was openly sold and smoked here until the trade was outlawed in 2004.

⑫ Operaen

Ekvipagemestervej 10. **Map** 2 F5. **Tel** 33 69 69 69. 🚌 66. ⛴ 901, 902. **Open** foyer: 3 hours before a performance. Jul–late Aug: 2pm and 4pm daily (in English).
Ⓦ **kglteater.dk**

The stunning Copenhagen Opera House opened in January 2005 on the island of Holmen in Copenhagen Harbour. For over a century the Danish Royal Opera shared a space with the ballet and theatre companies at Det Kongelige Teater. The auditorium was designed by the prominent Danish architect Henning Larsen, whose works include the Ny Carlsberg Glyptotek extension and the Danish Design Centre. The modern building is clad in German limestone and covers 41,000 sq m (441,300 sq ft). It includes a 1,500-seat auditorium with a gold leaf-gilded ceiling, as well as a second, smaller stage.

Striking façade of Copenhagen's opera house

FURTHER AFIELD

There is plenty to see outside the city centre. Some attractions, such as the Tycho Brahe Planetarium, are within walking distance. Others, like the Carlsberg Brewery, Zoological Garden or Assistens Kirkegård, can be reached by bus. Sights even further afield are served by a network of modern suburban trains.

A visit to one or more of these places provides an alternative to the bustle of inner-city Copenhagen. Charlottenlund, in an affluent coastal suburb, has a patch of surrounding woodland that is perfect for gentle walks, as is the park area around Frederiksberg Slot. And, thanks to the bridge and tunnel that spans the Øresund (Sound), the sandy beach and many attractions of Malmö in Sweden are only half an hour away. The bridge is a marvel of modern engineering and can be admired from the harbour of the charming fishing village of Dragør.

Sights at a Glance

Historic Buildings

4 Frederiksberg Slot and Have

Places of Interest

1 Tycho Brahe Planetarium
2 Carlsberg Brewery
5 Cisternerne
8 Experimentarium City
10 Den Blå Planet
11 Øresund Bridge
12 Amager and Ørestad
13 Dragør

Parks and Gardens

3 Zoologisk Have
9 Charlottenlund

Museums

14 Arken Museum For Moderne Kunst

Churches

7 Grundtvigs Kirke

Cemeteries

6 Assistens Kirkegård

Key

City centre
Motorway
Major road
Other road
Railway

0 kilometres 4
0 miles 2

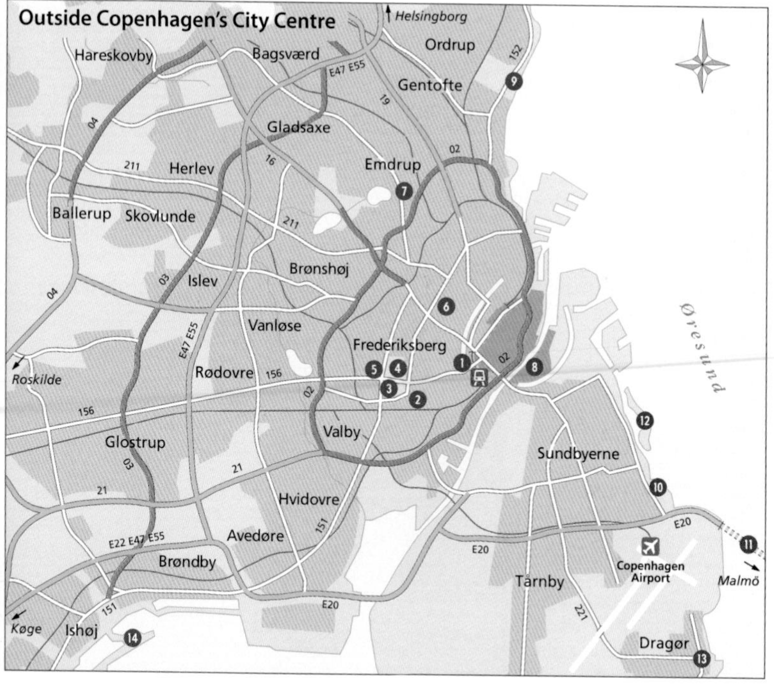

◀ Charlottenlund Slot, the grand former summer residence of Princess Charlotte Amalie

For keys to symbols see back flap

Tycho Brahe Planetarium in the shape of a sliced-through cylinder

❶ Tycho Brahe Planetarium

Gl. Kongevej 10. **Tel** 33 12 12 24. Ⓢ Vesterport. 🚌 14, 15, 29. **Open** daily; check website for times. **planetariet.dk**

Copenhagen's planetarium is the largest of its kind in western Europe and is named after Tycho Brahe (1546–1601), the renowned Danish astronomer. Brahe is credited with the discovery of a new star in the constellation of Cassiopeia, in 1572, and with making important advances in our knowledge of planetary motion. These impressive advances were made before the invention of the telescope.

The planetarium opened in 1989 in a cylindrical building designed by Knud Munk. Built from sand-coloured brick, it appears at its most attractive when viewed from across the small lake, which is one of a series that continues right up to Østerbro and that was created in the late 18th century by damming the local river. The planetarium is located on the Old Royal Route (Gammel Kongevej), which was once travelled by royal processions heading for Frederiksberg Slot.

The planetarium is Denmark's most advanced centre for popularizing astronomy and space research as well as promoting knowledge on natural science. A huge IMAX® cinema screens films daily, including one on the wonders of space travel.

❷ Carlsberg Brewery

Carlsberg Visitors Centre & Jacobsen Brewhouse: Gamle Carlsberg Vej 11. **Tel** 33 27 12 82. Ⓢ Enghave, Valby. 🚌 18, 26. **Open** May–Oct: 10am–5pm daily; Nov–Apr: 10am–5pm Tue–Sun. **visitcarlsberg.dk**

Carlsberg Brewery was founded in 1847 by Jacob Christian, whose father had worked at the king's brewery in Copenhagen. Jacob Christian chose this site on Valby Hill because of the quality of the water nearby, and named his company Carlsberg (Carl's Hill) after his son. By the late 19th century the business had an international reputation. In 1882 Carl founded his own brewery, Ny (New) Carlsberg, while his father's brewery continued as Gamle (Old) Carlsberg. The two merged in 1906.

East entrance gate to the Carlsberg Brewery

In 2005, the Jacobsen Brewhouse opened in part of the old brewery, with the aim of developing speciality beers. This brand is now the only one still produced at this site.

The rest of the brewery is an exhibition centre where visitors can learn about the manufacturing process and history of beer during a 90-minute self-guided tour that ends with a beer tasting in a bar overlooking the shining copper kettles used in the brewing process.

In addition to the Visitors' Centre, there is a cluster of small art galleries, the exhibition space Fotografisk Center and Europe's largest centre for modern dance, Dansehallerne.

The brewery site also features many interesting examples of industrial architecture, including the intriguing Elephant Gate (1901), which consists of four 5-m (16-ft) high granite elephants shipped from Bornholm.

Giraffes in the city zoo, near Frederiksberg Have

❸ Zoologisk Have

Roskildevej 32. **Tel** 72 20 02 00. Ⓢ Valby. Ⓜ Frederiksberg. 🚌 4A, 6A, 18, 26. **Open** Jan–Mar, Nov & Dec: 10am–4pm daily (Mar: to 5pm Sat & Sun); Apr, May & Sep: 10am–5pm daily (to 6pm Sat & Sun); Jun & mid-Aug–late Aug: 10am–6pm daily; Jul–mid-Aug: 10am–8pm daily; Oct: 10am–5pm daily. **zoo.dk**

Copenhagen's zoological garden was established close to Frederiksberg Slot in 1859, making it one of Europe's oldest zoos. In the 1940s it was expanded to include part of Søndermarken, with the two

Frederiksberg Slot, headquarters of the Danish Military Academy

areas connected by a tunnel under Roskildevej. Although not large by international standards, the zoo has a good record of breeding in captivity. A wide selection of animals are kept here, including giraffes, polar bears, hippos, elephants and lions. The Norman Foster-designed Elephant House is especially noteworthy for its large glass domes and groundbreaking architecture. An enclosure for seals, elks and polar bears, The Arctic Ring, opened in 2012.

A tropical section houses butterflies and birds, as well as some crocodiles. Smaller children will enjoy the petting zoo, which offers close-up contact with domestic animals, pony rides and the chance to let off steam in a large play area laid out like a child-size rabbit warren. The 42-m (138-ft) high wooden observation tower, built in 1905, affords views as far as the coast of Sweden.

4 Frederiksberg Slot and Have

Roskildevej 28. **Tel** 36 13 26 00. M Frederiksberg. 4A, 6A, 18, 26. Palace: **Open** for tours only at 11am & 1pm on last Sat of month (except Jul & Dec). Garden: **Open** daily.

Built between 1700 and 1735 this palace was the summer residence of Frederik IV who used it to entertain visitors including, in 1716, the Tsar of Russia, Peter the Great. The king is said to have enjoyed sailing along the park canals, while Copenhagen's inhabitants lined the banks and cheered.

The palace was designed in the Italian style by the architect Ernst Brandenburger following the king's visit to Italy. During the reign of Christian IV the building was enlarged with two additional wings, giving it its present horseshoe shape.

Since 1869 Frederiksberg Slot has been used by the Danish Military Academy. Having its origins in the Cadets' Corp established by Frederik IV in 1713, the school's emblem still bears the king's monogram. The school is not open to the public except for guided tours, though visitors are free to explore the grounds. The palace gardens, known as Frederiksberg Have, were laid out in a French style in the early 18th century. Later on they were transformed into a romantic rambling English park, criss-crossed with a network of canals and tree-lined paths, and dotted with statues and benches.

Frederiksberg Slot stands on top of a hill and, for the people of Copenhagen, marks a notional boundary of the city. In the 18th century, when it was built, the palace stood outside the city limits.

5 Cisternerne

Søndermarken. **Tel** 30 73 80 32. S Enghave, Valby. 4A, 6A, 18, 26, 171E. **Open** 1am–5pm Thu– Sun. **Closed** Jan, Feb & Dec. W **cisternerne.dk**

Praised by *Forbes* magazine as one of the most unique museums in Europe, the cisterns is a long forgotten subterranean reservoir that once contained the supply of drinking water for the Danish capital. Today, the cisterns acts as a venue for art exhibitions and other events. The cisterns is located under Frederiksberg Hill in the heart of Søndermarken Park; at ground level, the presence of the museum is given away only by two modern glass pyramids. Guided tours lasting an hour take in the current exhibition at Cisternerne, as well as the geology and architecture of the cisterns.

Colourful glass artwork on display at Cisternerne

Flora Danica

This dinner service, decorated with floral designs copied from the *Flora Danica* encyclopedia of plants, was ordered in 1790 by Christian VII. The set was intended as a present for Catherine II of Russia. However, during the 12 years when the first *Flora Danica* was in production the Tsarina died, and the king decided to keep the set for himself. It was used for the first time in 1803 during a reception to celebrate the king's 37th birthday. Over 1,500 of the original 1,802 pieces have survived and are now in the possession of Queen Margrethe II. Copies of individual items are made to order and the methods of production hardly differ from those employed over 200 years ago. The pieces are hand-painted by artists who train for over 10 years to master the exquisite flower paintings. This kind of quality is expensive – a plate costs upwards of 5,000 Dkr.

An example of *Flora Danica* tableware

Assistens Kirkegård, both a park and a cemetery

6 Assistens Kirkegård

Kapelvej 2. **Tel** 35 37 19 17. Ⓢ Ⓜ Nørreport. 🚌 3A, 5A, 12, 18, 66, 250S 350S. **Open** Oct–Mar: 7am–7pm daily; Apr–Sep: 7am–10pm daily. **W assistens.dk**

In 1760 Copenhagen's graveyards were too small to accommodate victims of a plague that was assailing the city at this time. The plague first struck in 1711 and claimed 23,000 lives in all, reducing the city's population by a third. Assistens Kirkegård was established to supplement the existing provisions for burials.

Initially the cemetery was used only for burying the poor but, from the late 18th century, burial plots at Assistens came into fashion. The list of famous people who are buried here include Søren Kierkegaard, Niels Bohr and Hans Christian Andersen, as well as the artists Christoffer Wilhelm Eckersberg and Christian Købke. The cemetery is also a pleasant park, and popular with many locals. Visitors are as likely to see buskers, joggers, cyclists and sunbathers as people tending the graves.

7 Grundtvigs Kirke

På Bjerget 14B. **Tel** 35 81 54 42. Ⓢ Emdrup. 🚌 6A, 42, 43, 66, 69. **Open** 9am–4pm Mon–Sat (to 6pm Thu), noon–4pm Sun (to 1pm in winter). **W grundtvigskirke.dk**

This unusual yellow brick church, remarkable not only for its size but also its highly original shape, was designed in 1913 by P.V. Jensen Klint. Standing almost 49 m (161 ft) high, it ranks as one of Denmark's largest churches and is designed in a Danish Modernist style. It was built between 1921 and 1940 on Bisperbjerg, the highest hill in Copenhagen, and paid for by public donations to honour the memory of Nicolai Frederik Severin Grundtvig (1783–1872) – a prominent clergyman, theologist and philosopher. In addition to his social work, this versatile man found time to write books and treatises, and composed some 1,500 hymns, many of which are sung to this day in Danish churches. For more than 10 years Grundtvig was a member of the Danish Parliament, and in 1861 he became an honorary bishop of the Danish Church.

Front elevation of Grundtvigs Kirke, inspired by small village churches

The charismatic clergyman became famous in his country as the founder of the Danish Folkehøjskole (People's High School), a system that enabled those from the lower ranks of society to gain access to education. The shape of the church building symbolizes this sphere of his activities, being reminiscent of a typical Danish village church. In addition, the top of the tower is designed to resemble a church organ and alludes to the many religious hymns written by Grundtvig.

A climbing wall, one of the many popular attractions at Experimentarium City

8 Experimentarium City

Trangravsvej 10–12. **Tel** 39 27 33 33. Ⓢ Hellerup or Svanemøllen. 🚌 9A. ⛴ 993. **Open** 10am–5pm daily. **Closed** 1 Jan, 24, 25 & 31 Dec. **W experimentarium.dk**

This innovative science centre is temporality located at Christianshavn while the original site in the Hellerup district is being redeveloped. The main idea behind the centre is to bring science to life through hands-on exploration. Almost all the exhibits are of the interactive kind and the experiments can be independently performed by anyone.

The place is hugely popular with children who run about trying out all the exhibits. Adults, too, will find much of interest, whether it be testing the latest in virtual technology, programming robots or playing ball with blow pipes.

Some of the many aquatic creatures to be found at Den Blå Planet

At Experimentarium City science is for everybody and visitors can learn about the wonderful world that surrounds them through play and exciting experiences. There are enough activities to fill several hours of exploration. At every point, children are confronted with exhibits and puzzles to fire their curiosity, and tested with different kinds of challenges such as drawing the outline of a figure while looking in the mirror, and seeing if they can make all the muscles in their lower body work together to keep their balance on a special board. Kids can try their hand at guiding a cargo vessel into harbour, test their emotions, check their hearing from the lowest to the highest frequencies, and see which kind of ball runs the fastest in the zigzag track.

The Kids' Pavillion is a section where younger visitors between 3 and 6 years old can experiment with magnetism, build a house using a crane, hear what their voice sounds like backwards and much more.

The large outdoor area, right beside the harbour, is in use all year around with different activities depending on the season. There are also activities during which entertaining chemistry and physics experiments are carried out, and demonstrations and dissections where audience participation is encouraged. All the exhibits are labelled in Danish and English, and there are numerous lectures and special exhibitions staged throughout the year.

❾ Charlottenlund

Jægersborg Allé. 🚌 14. Ⓢ Charlottenlund St. Palace: **Closed** to the public. Gardens: **Open** to the public.

A royal residence has stood on this site since 1690, but the present palace was built between 1731 and 1733 on the orders of Princess Charlotte Amalie. The princess, who remained single all her life, liked the place so much that it was soon named after her. She used it as her summer residence until her death in 1782.

The building was remodelled in the 19th century, when its Baroque character gave way to a Renaissance style. A number of other Danish royals have enjoyed staying here including Frederik VIII and his wife, Princess Louise, who remained here until her death in 1926. The couple are commemorated by an obelisk located at the rear of the building.

The palace is now used by the Danish Institute for Fisheries, but it is still possible to stroll in its surrounding gardens. The appearance of the park, with its pruned conifers and pleasant avenues, dates from the 1990s, though marked pathways and ponds remain from the 17th century. The vegetable garden dates from 1826 and once grew herbs and produce to be used in the palace kitchen. There are a number of ancient trees in the grounds, notably two larches that stand at the rear of the palace and are considered to be the oldest of their kind in Denmark.

❿ Den Blå Planet

Jacob Fortlingsvej 1. **Tel** 39 62 32 83. 🚌 5A, 14. Ⓜ Kastrup. **Open** 10am–9pm Mon, 10am–6pm Tue–Sun. **Closed** 1 Jan, 24, 25 & 31 Dec. W **denblaaplanet.dk**

Copenhagen's aquarium, Den Blå Planet (The Blue Planet), opened in spring 2013 in a modern building in Kastrup harbour, on the island of Amager. Although not as large as Nordsøen Oceanarium in Hirtshals *(see p208)*, it offers the chance to admire a wide variety of marine life; it also plays a major role in conservation, research and education.

The aquarium contains more than 90 glass tanks, the largest holding 85,000 litres (18,700 gallons) of water. The five main sections are the Amazon, the African Great Lakes, the Warm Ocean, Cold Water, and Evolution and Adaptation. The tanks are populated by over 300 species of fish from all over the world including sharks and sharp-teethed piranha. Among the other aquatic wildlife are a giant octopus, crocodiles and an electric eel (capable of producing up to 2,000 volts), as well as turtles and many hundreds of brightly coloured tropical fish.

Feeding times (displayed on the aquarium website and at the entrance) are especially animated. In the basement, kids can come close to small marine life in the touch pools.

Charlottenlund Slot, surrounded by parkland

⓫ Øresund Bridge

Tel 70 23 90 60. Toll charge: 188–800 Dkr, depending on vehicle size; no bicycles allowed; toll and passport control points are located on the Swedish side.
W oresundsbron.com

In 2000, when Queen Margrethe II and King Carl XVI of Sweden jointly opened the Øresund Bridge, it was the first time that the Scandinavian peninsula had been connected to mainland Europe since the Ice Age. Now, thanks to the bridge, the delights of Malmö, the largest city in southern Sweden, are only 35 minutes away from Copenhagen.

The bridge is the second longest fixed-link bridge in the world. The entire crossing is 16 km (10 miles) long and consists of (from the Danish side): a 430-m (1,411-ft) long artificial peninsula, a tunnel measuring more than 3.5 km (2.2 miles) and running 10 m (33 ft) below the water, a 4-km (2-mile) long artificial island and a 7,845-m (25,738-ft) long cable-stayed bridge. From either side of the sound, the sight of the structure, with its huge 204-m (670-ft) high pylons, is truly impressive.

The bridge is a marvel of modern engineering. It has a two-level structure; the top is for motor traffic, the bottom for rail. At its highest point the bridge is suspended 57 m (187 ft) above the water. At the tunnel entrance, on both sides, are light filters designed to allow drivers to adjust to the dimmer conditions. About one thousand sensors are installed along the route as part of a fire alarm system.

Wind turbines rising from the seabed east of Amager

The bridge has proved to be popular and over 20,000 rail passengers and 10,000 cars make the crossing every day. It also forms part of an annual marathon run, the first of which took place in June 2000, before the official opening.

⓬ Amager and Ørestad

3 km (2 miles) southeast of Copenhagen city centre.

For a great number of visitors arriving by plane, the island of Amager, southeast of Copenhagen's city centre, is the starting point of their exploration of Denmark, since it is the site of Copenhagen's international airport.

Since the opening of the Øresund Bridge in 2000, Amager has gone from being a relatively undeveloped area to one characterized by groundbreaking architecture and housing developments. The urban conglomeration of Amager, with its residential blocks, shops and restaurants, blends into the almost futuristic Ørestad. Landmark buildings here include the 23-floor skyscraper Bella Sky Comwell Hotel, whose two towers lean away from each other with insulating, alternating glass panels, and the DR Koncerthuset *(see p106)*. This world-class performance venue and studio space was designed in the shape of a giant blue cube by acclaimed French architect Jean Nouvel. Its glass façade, opaque by day, acts like blue-screen technology at night, projecting images of the activity within. Most of the University of Copenhagen *(see p76)* is now based on Amager, and Scandinavia's largest shopping centre, Fields *(see p105)*, can be found right next to Ørestad metro station. Convenient metro connections to Copenhagen have further helped rejuvenate the district. Those looking for outdoor

Øresund Bridge linking Denmark and Sweden

attractions can still find them here, however: Naturcenter Vestamager is an oasis for families, with play areas, pony rides and a lake, while the recreated Amager Strandpark, which replaced the former 1930s bathing huts, is a landscaped area of man-made beaches, including a lagoon and an island.

⓭ Dragør

12 km (7 miles) southeast of Copenhagen. Museum: Havnepladsen 2. **Tel** 32 53 93 07. **Open** Jun–Sep: noon–4pm Wed, Thu, Sat & Sun.
museumamager.dk

This picturesque town to the southeast of Amager used to be the place to catch a ferry for Limhamn, on the Swedish side of the Øresund (Sound), which ran from 1934 until 1999. The opening of a bridge brought about the closing of this route, and Dragør has since become a destination for those wishing to escape the hustle of central Copenhagen.

As far back as the Middle Ages, Dragør was a major centre for the Baltic herring trade. Later on, its inhabitants profited by piloting the boats that sailed across the Øresund. Many houses in Dragør still have distinctive observation towers, known as "Kikkenborg". The biggest of these (now a museum) stands by Lodshuset, a building that houses the local pilot service headquarters, which was established in 1684. Surprisingly, for a long time Dragør had no proper harbour and the boats were simply dragged ashore. The word "dragør" means a sandy or pebbly strip of land up which the boats were hauled. It was not until 1520 that Dutch settlers, inhabiting nearby Store Magleby, built a proper harbour. Once built, it developed fast and by the 19th century it was the third-largest port in Denmark (after Copenhagen and Helsingør), receiving large sailing ships. Today these maritime traditions are kept alive by a pleasant marina overlooking nearby Sweden and the stunning bridge.
The town is a pleasant place for a stroll with cobbled streets and pretty 18th-century yellow-walled houses decorated with flowers. The local museum, housed in the old town hall building and a 17th-century harbour warehouse, has a collection of items devoted to Dragør's rich maritime past.
A combined ticket allows admission to four museums in the area: the Dragør Museum, the Amagermuseet in Store Magleby, the Lodshuset building and the Mølsted Museum, which is dedicated to the Danish seascape painter Christian Mølsted.

Cutters moored in Dragør's harbour

An exhibit from Dragør's museum

⓮ Arken Museum For Moderne Kunst

20 km (12 miles) south of Copenhagen city centre. Ishøj, Skovvej 100. **Tel** 43 54 02 22. to and from Ishøj. 128. **Open** 10am–5pm Tue–Sun (to 9pm Wed).
arken.dk

Located a stone's throw from the beach, Arken Museum For Moderne Kunst (Arken Museum of Modern Art) is housed in a building intended to resemble a marooned ship.

The museum's permanent collection is comprised of contemporary Danish, Nordic and international art, with an emphasis on installations, sculpture and graphic art. Many of the works on display are by Danish artists such as Asger Jorn, Jeppe Hein and Per Kirkeby. One of the most fascinating installations in the gallery is Ai Weiwei's *Circle of Animals/Zodiac Heads*, which represents 12 animals of the Chinese zodiac. There are also nine huge, abstract paintings by German artist Anselm Reye, whose neon colours reference Pop Art, Minimalism and Expressionism, and ten works by Damien Hirst, which are exhibited separately in the Damien Hirst Room. In addition, the museum presents at least two major temporary exhibitions a year, ranging from international retrospectives to large group shows.

Opened in 1996, the building has proved to be as controversial as much of the work inside. Designed by Søren Robert Lund when he was 25 years old and still a student, it follows few conventional rules. Extensions built in different materials have softened the original raw finish and provide a more welcoming exterior.

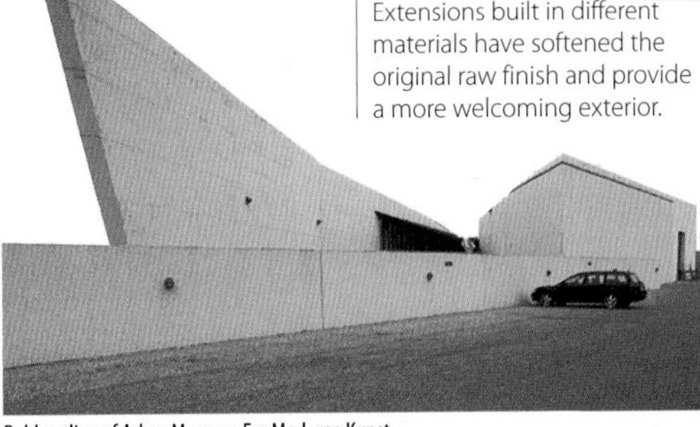

Bold outline of Arken Museum For Moderne Kunst

SHOPPING IN COPENHAGEN

Copenhagen has long been the commercial centre not only of Denmark, but also of an entire region that includes Zealand and, on the Swedish side, Skåne (Skania). Shopping here is a pleasurable experience, with many of the most interesting stores concentrated in just a few areas, often in buildings as interesting as their merchandise. Strøget and the adjacent pedestrian streets offer everything from designer labels and casual fashion, to porcelain, crystal and antiques. Copenhagen is synonymous with the best in interior style and the decorative arts, while young Danish talent has turned the city into a fashion capital, too. An array of hip boutiques and quirky shops have helped to revitalise some previously run-down areas of the city and they deserve to be explored. Along the way, dozens of picturesque squares and cafés offer welcome respite for tired feet.

Magasin du Nord, one of Copenhagen's best-known department stores

What to Buy

Denmark is the home of applied design, and those looking for homewares are spoilt for choice by the vast array of ingenious, smart, unusual and extravagant items on offer. The Danes like to dress smartly too, without spending a fortune, so it is worth checking out the sales for good quality clothes and footwear at bargain prices. The best times are in July and January.

While all the high-profile international designer labels are available, one of the pleasures of shopping in Copenhagen is discovering unusual and unique items unavailable back home.

Where to Shop

Most of the major international brands can be found along the city's two longest pedestrian streets, Strøget *(see p74)* and Købmagergade. Shops range from cheerful and inexpensive to designer and upmarket department stores (towards Kongens Nytorv). If you take detours into the side streets there is plenty of more alternative shopping on offer. On parallel Læderstræde and Kompagnistræde you will discover a variety of small independent shops; the latter is especially good for antiques. Those on tighter budgets should head west of Strøget, to Larsbjørnsstræde and Studiestræde for street fashion, secondhand shops and music stores.

On the outskirts of the old town, the Nansensgade area mixes traditional and trendy boutiques with attractive bars and cafés. There is everything here from sushi restaurants and chocolate shops to vintage clothes and accessories.

To the west of the central station, the former red light district of Vesterbro has undergone a complete transformation and is now one of Copenhagen's most vibrant areas. At its centre, Halmtorvet is a trendy café-filled square. Head to Istedgade for art and speciality shops.

Those in search of a quirky bargain should try the multi-cultural Nørrebro district, north of the city. Elmegade and Fælledvej are lined with secondhand stores, new Danish design and recycled goods. For secondhand jewellery try Ravnsborggade.

Opening Hours

It is not worth trying to shop in Denmark for anything other than foodstuffs before 10am. Early in the week most shops close at around 5:30pm, although many stores remain open on Fridays until 6 or 7pm. On Saturdays some shops close at 2pm, but the majority now stay open until 4 or 5pm. Department stores tend to have the longest opening hours. While smaller shops in Denmark stay closed on Sundays, larger stores and shopping centres now open Sundays though hours may vary.

How to Pay

The country's currency is the Danish krone (Dkr). Some shops also accept the Swedish krone and the euro, although the rate of exchange applied in such cases may not be advantageous. A few of the smaller shops may expect payment in cash, however the vast majority of outlets accept credit cards. The prices quoted always include VAT and excise tax. Non-EU residents are entitled to a VAT refund *(see p278)*.

Department Stores and Shopping Centres

Magasin du Nord was Scandinavia's first department store and is still a huge favourite. As well as clothes, cosmetics and luxury household goods it sells books, jewellery, delicious chocolate and foodstuffs. Also popular is the light and airy **Illum** on Strøget, which has several elegant floors selling high-quality goods under a glass dome, and the added advantage of a rooftop café.

Copenhagen has several shopping centres, with shops, cafés, restaurants, and cinemas under one roof. Vesterbro's **Fisketorvet**, situated on the site of an old fish market facing the Sound, is arguably one of the best. It is also worth taking a trip out to **Fields**, one of the biggest shopping centres in Scandinavia with a total of 150 shops under one roof. Although a little way out of the city, it is conveniently situated at the Ørestad metro station.

Design and Interior Decoration

Denmark is justly famous for combining attractive design with functionality and quality materials. Most of its best-known brands have their own shops in the city centre. The **Bang & Olufsen** showroom has listening rooms where customers can appreciate the quality of its audio products. For a good selection of interior design under one roof, head for **Illums Bolighus**, which keeps an eye on tradition while displaying the latest trends in furnishing and lighting.

Winner of numerous awards for innovative design, **Normann Copenhagen** has converted an old cinema in Østerbro into a stunning showroom. As well as its own collection of kitchen accessories, here you can find a variety of contemporary lifestyle products and high-profile fashion brands from around the world – all in a truly unforgettable setting.

The **Louis Poulsen** showroom offers various designer lighting solutions set against a minimalist background, and young furniture designers display their talent for creating classics with a contemporary twist at **Hay Cph**, which has two branches in the city centre. Another sleek furniture store is **Paustian** in the dock area. Designed by architect Jørn Utzon, of Sydney Opera House fame, there is also a stylish restaurant.

Back in town, the interior design centre **Casa Shop** is well worth a look, as is the **Danish Design Centre (DDC)**, which hosts changing exhibitions showcasing Danish innovation. **Designer Zoo**, in Vesterbro, is a working design store for eight Danish designers who create furniture, jewellery, knitwear and artistic glass. **Bolia** is a nationwide interior design store that celebrates Scandinavian traditions.

Interior of a shop selling Bodum kitchenware, a popular Danish product

Minimalist interior of leading fashion store Munthe plus Simonsen

Clothes and Accessories

From high fashion to secondhand chic, Copenhagen has it all. Top international designers congregate at the Kongens Nytorv end of Strøget, while less expensive labels stretch down the street towards the town hall. Købmagergade is good for mid-price clothes while Kronprinsensgade, which runs off it, is known as "Copenhagen's Catwalk" for the cutting-edge clothes shops located here. **Bruuns Bazaar** is a favourite, selling men's and women's modern designs.

The narrow streets of the Grønnegade quarter are lined with half-timbered buildings housing Danish streetwear and classic labels. **Munthe plus Simonsen**, renowned for classy yet casual ladieswear, is found here. Nearby, on Pilestræde, **Designers Remix** have opened a large flagship store of their sexy, edgy womenswear. **Day Birger et Mikkelsen**, has also gathered all of their seven lines under one roof here: women's, men's and children's wear, lingerie, jewellery, accessories and home. **Holly Golightly** sells elegant Danish womenswear and accessories.

Secondhand chic lies in the "Pisserenden" area adjacent to Strøget, on streets like Læderstræde and Studiestræde; **Carmen & Fantasio** is one of the best. For vintage frocks and clever accessories, head to Nansensgade or try **Glam Vintage** in Silkegade 7. The collection of high-end 1960–70s glad rags is particularly pleasing.

Jewellery

Danish jewellery has a reputation for fine design and attention to detail. The city's most famous jewellery shop is silversmith **Georg Jensen**, but Julie Sandlau (stocked at **Magasin du Nord**), who creates pretty gold designs, is the name on many a celebrity's lips. Similarly trendy (and expensive) are the gold and silver creations of Marlene Juhl Jørgensen at **Figaros Bryllup**. For jewellery fit for Denmark's Queen, visit **Peter Hertz**. Amber washed up on Denmark's west coast makes its way into jewellery at **The Amber Specialist** and branches of **House of Amber**, which also has an amber museum.

Royal Shopping

While historic royals have left their mark on Copenhagen's architecture, fans of today's very popular royal family like to follow in their footsteps to the shops. The Queen, a talented artist, book illustrator, and designer of ecclesiastical textiles and stage costumes, can often be seen shopping in the city centre while several family members frequent Copenhagen's two big department stores, **Illum** and **Magasin du Nord**.

Grand stores carrying the coveted words "Purveyors to her Majesty, the Queen of Denmark" cluster together on the Amagertorv section of Strøget – the great silversmith **Georg Jensen**, **Royal Copenhagen**, which also boasts a charming tea room, and **Illums Bolighus**, a shrine to modern design.

Crown Princess Mary is a fashion and style icon in Denmark. Among her favourite clothes designers are Julie Fagerholt at **Heart Made**, known for her subtle detailing, the sexy and sophisticated look of **By Malene Birger**, and the innovative yet classic lines of Baum und Pferdgarten, stocked at **Urban Factory**.

Should you wish to take home wine bottled on Prince Henrik's estate in France, visit **Kjaer & Sommerfeldt**.

Markets

Hours can be spent bargain hunting in Copenhagen's outdoor flea markets that pop up around the city between April or May and mid-October. The flea market on **Thorvaldsens Plads**, in front of the museum, sells antiques, Danish design, posters, paintings and ceramics. It is particularly popular with its canalside setting and outdoor cafés.

Torvehallerne København (KBH), the purpose-built covered food market on Israel Plads, offers more than 60 stands, from fruit and vegetables to meat and fish, and from handmade chocolate and cupcakes to gourmet ready meals.

Flea market in one of Copenhagen's picturesque squares

Art and Antiques

Bredgade, in the financial district, and Ravnsborggade in Nørrebro are packed with antiques shops, bric-a-brac sellers and collectibles, especially modern Danish classics and funky retro designs. Come here for pieces by the great names in 20th-century Danish design, such as Arne Jacobsen, famed for his Egg, Ant and Swan chairs, Hans J Wegner, Kaare Klint and lighting by Poul Henningsen. Out of town but worth the trek, **Dansk Møbelkunst**, in Østerbro, and **Green Square**, out on Amager, are essential browsing territory for collectors of modern Danish classics.

Great furniture and style from the 1950s, 60s and 70s can also be found at **Klassik**, while **Lysberg** is popular for the timeless quality of its designs. Bredgade is also the home of the traditional art galleries and auction houses. Sotheby's have a house here as do the long-established Danish auction houses, such as **Bruun Rasmussen**. These offer a good potential source of finds in art, antiques, furniture and jewellery.

In vibrant Vesterbro, the side streets off Istedgade and the meat-packing district of Kødbyen are the places to look for galleries displaying work by up-and-coming artists. The small streets in the Islands Brygge area are a hotbed of galleries specialising in experimental art. Off Strøget, Kompagnistræde is a quiet haven for collectors. Among the cluster of antiques shops there are specialists in porcelain and china, vintage watches and books, prints and comics. For the finest porcelain, silver and crystal, visit **Royal Copenhagen**.

Specialist Shops

The array of individual and innovative little shops make strolling Copenhagen's streets a pleasure. They are also a great way to find gifts and souvenirs to take home from the city. Buy specialist teas in one of Europe's oldest teashops, **A.C. Perch's Thehandel**, which dates from 1834. Having retained its original interior, the shop and tearoom are a highlight on fashionable Kronprinsensgade. **Sømods Bolcher** is an old-fashioned sweet shop where you can watch traditional treats being made in time-honoured fashion. For the finest foods, take a look at the delicious pastries at **Lagkagehuset** and the specialist breads at **Meyers Bakery**, or explore Vaernedamsvej in Vesterbro, a great street for gourmets, with specialist cheese, wine, fish and chocolate shops, as well as cafés and grocers.

Buy a posy, or just soak up the colour and scent of **Bering Flowers**, who not only provide the flowers for the Royal Theatre but for royal weddings and other glitzy occasions too.

DIRECTORY

Department Stores and Shopping Centres

Fields
Arne Jacobsens Allé 12.
Tel 70 20 85 05.
fields.dk

Fisketorvet
Kalvebod Brygge 59.
Map 3 A5.
Tel 33 36 64 00.
fisketorvet.dk

Illum
Østergade 52.
Map 3 C1.
Tel 33 14 40 02.
illum.dk

Magasin du Nord
Kongens Nytorv 13.
Map 4 D1.
Tel 33 11 44 33.
magasin.dk

Design and Interior Decoration

Bang & Olufsen
Østergade 18.
Map 4 D1.
Tel 33 11 14 15.

Bolia
Christian IX Gade 7.
Map 1 C5.
Tel 70 10 00 55.

Casa Shop
Store Regnegade 2.
Map 1 C3.
Tel 33 32 70 41.

Danish Design Centre
H.C. Andersens Blvd 27.
Map 3 B2.
Tel 33 69 33 69.
ddc.dk

Designer Zoo
Vesterbrogade 137.
Tel 33 24 94 93.
dzoo.dk

Hay Cph
Pilestræde 29–31.
Map 3 C1.
Tel 42 82 08 20.

Hay House
Østergade 61, 2nd/3rd Floors.
Map 3 C1.
hay.dk

Illums Bolighus
Amagertorv 10.
Map 3 C1.
Tel 33 14 19 41.

Louis Poulsen
Gammel Strand 28.
Map 3 C1.
Tel 70 33 14 14.

Normann Copenhagen
Østerbrogade 70.
Map 1 C1–C2.
Tel 35 27 05 40.

Paustian
Kalkbrænderiløbskaj 2.
Tel 39 16 65 65.
paustian.dk

Clothes and Accessories

Bruuns Bazaar
Kronprinsensgade 8–9.
Map 3 C1.
Tel 33 32 19 99.

Carmen & Fantasio
Larsbjørnsstræde 11.
Map 3 B1. **Tel** 33 14 30 36.

Day Birger et Mikkelsen
Pilestræde 16. **Map** 3 C1.
Tel 33 45 88 80.

Designers Remix
Pilestræde 8D. **Map** 3 C1.
Tel 33 14 33 00.

Glam Vintage
Silkegade 7. **Map** 3 C1.
Tel 35 38 50 41.

Holly Golightly
Gammel Mønt 2.
Map 1 C5.
Tel 33 14 19 20.

Munthe plus Simonsen
Grønnegade 10. **Map** 2 D5. **Tel** 33 32 00 12.

Jewellery

The Amber Specialist
Frederiksberggade 28.
Map 3 B2. **Tel** 33 11 88 03.

Figaros Bryllup
Store Regnegade 2.
Map 1 C3.
Tel 33 93 09 92.

Georg Jensen
Amagertorv 4.
Map 3 C1.
Tel 33 11 40 80.

House of Amber
Kongens Nytorv 2.
Map 4 D1.
Tel 33 11 67 00.

Magasin du Nord
(See Department Stores)

Peter Hertz
Købmagergade 34.
Map 3 C1.
Tel 33 12 22 16.

Royal Shopping

By Malene Birger
Antonigade 10.
Map 3 C1.
Tel 35 43 22 33.

Georg Jensen
(See Jewellery)

Illum
(See Department Stores)

Illums Bolighus
(See Design and Interior Decoration)

Heart Made
Pilestræde 45.
Map 3 C1.
Tel 33 38 08 80.

Kjaer & Sommerfeldt
Gammel Mønt 4.
Map 1 C5.
Tel 70 15 65 00.

Magasin du Nord
(See Department Stores)

Royal Copenhagen
Amagertorv 6.
Map 3 C1.
Tel 33 13 71 81.

Urban Factory
Store Regnegade 2. **Map** 1 C3. **Tel** 33 91 70 75.

Markets

Thorvaldsens Plads Antique Market
Bertil Thorvaldsens Plads 2 (in front of Thorvaldsens Museum).
Map 3 C2. **Open** May–Oct: Fri & Sat.

Torvehallerne København
Frederiksborggade 21.
Map 1 B5.
Tel 70 10 60 70.
torvehallerne kbh.dk

Art and Antiques

Bruun Rasmussen
Bredgade 32.
Map 2 E5.
Tel 88 18 11 11.

Dansk Møbelkunst
Aldersrogade 6C.
Tel 33 32 38 37.

Green Square
Strandlosvej 11B.
Tel 32 57 59 59.

Klassik
Bredgade 3.
Map 2 D5.
Tel 33 33 90 60.

Lysberg
Bredgade 77.
Map 2 E4.
Tel 33 14 47 87.

Royal Copenhagen
(See Royal Shopping)

Specialist Shops

A.C. Perch's Thehandel
Kronprinsensgade 5.
Map 3 C1.
Tel 33 15 35 62.

Bering Flowers
Landemærket 12.
Map 1 C5.
Tel 33 15 26 11.

Lagkagehuset
Torvegade 45.
Map 4 D2.
Tel 32 57 36 07.

Meyers Bakery
Store Kongensgade 46.
Map 2 D5.
Tel 25 10 75 79.

Sømods Bolcher
Nørregade 36B.
Map 1 B5.
Tel 33 12 60 46.

ENTERTAINMENT IN COPENHAGEN

Copenhagen has a vibrant cultural life, from world-class opera and ballet staged at the magnificent Operaen, to jazz clubs and street performance. Nightclubs range from small café-style venues to major nightspots, where live bands and international DJs play the latest sounds, and the gay scene is one of Europe's best. Festivals come in all sizes, especially during the summer months when the city seems to breathe enjoyment. In July and August, locals make the most of the beaches, open-air swimming pools and sunbathing spots which open up along the harbour, including an urban beach on Amager island. Copenhagen is incredibly child-friendly and there is plenty to entertain young visitors, from the thrills and spills on offer at the ever-popular Tivoli amusment park to interactive fun at some of the country's top museums.

Practical Information

The first place to look for up-to-date information is the free magazine *Copenhagen This Week* (which despite its name comes out monthly) for the latest news on cultural events and club listings. It also has its own website: www.ctw.com.

Booking Tickets

Tickets for theatre, opera, concerts, festivals and sport events can be booked via **Billetnet**, by phone, online, or at a post office. The **Royal Theatre/ Opera Box Office** on Kongens Nytorv opens at 4pm for the sale of half-price tickets for that day's performances. Get there early, as queues can be long. Under-25s and over-65s are eligible for half-price tickets when booking for shows more than a week in advance.

Cinema tickets tend to be cheaper for matinee and weekday performances; these can be booked online at www.biobooking.dk.

Opera and Classical Music

Opera fans should not miss a performance of the Royal Opera at the striking **Operaen** *(see p93)* which also hosts classical music concerts. From early June until late August, **Det Kongelige Teater** (The Royal Theatre) has an open-air stage Ofelia Beach, on the waterfront outside Skuespilhuset. It hosts free cultural events, including opera performances by the Royal Danish Opera Academy. For eight days in late July and early August, the **Copenhagen Opera Festival** organizes shows at several venues across the city. Many events are free and take place outside, while others are produced specially for children. National broadcaster Danmarks Radio's world-class **DR Koncerthuset** houses a number of concert halls, the largest of which can seat 1,800 people.

Those who enjoy classical music will be thrilled by the concerts given at the **Tivoli Koncertsal**. Throughout the summer season, Danish and international conductors and soloists join the 80-strong Tivoli Symphony Orchestra for the **Tivoli Festival**'s varied programme. During the winter months, the orchestra becomes the Copenhagen Philharmonic.

Tivoli Koncertsal, home to the Tivoli Symphony Orchestra

Ballet performance at Det Kongelige Teater

For a less formal occasion, students from the Royal Danish Academy of Music give free concerts on Wednesday afternoons during spring and autumn in various venues. See www.onsdagskoncerter.dk for more details.

Ballet and Contemporary Dance

Det Kongelige Teater is home to the Royal Danish Ballet, whose season runs August–June, finishing with a free open-air performance in the grounds of Kastellet *(see p58)*.

The main venue for contemporary dance is **Dansescenen**, located in Northern Europe's largest centre for modern dance, the vast Dansehallerne complex, in the Carlsberg Brewery *(see p96)*. With a large stage (Store Carl) and the smaller Lille Carl, this venue is devoted to the best in Danish and international dance, as well as hosting a number of festivals to showcase young dance companies and choreographers.

Dansehallerne is also home to **Dansk Danseteater**, an experimental dance company founded in 1981 by the British dancer and choreographer Tim Rushton. Every August the company presents its popular festival Copenhagen Summer Dance, with free performances in the colonnaded courtyard of the Copenhagen City Police headquarters.

Jazz quintet playing at the Copenhagen Jazz House

Jazz Clubs and Live Music

International performers are regulars at the atmospheric **Copenhagen Jazzhouse** and at the legendary **Jazzhus Montmartre**. At **The Standard** you can experience an intimate jazz performance of the highest international level. Many bars host their own jazz sessions – like gritty **La Fontaine**, the oldest jazz venue in Copenhagen, which has live sessions every weekend. In July, the **Copenhagen Jazz Festival** fills the streets and venues all over the city, attracting some of the world's finest jazz musicians. Many of the 800 or so performances are free.

For blues fans, there is live music every night at **Mojo Blues Bar** and, in September, the **Copenhagen Blues Festival**.

For up-and-coming bands as well as international acts, **VEGA**, in Copenhagen's rejuvenated Vesterbro district, is a popular venue housed in a 1950s trade union building. The large hall (Store Vega) has seen many international bands, while the smaller room (Lille Vega) is ideal for more intimate, acoustic concerts. A great place to see the best young indie bands is **Loppen**, in alternative Christiania.

Last but by no means least is **Tivoli** *(see pp80–81)*, where in summer, world-famous rock and pop acts perform on the open-air stage. Friday night rock concerts kick off at 10pm during the summer, and entrance is included in the Tivoli admission. Musicals also run in both summer and Christmas seasons.

Nightlife Venues

Copenhagen's clubs start getting lively only after midnight, so many people head first to a pre-club bar, such as the trendy **Zoo Bar** or Ideal Bar in **VEGA**. **Rust**, in the vibrant Nørrebro district, has club nights from midweek on three floors; indie rock and hip hop dominate the live music, while in the basement DJs play indie, punk and electro. **Culture Box** is a purist techno club. The converted warehouses and cattle stalls of the former meat-packing district in Kødbyen come alive on weekend nights. The vast **KB3** attracts the hippest locals, as well as visiting DJs, to its dance nights.

For something completely different, head to **Wallmans Saloner**, where you can enjoy a seated dinner show with artists performing on different stages around the restaurant.

Theatre

Most theatre in Copenhagen is performed in Danish, and while there are a number of English-language theatre companies, none have venues of their own. The best known of these is **London Toast**, whose pre-Christmas pantomime in Tivoli's Glassalen is a Copenhagen tradition. Most of the drama performed by the Royal Danish Theatre is now staged at the company's playhouse Skuespilhuset *(see p75)*. Housed in an 1807 listed building in the Latin Quarter, **Københavns Musikteater** is a lively venue for experimental musical theatre and avant-garde opera.

Cinema

There are scores of cinemas in and around Copenhagen, ranging from art-house theatres to huge multiplexes. Most films are shown in their original language, with Danish subtitles.

To catch the latest blockbusters, the big **Cinemaxx**, part of the Fisketorvet shopping centre down by the harbour, shows all the major releases on ten screens. The **Imperial** is used for all the Danish premieres and charges a little extra for its luxurious seats. Around the corner, the **Dagmar** has a diverse programme and a pleasant atmosphere, while the independent **Empire Bio**, in a former locomotive factory, is popular with locals for its late-night shows.

To get away from the mainstream, the long-established **Grand Teatret**, with its repertoire of European films, and **Cinemateket**, which is attached to the Danish Film Institute, are traditional art-house cinemas. For off-circuit and low-budget films, try **Vester Vov Vov**, in the Vesterbro district, or the tiny **Gloria** on Rådhuspladsen.

Entrance to Cinemaxx, one of Copenhagen's main cinemas

Gay and Lesbian

Copenhagen is a city with a long tradition of openness and acceptance: the city's first gay bar, **Centralhjørnet**, opened its doors in the 1930s and is still going strong. Famed for its annual Gay Pride Parade in August and for Mix, a well-established gay, lesbian, bi-sexual and transgender film festival in October, the city has a stream of other events year-round, including the Sankt Hans mid-summer bonfire and beach party on Amager Island in June.

The city centre gay club, bar and restaurant scene is concentrated in quite a small area, so everything is pretty much within walking distance. **Club Cristopher** is Copenhagen's biggest gay club, with several dance floors, resident as well as visiting DJs and an open bar. **Jailhouse** is a popular concept bar and restaurant with booths kitted out as prison cells and staff dressed in police uniforms. On Friday evenings, DJs and a good atmosphere are available at the lounge-style **Oscar Bar & Café**. Young gay men favour **Masken Bar**, where the shows span live music and drag. **Mens Bar** is for the leather-clad contingent. For the really late night scene, head on to the aptly named **Never Mind**, open daily until 6am, or the darker, dingier **Dunkel**, where closing time is when the manager feels like closing. **Café Intime** is a piano bar near Frederiksberg Have that attracts theatrical types.

Tables on the pavement outside the Oscar Bar and Café

For up-to-date listings of gay events in the city, see the **Copenhagen Gay Life** website.

Beaches

Clean and spacious harbour swimming pools, with beaches and sports activities, are a great summer feature and only a short walk from the centre of Copenhagen. The harbour area has been revitalised with apartments, hotels and restaurants and the water really is clean enough for swimming. The pools are open from June until early September.

Havnebadet, just across the ramparts from Christianshavn at Islands Brygge, has five pools and a large grassy bathing "beach". The smaller **Copencabana** pool is by the Fisketorvet shopping centre and comes complete with sand beach and palm trees.

Further afield, the north end of **Bellevue Strand**, at Klampenborg, is a short train or bike ride from town. It's a gay-friendly place with a nudist area at the top end. **Amager Strandpark** *(see pp100–101)* on Amager Island is divided into two parts: an "urban" beach with a range of fitness activities, bars, food stalls, even a Bedouin tent; and a "wild" section with wide sandy beaches and small sand dunes. A lagoon between the island and the mainland has child-friendly shallow water.

Children's Entertainment

No child visiting Copenhagen should miss **Tivoli** amusement park *(see pp80–81)*, which has enough rides and attractions to keep even the most demanding young person happy. **Bakken** *(see p124)* in a wooded area north of the city near Klampenborg, claims to be the oldest fun park in the world and has over 100 rides. **Zoologisk Have** *(see pp96–7)* is the city's zoo and includes a mini zoo for smaller children and a large play area. **Den Blå Planet** *(see p99)* allows children to see weird and wonderful marine life up close.

Miniature classic car ride in Tivoli Gardens

Several museums in or near Strøget are especially suitable for children, including **Ripley's Believe It or Not!** *(see p77)*, **Hans Christian Andersen's Wonderful World** and **Guinness World Records Museum** *(see p73)*. These are all part of the same group, and it's possible to pay a joint entry price. There is also the **Experimentarium City** *(see pp98–9)*, a science-based museum with plenty of hands-on fun; or the chance to be dazzled by a 3D movie in the IMAX Space Theatre of the **Tycho Brahe Planetarium** *(see p96)*. The **Nationalmuseet** *(see pp88–9)* has a separate children's wing, and families and children have their own exhibitions and guided tours at the **Statens Museum for Kunst** *(see pp66–7)*.

Children's theatre is very popular in Denmark, with a number of international festivals held annually or bi-annually. Kids even have their own theatres, with child-size seats or centrally placed stages. **Zebu** in Amager has performances for kids aged one and upwards; most of them are virtually wordless.

Free puppet shows take place from June to mid-August at the **Marionet Teatret** at the foot of Kongens Have *(see p62)*, a lovely green space in front of the fairytale Rosenborg Palace. There are plenty of other playgrounds, including many in natural settings, like the one in Naturcenter Vestamager *(see p101)*. The harbour swimming pools *(see Beaches)* have areas reserved for kids and events during July's summer holidays.

DIRECTORY

Booking Tickets

Billetnet
Tel 70 15 65 65.
W billetnet.dk

Royal Theatre/ Opera Box Office
Kongens Nytorv. **Map** 4 D1. **W kglteater.dk**

Opera and Classical Music

Copenhagen Opera Festival
W copenhagenopera festival.com/en

Det Kongelige Teater
August Bournonvilles Passage, Kongens Nytorv. **Map** 4 D1. **Tel** 33 69 69 69. **W kglteater.dk**

DR Koncerthuset
Emil Holms Kanal 20, Ørestad. **Tel** 35 20 62 62. **W dr.dk/koncerthuset**

Operaen
Ekvipagemestervej 10. **Map** 2 F5. **Tel** 33 69 69 69. **W operahus.dk**

Tivoli Festival
W tivolifestival.dk/en

Tivoli Koncertsal
Vesterbrogade 3. **Map** 3 A3. **Tel** 33 15 10 12. **W tivoli.dk**

Ballet and Contemporary Dance

Dansescenen
Pasteursvej 20. **Tel** 33 88 80 00. **W dansehallerne.dk**

Dansk Danseteater
Tel 35 39 87 87. **W danskdanseteater. dk**

Det Kongelige Teater
(See Opera and Classical Music)

Jazz Clubs and Live Music

Copenhagen Blues Festival
W copenhagenblues festival.dk

Copenhagen Jazz Festival
W jazz.dk

Copenhagen Jazzhouse
Niels Hemmingsens Gade 10. **Map** 3 C1. **Tel** 33 15 47 00. **W jazzhouse.dk**

Jazzhus Montmartre
Store Regnegade 19A. **Map** 1 C5. **W jazzhusmontmartre. dk**

La Fontaine
Kompagnistræde 11. **Map** 3 C1. **Tel** 33 11 60 98. **W lafontaine.dk**

Loppen
Bådsmandsstræde 43, Christianshavn. **Map** 4 E2. **Tel** 32 57 84 22. **W loppen.dk**

Mojo Blues Bar
Løngangstræde 21. **Map** 3 B2. **Tel** 33 11 64 53. **W mojo.dk**

Tivoli
(See Opera and Classical Music)

VEGA
Enghavevej 40. **Tel** 33 25 70 11. **W vega.dk**

Nightlife Venues

Culture Box
Kronprinsensgade 54. **Map** 1 C5. **Tel** 33 32 50 50. **W culture-box.com**

KB3
Kødboderne 3, Kødbyen. **W kb3.dk**

Rust
Guldbergsgade 8. **Tel** 35 24 52 00. **W rust.dk**

The Standard
Havnegade 44. **Map** 4 E1. **Tel** 72 14 88 08. **W thestandardcph.dk**

VEGA
(See Jazz Clubs and Live Music)

Wallmans Saloner
Wallmans Cirkusbygningen, Jernbanegade 8. **Map** 3 A2. **Tel** 33 16 37 00. **W wallmans.dk**

Zoo Bar
Sværtegade 6. **Map** 3 C1. **Tel** 33 16 37 00. **W zoobar.dk**

Theatre

Københavns Musikteater
Kronprinsensgade 7. **Map** 3 C1. **Tel** 33 32 55 56. **W kobenhavns musikteater.dk**

London Toast
Tel 33 22 86 86. **W londontoast.dk**

Cinemas

Cinemateket
Gothersgade 55. **Map** 1 C5. **Tel** 33 74 34 12. **W dfi.dk/filmhuset**

Cinemaxx
Kalvebod Brygge 59. **Map** 3 A5. **Tel** 70 10 12 02. **W cinemaxx.dk**

Dagmar
Jernbanegade 2. **Tel** 70 13 12 11. **W nfbio.dk**

Empire Bio
Guldbergsgade 29F. **Tel** 35 36 00 36. **W empirebio.dk**

Gloria
Rådhuspladsen 59. **Map** 2 A2–B2. **Tel** 33 12 42 92. **W gloria.dk**

Grand Teatret
Mikkel Bryggersgade 8. **Map** 3 B2. **Tel** 33 15 16 11. **W grandteatret.dk**

Imperial
Ved Vesterport 4. **Tel** 70 13 12 11. **W nfbio.dk**

Vester Vov Vov
Absalonsgade 5. **Tel** 33 24 42 00. **W vestervovvov.dk**

Gay and Lesbian

Café Intime
Allegade 25, Frederiksberg. **Tel** 38 34 19 58.

Centralhjørnet
Kattesundet 18. **Map** 3 B2. **Tel** 33 11 85 49. **W centralhjornet.dk**

Club Christopher
Knabrostræde 3. **Map** 3 B1. **Tel** 60 80 71 76. **W clubchristopher.dk**

Copenhagen Gay Life
W copenhagen-gay- life.dk

Dunkel
Vester Voldgade 10. **Map** 3 B2. **Tel** 33 14 13 30.

Jailhouse
Studiestræde 12. **Map** 3 B1. **Tel** 33 15 22 55. **W jailhousecph.dk**

Masken Bar
Studiestræde 33. **Map** 3 A1. **Tel** 33 91 09 37. **W maskenbar.dk**

Mens Bar
Teglgårdsstræde 3. **Map** 3 A1. **Tel** 33 12 73 03. **W mensbar.dk**

Never Mind
Nørre Voldgade 2. **Map** 3 A1. **W nevermindbar.dk**

Oscar Bar & Café
Rådhuspladsen 77. **Map** 3 B2. **Tel** 33 12 09 99. **W oscarbarcafe.dk**

Beaches

Bellevue Strand
Strandvejen 340, Klampenborg.

Copencabana
Kalvebod Brygge. **Map** 3 A5.

Havnebadet
Islands Brygge. **Map** 3 C3.

Children's Entertainment

Hans Christian Andersen's Wonderful World
Rådhuspladsen 57. **Tel** 33 32 31 31. **W topattractions.dk**

Marionet Teatret
Tel 33 12 12 29. **W marionetteatret.dk**

Zebu
Øresundsvej 4, Amager. **Tel** 38 77 38 77. **W zebu.nu**

STREET FINDER

The map references given for all of Copenhagen's sights, hotels, restaurants, bars, shops and entertainment venues included in this guide refer to the maps in this section. All major sights, famous historic buildings, museums, galleries, railway, bus, metro and suburban train stations have been marked on the map. Other features are indicated by symbols explained in the key below. The names of streets and squares contained on the map are given in Danish. The word *gade* translates as street; *plads* means square, *allé* translates as avenue and *have* means park or garden.

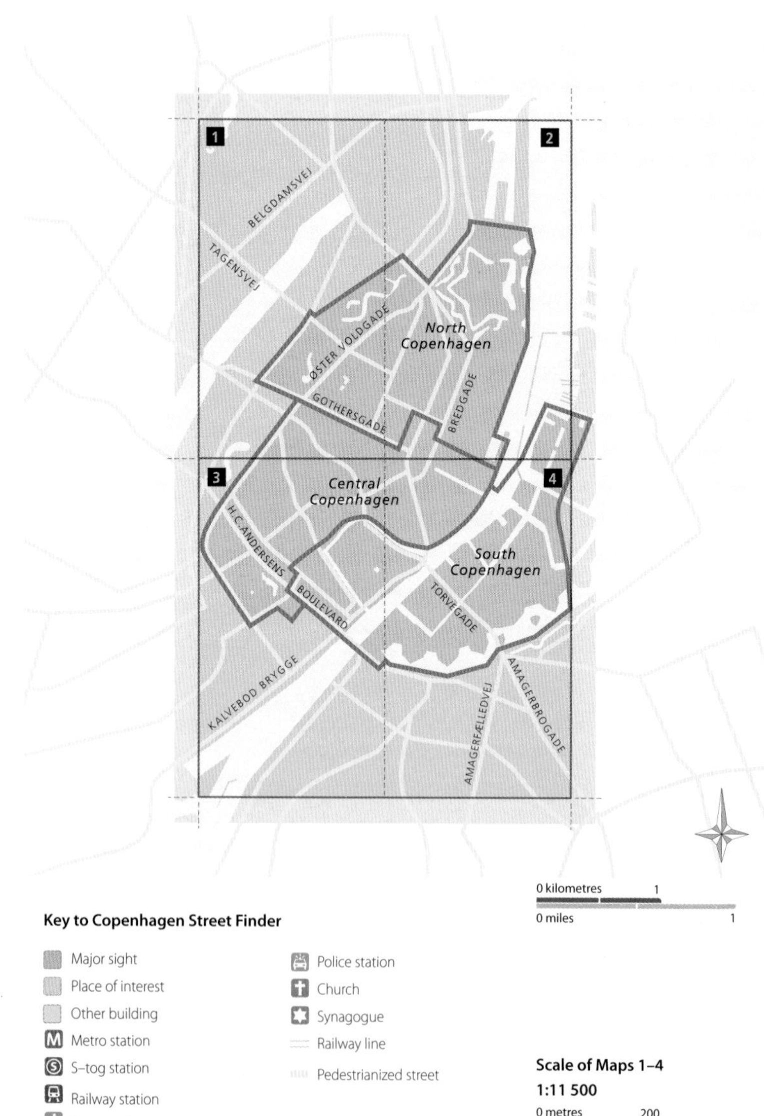

Key to Copenhagen Street Finder

- Major sight
- Place of interest
- Other building
- Metro station
- S-tog station
- Railway station
- Tourist information
- A&E hospital
- Police station
- Church
- Synagogue
- Railway line
- Pedestrianized street

Scale of Maps 1–4

1:11 500

0 metres 200

0 yards 200

Street Finder Index

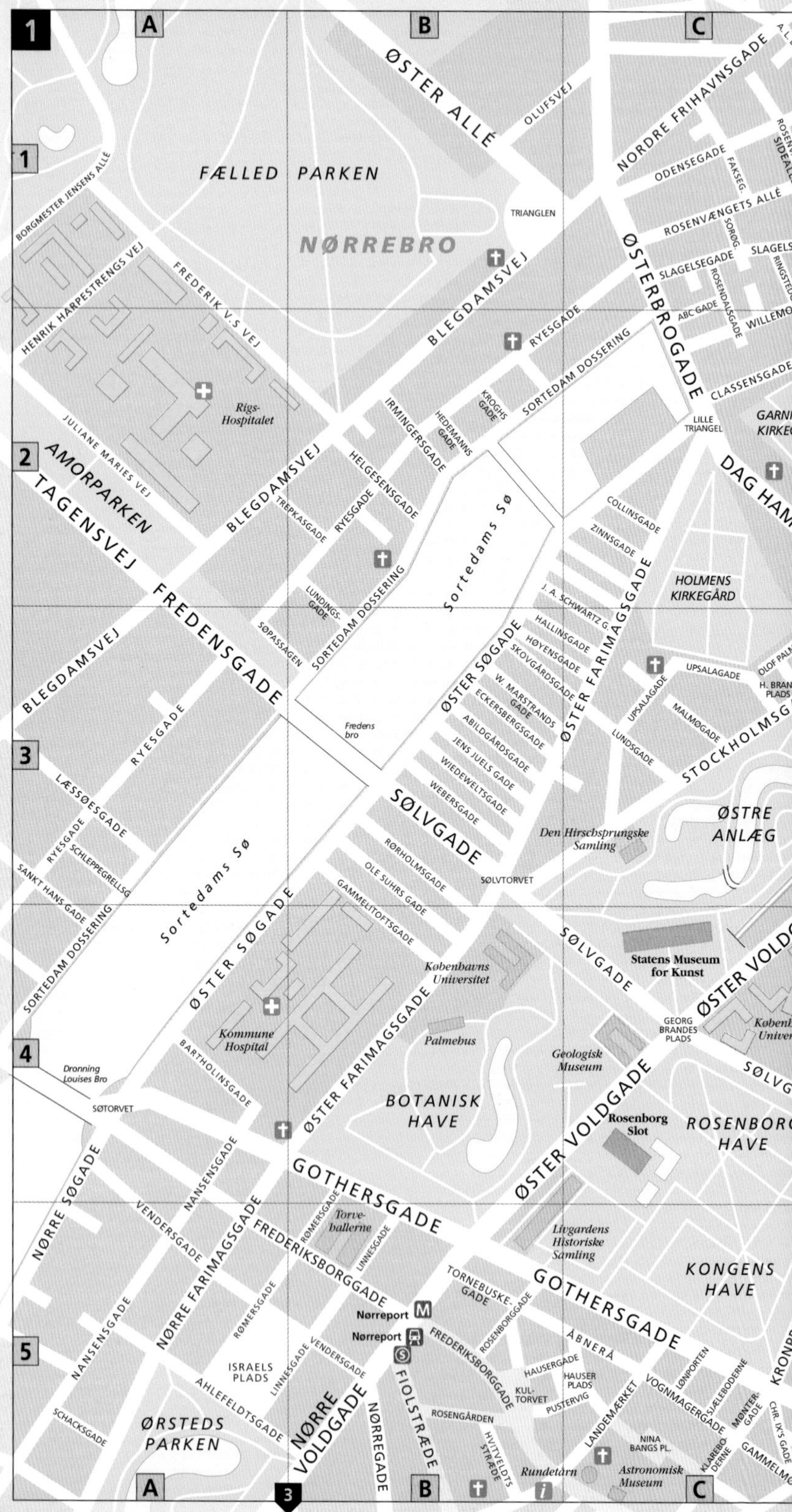

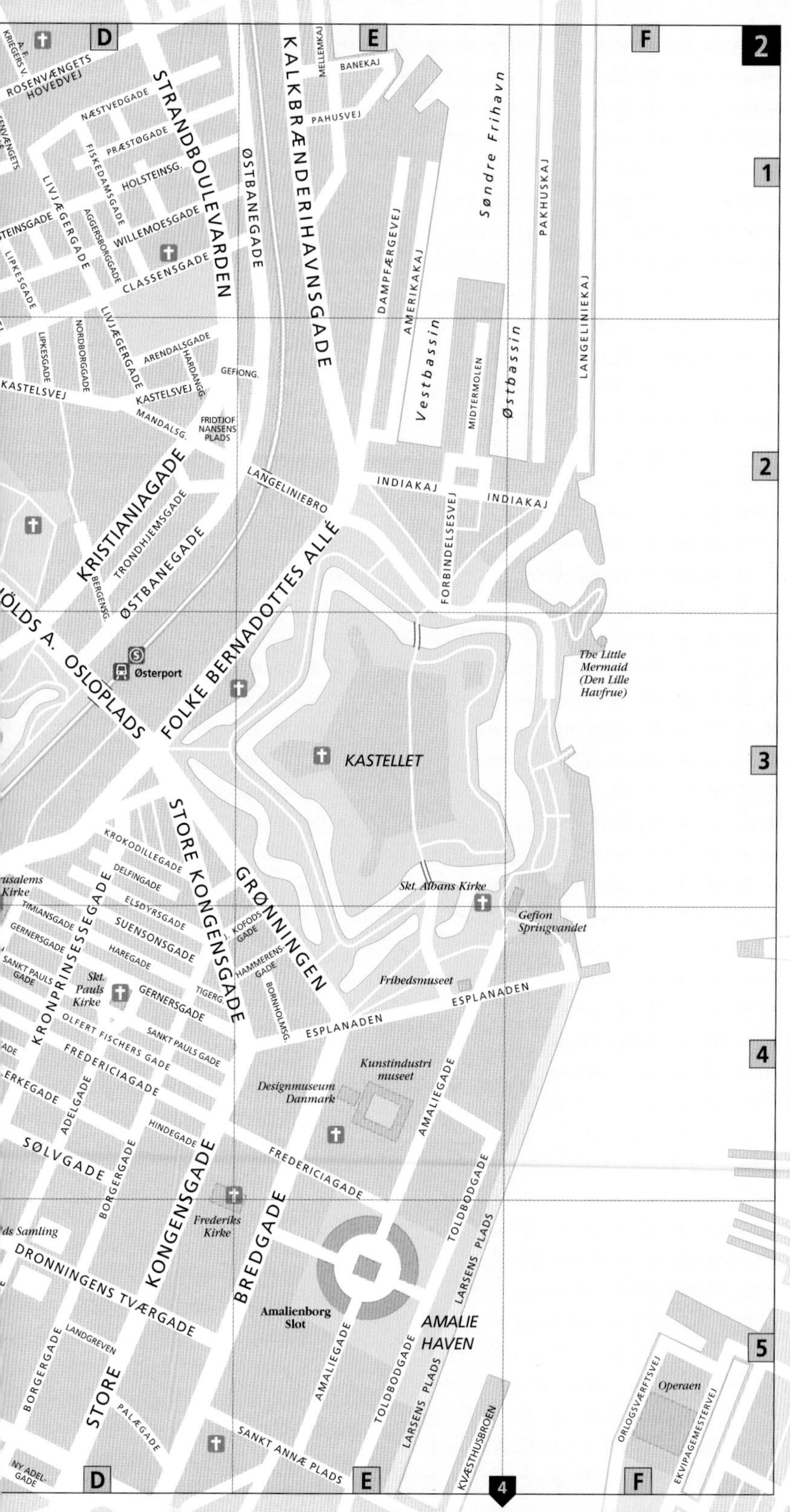

D
E
F
2
1
2
3
4
5
A. F. KRIEGERS V.
ROSENVÆNGETS HOVEDVEJ
NÆSTVEDGADE
PRÆSTØGADE
HOLSTEINSG.
FISKEDAMSGADE
LIVJÆGERGADE
AGGERSBORGGADE
WILLEMOESGADE
CLASSENSGADE
LIPKESGADE
NORDBORGGADE
ARENDALSGADE
HARDANGG.
GEFIONG.
KASTELSVEJ
MANDALSG.
FRIDTJOF NANSENS PLADS
STRANDBOULEVARDEN
ØSTBANEGADE
KALKBRÆNDERIHAVNSGADE
MELLEMKAJ
BANEKAJ
PAHUSVEJ
DAMPFÆRGEVEJ
AMERIKAKAJ
Vestbassin
MIDTERMOLEN
Østbassin
Søndre Frihavn
PAKHUSKAJ
LANGELINIEKAJ
INDIAKAJ
FORBINDELSESVEJ
LANGELINIEBRO
KRISTIANIAGADE
TRONDHJEMSGADE
BERGENSG.
ØSTBANEGADE
FOLKE BERNADOTTES ALLÉ
OSLOPLADS
Østerport
KASTELLET
The Little Mermaid (Den Lille Havfrue)
Skt. Albans Kirke
Gefion Springvandet
Frihedsmuseet
ESPLANADEN
STORE KONGENSGADE
GRØNNINGEN
KROKODILLEGADE
DELFINGADE
ELSDYRSGADE
SUENSONSGADE
HAREGADE
GERNERSGADE
TIGERG.
J. KOFODS GADE
HAMMERENS-GADE
BORNHOLMSG.
Jerusalems Kirke
TIMIANSGADE
GERNERSGADE
SANKT PAULS GADE
KRONPRINSESSEGADE
Skt. Pauls Kirke
OLFERT FISCHERS GADE
SANKT PAULS GADE
FREDERICIAGADE
ADELGADE
SØLVGADE
HINDEGADE
BORGERGADE
KONGENSGADE
Kunstindustri museet
Designmuseum Danmark
AMALIEGADE
FREDERICIAGADE
TOLDBODGADE
LARSENS PLADS
Frederiks Kirke
BREDGADE
DRONNINGENS TVÆRGADE
Amalienborg Slot
AMALIE HAVEN
LANDGREVEN
BORGERGADE
STORE
PALÆGADE
SANKT ANNÆ PLADS
KVÆSTHUSBROEN
NY ADELGADE
ORLOGSVÆRFTSVEJ
Operaen
EKVIPAGEMESTERVEJ

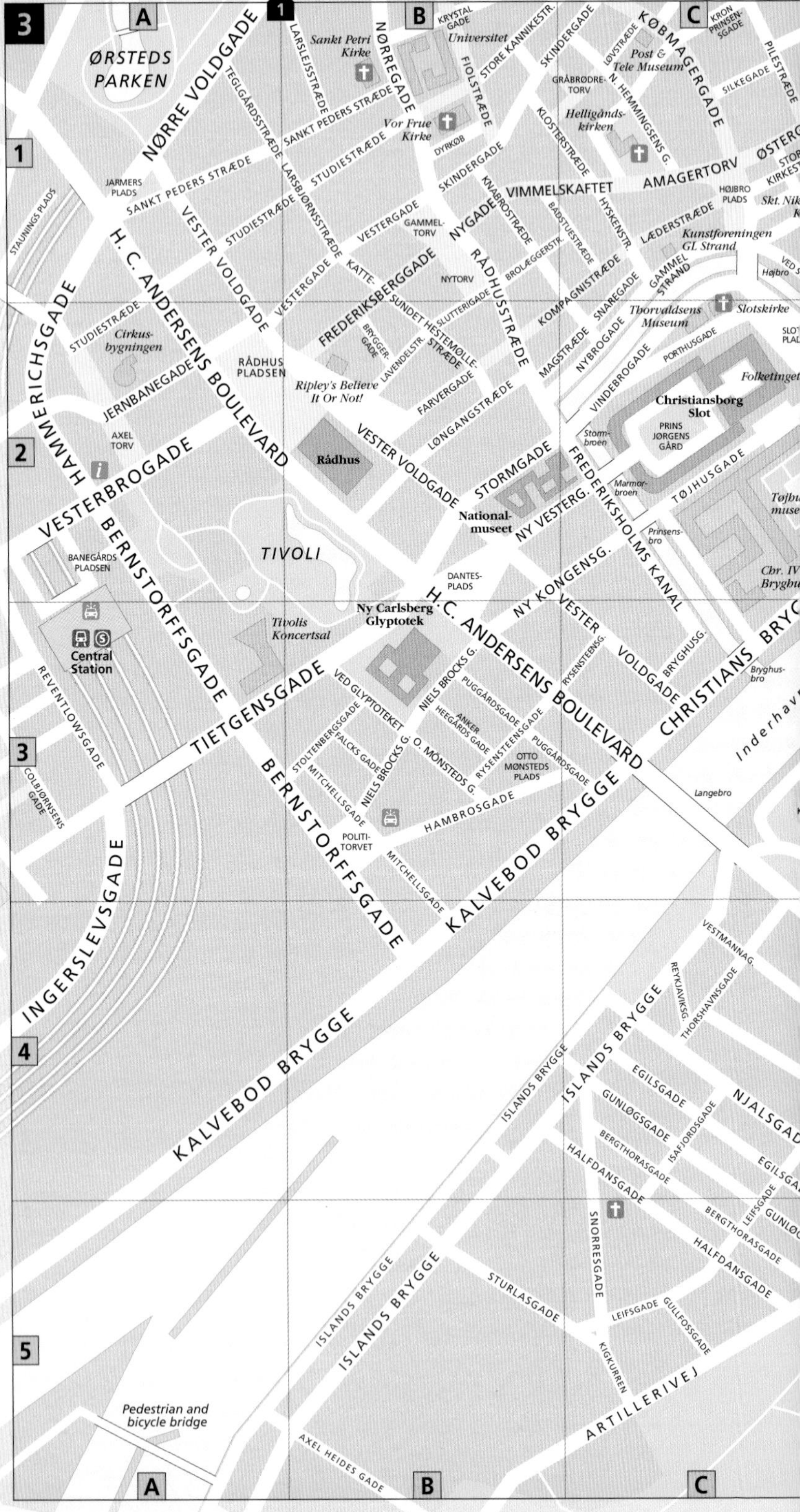

3
ØRSTEDS PARKEN
NØRRE VOLDGADE
Sankt Petri Kirke
Universitet
Post & Tele Museum
KØBMAGERGADE
Vor Frue Kirke
Helligånds-kirken
AMAGERTORV
VIMMELSKAFTET
NYGADE
FREDERIKSBERGGADE
RÅDHUSSTRÆDE
H. C. ANDERSENS BOULEVARD
VESTER VOLDGADE
HAMMERICHSGADE
VESTERBROGADE
Cirkus-bygningen
RÅDHUS PLADSEN
Ripley's Believe It Or Not!
Rådhus
Kunstforeningen GL Strand
Thorvaldsens Museum
Slotskirke
Folketinget
Christiansborg Slot
PRINS JØRGENS GÅRD
National-museet
TIVOLI
Tivolis Koncertsal
Ny Carlsberg Glyptotek
Central Station
BERNSTORFFSGADE
TIETGENSGADE
KALVEBOD BRYGGE
CHRISTIANS BRYGGE
INGERSLEVSGADE
ISLANDS BRYGGE
ARTILLERIVEJ
Pedestrian and bicycle bridge

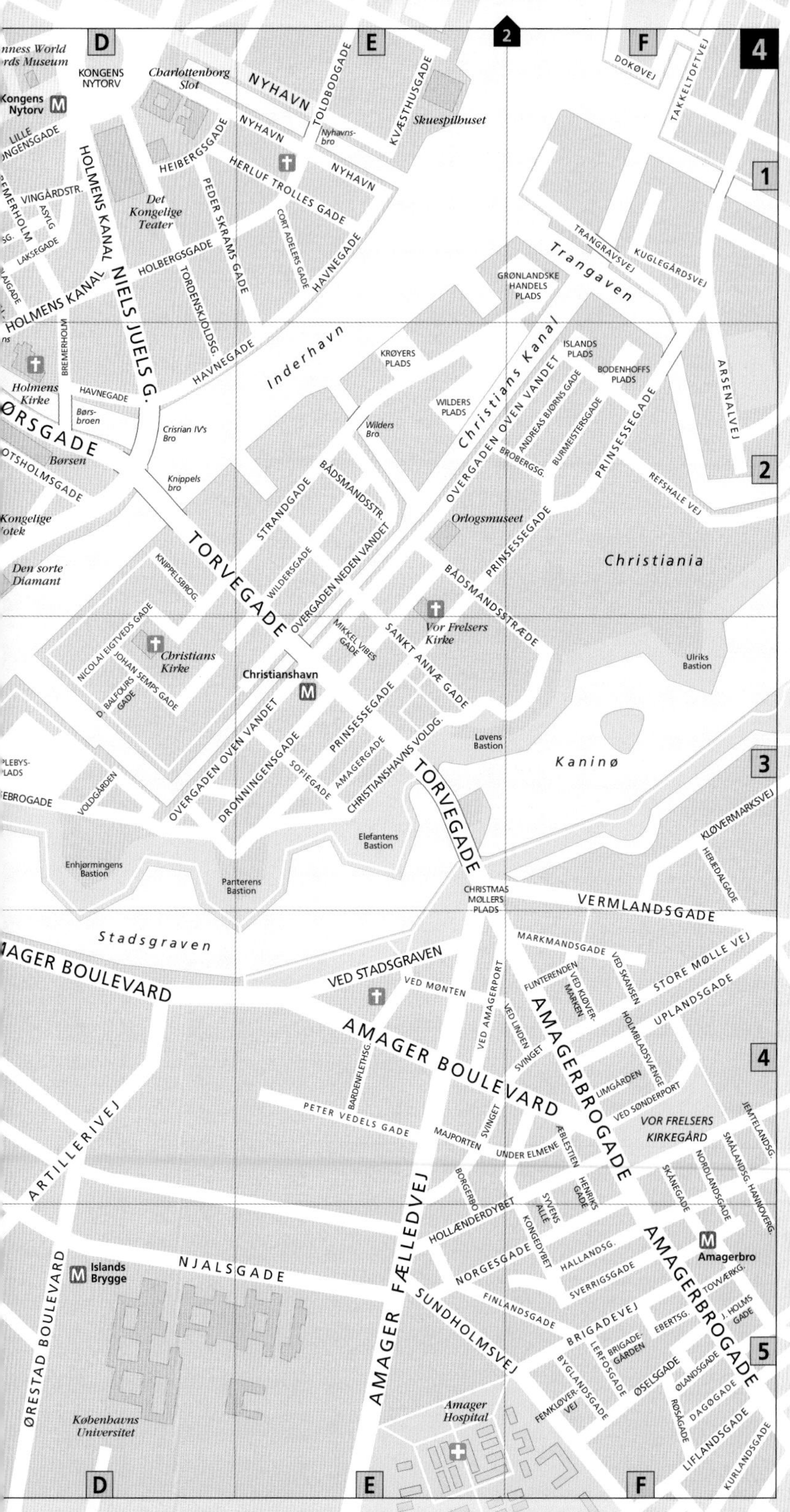

D
E
2
F
4
1
2
3
4
5
KONGENS NYTORV
Kongens Nytorv
Charlottenborg Slot
NYHAVN
TOLDBODGADE
KVÆSTHUSGADE
Skuespilhuset
DOKØVEJ
TAKKELTOFTVEJ
LILLE KONGENSGADE
HOLMENS KANAL
HEIBERGSGADE
HERLUF TROLLES GADE
Nyhavns-bro
VINGÅRDSTR.
ASYLG
LAKSEGADE
Det Kongelige Teater
PEDER SKRAMS GADE
CORT ADELERS GADE
HAVNEGADE
HOLBERGSGADE
TORDENSKJOLDSG.
NIELS JUELS G.
BREMERHOLM
Holmens Kirke
Inderhavn
TRANGRAVSVEJ
KUGLEGÅRDSVEJ
Trangaven
GRØNLANDSKE HANDELS PLADS
KRØYERS PLADS
ISLANDS PLADS
BODENHOFFS PLADS
ARSENALVEJ
Christians Kanal
OVERGADEN OVEN VANDET
ANDREAS BJØRNS GADE
BURMEISTERSGADE
PRINSESSEGADE
WILDERS PLADS
Wilders Bro
Børs-broen
Crisrian IV's Bro
Knippels bro
BØRSGADE
Børsen
SLOTSHOLMSGADE
Kongelige Bibliotek
Den sorte Diamant
STRANDGADE
BÅDSMANDSSTR.
BROBERGSG.
REFSHALE VEJ
Orlogsmuseet
Christiania
TORVEGADE
KNIPPELSBROG.
WILDERSGADE
OVERGADEN NEDEN VANDET
BÅDSMANDSSTRÆDE
Vor Frelsers Kirke
MIKKEL VIBES GADE
SANKT ANNÆ GADE
Ulriks Bastion
NICOLAI EIGTVEDS GADE
JOHAN SEMPS GADE
Christians Kirke
D. BALFOURS GADE
Christianshavn
DRONNINGENSGADE
SOFIEGADE
AMAGERGADE
CHRISTIANSHAVNS VOLDG.
Løvens Bastion
Kaninø
VOLDGÅRDEN
KLØVERMARKSVEJ
HERJÆDALGADE
Elefantens Bastion
Enhjørningens Bastion
Panterens Bastion
CHRISTMAS MØLLERS PLADS
VERMLANDSGADE
Stadsgraven
AMAGER BOULEVARD
VED STADSGRAVEN
VED MØNTEN
MARKMANDSGADE
FLINTERENDEN
VED KLØVER-MARKEN
VED SKANSEN
STORE MØLLE VEJ
UPLANDSGADE
HOLMBLADSVÆNGE
VED AMAGERPORT
VED LINDEN
SVINGET
AMAGERBROGADE
LIMGÅRDEN
VED SØNDERPORT
BARDENFLETHSG.
PETER VEDELS GADE
MAJPORTEN
UNDER ELMENE
ÆBLESTIEN
VOR FRELSERS KIRKEGÅRD
JEMTELANDSG.
SMÅLANDSG.
HANNOVERG.
NORDLANDSGADE
SKÅNEGADE
ARTILLERIVEJ
AMAGER FÆLLEDVEJ
BORGERBO
HOLLÆNDERDYBET
KONGEDYBET
SYVENS ALLÉ
HENRIKS GADE
Amagerbro
ØRESTAD BOULEVARD
Islands Brygge
NJALSGADE
NORGESGADE
HALLANDSG.
SVERRIGSGADE
TOVÆRKG.
SUNDHOLMSVEJ
FINLANDSGADE
BRIGADEVEJ
EBERTSG.
J. HOLMS GADE
BRIGADE-GÅRDEN
LERFOSGADE
BYGLANDSGADE
ØSELSGADE
ØLANDSGADE
RØSAGADE
DAGØGADE
LIFLANDSGADE
KURLANDSGADE
FEMKLØVER-VEJ
Amager Hospital
Københavns Universitet

DENMARK REGION BY REGION

Denmark at a Glance

Denmark has a host of attractions for visitors. Small rural farms, rolling fields of wheat, lush woodlands and fine beaches are just some of the things that make the country especially popular with nature lovers. Those favouring outdoor activities will enjoy the many trails and cycle routes. Many of these are themed and designed to take in some of the country's best historic churches, castles and palaces. For sightseers, there are Neolithic ruins, Viking remains and medieval villages to explore, while the various delights on offer at amusement parks such as Bakken or LEGOLAND® will thrill most children.

Northern Jutland has some beautiful beaches, as well as fine buildings such as Voergård Slot. The works on display in the Skagens Museum perfectly capture the shimmering Nordic light found in this part of the country.

Southern Jutland is famous for towns such as Ribe, which survived flood and fire, and retains some of the best-preserved medieval architecture in Denmark. The level to which the waters of the Ribe Å River rose during a flood in 1634 are marked on a wooden column.

Funen has been nicknamed the "Garden of Denmark". The charm of this island resides mainly in its scenery, which includes flower-filled fields and meadows, ancient castles and half-timbered houses.

◀ Rosnaes lighthouse near the mouth of Kalundborg Fjord

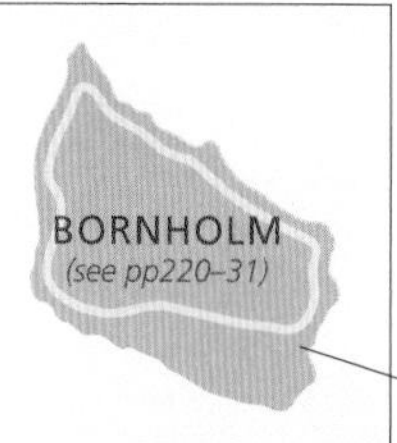

Bornholm is sometimes described as "Scandinavia in a nutshell" because it combines many typically Scandinavian features, such as rocky shores, picturesque villages and peaceful forests.

Northwestern Zealand is known for its royal castles and palaces. Among these is the magnificent Kronborg Slot on the Øresund coast, which was used by William Shakespeare as the setting for *Hamlet*. The castle now contains a museum.

Copenhagen is Denmark's capital and its largest city. It has many sights, both modern and old, including the magnificent Marmorkirken, which offers splendid views from its grand dome. *(See pages 50–115.)*

Grenå
oft
Helsingør
Hillerød
Copenhagen
(København)
Holbæk
dborg
Roskilde
NORTHWESTERN
ZEALAND
(see pp120–55)
Køge
Slagelse
Ringsted
org
Næstved
org
SOUTHERN ZEALAND
& THE ISLANDS
(see pp156–75)
Nakskov
Nykøbing F.
Rødbyhavn
Gedser
0 km 30
0 miles 30

Southern Zealand is a mix of farmland, woodland and glorious coastal scenery. There is much to see, including a 1,000-year-old Viking fortress at Trelleborg and the 12th-century Sankt Bendts Kirke, which is the oldest brick church in Denmark.

NORTHWESTERN ZEALAND

Zealand is the largest of the Danish islands and has an area of 7,500 sq km (2,895 sq miles). On its eastern shore lies Copenhagen (*see pp50–115*) – the country's capital city as well as its cultural and commercial centre. Away from the city, there is much to enjoy, from mighty castles and historic towns to sandy beaches, rural villages and beautiful countryside.

The island's scenery is typical of the lowland regions: idyllic meadow scenery broken here and there by beech forests and coastal fjords that cut deep into the land. Much of the region's wildlife can be seen around Arresø, Denmark's largest lake.

Most of the port towns were once Viking settlements. A reconstructed 10th–11th-century Viking camp can be visited in Trelleborg, while Viking ships can be seen at Roskilde's Viking Ship Museum. A visit to Sagnlandet Lejre, an experimental camp where Danish families volunteer to spend a week living in an Iron Age village, provides a glimpse into the past, as do the Viking plays staged at Frederikssund.

Northwestern Zealand has played an important part in the history of Denmark. Lejre was one of the first centres of Danish administration; later on this function was assumed by Roskilde, which in 1020 became a bishopric and the capital of Denmark. This lasted until 1443 when the role of the country's capital was taken over by Copenhagen. Traditionally, this area has been favoured by wealthy Danes and some of the most impressive royal castles can be found here including Kronborg, Fredensborg and Frederiksborg. In addition, there is a variety of more modest establishments worthy of a visit, such as Ermitagen, a royal hunting lodge a short way west of Klampenborg.

Hundested's popular beach

◀ Neptune's Fountain, Frederiksborg Slot, symbolizing Denmark's power in the 17th century

Exploring Northwestern Zealand

Most visitors to Zealand never stray beyond the limits of Copenhagen. There are, however, many other parts of the island that are well worth exploring. The list of sacral buildings includes Roskilde Domkirke (Cathedral) and Vor Frue Kirke, in Kalundborg, a 12th-century church with five spires. The region also has several areas that are conducive to carefree holidays. The northern shores, washed by Kattegat's waters, are famous for their beautiful sandy beaches, while the forests, criss-crossed with a network of trails, are perfect for cyclists and hikers.

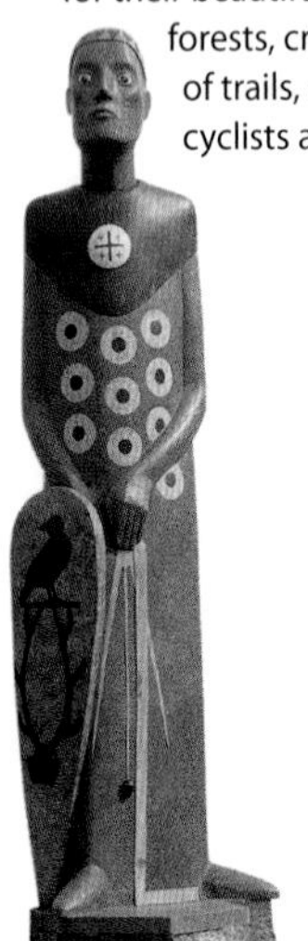

A statue of Esbern Snare, 12th-century founder of Kalundborg

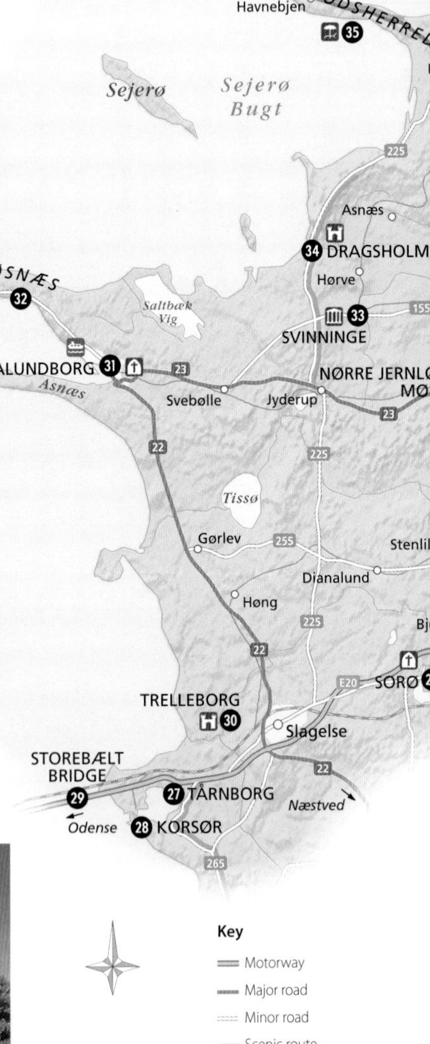

Getting Around

Denmark's capital, served by Copenhagen International Airport, is a good starting point for exploring Zealand. Central Station in Copenhagen is the island's main railway hub. Northwestern Zealand has a well-developed network of motorways and major roads, which make getting around by car straightforward.

The tall spires of Roskilde Domkirke

Sights at a Glance

1. Jægersborg Dyrehave
2. Bakken
3. Frilandsmuseet
4. Rungstedlund
5. *Louisiana Museum pp126–7*
6. *Helsingør pp128–9*
7. *Kronborg Slot pp130–31*
8. Hornbæk
9. Gilleleje
10. Fredensborg Slot
12. *Frederiksborg Slot pp136–7*
13. Grønnesse Skov
14. Hundested
15. Nordskoven
16. Jægerspris Slot
17. Frederikssund
18. Selsø Slot
19. Skibby
20. *Roskilde pp144–7*
21. Lejre
22. Ledreborg Slot
23. Holbæk
24. Tveje Merløse Kirke
25. Nørre Jernløse Mølle
26. Sorø
27. Tårnborg
28. Korsør
29. Storebælt Bridge
30. Trelleborg
31. Kalundborg
32. Røsnæs
33. Svinninge
34. Dragsholm

Tours

11. Esrum Sø and Arresø
35. Odsherred

Stately Dutch Renaissance entrance to Frederiksborg Slot

For keys to symbols *see back flap*

❶ Jægersborg Dyrehave

Road map: F4.

The beech forests and parkland covering an area between the motorway that runs from Copenhagen towards Helsingør and the shore of the Øresund (Sound) is one of the favourite places for weekend forays out of Copenhagen. This area, which is criss-crossed with paths and cycle routes, was established as a royal hunting ground in 1669. The park still supports a herd of some 2,000 deer. A good vantage point from which to view them is the Ermitagen hunting lodge at the centre of the park, which was built in 1736 for Christian VI.

Among the park's other attractions are Bakken amusement park *(see below)*, Kirsten Pils Kilde (a holy spring that was a pilgrimage destination in the 16th century) and, nearby, Bellevue (one of the area's best beaches). Horse-drawn carriages offer rides through the park and there is also a golf course and a horse-racing track just to the south of Bakken.

Ermitagen hunting lodge

❷ Bakken

Road map: F4. Dyrehavevej 62. Ⓢ Klampenborg. **Tel** 39 63 35 44. **Open** May–Aug. Opening hours vary; consult the website before visiting. **W** **bakken.dk**

Bakken was founded in 1583 and is considered to be the world's oldest amusement park. Located just a short way out of Copenhagen, it is on the edge of the Jægersborg Dyrehave deer park.

One of the many rides to be enjoyed at Bakken

The present amusement park has 100 or so rides, including rollercoasters and merry-go-rounds, as well as circus shows and a cabaret-style revue. There are 40 cafés and restaurants on site, although people can bring their own supplies for a picnic. Entrance to the park is free though rides must be paid for. Bakken opens on 1 May and closes on 31 August; both occasions are cause for a huge motorcycle parade up to the park from north Copenhagen.

❸ Frilandsmuseet

Road map: F4. Kongevejen 100, 2800 Lyngby. **Tel** 33 47 38 55. **Open** May–Oct: 10am–4pm Tue–Sun (Jul–mid-Aug: to 5pm). **W** **natmus.dk/frilandsmuseet**

This open-air museum, founded in 1897, contains virtually every kind of Danish country dwelling imaginable. Originally situated near Rosenberg Slot in Copenhagen, it was relocated to its present site in 1901 and is now run as part of the Nationalmuseet. Over 100 buildings are arranged into 40 groups and include many examples of rural architecture from cottages to grand manor houses, many of which are furnished and decorated in keeping with the period in which they were built. Visitors should allow a day to look round the collection, which includes fishermen's cottages, windmills, peasant huts, a post mill (still with working sails) and a smithy (kitted out with irons and a hearth). Many of the staff dress in traditional costume and demonstrate such fading arts as turning clay pots and weaving cloth. The ticket also allows entry to Brede Værk, by the northern entrance of Frilandsmuseet. This textile mill, which closed in 1956, is now preserved as an industrial village complete with cottages, a school, an "eating house" and the owner's country house.

A meticulously reconstructed house interior, Frilandsmuseet

❹ Rungstedlund

Road map: F4. 2960 Rungsted Kyst. **Tel** 45 57 10 57. Karen Blixen Museum: **Open** May–Sep: 10am–5pm Tue–Sun; Oct–Apr: 1–4pm Wed–Fri, 11am–4pm Sat–Sun. **W** **karen-blixen.dk**

Made famous by Karen Blixen, author of *Out of Africa,* Rungstedlund is the author's birthplace and was where she grew up and wrote most of her works under the pen name Isak Dinesen.

Karen Blixen's house was built around 1500 and was first used as an inn. In 1879 her father bought the property. It is now maintained by a foundation established by the writer, and in 1991 was converted into a museum devoted to Blixen's life and work. The rooms remain little changed from the period when she lived here, and manuscripts, photographs and personal belongings are on display. Blixen's grave is in the surrounding park.

Karen Blixen

Karen Blixen was born in 1885. The most colourful period in the Danish writer's life was her stay in Africa. Blixen left for Kenya at the age of 28 with her Swedish husband, Baron Bror von Blixen-Finecke, to establish a coffee plantation. While in Kenya she wrote *Seven Gothic Tales,* a collection of stories that launched her career. Safari expeditions, the raptures and miseries of her affairs, the breakdown of her marriage and the eventual failure of the plantation are all themes of her best-known work, *Out of Africa,* which established her reputation. The author returned to Rungsted in 1931 and lived here until her death in 1962. Among Blixen's other famous stories is *Babette's Feast,* which was made into a film in 1987.

Karen Blixen's House
Only part of the original house is still standing; two wings burned down when Blixen was 13 years old.

Blixen's Grave
The park behind the house contains a beech tree, with a modest gravestone underneath. This is the final resting place of Karen Blixen, who died at the age of 77.

African Room
Displayed in the room are Masai shields and spears as well as other mementos brought back from Africa.

Karen Blixen
Karen von Blixen-Finecke was also known by her pen name Isak Dinesen. Other pen names she wrote under were Tania Blixen, Osceola and Pierre Andrézel.

The Film Version
The screen version of *Out of Africa* stars Robert Redford and Meryl Streep. It was directed by Sydney Pollack (above) and departs markedly from the novel.

Out of Africa
Out of Africa was first published in 1937. It was originally written by the author in English and then translated by Blixen herself into Danish. The cover seen here is of the rare first Danish edition.

5 Louisiana Museum

This striking museum was established in 1958 to house a collection of modern Danish art. The museum's remit has expanded considerably since then and the collection now concentrates on modern American and European paintings, graphic art and photography. The location and architecture are equally impressive. Light-filled galleries form a semi-circle round a 19th-century villa and open out onto a tranquil park filled with sculpture and offering stunning views of the Øresund. Among the many artists represented here are Giacometti, Henry Moore, Picasso and Warhol.

★ Big Thumb (1968)
The French artist César was fascinated by the shape of his thumb. This bronze image is 185 cm (73 inches) high.

Le Déjeuner sur l'Herbe (1961)
Picasso's painting is in homage to a famous work by Edouard Manet painted nearly 100 years earlier.

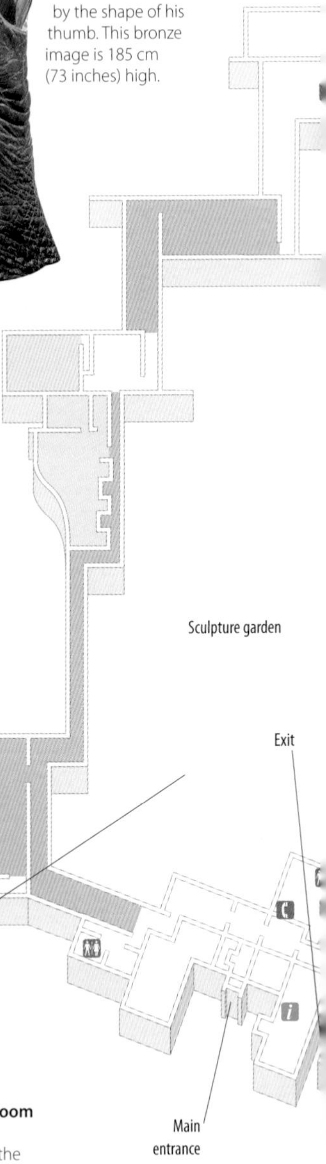

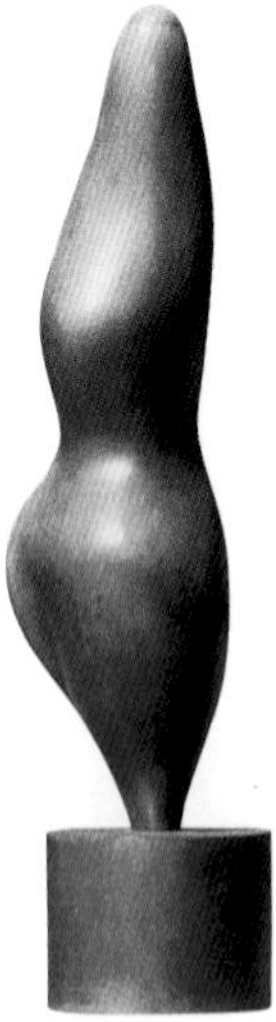

Sculpture garden

Exit

★ Vénus de Meudon (1956)
This work by the French sculptor and painter Jean Arp depicts a woman's body reduced to its simplest form.

Main entrance

Asger Jorn Room
This gallery is dedicated to the abstract works of Asger Jorn (1914–73), an important figure in 20th-century Danish art.

Key

- Exhibition space
- Cinema
- Giacometti collection
- Children's wing

Concert hall

VISITORS' CHECKLIST

Practical Information
Road map: F4. Humlebæk Gl. Strandvej 13. **Tel** 49 19 07 19.**Open** 11am–10pm Tue–Fri, 11am–6pm Sat, Sun & hols.
louisiana.dk

Transport
Humlebæk.

Café
On sunny days you can eat outside, enjoying coastal views and the works in the sculpture garden.

Marilyn Monroe (1967)
Obsessed by the legendary actress's suicide in 1962, Andy Warhol set about immortalizing the film star by endlessly duplicating her image, using a silk-screen process to transfer the picture onto canvas.

Two Piece Reclining Figure No. 5 (1963–64)
This Henry Moore bronze is in the sculpture garden, in keeping with the artist's intention to blend the female figure with the landscape.

The Graphics Wing, opened in 1991, was built underground to protect its displays from daylight.

Ground floor

★ South Wing
The south wing of the museum was added in 1982 and is half buried in a hillside facing the Øresund. It houses temporary and special exhibitions.

Gallery Guide

Single-storey galleries are connected by a corridor to the south wing and underground galleries. Works are on rotation apart from a room devoted to Giacometti and Japanese artist Kusama. A children's wing has workshops, art materials and computers for kids and their families.

❻ Helsingør

Helsingør owes its prosperity to its location on the sound that links the North Sea with the Baltic. The town was a centre of international shipping during the 1400s, when Erik of Pomerania levied a tax on every ship passing through its local waters. In 1857 the dues were abolished, causing a temporary economic decline in the town's fortunes. This downturn was reversed in 1864 with the opening of a railway line and ferry services to Sweden. Today, most people visit Helsingør to see Kronborg Slot *(see pp130–31)*, a late-16th-century castle that was used by William Shakespeare as the setting for *Hamlet*.

Old apothecary on display in the town museum

Exploring Helsingør

When sightseeing in Helsingør it is a good idea to start with a visit to the Carmelite Monastery and the Municipal Museum, and then continue with a walk along Biergegade promenade, turning occasionally into side streets (Stengade in particular). Further south is the tourist information centre in Havnepladsen and, a little further on, the ferry terminal.

Gothic cloisters surrounding the Karmeliterklosteret's courtyard

Karmeliterklosteret Sankt Mariæ Kirke

Sankt Anna Gade 38. **Tel** 49 21 17 74. **Open** mid-May–mid-Sep: 10am–3pm Tue–Sun; mid-Sep–mid-May: 10am–2pm Tue–Sun. **sctmariae.dk**

This Gothic building once belonged to the Carmelites and was erected in the second half of the 15th century. It is considered to be one of the best-preserved medieval monasteries anywhere in Scandinavia and was described by H.C. Andersen as "one of the most beautiful spots in Denmark". Among its many features are the chapterhouse with its barrel vault and the "Bird Room" decorated with ornithological frescoes. Christian II's mistress, Dyveke, who died in 1517, is believed to be buried in the grounds.

Helsingør Bymuseum

Sankt Anna Gade 36. **Tel** 49 28 18 00. **Open** noon–4pm Sun–Fri, 10am–2pm Sat.

The building that currently houses the town museum was erected by friars from the neighbouring monastery, who used it as a hospital for sailors arriving at the local harbour. Some of the instruments once used by the friars for brain surgery in the hospital are on display together with other exhibits relating to the town's past including a model of Kronborg Slot as it was in 1801. Visitors to the museum can also learn about the origin of the region's name: Øresund refers to the levy demanded by Erik of Pomerania which translates as "Penny Sound" (an "øre" is a Danish penny, and "sund" means "sound").

Axeltorv

Helsingør's main square has a number of restaurants and bars. On Wednesday and Saturday mornings there is a colourful local market here that sells flowers, vegetables, fresh fish, handicrafts, cheese and souvenirs.

The statue in the centre depicts Erik of Pomerania – the Polish king and nephew of Margrethe I who occupied the throne of Denmark between 1397 and 1439. Following the break-up of the Kalmar Union and his subsequent dethronement in 1439 in favour of Christoffer III of Bavaria, the ex-monarch moved to the Swedish island of Gotland. Here, he began to occupy himself with piracy and he is sometimes referred to as "the last Baltic Viking".

In his old age Erik returned to Pomerania and is buried in the Polish seaside town of Darlowo. One legend has it that Darlowo's castle still

Monument to Erik of Pomerania in Axeltorv

contains hidden treasure plundered from Denmark.

Stengade

Helsingør's medieval quarter includes Stengade, a pedestrianized street that is linked by various alleyways to Axeltorv. Many of the colourful half-timbered houses once belonged to merchants and ferrymen and date from the 17th and 18th centuries. Oderns Gård, at Stengade No. 66, was built in 1459.

Sankt Olai Kirke

Sankt Anna Gade 12. **Tel** 49 21 04 43. **Open** May–Aug: 10am–4pm Mon–Fri; Sep–Apr: 10am–2pm Mon–Fri.

This building was consecrated around 1200 and served for centuries as a parish church. It was elevated to the rank of cathedral in 1961. Numerous elaborate epitaphs can be seen commemorating the many rich merchants and distinguished citizens of Helsingør who are buried here. The church's present-day appearance dates from 16th-century modifications when it also acquired its current furnishings. Among its most precious possessions are a 15th-century Gothic crucifix, a Renaissance pulpit (1568) and a carved wooden altar.

Statue of the Virgin Mary, Skt Olai's Kirke

Museet for Søfart

Ny Kronborgvej 1. **Tel** 49 21 06 85. **Open** Jul & Aug: 10am–5pm daily; Sep–Jun: 11am–5pm Tue–Sun. **mfs.dk**

The spectacular Maritime Museum of Denmark was built around an old dry dock in front of Kronborg Castle by the internationally acclaimed architecture company BIG – Bjarke Ingels Group.

Leaving the over 60-year-old dock walls untouched, the galleries are located below ground and arranged in a continuous loop around the dry dock walls, making the dock the centerpiece of the exhibition. Visitors can experience the scale of ship building, and follow the sloping bridges down to an underground maritime world that traces the story of Denmark as one of the world's leading shipping nations.

VISITORS' CHECKLIST

Practical Information
Road map: F4. 40,000.
Havnepladsen 3. **Tel** 49 21 13 33. **visitnordsjaelland.com**

Transport
Helsingør.

Øresundakvariet

Strandpromenaden 5. **Tel** 49 21 37 72. **Open** Jun–Aug: 10am–5pm daily; Sep–May: 10am–4pm Mon–Fri, 10am–5pm Sat & Sun. **oresunds akvariet.ku.dk**

In addition to a colourful collection of tropical fish from around the world, Helsingør's aquarium contains many species taken from the waters of the Øresund (Sound). These local varieties include Baltic jellyfish and seahorses.

A model ship at the Maritime Museum

Helsingør Town Centre

1. Karmeliterklosteret
2. Helsingør Bymuseum
3. Axeltorv
4. Stengade
5. Sankt Olai Kirke
6. Museet for Søfart
7. Øresundakvariet

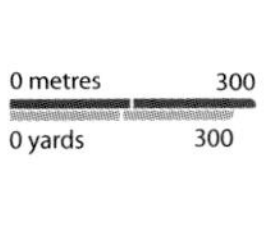

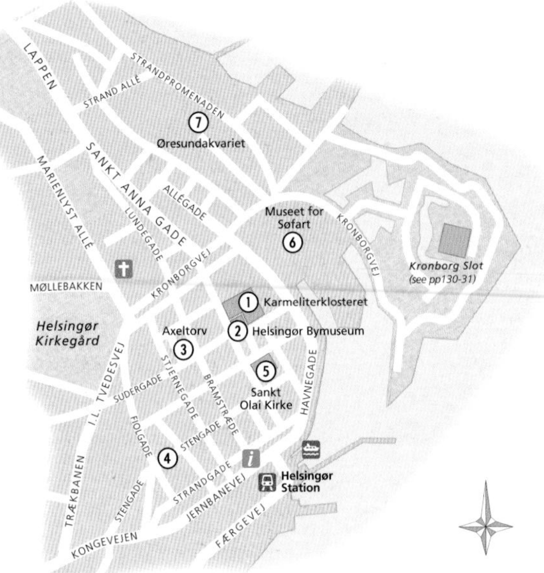

❼ Kronborg Slot

Hamlet's "Castle of Elsinore" was originally built by Erik of Pomerania in the early 15th century. It was remodelled by Frederik II and later by Christian IV but still retains an eerie quality that makes it perfect for the many productions of Shakespeare's play performed here. Among the most impressive rooms are the 62-m (203-ft) Great Hall, the King's Chamber, which has a ceiling painted by the Dutch artist Gerrit van Honthorst, and the "Lille Sal" containing 16th-century silk tapestries by the Flemish painter Hans Knieper. The castle was added to UNESCO's World Heritage List in 2000.

Exterior
Originally constructed using red brick, in 1580 the castle was remodelled on the orders of Frederik II and faced with attractive sandstone.

Viking Chief
The dungeons contain a sleeping statue of Holger Danske, a Viking chief. According to legend he will wake up should Denmark find itself in peril.

★ Ballroom
Once the longest hall in northern Europe, it was completed in 1582 and is decorated with paintings from Rosenborg Slot. The chandeliers date from the 17th century.

Hamlet

Shakespeare probably never visited Kronborg, but it is here that he set one of his best-known plays. The prototype for the fictional Danish prince was Amlet, whose story is recounted by the 12th-century Danish chronicler Saxo Grammaticus in his *Historia Danica* (Danish History). Shakespeare may have encountered this classic tale of murder and revenge via Francois de Belleforest's *Histoires Tragiques* (Tragic Histories), published in 1570. A festival is held in the castle each year in August during which *Hamlet* and other works by Shakespeare are performed.

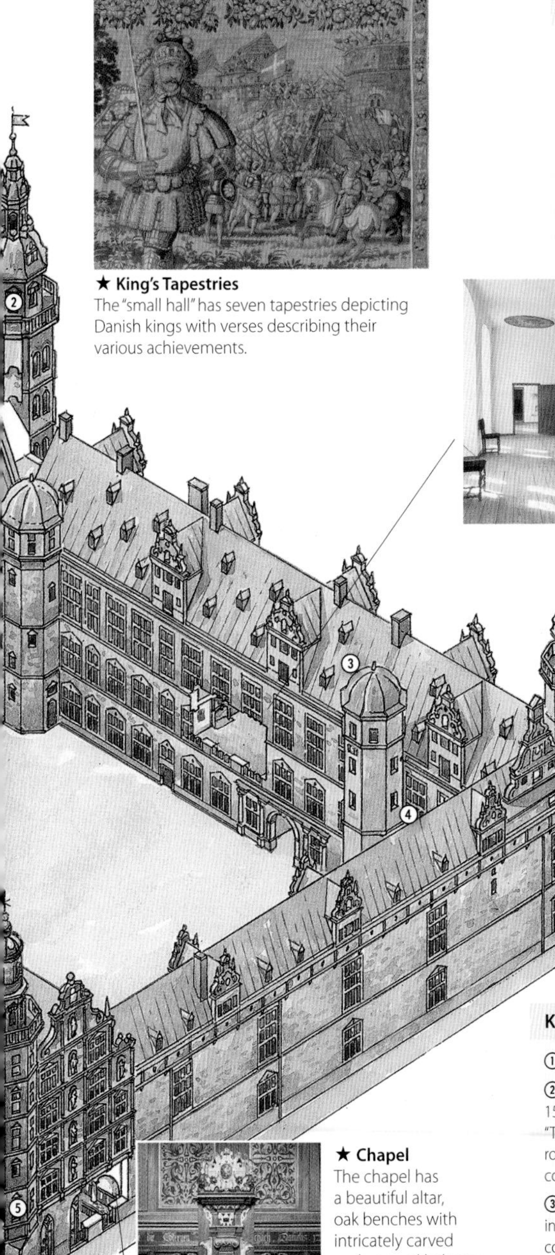

★ King's Tapestries
The "small hall" has seven tapestries depicting Danish kings with verses describing their various achievements.

Royal Chambers
These rooms contain ornate ceiling decorations and marble fireplaces. At one time the walls would have been lined with gold-embossed leather.

★ Chapel
The chapel has a beautiful altar, oak benches with intricately carved ends, a royal balcony and an organ dating from the early 18th century.

VISITORS' CHECKLIST

Practical Information
Road map: F4. Ny Kronborgvej, DK 3000, Helsingør.
Tel 49 21 30 78. Fax: 49 21 30 52.
Open Apr, May, Sep & Oct: 11am–4pm daily; Jun–Aug: 10am–5:30pm daily; Nov–Mar: 11am–4pm Tue–Sun.
W kronborg.dk

KEY

① **Trumpeter's Tower**

② **King's Tower,** built during 1584–5, this was also known as the "Turner's Tower" because one of its rooms housed Frederik II's turnery containing lathes.

③ **The North Wing** was completed in 1585. Its western section contained the castle offices.

④ **The Queen's Chambers** at the corner of the north wing had direct access to the chapel, via the east wing.

⑤ **The Pigeon Tower** housed birds that were used for sending important royal messages.

Clean sandy beaches of Hornbæk

8 Hornbæk

Road map: F4. Vestre Stejlebakke 2A. **Tel** 49 70 47 47. **visitnordsjaelland.com**

The northern shore of Zealand is famous for its pleasant sandy beaches, clean water and the small town of Hornbæk, which has for years been a favoured resort. A large number of visitors come from Copenhagen, many of whom have built holiday homes here. In summer the resort fills with holiday-makers enjoying various outdoor pursuits, including sailing and swimming.

Former Cistercian monastery buildings

Environs

Esrum, situated southwest of Hornbæk, is famous mainly for its Cistercian monastery, Esrum Kloster. Founded in 1151, it was regarded as one of the most important monasteries in Denmark during the Middle Ages. Its prominence was acknowledged even by the monarchy: in 1374 Queen Helvig, wife of Valdemar IV, was buried here. Even the fires that plagued the establishment (in 1194 and 1204) did not prevent the monastery from becoming one of the largest buildings in Scandinavia. During the Lutheran Reformation in the 16th century much of the church was demolished and the materials were used to build Kronborg Slot *(see pp130–31)*. What remained of the buildings passed into the hands of the monarch and the premises were used first as a hunting base and later as warehouses before being turned into army barracks. In the 20th century they were used as offices, as a post office and then as an orphanage. During World War II they became an air-raid shelter and a fireproof store for valuable documents brought here from the National Archives, and for the Royal Library collection. This chequered history came to an end when a decision was reached to renovate the ancient walls and in 1997 the former monastery opened to visitors. Its main building now houses an exhibition devoted to the Cistercian order while the vaults have been transformed into a café. Also open to visitors is the herb garden, where medicinal plants are grown and used, as they once were when the monastery flourished. Some of the plants are used to produce a flavoured beverage, which is on sale in the shop.

Not far from the monastery is **Esrum Møllegard**, a 400-year-old mill. The mill was first used to grind grain, and later to generate electricity. Today, it houses a centre for environmental awareness.

9 Gilleleje

Road map: F4. 6,000. Hovedgade 6F. **Tel** 48 30 01 74. **visitnordsjaelland.com**

The northernmost town in Zealand is also one of the oldest Danish fishing ports and contains the island's largest harbour. From historical records it has been established that the local inhabitants were engaged in fishing here as early as the mid-14th century. Today, Gilleleje is an attractive town with thatched houses, a busy harbourside fishing auction and a colourful main street that has been turned into a promenade. Rising above the fisherman's cottages is the town's church – Gilleleje Kirke. During the German occupation locals used the church as a hiding place for Danish Jews who were then smuggled into neutral Sweden aboard fishing boats under cover of darkness.

Other places of interest include **Gilleleje Museum**, devoted to the town's history, and **Det Gamle Hus**, an old fisherman's house that illustrates the realities of everyday life for a mid-19th-century fishing family. A coastal trail from the town centre leads east to the Nakkehoved Østre Fyr lighthouse. Built in 1772, this is one of a very few coal-fuelled lighthouses in the world to have survived to this day. This historic building is now open to visitors. **Environs:** The Gilbjergstien is a 2.5-km (1.5-mile) foot- and

Nakkehoved Østre Fyr, a coal-fired lighthouse near Gilleleje

Fishing boats in Gilleleje's harbour, the largest in Zealand

cycle path leading from Vesterbrogade, in Gilleleje, all the way to Gilbjergshoved, Zealand's northernmost point. The path offers splendid views across the water to Sweden from the cliffs. En route you can admire the Gilbjergstenen rock, which has a natural seat and back support, and a monument to the Danish philosopher Søren Kirkegaard.

Gilleleje Museum
Vesterbrogade 56. **Tel** 72 49 99 50. **Open** Jun–Aug: 1–4pm Wed–Mon; Sep–May: 1–4pm Wed–Fri, 10am–2pm Sat. includes a visit to the lighthouse.

Det Gamle Hus
Hovedgade 49, Gilleleje. **Tel** 48 30 16 31.

⑩ Fredensborg Slot

Road map: F4. **Tel** 33 40 31 87. Palace, Chapel, Orangery and Herb Garden: **Open** Aug: 1–4:30pm daily. compulsory; every 15 mins (duration about 35 mins). Gardens: **Open** 9am–5pm daily. **slke.dk**

Frederik IV decided to build Fredensborg Castle in order to commemorate the 1720 peace treaty between Denmark and Sweden at the end of the Nordic Wars (Fredensborg means "Palace of Peace"). The building was originally used as a hunting lodge. Nowadays the castle is one of the main residences of the Danish royal family and is often used to receive VIPs from all over the world. According to tradition, guests who spend the night at the palace must sign their name on a glass pane using a diamond pen.

The original design was modelled on French and Italian castles and the long list of contributors who influenced its final shape includes renowned architects such as Niels Eigtved, Lauritz de Thurah and Caspar Frederik Harsdorf. The present-day complex consists of 28 separate buildings. At its centre is the Dome Hall (Kuppelsalen), surmounted by a dome crowned with a lantern. The magnificent room is encircled by a gallery, which divides the hall into two levels. It is used for formal royal family occasions and also for entertaining special guests.

One of the most interesting rooms in the palace is Havesaln, or the Garden Room, which features a wide door leading to the castle gardens. Its ceiling is decorated with a painting by Henrik Krock depicting Denmark and Norway begging the Olympian gods for help against Sweden.

Fredensborg's gardens decorated with numerous statues

Fredenborg Slot's ornate Chinese Dining Room (Kinesisk Spisesalon) is another notable room. It is decorated in yellow and red and houses a collection of Chinese porcelain.

The palace garden was established in the 1760s, and contains a lane decorated with a sculpted group of 70 figures, created by J.G. Grund, of fishermen and farmers from Norway and the Faroe Islands. Plants sensitive to cold, including a 250-year-old myrtle shrub, are shielded from low temperatures in a greenhouse built in 1995.

Fredensborg Slot, used as a residence by the Danish royal family

⓫ A Tour Around Esrum Sø and Arresø

These beautiful lakes are the two largest in Denmark and attract a great many visitors, especially in summer. Gribskov, on the west bank of Esrum Sø, is a forested area where marked paths and bicycle trails lead through thick clusters of ancient beech and spruce trees. Arresø, to the east of Esrum Sø, is Denmark's largest lake and reaches depths of 22 m (72 ft). Ospreys and cormorants can occasionally be spotted diving for fish. As well as being perfect for anglers, bathers and enthusiastic sailors, a tour around the area takes in lush farmland, ancient church ruins, picturesque towns and historic medieval villages.

③ Ramløse
Situated on Arresø's north bank, the town's most interesting feature is its Dutch-style windmill (1908) that can be seen working on traditional "Mill Days".

② Asserbo
Scenic ruins surrounded by a wind-blown forest are all that remains of this former fortress, built in 1100 on the orders of Bishop Absalon.

① Frederiksværk
Frederiksværk, built alongside a canal, is Denmark's oldest industrial town. A museum in a former gunpowder factory has exhibits on the town's industrial past.

⑩ Æbelholt Kloster
This 12th-century Augustinian abbey was once a hospital. Today, as well as viewing the ruins, visitors can examine the museum's collection of surgical instruments.

⑤ **Esrum** The restored buildings of this former Cistertian monastery house a museum devoted to the community that lived here, giving visitors an idea of the monk's day-to-day life *(see p132)*.

Tips for Drivers

Length: about 100 km (62 miles).
Stopping-off points: There is a large choice of restaurants and accommodation in Fredensborg.
W visitdenmark.com
W visitnordsjaelland.com

④ **Annisse Nord**
Annisse Nord is a sleepy village but was strategically important for the surrounding area in medieval times; at that time numerous watchtowers were erected along the fjord.

⑥ **Fredensborg Slot**
The castle gardens are arranged in a Baroque style and are open to the public all year round *(see p133)*.

⑦ **Fredensborg**
This historic town has a long tradition of hunting and holds regular demonstrations of falconry.

⑨ **Gribskov**
Growing along the undulating western shoreline of Esrum Sø, Gribskov is the second largest forest in the country.

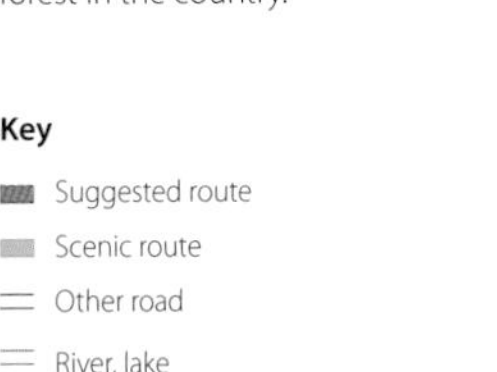

0 km 2
0 miles 2

⑧ **Nødebo**
The tiny village of Nødebo is on the banks of Esrum Sø (left) and surrounded by Gribskov. The pretty village church is decorated with 15th-century frescoes.

Key

- Suggested route
- Scenic route
- Other road
- River, lake

⓬ Frederiksborg Slot

The first royal residence was constructed on this site by Frederik II in 1560. A fire in 1859 destroyed most of the castle, which may well have remained a ruin were it not for Carlsberg boss J.C. Jacobsen who restored the building and helped found a national history museum shortly after the fire. The museum now takes up 80 or so of the palace rooms. Jacobsen also donated many of his own paintings which, along with others, are arranged chronologically to chart Denmark's history. Period furnishings and some magnificent architecture help to conjure up a feel for the country's past.

★ Slotskirken
From 1671 until 1840 the castle chapel was used to crown Denmark's monarchs. Its ebony altar dates from 1606 and is the work of Jakob Mores, a German goldsmith.

★ Riddersalen
The Knights' Hall has a carved wooden ceiling. The gilded ornaments, a 19th-century black marble fireplace and intricate tapestries add to the splendour.

Audienssalen
The Audience Chamber was completed in 1688. Among the paintings lining the walls is a portrait of a proud-looking Christian V, depicted as a Roman emperor surrounded by his children.

Chapel Portal
The oak door, set within a sandstone portal in the shape of a triumphal arch, survived the fire of 1859 and looks as it would have done in Christian IV's day.

For hotels and restaurants see pp248–55 and pp262–77

VISITORS' CHECKLIST

Practical Information
Road map: F4. 3400 Hillerød, Slotsgade 1.
Tel 48 26 04 39.
Open Apr–Oct: 10am–5pm daily; Nov–Mar: 11am–3pm daily.
Baroque gardens: **Open** 10am–sunset daily.
dnm.dk

Queen Sophie's Room
During the reign of Christian IV this room was used by the king's mother. When the palace became a museum, it was hung with paintings associated with Frederik III.

The Royal Wing has a gallery of statues symbolizing the influence of planets on human life and is an excellent example of Dutch Mannerism.

Room 42
This example of over-blown Baroque is typical of the taste associated with Denmark's era of absolute monarchy *(see pp42–3)*. The bed with silk draperies was made in France in 1724.

Room 46
All the items in this room, such as this ornate wall clock, are in perfect accord with the colours and Rococo excess of the overall design.

Gardens
The castle gardens were established in the 1720s and restored in 1996. The carefully trimmed shrubs create a symmetrical pattern typical of a Baroque garden.

⓭ Grønnesse Skov

Road map: E4.

The ancient forest of Grønnesse Skov is about 5 km (3 miles) east of Hundested, on the shores of Roskilde Fjord. Archaeological excavations indicate that during the Neolithic era this area was one of the more important sites of early culture in Zealand and the site now attracts thousands of visitors every year.

One of the most important relics of Denmark's Neolithic past is an extraordinary burial chamber known as a dolmen. It is one of many such tombs in Denmark and consists of a huge flat stone resting on three chunky pillars. The dolmen is referred to locally as Carlssten ("Carl's Stone") and is one of the biggest and best preserved of its type anywhere in Denmark. It must be reached on foot but the forest car park is only a short distance away.

Prehistoric Carlssten, Grønnesse Skov

⓮ Hundested

Road map: E4. Jernbanegade 8. **Tel** 47 93 77 88.
visitnordsjaelland.com

This small town lies on a slender peninsula. Its name translates literally as "dog's place" and derives from a species of local seal commonly known as a sea dog because of its canine-like barking. The main reason to come to Hundested is to take a look around **Knud Rasmussens Hus**, which is situated on a high cliff close to Spodsbjerg lighthouse. The house was built in 1917 by the intrepid Arctic explorer, Knud Rasmussen, and now houses a museum devoted to his life and travels. Close by is a monument to him erected in 1936 made of stones brought over from Greenland.

Environs

A short way northeast is **Kikhavn**, the oldest fishing village on the Halsnæs peninsula, which dates back to the 13th century. In the 18th century there were many small farms here, some of which were partly destroyed by a fire in 1793. The remaining farms and buildings have been preserved, and form a picturesque village. Kikhaven is also the starting point of a footpath, **Halsnæsstien**,

Knud Rasmussen's house, now a popular museum

that links the shores of Isefjord and Kattegat.

Another place worth visiting is **Lynæs**, just south of Hundested. The local church, built in 1901 from granite blocks, serves as a navigational guide for returning fishermen. A monument standing by the church commemorates those who lost their lives at sea.

Knud Rasmussens Hus
Tel 47 72 06 05. **Open** Easter–Oct: 11am–4pm Tue–Sun.
indmus.dk

Knud Rasmussen

Knud Rasmussen was born in 1879. Part Inuit himself, Rasmussen was fascinated by Inuit culture and language and resolved to become a polar explorer at an early age. He took part in his first scientific expedition in 1902 and soon began organizing them himself. In 1910, together with Peter Freuchen, he founded the Thule settlement in the north of Greenland. Between 1921 and 1924 Rasmussen completed a grand expedition from Greenland to the Bering Strait, covering 18,000 km (11,185 miles) by dog-sleigh. From each of his expeditions the explorer brought back many artefacts; most of these are now in the Nationalmuseet in Copenhagen *(see pp88–9)*. In the course of his seventh expedition Rasmussen fell seriously ill. He died in 1933, aged 54.

The explorer's house, full of reminders of his expeditions

Kongeegen, believed to be the oldest living oak tree in Europe

⓯ Nordskoven

Road map: F4.

The peninsula that separates Roskilde Fjord from Isefjord contains one of Denmark's most beautiful beech forests. The forest has two sections, known as Fællesskoven and Studehaven. Running between them is a 15-km- (9-mile-) long bicycle trail with views over Roskilde Fjord. At its highest

Statue of a deer in front of Jægerspris Slot

point, called Frederikshøj, is a hunting pavilion built by Frederik VII in 1875. A number of ancient trees can be found in the forest including three famous oaks: Kongeegen, Storkeegen and Snoegen, which have inspired many artists. Kongeegen, the most ancient of the three trees, is believed to be 1,500–1,900 years old. In 1973 its last bough broke away, leaving only the vast trunk, which has a circumference of 14 m (46 ft).

⑯ Jægerspris Slot

Road map: F4. Jægerspris Slot, Slotsgården 20. **Tel** 47 53 10 04. **Open** Easter–Oct: 11am–4pm Tue–Sun. Park: **Open** all year round. **kongfrederik.dk**

This medieval castle, situated about 6 km (4 miles) west of Frederikssund, has been used by Danish royalty since the early 14th century and is now open to the public. The first royal building, known as Abrahamstrup, still exists although it has been swallowed by the north wing of the present complex. A life-size statue of a deer standing before the entrance to the castle is by Adelgund Vogt, a pupil of Bertel Thorvaldsen.

In the mid-19th century Frederik VII made the palace his summer residence. After his death in 1863 the monarch's widow, Countess Danner, turned part of the palace into a refuge for poor and unwanted girls. The centre became the first children's home in Denmark. A special exhibition illustrates the often austere way of life in an early 20th-century Danish orphanage.

Much of the house retains its royal character, and visitors can take a look at magnificent rooms arranged by Frederik VII. There is also an exhibition of archaeological finds reflecting one of Frederik VII's abiding passions.

The gardens stretching to the rear of the castle include Zealand's largest collection of rhododendrons; standing among them are 54 obelisks with busts of famous Danish personages. The tomb of countess Danner is also in the castle gardens. The forests around Jaegerspris offer walking and cycling opportunities.

⑰ Frederikssund

Road map: F4. 15,700. Havnegade 5A. **Tel** 47 31 06 85. Viking Festival (mid-Jun–early Jul). **visitfrederikssund.dk**

This town was founded in 1655 on the orders of Frederik III. The choice of site was not accidental, as it overlooks the narrowest part of the Roskilde Fjord and was used for many years by boats crossing to the other side.

In the town centre is the **J.F. Willumsens Museum**. Willumsen (1863–1958), a prominent Danish Symbolist painter, donated his paintings, sculptures and drawings to Frederikssund on condition that a suitable building be erected to display them. The museum also contains works by other artists that were collected by Willumsen.

Frederikssund is primarily known, however, for its reconstructed **Viking Village**, located near the town's harbour. The village is open to visitors all year round but the best time to visit is during the summer Viking Festival, when events are held that involve the whole town. The most popular are the evening Viking plays that feature more than 250 actors, many of them local residents and children; the final night is celebrated with a grand banquet.

J.F. Willumsens Museum
Jenriksvej 4. **Tel** 47 31 07 73. **Open** 10am–5pm Tue–Sun. **jfwillumsensmuseum.dk**

Danes dressed as Vikings during Frederikssund's summer festival

Selsø Slot, built in 1578

⓲ Selsø Slot

Road map: F4. Selsøvej 30A, 4050 Skibby. **Tel** 52 17 20 60. **Open** May–mid-Sep: 11am–4pm Tue–Sun. **selsoe.dk**

This property's history dates back to the 12th century. According to records, Bishop Absalon became interested in the site in about 1170 and by 1228 a sumptuous residence had been built here.

The present castle was built in 1578. It was reworked in 1734 and much of its original Renaissance style was replaced with Baroque details. The castle is now a museum and gives visitors an idea of what aristocratic life was like in the 1800s. The castle's stern, simple exterior hides a richer interior, including the "Grand Ballroom". With original marble panels and a decorated ceiling, it is used as a venue for classical music concerts. Wine-tasting sessions are held in the castle vaults. The castle church has an altarpiece dating from 1605.

The property owes much of its charm to its location on the banks of Selsø lake. A bird reserve established in the gardens is one of the premium places for birdwatching in Denmark. A viewing tower standing in the garden was built specifically for this purpose.

⓳ Skibby

Road map: F4. Havnegade 5A, 3600 Frederikssund. **Tel** 47 31 06 85. **visitfrederikssund.dk**

The main town of the peninsula between Roskilde Fjord and Isefjord, Skibby is known mainly for its early 12th-century church, which is decorated with some well-preserved frescoes. The oldest of these were found in 1855 in the Romanesque apses and date from the second half of the 12th century. Similar decorations can be found in other churches in the district, including some at nearby Dråby. In 1650 a manuscript, known as the *Skibby Chronicle*, was found buried behind the altar. The work, written in Latin, recounts the history of Denmark between 1046 and 1534. It is uncertain why the chronicle was found here. Its style points to the authorship of Paul Helgsen, a Carmelite monk and orator. Helgsen was a native of Helsingør, however, and since the work is unfinished, its discovery has provoked debate as to the fate of its author. Skibby's other claim to fame is as the location of Scandinavia's first nudist swimming pool.

Dråby Kirke, situated near Skibby

Environs

Northeast of Skibby, in the town of Skuldelev, is a **doll museum** with a 6,000-strong collection. Also on display are antique baby carriages, dolls' prams and a working model railway from 1940 (runs from March to October).

⓴ Roskilde

See pp144–7.

Trying out a dugout canoe at Lejre's Stone Age village

㉑ Lejre

Road map: F4. Open-air museum: Slangealleen 2, 4320 Lejre. **Tel** 46 48 08 78. **Open** May–Jun & late Aug–mid-Sep: 10am–4pm Tue–Fri, 11am–5pm Sat & Sun; end Jun–late Aug: 10am–5pm daily. **sagnlandet.dk**

A reconstructed village that takes visitors back to the Iron Age is the main attraction of Lejre, which is situated 8 km (5 miles) to the southwest of Roskilde. In summer Sagnlandet Lejre ("Land of Legends") is populated by volunteer Danish families who, in the name of research, dress in prehistoric furs

◀ The chapel at Frederiksborg Slot, with stunning decor dating back to Christian IV

Ledreborg Slot, surrounded by beautiful, well-kept gardens

and skins, use traditional tools and carry out all-but-forgotten chores such as chopping firewood and making clay pots.

The village is popular with children, especially in summer, when it is possible for them to take part in activities such as archery, dying clothes and paddling a dugout canoe. The centre also has a 19th-century cottage farm that re-creates the lives of Danish farmers of that period.

Lejre was one of the earliest centres of government in Denmark. Legend has it that it was the seat of a royal Stone-Age clan, the Skjoldungs, although the building shown to the visitors, once home of the supposed sovereign, is an 18th-century re-creation. It is quite likely, however, that the nearby grave-mound dates from the Stone Age period. The **Lejre Museum** has displays on the Skjoldung clan and artifacts from Viking times, as well as from the Stone and Iron ages.

Lejre Museum
Orehøjvej 4B. **Open** 11am–4pm Sat & Sun (Jul & Aug: 11am–4pm daily).

㉒ Ledreborg Slot

Road map: F5. Ledreborg Alle 2, 4320 Lejre. **Tel** 46 48 00 38. **Open** only for events. Park: **Open** 11am–4pm daily (all year round). can be pre-booked in summer.
ledreborg-slot.dk

Elegant on the outside and opulent on the inside, Ledreborg Slot is one of the foremost examples of Baroque architecture in northern Europe. It was built in 1739 on the orders of Count Johan Ludvig Holstein. In 1745 this exclusive residence acquired a chapel, which until 1899 served as a parish church.

The palace is closed to the public, but it is possible to explore the gardens that surround it. The neatly trimmed hedges make it one of the most enchanting Baroque gardens in Scandinavia. The grounds host a lifestyle exhibition in May and an outdoor chamber music concert in August.

㉓ Holbæk

Road map: E4. 27,000.
Klosterstræde 18, 59 43 11 31.
visitholbaek.dk

An important port, Holbæk is also the main commercial town for the area. It serves as a good starting point for people wishing to visit Øro island, which lies just 7 km (4 miles) away. The area has several bicycle trails, and Holbæk itself is popular with cyclists.

Holbæk was granted municipal privileges in the late 13th century, making it one of the oldest of Zealand's towns. At that time it was the site of a dynamic Dominican monastery, although the oldest surviving remains are those of a Franciscan monastery, which is located next to the Neo-Gothic Sankt Nicolaj Kirke in the medieval part of the town.

Not far from this church is **Holbæk Museum**, which consists of a dozen or so period houses dating from 1660 to 1867. Their interiors include typical items and furnishings from rural and urban dwellings of the 17th and 18th centuries. There is also a reconstructed grocery shop, a merchant's yard, café, toy shop and pottery exhibition. The tiny market square between the houses is a venue for numerous events staged during summer months, which often feature people dressed in period costumes.

Holbæk has some good local parks, such as Østre Anlæg and Bysøparken, which has a charming fountain. Just ouside the city is **Andelslandsbyen Nyvang**, an open-air museum that re-creates country life as it was from the 1870s to the 1950s.

Holbæk Museum
Klosterstræde 18. **Tel** 59 43 23 53. **Open** 10am–4pm Tue–Fri, noon–4pm Sun. **holbmus.dk**

Andelslandsbyen Nyvang
Oldvejen 25. **Tel** 59 43 40 30. **Open** Apr–Oct: 10am–4pm Mon–Thu, 10am–5pm (4pm in Oct) Sat & Sun. **adlbn.dk**

Period interior in Holbæk Museum

For hotels and restaurants see pp248–55 and pp262–77

20 Roskilde

Founded in the 10th century by the Vikings, Roskilde was Denmark's first capital. In AD 980 Harald I (Bluetooth) built Zealand's first church here, making the town an important religious centre and from the 11th century it was a bishopric. In the Middle Ages Roskilde had a population of 10,000 and was one of the largest towns in northern Europe. When Erik of Pomerania moved the capital, the town lost much of its status but it flourishes today as a market centre for the region and is popular with visitors in summer who come to see the historic Viking ships and the ancient cathedral.

Exploring Roskilde

All of the town's attractions are within easy reach. The most prestigious streets, lined with shops and cafés, are Skomagergade and Algade. The Vikingeskibsmuseet (Viking Ship Museum) is by the harbour.

Roskilde Domkirke

See pp146–7.

Fountain in front of the town hall in Stændertorvet

Stændertorvet

This small square situated by the town's main promenade has for centuries been the heart of Roskilde. In the Middle Ages it was the site of fairs. Sankt Laurence, a Romanesque church, was demolished in the mid-16th century to provide more space for the growing market. A few remaining parts of the church can be seen today including the tower, which now adorns the town hall (built in 1884) and what remains of the church foundations. The foundations are open to the public and are in the town hall's vaults. In the square is a monument depicting, among others, Roar, the legendary father of Roskilde, who established Roskilde as homage to the two pagan gods, Thor and Odin.

Roskilde Palace and the Museum of Contemporary Art

Stændertorvet 3. **Tel** 46 31 65 70. Art Museum: **Open** noon–4pm Tue–Sun (to 8pm Wed). **samtidskunst.dk**

Built in 1733 by the Danish architect Laurits de Thurah, this yellow Baroque palace is the former seat of Roskilde's bishops. It is linked to the neighbouring cathedral by the Arch of Absalon. Part of the palace houses the Museum of Contemporary Art (Museet for Samtidskunst), which organizes temporary exhibitions of Danish and foreign artists. Another wing is used by a local art association.

Roskilde Museum

Sankt Ols Gade 18. **Tel** 46 31 65 29. **Open** 11am–4pm daily. **roskildemuseum.dk**

The municipal museum in Roskilde is an excellent place for anyone interested in the town's history. Its collection – including documents, photographs, archaeological finds and works of art – explains the region's past, from the Stone Age up to the present day (which is aptly symbolized by a display devoted to the prestigious rock festival organized every year in Roskilde since 1971). The museum also includes a building in Ringstedgade, named Brødrene Lützhøfts Købmandsgård, which is simply a shop furnished in a manner typical of a century or so ago, where potash soap and dried cod can be purchased.

Hussar's uniform, Roskilde Museum

Roskilde Kloster

Sankt Peder Stræde 8. **Tel** 46 35 02 19. **Open** for tours only. Easter & July: 11am & 2pm Wed (in Danish; book in advance for tours in English). **roskildekloster.dk**

In the Middle Ages Roskilde had about 20 churches and monasteries, not counting the cathedral. Their sacral functions ceased as the Reformation swept through the country in 1536.

This brick-built monastery, which stands in its own grounds, was built in 1560 and, in 1699, became Denmark's first refuge for unmarried mothers from well-to-do families. It has some fine interiors including a chapel, extensive library and a banqueting hall.

Brick monastery buildings of Roskilde Kloster

Gråbrødre Kirkegård

The former cemetery, where prominent and wealthy citizens of the town were buried during the Middle Ages, is now used as a park and is located near the railway station. The station was built in 1847 to serve the Copenhagen–Roskilde line and is one of the oldest train stations in Denmark.

Roskilde Jars commemorating the city's 1,000-year anniversary

Hestetorvet

The main landmark of the market square, used in medieval times for horse trading, are the three 5-m (16-ft) tall jars. These were put in place in 1998 as part of the town's millennium celebrations. Engraved on one of the jars are verses from a poem written by Henrik Nordbrandt, dedicated to Roskilde and to Margrete I. The jars' creator, Peter Brandes, intended them to symbolize life and death.

Vikingeskibsmuseet

Vindeboder 12. **Tel** 46 30 02 00. **Open** Jul & Aug: 10am–5pm daily; Sep–Jun: 10am–4pm daily. **vikingeskibsmuseet.dk**

About 1,000 years ago the ships now exhibited at the Viking Ship Museum were filled with stones and sunk in the fjord in order to block the passage of enemy ships. In 1962 five of the vessels were recovered. Although they had been underwater for so long, they are in remarkably good condition and give a good indication of Viking boat-building skills. The largest of them is a 30-m (98-ft) long warship with the capacity to carry a crew of 70 to 80 Vikings. The best preserved is a 14-m- (46-ft-) long merchant ship, which sailed around the Baltic and Danish sounds. The other ships are a deep-sea trader, a longship and a fishing boat. The museum also has an exhibition devoted to the Vikings and a working boatyard, where replicas of old Viking ships, including those in the museum, are built using traditional methods and materials. In summer it is possible to sail on a replica ship on the Roskilde Fjord. The museum also has a pleasant café, plus themed activities for children and adults.

VISITORS' CHECKLIST

Practical Information
Road map: F4. 50,000.
Stændertorvet 1. **Tel** 46 31 65 65. Roskilde Rock Festival (late Jun–early Jul). **visitroskilde.com**

Transport
Roskilde.

Historic boat at Vikingeskibsmuseet

Roskilde Town Centre

1. Roskilde Domkirke
2. Stændertorvet
3. Roskilde Palace
4. Roskilde Museum
5. Roskilde Kloster
6. Gråbrødre Kirkegård
7. Hestetorvet
8. Vikingeskibsmuseet

For keys to symbols see back flap

Roskilde Domkirke

The twin towers of this magnificent brick cathedral, begun in the 12th century on the orders of Bishop Absalon, are a landmark of Roskilde. The cathedral is an organic mix of styles. For centuries it was used as the burial site of Danish monarchs, 39 of whom are interred here. The remains of Harald I (Bluetooth), a 10th-century Viking king, are said to be inside one of the columns to the side of the main altar. In view of its historic value the cathedral has been declared a UNESCO World Heritage Site.

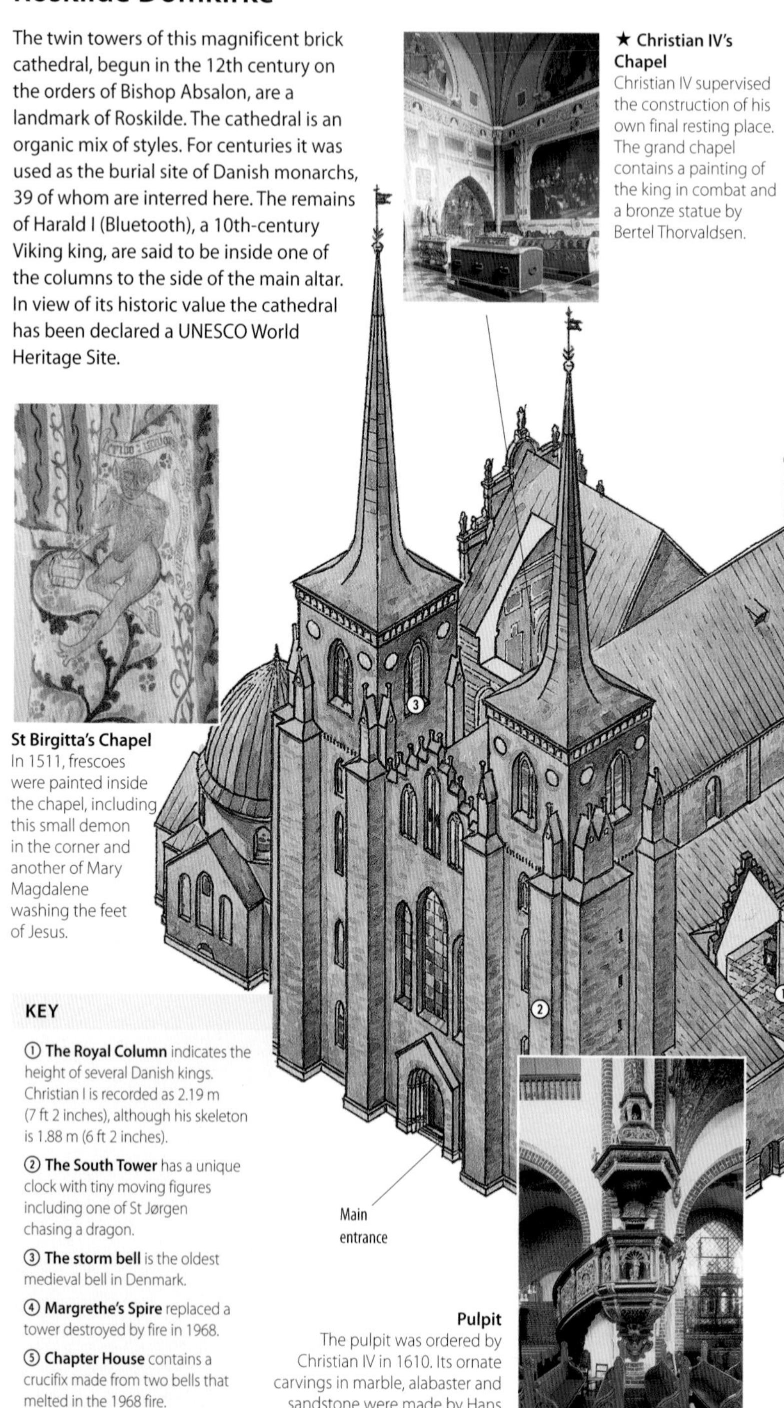

★ Christian IV's Chapel
Christian IV supervised the construction of his own final resting place. The grand chapel contains a painting of the king in combat and a bronze statue by Bertel Thorvaldsen.

St Birgitta's Chapel
In 1511, frescoes were painted inside the chapel, including this small demon in the corner and another of Mary Magdalene washing the feet of Jesus.

KEY

① **The Royal Column** indicates the height of several Danish kings. Christian I is recorded as 2.19 m (7 ft 2 inches), although his skeleton is 1.88 m (6 ft 2 inches).

② **The South Tower** has a unique clock with tiny moving figures including one of St Jørgen chasing a dragon.

③ **The storm bell** is the oldest medieval bell in Denmark.

④ **Margrethe's Spire** replaced a tower destroyed by fire in 1968.

⑤ **Chapter House** contains a crucifix made from two bells that melted in the 1968 fire.

Pulpit
The pulpit was ordered by Christian IV in 1610. Its ornate carvings in marble, alabaster and sandstone were made by Hans Brokman of Copenhagen.

Stalls
Set near the altar these wooden pews are beautiful examples of Gothic carving.

VISITORS' CHECKLIST

Practical Information
Domkirkestræde 1. **Tel** 46 35 16 24. **Open** Apr–Sep: 9am–5pm daily (from 12:30pm Sun & hols); Oct–Mar: 10am–4pm Tue–Sat, 12:30–4pm Sun & hols.
roskildedomkirke.dk

4

5

★ Altarpiece
The altar, depicting scenes from the life of Christ, was produced in Antwerp in the 1500s.

★ Sarcophagus of Margrete I
The sarcophagus bearing an alabaster effigy of Margrete I as a young girl is considered to be the most beautiful sculpture in the cathedral.

Interior
The cathedral has been rebuilt several times, acquiring features typical of the styles that were then in fashion. The last major works were carried out following a fire in 1968.

㉔ Tveje Merløse Kirke

Road map: E4. Holbæk, Tveje Merløse 14. **Tel** 59 43 24 53. **Open** 8am–4pm daily. **tvejemerloesekirke.dk**

As a miniature version of Roskilde's original 12th-century cathedral, the church in Tveje Merløse, south of Holbæk, is one of the most interesting Romanesque sacral buildings in Denmark. Its most distinctive features are the two almost identical square towers. The history of the site as a place of worship is believed to date back to the Viking era; some records suggest it was used for worship in the 3rd century.

The church's interior has an altarpiece by Joakim Skovgaard. At one time the church contained some colourful 13th-century frescoes depicting, among other things, the devil and the motif of God's Majesty, a typical medieval theme found particularly in the region of Øresund. These have been removed and are now on display in Copenhagen's Nationalmuseet *(see pp88–9)*. A small cemetery is in the church grounds.

㉕ Nørre Jernløse Mølle

Road map: E4. Windmill: Møllebakken 2, Regstrup. **Tel** 23 40 30 03. **Open** Apr–Oct: 2–4pm 1st Sun of each month. **nrjernlosemolle.dk**

The small village of Nørre Jernløse, located some 25 km (16 miles) west of Roskilde, has a 12th-century church containing 16th-century frescoes. The town is best known, however, for its 19th-century windmill, which is set on an sturdy octagonal base surrounded by a distinctive gallery.

The Dutch-style windmill was built in 1893 in Nørrevold, near Copenhagen, where it was known as Sankt Peders Mølle. When financial difficulties forced its owners to sell the mill it was bought by Niels Peter Rasmussen, a miller, who dismantled it and transported it in pieces on a horse cart to Jernløse, 70 km (43 miles) away. In 1899 the windmill was bought by Ole Martin Nielsen, whose family used and maintained it for the next 60 years. Finally, in 1979 the windmill was handed over to the parish of Jernløse. Built on a stone base, the Nørre Jernløse mill has a timber structure with a shingled roof crowned with a wooden, onion-shaped cupola. Its sails were once cloth covered and could be operated directly from the gallery. The mill, which is no longer used to grind flour, now has an information centre where visitors can learn about the mill's history and about early methods of flour production.

Dutch-style windmill in Nørre Jernløse

Well in front of the monastery in Sorø

㉖ Sorø

Road map: E5. 7,000. Storgade 15. **Tel** 57 82 10 12. **soroe.dk**

Located on the banks of the Tuel and Sorø lakes, Sorø is one of the most beautiful towns in Zealand. In 1142 Bishop Absalon, the founder of Copenhagen, began to build a monastery here. When it was complete, the Klosterkirke was the largest building of its kind in Scandinavia and one of the first brick structures ever to be built in Denmark. This 70-m (230-ft) long Romanesque-Gothic church contains the remains of Bishop Absalon in a tomb at the rear of the main altar. The church also contains the sarcophagi of Christian II, Valdemar IV and Oluf III.

Attractions in Sorø include the **Museum Vestsjælland** (Museum of Southwest Zealand), which displays exhibits from the Stone Age right up to the present time. Next to the museum is the Bursers Apotekerhave (Apothecary Garden), with plants from the herbarium of Joachim Burser, a pharmacist linked to the Danish royal family in the 1600s.

Sorø is perhaps best known for its Akademiet, which is set in a picturesque spot on Lake Sorø. This establishment, dedicated to the education of the sons of the nobility, was founded in 1623 by Christian IV in the monastery buildings left empty as a consequence of the Reformation. The Akademiet is surrounded by a park which contains a monument depicting the writer Ludwig Holberg, who bequeathed his considerable fortune and library to the school after his death in 1754. The school still operates though it is no longer reserved only for the country's nobility.

Environs

Tystrup-Bavelse is a national wildlife reserve with two connected freshwater lakes that attract a variety of birdlife; more than 20,000 water birds winter here. The forests contain many prehistoric grave-mounds, including **Kelleroddysen**, Zealand's largest megalithic stone formation, which is over 120 m (394 ft) in length. **Bjernede**, near Sorø, has the only surviving round church in Zealand. Constructed of stone and brick, it is quite unlike Bornholm's round churches *(see p225)* and was built around 1175 by Sune Ebbesøn, a provincial governor to Valdemar I (The Great).

Museum Vestsjælland
Storgade 17. **Tel** 57 83 40 63.
Open 1–4pm Tue–Thu & Sun, 11am–2pm Sat.

㉗ Tårnborg

Road map: E5.

This ancient parish on the shores of Korsør bay, with the rising outline of a white 13th-century church, was once occupied by a castle and

Distinct white exterior of the 13th-century church in Tårnborg

settlement. Tårnborg appeared as a place name for the first time in a royal land survey completed in the first half of the 13th century, though it is likely that a stronghold existed at least one hundred years prior to this and that, together with the forts at Nyborg and Sprogø, it controlled the passage across the Store Bælt *(see pp150–51)*. From the 13th century it was also a major centre of commerce and in the 14th century Tårnborg forged links with neighbouring estates, helping to intensify foreign trade. The castle was demolished in the 15th century following a financial crisis.

Bjernede Rundkirke – the only round church in Zealand

Archaeological excavations suggest that Tårnborg's original stronghold measured approximately 30 m (98 ft) in diameter, with an 8-m (26-ft) high tower at its centre.

㉘ Korsør

Road map: E5. 20,000. **Tel** 70 25 22 06. **visitvestsjaelland.dk**

The earliest records of this town date from 1241. The most prominent building in Korsør is a 13th-century fortress (Korsør Fæstning), which played a crucial role in the town gaining control of the Storebælt. In 1658 the constantly enlarged fortress was captured by the Swedes, but returned to Danish control a year later. Its 25-m-(82-ft-) high tower now houses the **Korsør By-og Overfarts-museet** (Town and Ferry Service Museum), which has a collection that includes models of ships that once sailed across the Storebælt.

Clusters of historic buildings, mainly from the 18th century, can be seen in the environs of Algade, Slottensgade and Gavnegade. The Rococo mansion at No. 25 Algade dates from 1761 and was built by Rasmus Langeland, a shipowner. It was originally used as an inn for sailors who were waiting for the right conditions to cross the Storebælt. Its front is adorned with allegories of the four seasons. Inside is a small art museum displaying, among other things, sculptures by artist Harald Isenstein who died in 1980.

Korsør By-og Overfartsmuseet
Søbatteriet 7. **Tel** 58 37 47 55. **Open** Apr–Dec: 11am–4pm Tue–Sun.
byogoverfartsmuseet.dk

Cannons outside Korsør Fæstning (Fortress)

29 Storebælt Bridge

Until the late 20th century, the only way of travelling to Zealand was by air or ferry across the Storebælt (Great Belt). In 1998, after 12 years of construction work, the two biggest Danish islands – Zealand and Funen – were joined together. The link consists of two bridges with an artificial island in between. The journey time has now been cut to 10 minutes and the bridge is open 24 hours a day. Of the two bridges, the Østbro (Eastern) suspension bridge presents a more impressive sight. A toll charge of around 235–360 Dkr, depending on the size of your vehicle, is payable at the toll station on the Zealand side. Head to the yellow *Manuel* lanes for payment by credit card or cash.

VISITORS' CHECKLIST

Practical Information
Road map: E5. **Tel** 70 15 10 15.
storebaelt.dk

Bridges
The Østbro is 7 km (4.4 miles) long and carries cars (trains run in a tunnel). The Vestbro is 6.6 km (4.1 miles) long and carries cars and trains.

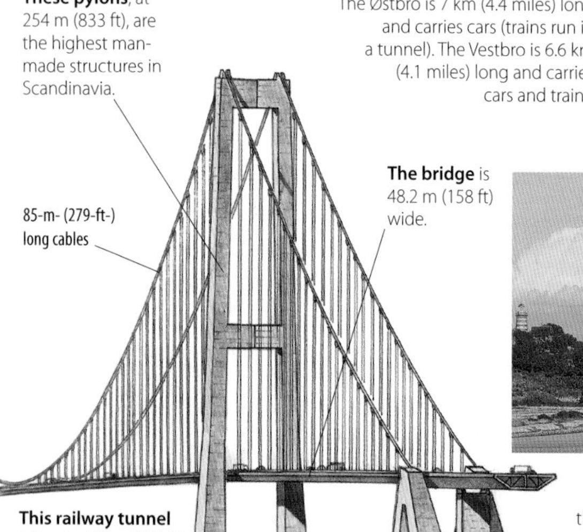

These pylons, at 254 m (833 ft), are the highest man-made structures in Scandinavia.

85-m- (279-ft-) long cables

The bridge is 48.2 m (158 ft) wide.

This railway tunnel is located 75m (246 ft) underground

Sprogø
This small island in the middle of the Storebælt is the junction where the Østbro motorway and the railway track meet.

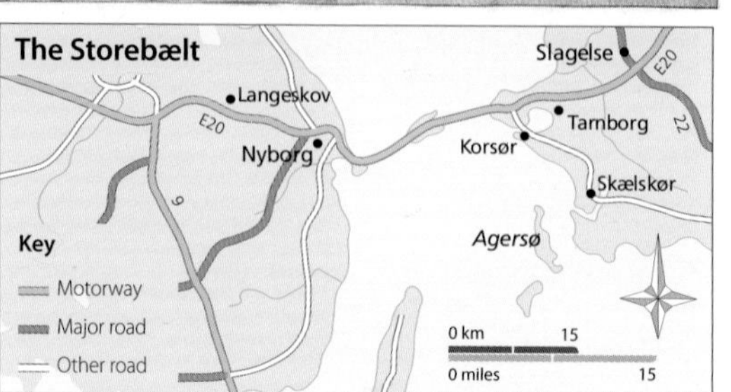

Tunnel
An 8-km- (5-mile-) long rail tunnel, measuring 7.7 m (25 ft) in diameter, descends 75 m (246 ft) below the surface. It is the second largest underwater tunnel in Europe.

A display of Viking archery in Trelleborg

30 Trelleborg

Road map: E5. 7 km (4 miles) east of Slagelse. Tower: Trelleborg Allé 4, 4200 Slagelse. **Open** Jun–Aug: 10am– 5pm Tue–Sun; Apr–May & Sep–Oct: 10am–4pm Tue–Sun.
vikingeborgen-trelleborg.dk

The best-preserved of Denmark's Viking fortresses was founded in the 10th century by Harald I (Bluetooth). At the height of its power it was manned by an estimated force of 1,000 warriors. Of the reconstructed buildings, the longhouse is the most impressive. It is built of rough oak beams and furnished with benches on which the Vikings slept.

Originally, there were 16 buildings in the main section of the fortress. Outside the fortress was a small cemetery, where archaeologists have counted about 150 graves.

In summer visitors can participate in fun and games. Some of the staff are dressed in Viking costume and are on hand to demonstrate such workaday jobs as grinding corn and sharpening tools. Daily workshops provide children with the opportunity to try their hand at archery and even dress up as Vikings.

A small museum exhibits finds excavated from the grounds such as jewellery and pottery. It also screens a 20-minute film about the history of Trelleborg.

31 Kalundborg

Road map: E4. 20,000.
Klosterparkvej 7. **Tel** 59 51 09 15. Museum: Adelgade 23. **Tel** 59 51 21 41. **Open** May–Aug: 11am–5pm daily; Sep–Apr: 11am–4pm Sat & Sun.
kalmus.dk or
visitvestsjaelland.dk

Kalundborg is one of Zealand's oldest towns and was populated by the Vikings as early as the 9th century. The town was also once used as a base by pirates but in 1168 a castle was built here and control of the fjord's waters was assumed by the crown.

The ruins in Volden square are all that remains of the castle. Its builder was Esbern Snare, the brother of Bishop Absalon. Snare was also the creator of the well-preserved 12th-century Vor Frue Kirke (Church of Our Lady), which has five octagonal towers and a Byzantine design based on a Greek crucifix.

Kalundborg's medieval quarter surrounds the church and includes cobbled streets and 16th-century buildings. One of these now houses the town museum. Most of the exhibits are devoted to local history and include a collection of costumes and the skeletons of two beheaded Vikings. Standing in the museum courtyard is a model of Kalundborg, providing a view of the town's 17th-century layout.

32 Røsnæs

Road map: E4. Kalundborg.

The Røsnæs peninsula, as well as the Asnæs peninsula that flanks the Kalundborg Fjord on the other side, were created by a continental glacier some 20,000 years ago. In the Middle Ages the Røsnæs peninsula, which thrusts into the Storebælt, was covered with thick forest, making it one of the favourite areas for royal hunting trips. One hunt, in 1231, organized at the request of Valdemar the Victorious, ended in a bitter tragedy when a stray arrow killed the king's son (who was also named Valdemar).

The peninsula's tip is the westernmost point of Zealand and is marked by a lighthouse erected in 1845. The light from its lantern, mounted 25 m (82 ft) above sea level, can be seen up to 40 km (25 miles) away. A short way before the lighthouse, in the village of Ulstrup, is a Dutch-style windmill built in 1894. It was still being used in the 1950s to grind flour but is now purely a visitor attraction.

At the base of the Asnæs peninsula is Lerchenborg Slot, a Baroque castle built in 1753 by General Christian Lerche. H.C. Andersen stayed here in 1862 and some of the rooms contain items relating to the famous writer.

The unusual five-towered church in Kalundborg

GILLELEJE

H 219

㉝ Svinninge

Road map: E4. Hovedgaden 7. **Tel** 59 21 60 09.

The main reason people come to this town, located at the base of the Odsherred peninsula, is to visit its model electric railway, which is one of the longest in Europe. **Svinninge Modeljernbane** is housed in a building measuring 8 m by 14 m (26 ft by 46 ft) and contains over 550 model railway coaches and nearly 90 locomotives. All of the rolling stock, as well as the convincing reconstructions of many Danish stations (including Svinninge, Hilbæk, Lisebro, Hjortholm and Egaa), are built to a scale of 1:87. The creators of this extraordinary display have meticulously and painstakingly recreated entire railway routes, including the link from Holbæk to Oxneholm.

The model railway was originally a private affair and was opened to the public after it was donated to the town by its original creator. The building of this impressive display involved a great deal of work by many people including model makers, carpenters, joiners and electricians. More than 80 m (262 ft) of cable were laid in order to supply current to over 2 km (1.3 miles) of track. The display continues to grow with new sections of track and locomotives added yearly.

Svinninge Modeljernbane
Stationen 2, 4520 Svinninge. **Tel** 59 21 60 09. **Open** end Apr–end Oct: 10am–4pm daily. **svmjk.dk**

Section of the model railway in Svinninge

Dragsholm Slot, seen from the courtyard

㉞ Dragsholm

Road map: E4. Dragsholm Allé, 4534 Hørve. **Tel** 59 65 33 00. tours only: Jul: 1:30pm Tue (in English). **dragsholm-slot.dk**

The castle in Dragsholm was once a fortress and later a royal residence. It is now used as a luxurious hotel and restaurant, but has lost none of its historical grandeur.

Situated on the shores of Nekselø bay, at the foot of Zealand's third highest hill – Vejrhøj (121 m/397 ft above sea level) – Dragsholm Slot is one of Denmark's oldest castles. Its origins date back to the beginning of the 13th century, when the Bishop of Roskilde decided to build a palace, which would also serve as a military fortress. The bishops owned the castle until 1536, when the king took possession of it following the Reformation. The king established a prison at the castle. The most famous prisoner was James Hepburn, the 4th Earl of Bothwell. He was married to the Scottish queen, Mary Stuart, but had to flee from Scotland. He was captured in Bergen and later sent to Dragsholm, where he was imprisoned for five years. Hepburn died in 1578, and his mummified body is located in the church in Fårevejle.

In 1657 Denmark declared war on Sweden. When Sweden won, the Swedish soldiers blew up parts of the castle. The castle was then given to Henrik Müller, who rebuilt the southern wing in 1675. In 1694 the castle was bought by Frederik Christian Adeler and his wife Henriette Margrethe von Lente. They rebuilt the rest of the castle as the Baroque building seen today. The Adeler family owned the castle until 1932, when the state had to take over. Since 1937 the property has been owned by the Bøttger family, who today run it as a hotel with a spa and two restaurants. The castle contains 34 rooms, all with unique and contemporary furnishings. Some rooms overlook the park, with others offering views of the fields, moat or beautiful cobblestone castle yard. The 1-m (3-ft) thick walls, high ceilings and sumptuously decorated interiors enhance the historic aura of the place. The most interesting rooms include the magnificent Banqueting Hall (Riddersalen) and Hunting Room (Jagtværelset).

Heraldic arms from Dragsholm Slot

The castle and its moat are surrounded by a large expanse of parkland that contains, among other plants, a collection of rhododendrons. Like all great castles, Dragsholm is reputed to be haunted. The three ghosts that are most frequently spotted are the White Lady, the Grey Lady and, of course, Lord von Bothwell.

◀ Boats moored at Gilleleje, the northernmost town in Zealand

35 Odsherred

Surrounded by the waters of the Kattegat, Isefjord and Sejerø bay, the Odsherred peninsula is one of the most popular holiday destinations in Denmark, visited annually by sun-seekers and water sports enthusiasts. Its wide sandy beaches, the lure of the sea and the varied landscape also make this region popular with artists, some of whom have established galleries here.

③ Sjælland Sommerland
This amusement park (open mid-May–Sep only) provides a good day out for families with kids. Among the many attractions are a mini train, a roller coaster and giant water slides ending in splash pools.

⑤ Havnebyen
Cutters in the harbour and the aroma from the local smokehouses make this fishing village a memorable place.

② Højby Sø
The banks of this small lake are inhabited by a wide variety of birds. The lake is also popular with anglers.

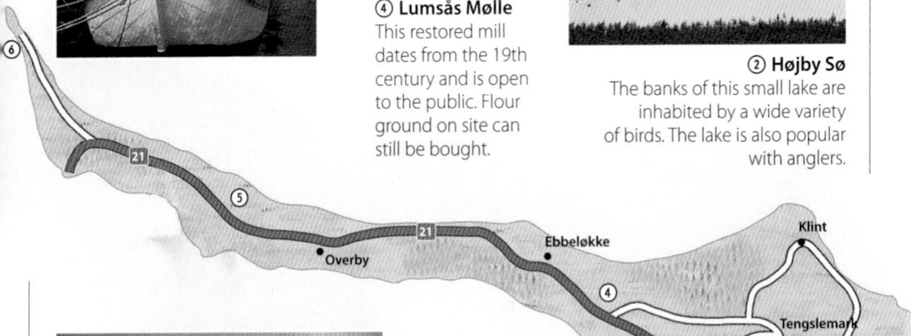

④ Lumsås Mølle
This restored mill dates from the 19th century and is open to the public. Flour ground on site can still be bought.

⑥ Gniben
The narrow strip of land stretching westwards has wide sandy beaches and is excellent for sunbathing. Gniben, situated furthest to the west, affords magnificent views of the sea.

0 km 2
0 miles 2

Key

Suggested route
Scenic route
Other road

① Højby
The interior of the local church is decorated with frescoes depicting, among others, Sankt Jørgen.

Tips for Drivers

Length of route: 50 km (31 miles). Nykøbing SJ: Algade 43. **Tel** 59 91 08 88. visitodsherred.dk

For hotels and restaurants see pp248–55 and pp262–77

SOUTHERN ZEALAND AND THE ISLANDS

The lowlands of southern Zealand are characterized by cultivated fields and beautiful lakes. Many visitors see only Vordingborg and Køge, two towns that have played a significant part in Denmark's history, but the islands of Lolland, Falster and Møn to the south are attractive holiday destinations and offer miles of sandy beaches, woodland and awe-inspiring views of coastal cliffs.

Southern Zealand (Sjælland) is an important region for the Danes. Vordingborg was the capital of the Valdemar dynasty and in the 12th century was used by Bishop Absalon as a staging post for his military expeditions to eastern Germany. The market town of Ringsted, in central Zealand, was for many years the venue of the *landsting*, a regional government assembly that formed the basis of the present-day parliament. In 1677, Køge Bay was the scene of a major naval engagement in which the Danish Admiral Niels Juel became a national hero when he dealt a crushing blow to the Swedish fleet.

The islands to the south of Zealand are more rural in character. Lolland is Denmark's third biggest island (1,243 sq km/480 sq miles) and also its flattest (at its highest point it is a mere 22 m/72 ft above sea level). The island has some pretty beaches and is popular with hikers in summer. Falster is only slightly smaller and is visited mainly for its wide beaches. Møn is the smallest of the islands and the hardest to reach. The journey is worth it, however, as Møn has rustic scenery, spectacular white cliffs, good beaches and some interesting sights including Neolithic burial places and a number of medieval churches containing some spectacular frescoes.

Tree-lined beach on the island of Møn

◀ Vallø Slot, an impressive Renaissance castle in Southern Zealand

Exploring Southern Zealand and the Islands

The largest town in southern Zealand is Næstved, which has a number of historic buildings. However, Køge, Ringsted and Vordingborg have more to offer in the way of outstanding buildings. This part of Denmark is particularly attractive to families because it has a slow, relaxed pace and a number of child-friendly attractions such as BonBon-Land, Knuthenborg Safari Park on Lolland and, on Falster, a recreated medieval village. Falster benefits from some of Denmark's best beaches; Lolland has a popular resort complex.

Brick-built Holsted Kirke, Næstved

Getting Around

Getting from southern Zealand to Falster and Lolland presents few problems thanks to the toll-free bridges. The main arterial road – the E47 motorway – runs from Copenhagen via southern Zealand to Falster and Rødbyhavn on Lolland. Most places are easily accessible from Copenhagen by train except for Møn, which has no railway.

Key

- Motorway
- Major road
- Minor road
- Scenic route
- Main railway
- Minor railway

For hotels and restaurants see pp248–55 and pp262–77

Neolithic burial site on the Knudshoved Odde peninsula

Sights at a Glance

1. Agersø
2. Ringsted
3. Suså
4. Glumsø
5. BonBon-Land
6. Næstved
7. Gavnø
8. Vordingborg
9. Knudshoved Odde
10. Sakskøbing
11. Maribo
12. *Knuthenborg Safari Park pp164–5*
13. Nakskov
14. Lalandia
15. Tågerup
16. Nysted
17. Fuglsang Kunstmuseum
18. Middelaldercentret
19. Nykøbing F
20. Eskilstrup
21. Marielyst
22. Væggerløse
23. Fanefjord Kirke
24. Kong Asgers Høj
25. Møns Klint
26. Liselund Slot
27. Elmelunde
28. Stege
29. Nyord
30. Fakse
31. Stevns Klint
32. Vallø Slot
33. Køge

For keys to symbols *see back flap*

Vaulted interior of Sankt Bendts Kirke, Ringsted

❶ Agersø

Road map: E5. **W** **agersoe.com**
Agersø Mølle: **Tel** 58 19 81 03.
Open Jul–early Aug: 2–4pm Fri–Sun.
W **agersoe-moelle.dk**

A 15-minute ferry trip from Stigsnæs, a small port 7 km (4.3 miles) southwest of Skælskør, takes visitors to the lovely island of Agersø. This strip of land is just 3 km (1.8 miles) wide and 7 km (4.3 miles) long, and it is home to a community of about 240 people.

Despite its small size, Agersø has a lot to offer, starting with the pretty harbour, which plays host to all manner of vessels, from ferries and yachts to fishing boats. There is also a comprehensive network of walking and cycling routes starting from the harbour and covering a length of 20 km (12.4 miles). The north of the island features several unspoiled beaches with good bathing opportunities.

The island's main attraction, however, is probably the Agersø Mølle, a mill built in 1892. Farmers from the surrounding areas would come here to grind their corn. Resting on a stone base, the octagonal uppermill is made of wood and covered with shingle. The mill was in use until 1959, when its owner, a baker called Erik Thomsen, gifted it to the people of Agersø. A bench was placed next to the mill in his honour.

❷ Ringsted

Road map: E5. 18,000.
Tvær Allé 1–3. **Tel** 57 62 66 00.
W **visitringsted.dk**

Owing to its location at the crossroads of two trading routes, Ringsted was once an important market town. It was the venue for regional government assemblies – the *landsting* – which took decisions and passed laws on major national issues. The three stones standing in the market square were used hundreds of years ago by members of the *landsting*.

Ringsted gained notoriety in 1131 when Knud (Canute) Laward, duke of southern Zealand, was murdered in the neighbouring woods by his jealous cousin Magnus. He is buried in Ringsted's Sankt Bendts Kirke (St Benedict's Church) along with a number of Danish kings and queens. Sankt Bendts Kirke was erected in 1170 and is believed to be the oldest brick church in Scandinavia. Its main altarpiece dates from 1699; its baptismal font is believed to be 12th century and was for a time used as a flower pot in a local garden until it was discovered quite by chance. The magnificent frescoes were painted in about 1300 and include a series depicting Erik IV (known as Ploughpenny for his tax on ploughs).

In the 17th century it was decided to open some of the coffins. The items found in them are on display in one of the chapels. The Dagmar Cross, dating from about AD 1000, is a copy. The original is on display in the Nationalmuseet in Copenhagen *(see pp88–9)*. The famous cross once belonged to Queen Dagmar, the first wife of Valdemar II. Depicted on its enamelled surface is a figure of Christ with his arms outstretched. On the other side of the cross, Christ is pictured with the Virgin Mary flanked by John the Baptist, St John and St Basil.

❸ Suså

Road map: E5.

At nearly 90 km (56 miles) long, Suså is one of Denmark's longest rivers. From its source near the town of Rønnede it flows through two lakes, Tystrup Sø and Bavelse Sø, to end its journey in Karrebæk Bay, near Næstved. The picturesque surroundings and slow-flowing current make the river particularly popular with canoeists. Canoe trips are usually taken over the final stretch of the river, where a canoe or a kayak can be hired for an hour or two. River traffic gets quite busy in summer, and many large family groups enjoy picnicking along the river banks.

Near Haslev are two magnificent properties. Gisselfeld Kloster, completed in 1575, is one of the finest Renaissance castles in northern Europe and is surrounded by gardens containing about 400 species of trees and shrubs. The castle was often visited by Hans Christian Andersen – it was here that he got his idea for *The Ugly*

Suså – Zealand's longest river

Canoeing on the Suså past the Gunderslev Kirke in Skelby

Duckling. The grounds are open to the public for opera concerts, classic car shows and market days. On the latter, there are also guided tours of the house. Bregentved Slot, on the outskirts of Haslev, was erected in the 1650s; however, the property was substantially modified in the late 1880s.

❹ Glumsø

Road map: E5.

Glumsø is a good base from which to embark upon a canoeing trip along the Suså. Located about 10 km (6 miles) south of Ringsted, its other main attraction is the **Dansk Cykel & Knallert Museum** (Museum of Bicycles and Motorbikes), which has a huge collection of two- and three-wheeled transportation, from vintage cycles to trendy modern scooters. Some bikes can even be ridden by visitors.

Environs

South of Glumsø, on the banks of the Suså, is **Skelby**. The main point of interest here is Gunderslev Kirke, a 12th-century church. Its sumptuously furnished interior was paid for by the former owners of the nearby Gunderslevholm estate.

Dansk Cykel & Knallert Museum
Sorøvej 8. **Tel** 57 64 77 94. **Open** May–Sep: 11am–5pm Sat & Sun.
W **dckm.dk/cykelmuseum**

❺ BonBon-Land

Road map: E5. Holme-Ostrup, Gartnervej 2. **Tel** 55 53 07 00. **Open** Apr–Oct. Opening hours vary; check the website before visiting. children up to 90 cm (3 ft) tall are admitted free. W **bonbonland.dk**

This amusement park attracts large numbers of visitors in the summer. The entrance fee covers all the 100 or so attractions. The greatest thrill is undoubtedly provided by a ride on the giant roller coaster, which races along at speeds up to 70 km/h (43 mph) and rises to a height of 22 m (72 ft) before hurtling back down again. A similar surge of adrenaline can be felt when dropping from the 35-m (115-ft) high tower. Gentler amusement can be had on the park's merry-go-rounds or mini racetracks. The queues lengthen for the water slides when the temperature rises, as do those for a raft trip down some white-water rapids. BonBon-Land has lots of attractions for smaller children too, including an adventure playground. It is attractively situated in woodland a short walk from Holme-Ostrup train station; expect queues in the summer, especially at the snack bars.

Environs

Every year more than 40,000 guests pay a visit to **Gisselfeld Kloster**. They come to enjoy the old Renaissance castle, the beautiful castle park, and the surrounding countryside. The name Gisselfeld can be traced back to the year 1370, but the red castle as it appears today was built during the period 1547–75 by Peder Oxe, the mightiest High Chancellor of Denmark. There has been a garden park around the castle since then. The present castle park of about 40 hectares (99 acres) was laid out towards the end of the 19th century by H.E. Millner, the famous English landscape architect. The English landscape garden with its beautiful oases and botanic rarities is definitely worth a visit.

Special events take place in the park throughout the year, including opera productions, a classic motor show and a Christmas market.

Gisselfeld Kloster
Godskontoret, Gisselfeldvej 12 A, 4690 Haslev. **Tel** 56 32 60 32. **Open** variable; check website before visiting.
W **gisselfeld-kloster.dk**

Children's attractions in BonBon-Land

6 Næstved

Road map: E5. 42,500. Sankt Peders Kirkeplads 14. **Tel** 55 72 11 22. **visitnaestved.com**

Southern Zealand's largest town, Næstved has been an important centre of trade since medieval times. The 15th-century town hall in Axeltorv, the main square, is one of the oldest in Denmark. The town has two Gothic churches. The 14th-century frescoes in Sankt Peder Kirke (St Peter's Church) depict Valdemar IV and his wife Helveg kneeling in prayer. Sankt Mortens is 13th century and has a beautiful altarpiece that was completed in 1667.

Other notable buildings include Kompagnihuset, a half-timbered guildhall (1493) and Apostelhuset (Apostles' House), built in the early 16th century. Its name derives from the figures of Christ and his 12 disciples placed between the windows.

Næstved's oldest building, however, is Helligåndhuset (House of the Holy Spirit), which dates from the 1300s and was used as a hospital and almshouse. It now houses part of the **Næstved Museum**, with a collection of medieval and contemporary woodcarvings. Another annex of the museum, in the Boderne houses near Sankt Peder Kirke, displays local handicrafts from the Holmegaard glass factory and nearby potteries (dating 1839–1970). The Løveapoteket (Pharmacy), on Axeltorv, dates back to 1640 – a herb garden is situated in the courtyard. Munkebakken Park (not far from Axeltorv) contains statues of seven monks which have been carved out of tree trunks.

English-style castle garden in Gavnø

Næstved Museum
Sankt Peders Kirkeplads 14. **Tel** 70 70 12 36. **Open** 10am–2pm Tue–Sat, 10am–4pm Sun.

7 Gavnø

Road map: E5. **Tel** 55 70 02 00. **Open** daily. Apr & early Aug–late Oct: 10am– 4pm; late Apr–late Jun: 10am–5pm; late Jun–early Aug: 10am–6pm. **gavnoe.dk**

Located a little way from Næstved and linked to Næstved by road, this tiny island had a castle used by pirates in the 12th century. In 1398 it was purchased by Queen Margrethe I, who established a convent here for unmarried women of noble rank. The convent church is said to be the most colourful church in Scandinavia.

Former Benedictine abbey in Næstved

Today Gavnø Castle is one of Denmark's finest Rococo castles with plenty to interest visitors. The art collection is the largest privately owned collection of paintings in Scandinavia. Also worth seeing are the Great Dining Room with its stunning French chandelier and the beautifully furnished guest rooms dating from the 1750s. The rooms are still used on special occasions.

Gavnø Castle Garden has been referred to as the most beautiful garden in Denmark. The grounds look spectacular in spring when there are displays of tulips and narcissus. The floral splendour continues into the autumn with a succession of summer flowers, rhododendrons, begonias, lilies and the beautifully landscaped rose garden at the northern end of the castle garden. In the centre of the garden is the "Skjærsommer" playhouse, which was built for the little Baroness Julie Reedtz-Thott in 1846. A part of the private doll collection is exhibited here. The gardens also have a butterfly house, a pirate-themed nature playground and a treasure hunt for both children and adults.

8 Vordingborg

Road map: F6. 9,300. Slotsruinen 1. **Tel** 55 34 11 11. **visitvordingborg.dk**

Vordingborg is on the strait between Zealand and Falster that leads to the Baltic, and was once Denmark's most important town. It was the royal residence of Valdemar I (The Great) who came to the throne in 1157 and built a castle here, ushering in a period of relative peace in the country's history. In 1241

Valdemar II sanctioned the Jutland Code in Vordingborg, which gave Denmark its first written laws. Subsequent monarchs from the Valdemar dynasty also took a liking to the castle and enlarged it over the years. The final length of its defensive wall was 800 m (2,625 ft) and its imposing appearance was emphasized by nine mighty towers.

Most of the towers are now in ruins except for the 14th-century Gåsetårnet (Goose Tower). This 36-m (118-ft) high tower has walls that are 3.5 m (11.5 ft) thick in places. Its name dates back to 1368 when Valdemar IV placed a golden goose on top of the tower in order to express his belief that the Hanseatic League's declaration of war was no more threatening than the cackling of geese. Though it has been modified, Gåsetårnet is important as the only intact building to remain from the Valdemar era. The building opposite the tower houses the remodelled **Danmarks Borgcenter** (Danish Castle Centre), which has displays on the castle's history and the three kings who lived there.

The 14th-century Gåsetårnet in Vordingborg

Algade is Vordingborg's main street and has been pedestrianized. It leads to Vor Frue Kirke (Church of Our Lady), a 15th-century church which contains a Baroque altarpiece dating from 1642.

Environs

The **Kalvehave Labyrintpark** features several exciting outdoor mazes and an area with brain-teasers and puzzles.

Goose Tower & Danmarks Borgcenter
Open 10am–5pm daily.
danmarksborgcenter.dk

Kalvehave Labyrintpark
Hovvejen 12, Kalvehave. **Tel** 55 34 47 71. **Open** May & Jun: 10am–5pm Sat & Sun; Jul–mid-Aug: 10am–6pm daily; mid-Aug-early Sep: 10am– 4pm daily; 10–18 Oct: 10am–5pm daily.
kalvehave-labyrintpark.dk

9 Knudshoved Odde

Road map: E5. The peninsula can be reached by car, from Oreby.

The narrow strip of the Knudshoved Odde peninsula is 20 km (12 miles) long and only 1 km (half a mile) at its widest point. The peninsula is owned by the Rosenfeldt Estate, which has managed to preserve the unique landscape. There are no towns or villages here, and the only road is closed to motor traffic after about 10 km (6 miles). This inaccessibility makes the Knudshoved Odde peninsula popular with people who wish to get away from it all and relax by indulging in simple activities such as sitting on the seashore, gathering blackberries and exploring the woods (which can be reached by foot from the car park halfway along the peninsula where the trail begins). The wood's marked walking trails are not taxing and range in distance from a short stroll to one that is just under 4 km (2 miles).

The peninsula is also known for its Neolithic burial mounds. One of these historic graves, which was dug about 5,500 years ago, can be seen close to the car park. Excavations have established that its ancient occupant was provided with all possible necessities for the after-life, including plenty of food and drink.

10 Sakskøbing

Road map: E6. Lolland. 4,700.
Torvet 4. **Tel** 54 70 56 30 (Jun–Sep).

One of Lolland's oldest settlements, Sakskøbing has few historic remains other than a Romanesque church (13th century). However, in view of the town's location on the E47, the main road linking Zealand to Falster and Lolland, it is a popular stopping-off point. The town's most striking feature is a water tower that resembles a smiling face. A distinctive landmark in the market square is the monument erected in 1939 for the Polish men and women who worked in the local fields. The town's links with Poland date back to the end of the 19th century when many Poles came here in search of work. Many settled permanently and some local Catholic churches still celebrate mass in Polish.

Monument to Polish workers in Sakskøbing

Shores of the Knudshoved Odde peninsula

⓬ Knuthenborg Safari Park

Knuthenborg Safari Park provides the chance to see such exotic creatures as zebras, camels, antelopes and giraffes. The parkland itself has been in the hands of the same family since the 17th century. It was landscaped in an English style in the 19th century and the first animals were transported by ship from Kenya in 1969. Today there are more than 1,000 animals. The park's botanical garden contains many rare trees and shrubs, and there is an attractive lake area that is ideal for picnics.

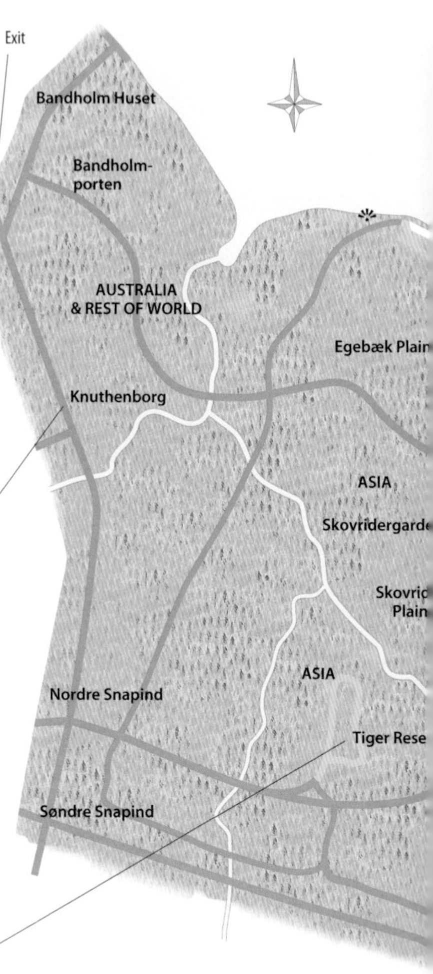

★ **Knuthenborg**
The house is surrounded by English-style parkland and was designed by Edward Milner. It bears clear signs of a Victorian influence. The main building is still inhabited by the Knuth family and closed to the public.

★ **Tiger Reserve**
The pride of the park are the Siberian tigers, the largest of all tigers. They enjoy bathing, which is unusual for cats. The deep marks visible on the trees in the reserve have been left by the tigers' sharp claws.

Congo Splash ride
The exhilarating Congo Splash ride allows visitors to experience the park from 16 m (52 ft) up in the air then take the plunge on Denmark's highest waterslide. Riders are guaranteed to get wet so towels and spare clothes are recommended.

Zebras
The zebras are allowed to roam freely and mingle with other animals in the park. They can run at speeds of up to 60 km/h (40 mph) when startled.

VISITORS' CHECKLIST

Practical Information
Road map: E6. Knuthenborg, Bandholm. Lolland. **Tel** 54 78 80 89. **Open** end Apr–early Sep: daily; early Sep–early Oct: Sat & Sun; for opening hours, visit the website.
W knuthenborg.dk

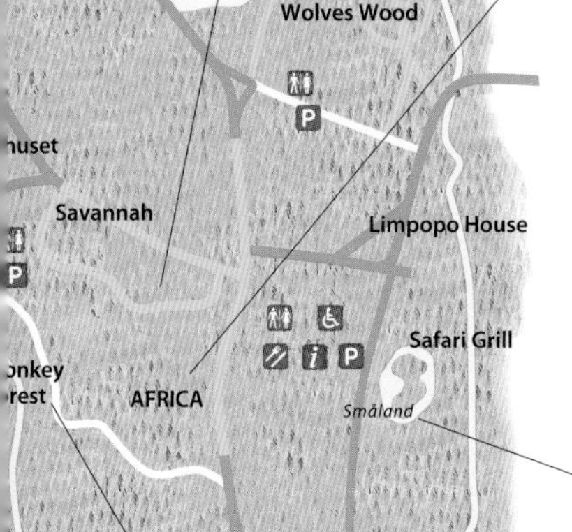

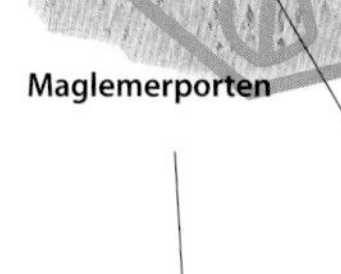

Giraffes
The giraffe can grow up to 5.5 m (18 ft) in height. The park's giraffes can sometimes be seen bending, with legs wide apart, to drink water.

Småland
This park for children in the old orchard features a water playground with geysers, water cannons and much more. There are also climbing courses, swings, playhouses and a formidable suspension bridge.

Cape Baboons
Take a free ride on a bus through the baboons' area, and watch them jump on and off the ride with you.

Half-timbered houses in Maribo

⓫ Maribo

Road map: E6. Lolland. 6,000. Torvet 1, Det Gamle Rådhus. **Tel** 54 78 04 96. **visitlolland-falster.com**

Situated on the northern shore of Maribo Søndersø, the largest of four inland lakes, Maribo is Lolland's commercial centre. The town was founded in 1416 by Erik of Pomerania and soon acquired a Gothic cathedral. All that remains of an original convent and monastery complex are the cathedral's bells (that toll six times a day) and a gallery where the nuns used to pray. The convent was dissolved following the Reformation.

The cathedral is located a short way from Torvet, the town's main square, which contains a 19th-century Neo-Classical town hall and several half-timbered houses.

Maribo has two museums, which offer separate, as well as joint admission fees. The **Lolland-Falster Stiftsmuseet** has a collection of church art and displays relating to Polish workers. **Frilandsmuseet**, a short way southwest of Maribo, is an open-air museum with a number of period cottages, as well as other buildings, including a windmill, a school and a smithy.

Lolland-Falster Stiftsmuseet
Frisegade 40. **Tel** 54 84 44 00.
Open 11am–4pm Thu–Sat.

Frilandsmuseet
Meinckesvej. **Tel** 54 84 44 00. **Open** May–Sep: 10am–4pm Tue–Sun.

⓬ Knuthenborg Safari Park

See pp164–5.

⓭ Nakskov

Road map: E6. Lolland. 14,000. Axeltorv 3. **Tel** 54 92 21 72.

Nakskov's origins date back to the 13th century. A reminder of its medieval past is the tower of Sankt Nikolai Kirke (Church), which rises above the old quarter. The oldest of Nakskov's houses are Dronningens Pakhus, a quayside warehouse that was built in 1590 and, at Tilegade 21, Den Gamle Smedje, a smithy where visitors can see a blacksmith working with 200-year-old tools.

Most of Denmark's sugar beet is grown on Lolland. Housed in a former factory, **Denmark's Sugar Museum** tells the story of the crop and the Polish immigrants who arrived to work in the fields.

There are 20 small islands in Nakskov Fjord, some of them inhabited. Post and other goods are still delivered using the **Postbåden**, a small boat that also welcomes tourists on its route (Jun–Aug). The route varies, but it always stops for a 1-hour lunch break at Albuen (The Elbow), an area with numerous natural attractions. It is well worth paying a little extra and bringing a bike; after cycling around one of the islands, you can catch another boat back to Nakskov. In addition to the daily morning excursions, there are also trips just before sundown.

Environs

Købelevhaven, about 6 km (4 miles) north of Nakskov, is a Japanese-style botanical garden. Established in 1975, it has a large rhododendron collection, a Japanese garden and some rare magnolia and Asian trees.

Denmark's Sugar Museum
Løjtoftevej 22. **Tel** 54 92 36 44.
Open Oct–May: 1–4pm Sat; Jun–Sep: 1–4pm Tue–Sun.
sukkermuseet.dk

Postbåden
Havnegade 2. **Tel** 54 93 12 36.
Open Jun–Aug: 9am daily.

Købelevhaven
Oddevej 116, Købelev. **Tel** 54 93 20 87.
Open May–Aug: 10am–5pm Tue–Sun.
koebelevhaven.dk

⓮ Lalandia

Road map: E6. Lolland. Rødby, Lalandiacentret 1. **Tel** 54 61 05 00.
lalandia.dk

Many families come to Lalandia – Denmark's largest holiday centre – for a short break. The resort is on the southern coast of Lolland and offers numerous attractions to visitors. The local beach competes for children's attention with the aquapark where swimming pools and slides are surrounded by artificial lakes and tropical vegetation. Regardless of the outside temperature, the water in the pools never falls below 28° C (82° F). For sports enthusiasts, there are tennis courts, a golf course, mini-golf, and, in the case of bad weather,

Palm trees enliven the aquapark area at Lalandia

Display in Polakkasernen, Tågerup

a vast leisure complex that includes a gymnasium, bowling alleys, amusement arcades and indoor tennis.

Visitors to Lalandia can stay in apartments that sleep up to eight people. All of the apartments have their own bathrooms and kitchens. There are also numerous restaurants and bars spread around the holiday complex.

⓯ Tågerup

Road map: E6. Lolland.

The main attraction of Tågerup, a small village situated a short way south of Maribo, is its Romanesque-Gothic church, which contains some fine 15th-century frescoes. At the entrance to the church is a runic stone. Many visitors are surprised to find a building displaying the Polish flag. This is **Polakkasernen**, or the Polish Barracks, and contains documents, fragments of diaries and various items left by Polish immigrants who from 1893 began arriving in Lolland in great numbers. Many Poles were on the move for political reasons as the Soviet Union had taken control of Poland. There were also economic reasons, however, and immigrants arrived from Poland between 1870 and 1920 in a bid to escape a feudal system that gave them few legal rights. Once they arrived, most Poles found employment as labourers in the local sugar-beet fields.

A short way from Polakkasernen is **Lungholm Gods**, an early 15th-century residence with English-style landscaped grounds. The house is now used as a conference centre and spa. The footpaths around it are ideal for a pleasant ramble.

Polakkasernen
Højbygårsvej 34. **Tel** 54 78 23 30. **Open** Easter, Whitsun, Jul–Aug: 2–4pm Tue–Sun.

Lungholm Gods
Rødbyvej 24. **Tel** 54 60 02 53.

⓰ Nysted

Road map: E6. Lolland. 1,500.

This small harbour town situated on the Rødsand bay was founded in the 13th century. Nysted's main historic monuments are a large Gothic church dating from the early 14th century, and a much later 17th-century tower. There are also a number of half-timbered houses and a water tower, which now serves as a viewpoint.

Environs

Ålholm Slot (Castle) is on the outskirts of Nysted and dates from the 12th century. It was crown property for many years and the rooms contain many royal furnishings. In 1332 Christian II was held prisoner in the dungeons here on the orders of his half-brother. The castle is now in private hands and is not open to the public.

About 3 km (2 miles) north of Nysted is **Kettinge**, a small village with an old Dutch windmill and a church containing magnificent frescoes dating from around 1500.

⓱ Fuglsang Kunstmuseum

Road map: E6. Nystedvej 71, Toreby, Lolland. **Tel** 54 78 14 14. **Open** Apr–May & Sep–Oct: 11am–4pm Tue–Sun; Jun–Aug: 11am–4pm daily; Nov–Mar: 11am–4pm Wed–Sun.
fuglsangkunstmuseum.dk

Located in the grounds of Fuglsang Manor, between Nysted and Nykøbing F, this art museum was designed by the British architect Tony Fretton. The modern white building provides a stark contrast to the green rural landscape. Inside is a collection of Danish art from the 18th century onwards, with a focus on art from 1850 until 1950. Golden Age painters such as P.C. Skovgaard and Kristian Zahrtmann are represented, as are the Funen artists, painters from the Skagen School and the CoBrA group *(see pp30-31)*.

Ålholm Slot seen from the water

NA
RVM
TOLLUNT:
REGIA:

Woman dressed in period costume at Middelaldercentret

18 Middelalder-centret

Road map: E6. Lolland. Sundby, Ved Hamborgskoven 2. **Tel** 54 86 19 34. **Open** May & Sep: 10am–4pm Tue–Sun; Jun & Aug: 10am–4pm daily; Jul: 10am–5pm daily.
middelaldercentret.dk

Lolland's Middle Ages Centre is a recreated medieval settlement that provides an insight into what life was like in the 14th century. Crafts and games from medieval times are displayed and explained by staff wearing costumes from the period, while the local inn serves a range of "medieval" food. A replica sailing ship lies in the harbour and a huge wooden catapult is ready for firing. Jousting tournaments are a regular feature in summer, and visitors can also try their hand at archery. A marked walking trail in the nearby forest explains medieval customs and includes a site where charcoal is made. Along the walk, visitors are warned about woodland spirits and are invited to throw a ghost-repelling stick at an appropriate spot – just in case.

The centre can easily be reached from Nykøbing F by crossing the bridge that connects Lolland and Falster.

19 Nykøbing F

Road map: F6. Falster. 16,500. Langgade 2. **Tel** 54 85 13 03.
visitlolland-falster.com

Falster's largest town and capital city was a busy commercial centre in medieval times and was granted municipal status in the early 13th century by Valdemar II. In order to distinguish it from two other Danish towns of the same name, this Nykøbing is followed by the letter F (standing for Falster).

Nykøbing F's main historic sight is a 15th-century brick church, which once formed part of a Franciscan monastery. Its richly decorated interior includes an eye-catching series of portraits of Queen Sophie (wife of Frederik II) together with her family, which were commissioned in 1627. Another notable sight is the half-timbered Czarens Hus (Tsar's House), which is one of the oldest buildings in town. In 1716 the Russian Tsar, Peter the Great, stopped here overnight on his way to Copenhagen. Today, the building is used as a restaurant and also houses a local history museum – **Falsters Minder**. Among the museum's exhibits are some reconstructed interiors including an 18th-century peasant cottage and a 19th-century burgher's house.

The most panoramic view of Nybøking F is from the early 20th-century yellow water tower. The town's **Guldborgsund Zoo** is a little way east of the train station and has a variety of animals including deer, monkeys, donkeys and goats.

Statue of a bear in Nykøbing F

Falsters Minder
Falsters Minder Færgestræde 1a.
Tel 54 85 13 03. **Open** 10am–4pm Tue–Fri, 10am–2pm Sat (Jul–Sep: 10am–5pm Mon–Fri, 10am–2pm Sat).

Guldborgsund Zoo
Øster Alle 92. **Tel** 54 85 20 76.
Open May–mid-Oct: 9am–5pm daily; mid-Oct–Apr: 10am–4pm daily.
guldborgsundzoo.dk

20 Eskilstrup

Road map: F6. Falster.

This small town is situated a short distance from the E47 motorway and has two rather unusual museums. The **Traktormuseum** is housed in a multi-storey brick building and contains over 200 tractors and engines dating from 1880 to 1960. Alongside a wide selection of vintage Fiats, Fords, Volvos and Fergusons are rare

Nykøbing F, as seen from the river

◄ A 13th-century fresco in the cupola of St Benedict

Beautiful white beaches around Marielyst

Czechoslovakian and Romanian tractors. The oldest tractor in the museum is American and was built in 1917. There is also a steam traction engine built in England in 1889. Until 1925 it was still being used as a threshing machine. A number of small pedal-tractors are also provided for the amusement of children.

About 3 km (2 miles) from the town centre is the **Krokodille Zoo**. This is the largest collection of crocodiles in Europe and includes 21 of the 23 species of these sharp-toothed reptiles that exist worldwide. The smallest among them is the dwarf cayman, which grows up to 159 cm (62 in) in length. At the other end of the scale, the zoo's giant Nile crocodile is called Samson and is currently the largest crocodile in Scandinavia.

As well as the many crocodiles, the zoo also contains a variety of other species including a green anaconda (the world's largest snake), turtles, tortoises and a number of rare clouded leopards. The zoo donates a percentage of the admission price to an international programme of scientific research and protection associated with crocodiles living in the wild.

Traktormuseum
Nørregade 17B. **Tel** 54 43 70 07.
Open Jun & Sep: 10am–4pm Tue–Fri, 10am–3pm Sat & Sun; Jul & Aug: 10am–5pm daily.
traktormuseum.dk

Krokodille Zoo
Ovstrupvej 9. **Tel** 54 45 42 42. **Open** mid-Jun–Aug: 10am–5pm daily; Sep–mid-Jun: noon–4pm Tue–Sun. **Closed** Jan, Dec. **krokodillezoo.dk**

21 Marielyst

Road map: F6. Falster. Marielyst Strandpark 3. **Tel** 54 13 62 98.
visitlolland-falster.com

Situated on the eastern end of the island, Marielyst gets its revenue mainly from its many summer visitors and is one of the foremost holiday resorts in the whole of Denmark. One of the main attractions is the fine white sand beach, which is a good length and easily accessible. It also benefits from clean and fairly shallow waters. The dunes running parallel to the coastline are an additional attraction and are fringed by an ancient beech forest. There are plenty of shops, restaurants and bars. Along with camp sites, guesthouses and hotels the town also has about 6,000 summer cottages.

Environs
Just south of Marielyst is the **Bøtø Nor bird sanctuary** where a variety of birds can be spotted including cranes, ospreys and plovers.

22 Væggerløse

Road map: F6. Falster. 

The small town of Væggerløse, situated a little way south of Nykøbing F, has an 18th-century windmill, which now houses a glass-blowing workshop, and ceiling paintings from the late Middle Ages in the church. Another nearby attraction is the **Sports Car Museum**. Road signs direct drivers to a private farmstead where one of the buildings houses a collection of motor cars. Although not as large as the car museum found at Ålholm Slot near Nysted on Lolland *(see p167)*, it is still worth visiting as it contains some interesting exhibits. Among the 65 vehicles on display are a 1917 Adler (which was capable of reaching the giddy speed of 35 km/h/ 22 mph), as well as a Jaguar (which could travel as fast as 240 km/h/149 mph).

Sports Car Museum
Stovby Tværvej 11. **Tel** 54 17 75 89.
Open 10am–5pm daily.
boesminde.dk

A zoo keeper at the Krokodille Zoo picking eggs from a nest.

Lime-based paintings in Fanefjord Kirke, painted around 1500–1520

㉓ Fanefjord Kirke

Road map: F6. Fanefjord Kirkevej 49, Askeby. **Open** 8am–6pm daily.
fanefjordkirke.dk

The small church of Fanefjord stands on top of an isolated hillock surrounded by green fields. It provides an excellent viewpoint and from here it is possible to look out over the Baltic and the island of Falster. Local folklore tells that the Gothic church derives its name from the Fanefjord bay, whose waters come close to the building. The fjord was in turn named after Queen Fane, wife of King Grøn Jæger, local rulers in the late Stone Age.

Built about 1250, the church was at that time far too big for the needs of the 300 or so parishioners, but its builders took into account worshippers from ships anchoring in the bay as this was a busy harbour in the Middle Ages. According to records it was probably here that Bishop Absalon gathered his fleet before embarking on his raids against the Wends on the south coast of the Baltic Sea.

Fanefjord Kirke is famous in Denmark for its frescoes. The oldest of them date from around 1350 and include an image of St Christopher carrying the infant Jesus. The later paintings date from the mid-15th century and include frescoes painted in warm colours by the Elmelunde master, an artist about whom virtually nothing is known. His mark, which is an arrow with a cross line, can be seen on one of the ribs of the first arch in the northeastern vault. A collection of votive ships hangs in the church. The oldest is a barquentine hanging above the entrance which commemorates a tragic shipwreck off the north coast of Møn.

㉔ Kong Asgers Høj

Road map: F6. Møn.

King Asgers mounds, located in a farmer's field near the village of Røddinge, are all that remain of Denmark's largest passage grave.

The Stone Age corridor consists of an 8-m (26-ft) long underground passage that leads to a large chamber, 10 m (33 ft) long by 2 m (6.5 ft) wide. It is dark inside, so it is advisable to take a torch.

Corridor leading to the burial chamber of Kong Asgers Høj

Environs

A short way south of Kong Asgers Høj stands yet another burial mound – the **Klekkendehøj**, which has two entrances placed side by side. The chamber is 7 m (23 ft) long. The mound has been restored and is now illuminated.

At the south end of Møn is **Grønjægers Høj**, another highly unusual tomb that is estimated to be about 4,000 years old. The burial site is one of the largest dolmens in Denmark and consists of 134 weighty stones arranged in an oval shape. According to one local legend, the site is the final resting place of Queen Fane and her husband, Grøn Jæger.

Chalk crags of Møns Klint, rising from the waters of the Baltic

㉕ Møns Klint

Road map: F6. Møn.

The white chalk cliffs soaring above the Baltic are one of Møn's main attractions. The cliffs are about 70 million years old and are formed mostly of calcareous shells. Stretching over a distance of about 7 km (4 miles), the crags reach 128 m (420 ft) in height to form a striking landscape. The highest point is near Dronningestolen (Queen's Throne). At one time these cliffs were mined for chalk but they are now a legally protected zone. **Geocenter Møns Klint**, a visitors' centre close to the cliffs, comprises geological exhibitions and hands-on activities. There is also a 3D-cinema and café.

After a clifftop hike many people head inland to explore Klinteskoven (Klint Forest), where about 20 types of orchid can be seen flowering from May to August.

Klintholm Havn is a port south of the cliffs. In the 19th century it was a private estate and later taken over by the local authorities. Small pleasure boats leave for 2-hour cruises from here and are a good way to take in the stunning coastal scenery.

Geocenter Møns Klint
Stengårdsvej 8, Borre. **Tel** 55 86 36 00. **Open** Apr–Oct: 11am–5pm daily (Jul–mid-Aug: 10am–6pm).
moensklint.dk

One of Stege's quieter shopping streets

㉖ Liselund Slot

Road map: F6. Møn. Palace: Langebjergvej 4. **Tel** 55 81 21 78. May–Sep: 10:30am, 11am, 1:30pm & 2pm Wed–Sun. free admission to the park. **liselundslot.dk**

The diminutive palace of Liselund was once crown property. A subsequent owner gave the building its present name in honour of his wife. The house is set in a large park, and its whitewashed walls are reflected in the waters of a small lake. The fairytale atmosphere is enhanced by the immaculate thatch on the building's roof (locals joke that this is the world's only thatched-roof palace). Liselund Ny Slot (New Castle), a 19th-century building in the midst of the estate, is now a hotel.

Sun dial at Liselund Slot

㉗ Elmelunde

Road map: F6. Møn. Churches in Emelunde and Keldby: **Open** May–Sep: 8am–5pm daily; Oct–Apr: 8am–4pm daily.
keldbyelmelundekirke.dk

Along with its famous cliffs, Møn boasts a number of churches with highly original frescoes. One of them can be visited in Elmelunde; another in Keldby, a little to the west. Built around 1075, the church in Elmelunde is one of the oldest stone churches in Denmark. The frescoes date from the 14th and 15th centuries and were whitewashed during the Reformation. Ironically this only served to preserve the paintings from fading. They were restored in the 20th century under the guidance of Copenhagen's Nationalmuseet (National Museum).

The frescoes depict scenes from the Old and New Testaments and include images of Christ and the saints as well as lively portrayals of demons and the flames of hell. Most of them are attributed to one artist, known simply as the Elmelunde Master. The paintings served to explain biblical stories to illiterate peasants and are characterized by their quirky static figures with blank faces devoid of any emotion. More frescoes can be seen in Keldby Kirke, which also has a sumptuously carved 16th-century pulpit.

Medieval fresco in Stege Kirke

㉘ Stege

Road map: F6. Møn. 4,000. Storegade 2. **Tel** 55 86 04 00.
visitmoen.com

Møn's commercial centre, Stege grew up around a castle built in the 12th century and reached the height of its power in the Middle Ages, when it prospered thanks to a lucrative herring industry. A reminder of those days is Mølleporten (Mill Gate), which spans the main street of the town and once served as Stege's principal entrance. Ramparts belonging to the fortress walls are another medieval relic. **Empiregården**, Stege's museum, is a short way from Mølleporten and has local history exhibits.

Stege Kirke is in the town centre. This Romanesque church was built by Jakob Sunesen, who ruled Møn in the 13th century. Its ceiling frescoes were painted over during the Reformation and exposed again in the 19th century.

Empiregården
Storegade 75. **Tel** 70 70 12 36. **Open** varies; check website.
empiregaarden.dk

Nyord island's meadows, with marshland beyond

29 Nyord

Road map: F5.

Until the late 1980s, the only way to reach the small island of Nyord was by boat. A bridge, built in 1986, now links Nyord with Møn and has made the island more accessible and so increasingly popular with visitors. Nevertheless, both the island and the pretty hamlet of the same name have changed little since the 19th century. Nyord is particularly favoured by bird-watchers – its salt marshes attract massive flocks of birds, especially in spring and autumn, when the island is used as a stopping-off place for winged migrants. The most numerous among them include arctic terns, curlews and swans. The birds can be best viewed from an observation tower situated near the bridge.

30 Fakse

Road map: F5. Postvej 3, Fakse Ladeplads. **Tel** 56 71 60 34. **visitfaxe.dk**

References to Fakse (also known as Faxe) can be found in late 13th-century records when it was an important area for limestone mining. Today the town is best known for its local brewery, Faxe Bryggeri, which produces over 130 million litres (28.6 million gallons) of beer each year.

The town's most historic building is the 15th-century Gothic church, which has a number of wall paintings dating from around 1500. **Geomuseum Faxe** has a collection of over 500 types of fossils including some 63 million-year-old remains of plants and animals found in the Fakse Kalkbrud quarry about 2 km (1 mile) outside the town. Visitors can collect their own fossils from the quarry.

Geomuseum Faxe
Kulturhuset Kanten, Østervej 2.
Tel 56 50 28 06. **Open** Apr, May, Sep & Oct: 1–4:30pm Tue–Sun; Jun–Aug: 11am–4:30pm daily; Nov–Mar: 1–4:30pm Sat & Sun. **Closed** Mon in Jul.

Fakse's brewery, producing millions of gallons of beer a year

31 Stevns Klint

Road map: F5. Rødvig, Havnevej 21. **Tel** 56 50 64 64. **visitstevns.dk**

Although Denmark's most famous cliffs are found on Møn, the limestone peninsula of Stevns Klint (a UNESCO World Heritage site) is as impressive. The cliffs from Rødvig to the harbour off Bøgeskov under the estate off Gjorslev where there is a 15th-century Gothic castle are the most picturesque, especially when the sun glints against the white chalk surface.

The area was for centuries known for its limestone quarries, which supplied building material for the first castle built by Bishop Absalon in Copenhagen; this castle became the nucleus of the royal residence, which in later times was given the name of Christiansborg Slot *(see pp90–1)*. Large-scale limestone quarrying was abandoned in the 1940s.

The strip of coastal cliffs is about 15 km (9 miles) long and 22 m (72 ft) tall. The best viewpoint can be found next to the old church of Højerup (Højerup Kirke). Legend has it that this 13th-century edifice, built close to the cliff's edge, moves inland each Christmas Eve by the length of a cockerel's jump.

Another local myth recounts a story about a king of the cliffs who lives in a cave in a crag south of the church. The king of the cliffs failed, however, to save the church from the destructive forces of nature. Over the years, due to constant erosion, the sea has advanced closer and closer towards the church and in 1928 the presbytery collapsed and crashed into the water.

A short distance from the church is the small town of Højerup. Here, the **Stevns Museum** has a local-history collection that includes workshops, Stone-Age tools, antique toys and a collection of fire-fighting equipment from the past including pumps and fire engines. There is also an exhibition dealing with the geology of the local cliffs.

Limestone cliffs of Stevns Klint on Zealand's east coast

Environs
A few kilometres inland is **Store Heddinge**, with one of Zealand's best Romanesque churches. The 12th-century church is made from limestone excavated in the nearby quarries. Its octagonal shape probably made it easier to defend.

Stevns Museum
Højerup Bygade 38, 4660 Store Heddinge. **Tel** 56 50 28 06. **Open** May, Jun, Aug, Sep: 11am–5pm Tue–Sun; Jul: 11am–5pm daily.

Vallø Slot, a moated 16th-century castle

32 Vallø Slot

Road map: F5. **Tel** 56 26 05 00. Castle: **Closed** to visitors, but it is possible to explore the courtyard 10am–6pm daily. Garden: 8am–sunset daily.

The secluded castle of Vallø is one of the most impressive Renaissance buildings in Denmark. As early as the 15th century the islet was surrounded by a moat and featured a complex of defensive buildings. The castle owes its present shape to the influence of two enterprising sisters, Mette and Birgitte Rosenkrantz, who in the 16th century owned the surrounding land. The sisters divided the estate in equal shares between themselves – the east part was managed by Birgitte, while the western section belonged to Mette.

In 1737 the castle was taken over by a trust that provided a home for unmarried daughters of noble birth during their later years. The castle is closed to visitors. The large park is open, however, as is the former stable block, which houses a museum containing a mix of agricultural implements and equestrian accessories.

33 Køge

Road map: F5. 40,000.
Vestergade 1. **Tel** 56 67 60 01.
visitkoege.com

One of Denmark's best-preserved medieval towns, Køge was granted a municipal charter in 1288 and grew quickly thanks to its large natural harbour at the mouth of a navigable river. Køge Bay entered the annals of Danish history in 1677, when the Danish fleet, led by Admiral Niels Juel, crushed a Swedish armada heading for Copenhagen. The battle and the victorious Admiral Niels Juel are commemorated by a 9-m (30-ft) tall obelisk by the harbour.

The heart of the town is its market square, which contains a monument to Frederik VI. The town hall standing in the cobbled square is the longest-serving public building of its kind in Denmark. The cobbled streets leading from the market square are lined with half-timbered houses for which Køge is famous. The most interesting street in this respect is Kirkestræde. The small house at No. 20, with only two windows, is the oldest dated half-timbered house in Denmark; the beam under its front door gives the year of construction as 1527.

Kirkestræde 10, now part of Køge library

Another impressive historic building is Sankt Nicolai Kirke, which dates from 1324. Its tower served for many years as a lighthouse and is now used as a viewpoint.

Køge Museum is located along Nørregade and occupies two early-17th- century buildings. Its exhibits include historic furniture, costumes and, as a reminder of the town's bloody past, the local executioner's sword. By the harbour is Kjøge Mini-by, an exact miniature version of Køge as it was in 1865.

Køge Museum
Nørregade 4. **Tel** 56 63 42 42. **Open** Jun–Aug: 11am–5pm Tue–Sun; Sep–May: 1–5pm Mon–Fri & Sun, 11am–3pm Sat.

The Aristocratic Ladies of the Castle

In 1737, Vallø's owner, Queen Sophie Magdalene, donated the castle to the Royal Vallø Foundation. From then on the castle become a home for unmarried women from noble families. The famously religious queen ensured the typically cloistral character of the place and promoted a lifestyle true to Christian principles. Initially it housed 12 women, some of whom were as young as 15. The convent was run by a prioress of high birth, and the mother superior was also descended from an aristocratic family. The male staff, an administrator, doctor and servants, lived opposite the castle. Some unmarried ladies still reside in Vallø Slot.

The imposing twin towers of Vallø Slot

FUNEN

Funen (Fyn in Danish) is Denmark's second largest island and occupies an area of about 3,000 sq km (1,158 sq miles). It has some of Denmark's best scenery including wide, sandy beaches, steep cliffs and lush pasture land and orchards. A number of neighbouring islands are considered to be part of Funen including Ærø and Tåsinge, which are themselves popular destinations.

Funen is separated from Zealand by the Store Bælt (Great Belt) and from Jutland by the Lille Bælt (Little Belt). Nearly half of Funen's inhabitants live in Odense, which is the island's capital, a lively cultural centre and the birthplace of Hans Christian Andersen. Aside from Odense there are no large towns on Funen and the island is sometimes described as the "garden of Denmark" because of the large amount of produce that grows in its fertile soil.

Thanks to the fact that the island has escaped most of Denmark's wars with other nations, Funen has an exceptionally high number of well-preserved historic buildings and palaces. The best-known of these is Egeskov Slot, a Renaissance castle encircled by a moat.

The relatively small distances, gently rolling landscape and the many interesting places to visit, make Funen an ideal area for cycling trips. The south-western part of the island features a range of wooded hills. The highest of these, rising to 126 m (413 ft), are found near the town of Faaborg. Central Funen is mostly flat and only becomes slightly undulated in the northeastern region. The south has most of the island's harbours and towns, while the northern and western parts are sparsely populated.

An archipelago of southern islets includes Langeland, Ærø and Tåsinge as well as a number of tiny islands inhabited only by birds. This area is popular with Danish yachtsmen and it is possible to explore the archipelago by joining an organized cruise on board a wooden sailing ship. Some of the islands can be reached by ferry.

The imposing façade of Egeskov Slot, one of Denmark's finest castles

◀ Picturesque Dukkehuset (Dolls' House) in Ærøskøbing, on the island of Ærø

Exploring Funen

Funen is known as the garden of Denmark and for its windy roads and cosy half-timbered houses. Throughout the centuries the Danish aristocracy built their opulent residences on the island, and Funen has over 120 beautifully preserved mansions, castles and palaces. The most impressive are Egeskov Slot and, on Tåsinge, Valdemars Slot. Funen's coastline is 11,000 km (6,800 miles) long and has some beautiful beaches. The lovely island of Ærø is a picturesque place with tiny villages and ancient farms. Odense, Denmark's third-largest city, is a university town and the birthplace of Hans Christian Andersen.

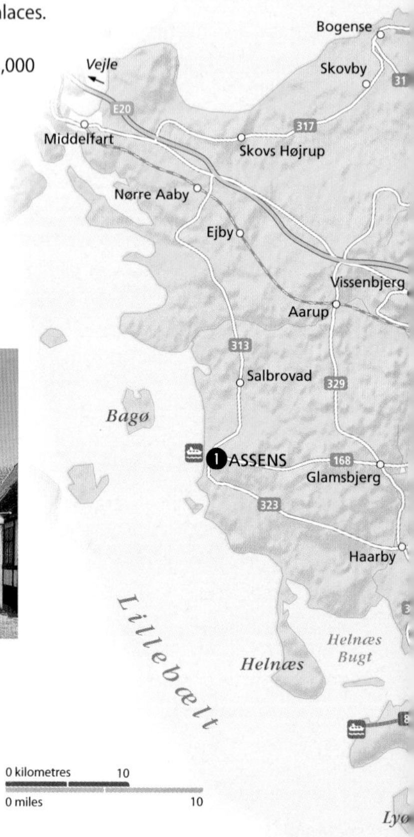

Bogense
Skovby
Vejle
E20
317
Middelfart
Skovs Højrup
Nørre Aaby
Ejby
Vissenbjerg
Aarup
313
Salbrovad
329
Bagø
1 ASSENS
168
Glamsbjerg
323
Haarby
Lillebælt
Helnæs
Helnæs Bugt
0 kilometres 10
0 miles 10

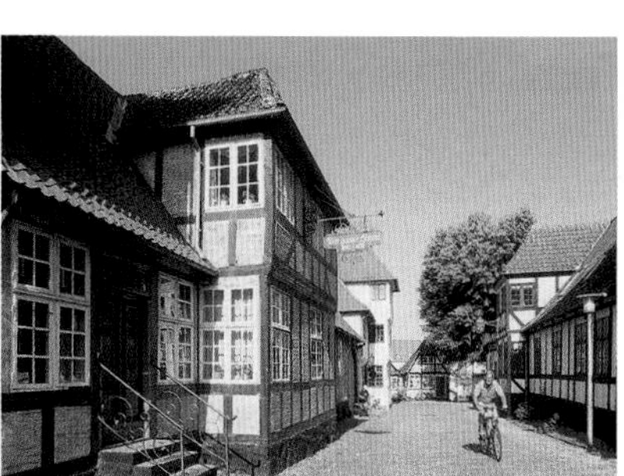

Den Gamle Gaard, a merchant's house in Faaborg

Key

- Motorway
- Major road
- Minor road
- Scenic route
- Main railway
- Minor railway

Sights at a Glance

1. Assens
2. *Odense pp182–3*
3. Kerteminde
4. Hindsholm
5. Nyborg
6. Egeskov Slot
7. Faaborg
8. Svendborg
9. Tåsinge
10. Langeland
11. Marstal
12. Ærøskøbing

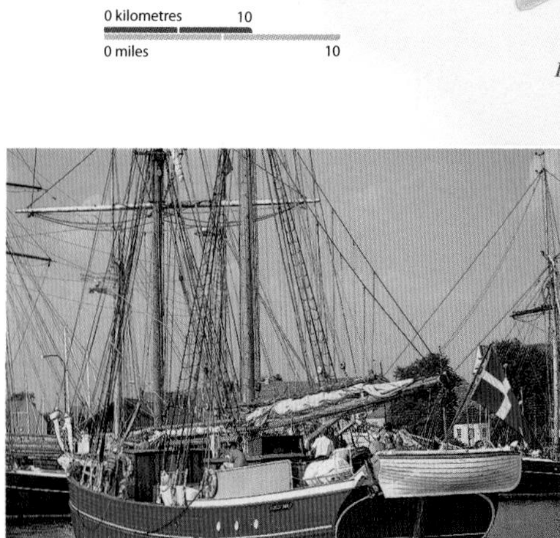

Traditional wooden boat moored in Svendborg harbour

For hotels and restaurants see pp248–55 and pp262–77

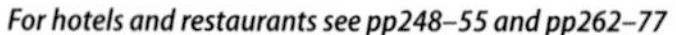

Imposing turrets and high walls of Egeskov Slot

Getting Around

Funen is linked to Jutland and Zealand by two bridges. There is a frequent (almost hourly) rail service from Copenhagen and Jutland. The island's main transport artery is the E20 motorway running from east to west (a railway line runs roughly parallel to this). The most important roads that lead from Odense towards other major towns are the No. 9 road to Svendborg and the No. 43 to Faaborg. Ferries sail to Ærø, while Langeland can be reached via a bridge.

For keys to symbols *see back flap*

Quiet yacht marina in Assens

❶ Assens

Road map: C5. 15,000.
Willemoesgade 15A. **Tel** 63 75 94 20. **visitassens.dk**

Situated on the shores of the Store Bælt (Great Belt), Assens was for centuries a busy harbour for ferries on the route between Funen and Jutland. Following the construction of a bridge across the strait, far north of the town, it lost its importance. Assens contains numerous historic buildings including 18th- and 19th-century merchants' houses, as well as the 15th-century Vor Frue Kirke (Church of Our Lady).

The best-known citizen of Assens was Peter Willemoes (1783–1808), a war hero who, in 1801, fought against Admiral Nelson during the Napoleonic Wars and distinguished himself during Nelson's bombardment of Copenhagen. Willemoes' birthplace, **Willemoesgården**, now houses a museum of cultural history. A monument to Willemoes has been erected near the harbour. A house by the monument was once a sailors' kitchen.

Nearby is the Ernsts Samlinger exhibition in the house of a local silversmith, Frederik Ernst, which has Denmark's largest collection of antique silver and glass.

Willemoesgården
Østergade 36. **Tel** 64 71 31 90.
Open Easter, May–mid-Oct: 10am–4pm Tue–Sun; mid-Oct–Apr: 10am–4pm Wed & Sat.

❷ Odense

See pp182–3.

❸ Kerteminde

Road map: D5. 5,500.
Hans Schacksvej 5. **Tel** 65 32 11 21. **visitkerteminde.dk**

Much of this pretty seaside town is clustered around the 15th-century Sankt Laurentius Kirke (Church). One of the town's main attractions is **Fjord&Bælt**, a sea-life centre built in 1997. A 50-m long tunnel with large windows allows visitors to walk beneath the fjord and enjoy the underwater view. The famous Danish painter Johannes Larsen (1867–1961) once lived in Kerteminde and the **Johannes Larsen Museum** contains many of his paintings.

Environs
Four kilometres (2 miles) south-west of Kerteminde is the **Ladbyskibet**, a 22-m (72-ft) long Viking ship that dates from the 10th century and was used as the tomb of a Viking chieftain.

Statue of St Laurentius, in Kerteminde

Fjord&Bælt
Margrethes Plads 1. **Tel** 65 32 42 00.
Open Feb–Nov: 10am–4pm Tue–Sun.
Closed Jan, Dec.
fjord-baelt.dk

Johannes Larsen Museum
Møllebakken 14. **Tel** 65 32 11 77.
Open Jun–Aug: 10am–5pm daily; Mar–May, Sep & Oct: 10am–4pm Tue–Sun; Nov–Feb: 11am–4pm Tue–Sun.
johanneslarsenmuseet.dk

❹ Hindsholm

Road map: D5.

Rising at the far end of the Hindsholm peninsula are 25-m (82-ft) high cliffs, which provide a splendid view over the coast and the island of Samsø. A little way inland is Marhøj knoll, a 2nd-century BC underground burial chamber.

The small town of Viby, north of Assens, has a 19th-century windmill and an Early-Gothic church. According to legend, Marsk Stig, a hero of Danish folklore, was buried here in 1293. Before setting off for war, Marsk Stig is said to have left his wife in the care of the king, Erik Klipping. The king took the notion of "care" somewhat too far and when the knight returned he killed the king and was outlawed. Even his funeral had to be held in secret.

Crops growing on the Hindsholm peninsula

Royal painting and suits of armour in the Knights' Hall, Nyborg Slot

❺ Nyborg

Road map: D5. 16,000.
Adelgade 3, 63 33 80 90.
visitnyborg.dk

The castle of **Nyborg Slot** was built around 1170 by Valdemar the Great's nephew as part of the fortifications that guarded the Store Bælt. For nearly 200 years the castle was the scene of the Danehof assemblies (an early form of Danish parliament). As a result, the city is considered to have been Denmark's capital from 1183 to 1413. The castle was also the venue of the signing, in 1282, of a coronation charter that laid down the duties of the king. Nyborg grew up around this fortress. Over the centuries the castle gradually fell into ruin; it was only after World War I that it was restored and turned into a museum. A number of rooms are open to the public including the royal chambers and the Danehof room. The castle ramparts and moat are now a park.

Nyborg Church, built in the late 14th century, has just one artifact from this time: a Gothic crucifix that is decorated to represent the Tree of Life.

During July and August, on Tuesdays at about 7pm, the Tappenstreg regiment marches through the streets of Nyborg. This regiment upholds an 18th-century tradition of checking whether all the town's entertainment venues have closed on time.

Nyborg Slot
Slotsgade 34. **Tel** 65 31 02 07.
Open Apr, May, Sep & Oct: 10am–3pm Tue–Sun; Jun–Aug: 10am–4pm daily. **nyborgslot.dk**

❻ Egeskov Slot

Road map: D5. Egeskov Gade 18, Kværndrup. **Tel** 62 27 10 16.
Open May & Sep–early Oct: 10am–5pm daily; Jun–Aug: 10am–6pm daily (1 Jul–9 Aug: to 7pm).
egeskov.dk

This magnificent castle was built in the mid-16th century and is one of Denmark's best-known sights. Egeskov means "oak forest" and the castle was built in the middle of a pond on a foundation of oak trees. The interior has some grand rooms containing antique furniture and paintings, and a hall full of hunting trophies that include elephant tusks and tiger heads.

Much of the grounds were laid out in the 18th century and include a garden adorned with various fountains, as well as a herb garden. Other additions to the layout are a bamboo maze and a vintage car museum.

Coat of arms from Egeskov Slot

❼ Faaborg

Road map: D5. 8,000.
Torvet 19, 63 75 94 44.
visitfaaborg.dk

Faaborg is a picturesque place with cobbled streets and half-timbered houses. The market square contains the town's most famous monument, Ymerbrønden, produced by the Danish painter and sculptor Kai Nielsen in the early 1900s. Its main figure is Ymer, a giant who according to Nordic mythology was killed by Odin.

The view from the 31-m (102-ft) tall Klokketårnet (Belfry) embraces the bay. The tower is all that remains of a medieval church.

Den Gamle Gaard is a wealthy merchant's house that dates from 1725.

Faaborg Museum, designed by Carl Petersen, has a number of works by the "De Fynske Malere" group of Danish artists, which included the likes of Peter Hansen, Johannes Larsen and Fritz Syberg.

Den Gamle Gaard
Holkegade 1. **Tel** 63 61 20 00. **Open** check website for latest information on opening hours.
ohavsmuseet.dk

Faaborg Museum
Grønnegade 75. **Tel** 62 61 06 45.
Open Apr, May, Sep & Oct: 10am–4pm Tue–Sun; Jun–Aug: 10am–4pm daily (to 6pm Wed); Nov–Mar: 11am–3pm Tue–Sun.
faaborgmuseum.dk

Collection of Danish art in Faaborg Museum

❷ Odense

One of the oldest cities in Denmark, Odense derives its name from the Nordic god Odin who was worshipped by the Vikings. In medieval times it was an important centre of trade and from the 12th century on it was a major pilgrimage destination. Since the 19th century, when a canal was built linking Odense with the sea, the city has been a major port. Odense has a rich cultural life and plenty to see including a cathedral and a museum devoted to the city's most famous son, Hans Christian Andersen.

Exploring Odense
Most attractions lie within the boundaries of the medieval district. Getting around Odense is made easy by the Citypass, which entitles the holder to free travel, free admission to museums and cut-price tickets for boat cruises.

Brandts

Brandts Passage 37–43. Mediemuseet: **Tel** 65 20 70 10. **Open** see website for opening hours. **Closed** Mon (except for weeks 7, 8 & 42). Museet for Fotokunst: **Tel** 65 20 70 10. **Open** see website for opening hours. Kunsthallen Brandts: **Tel** 65 20 70 10. **Open** see website for opening hours. **brandts.dk**

For more than fifty years Brandt's textile factory was the biggest company in Odense. After its closure in 1977 it stood empty for a number of years until it was renovated and transformed into a cultural centre. Today it houses museums, a cinema, art galleries, shops, restaurants and cafés. The **Mediemuseet** has displays on the history of print production and the latest electronic media. The **Museet for Fotokunst** exhibits works by Danish and international photographers, while the **Kunsthallen Brandts** shows contemporary art, craft, design and performance.

Childhood home of Hans Christian Andersen

H.C. Andersens Barndomshjem

Munkemøllestræde 3–5. **Tel** 65 51 46 01. **Open** Jan–Jun & Sep–Dec: 11am–3pm Tue–Sun; Jul & Aug: 10am–4pm daily. **museum.odense.dk**

The Andersen family moved to this small house close to the cathedral when Hans was two years old. Andersen lived here until the age of 14. The museum has only a few rooms, furnished with basic period household objects, but manages to conjure up what life was like for a poor Danish family in the early 19th century.

Art gallery in Brandts

Sankt Knuds Kirke

Klosterbakken 2. **Tel** 66 12 03 92. **Open** Apr–Oct: 10am–5pm daily; Nov–Mar: 10am–4pm daily. **odense-domkirke.dk**

Odense cathedral is named after Canute (Knud) II, who ruled Denmark from 1080–86. The king's skeleton is on public display in a glass case down in the basement. The

16th-century cathedral altarpiece by Claus Berg

present cathedral is one of Denmark's most beautiful examples of Gothic architecture. It stands on the site of an earlier Romanesque structure, which was destroyed by fire in 1248. The cathedral's ornate gilded altar is a masterpiece of 16th-century craftmanship by Claus Berg of Lübeck. The triptych is 5 m (16 ft) high and includes nearly 300 intricately carved figures within its design.

Flakhaven

Flakhaven derives its name from an old Danish word meaning an area surrounded by meadows and gardens. For centuries the square was used as a market venue and attracted merchants and farmers from all over Funen. The main building standing in the square is the Rådhus (city hall), which has a west wing dating from the 19th century. The remainder of the building is 20th century. Guided tours are available on Tuesdays and Thursdays in the summer and include access to the Wedding Room, the Town Council Chamber and a wall commemorating citizens who have made major contributions to the city's history.

Brandts 13

Jernbanegade 13. **Tel** 65 51 46 01. **Open** see website for opening hours. **brandts.dk**

This museum has a very large collection of Danish art, though only a fraction of it is on display at any one time. The Classical building is adorned on the outside with a frieze depicting scenes from Danish history and mythology. The interior is crammed with paintings, etchings and sculptures by Danish artists spanning a period

For hotels and restaurants see pp248–55 and pp262–77

of 250 years. One section of the museum contains works by local Funen artists, collectively known as Fynboerne.

H.C. Andersens Hus

Bangs Boder 29. **Tel** 65 51 46 01. **Open** Jan–Jun & Sep–Dec: 10am–4pm Tue–Sun; Jul & Aug: 10am–5pm daily. **museum.odense.dk**

Denmark's most famous writer was born in this house in 1805. It is now a museum, and it was greatly extended and modernized to celebrate the 200th anniversary of Andersen's birth. The exhibition includes a recreation of the author's study and numerous items belonging to Andersen, including his notes and letters. There is even an old rope – apparently Andersen was terrified by the thought of a fire and carried this with him wherever he went in readiness for an emergency evacuation. Hanging on one of the walls is a world map indicating the countries in which Andersen's tales have been published in translation. A special collection includes copies of his works in 120 languages.

Bust from Brandts 13

Close to the museum is Fyrtøjet (the Tinderbox), a children's cultural centre based on Andersen's stories.

Carl Nielsen Museet

Claus Bergs Gade 11. **Tel** 65 51 46 01. **Open** May–Aug: 11am–3pm Wed–Sun; Sep–Apr: 3–7pm Thu & Fri, 11am–3pm Sat & Sun.

This museum, devoted to the famous Danish composer Carl Nielsen (1865–1931), was opened in 1988 to celebrate the town's millennium. The exhibits, donated by the descendents of the composer, are all associated with Nielsen, who is mainly known for his operas, symphonies and violin concertos. In addition to handwritten scores of the artist's compositions, the collection includes Nielsen's piano and works by his wife, the sculptor Anne Marie Brodersen.

VISITORS' CHECKLIST

Practical Information
Road map: D5. 185,000.
City Hall, 63 75 75 20.
visitodense.com

Transport
Odense.

City hall façade, crowned with a statue of Justice

Odense City Centre

① Brandts
② H.C. Andersens Barndomshjem
③ Sankt Knuds Kirke
④ Flakhaven
⑤ Brandts 13
⑥ H.C. Andersens Hus
⑦ Carl Nielsen Museet

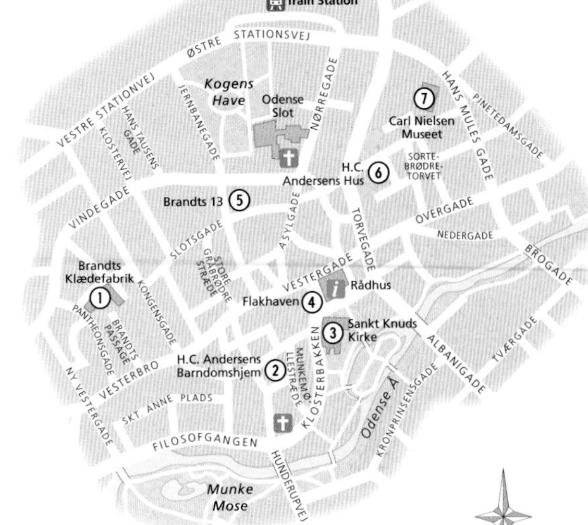

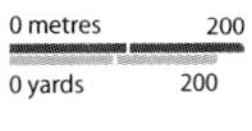

For keys to symbols see back flap

8 Svendborg

Road map: D5. 30,000.
Centrumpladsen 4. **Tel** 63 75 94 80. Fyn Rundt Regatta (Jul).
visitsvendborg.dk

Funen's second largest town, Svendborg is a busy port and has strong links with shipbuilding. In the 19th century its boatyards produced half of all Danish vessels.

Most of Svendborg's sights are within easy reach of Torvet, the market square. Closest to hand is the 13th-century Vor Frue Kirke, which has a carillon consisting of 27 bells. Sankt Nicolai Kirke is slightly older, though also 13th century. A short distance west of Vor Frue Kirke is Anne Hvides Gård, a half-timbered building dating from 1560. **SAK Kunstbygningen** (SAK Art Exhibitions) displays works by the Danish sculptor Kai Nielsen (1882–1924), who was born in Svendborg. Other museums include Naturama, a natural history museum, and **Forsorgsmuseet**, built in 1872 as a "poor farm". In 1906 there were 450 such institutions in Denmark; this, the only extant one, houses a museum telling the story of the country's poor.

SAK Kunstbygningen
Vestergade 27. **Tel** 62 22 44 70. **Open** mid-Feb–Apr: 10am–2pm Tue–Sun; May–Dec: 10am–4pm Tue–Sun.

Forsorgsmuseet
Viebæltegård Gruppemøllevej 13. **Tel** 62 21 02 61. **Open** May–Oct: 10am–4pm daily; mid-Feb–Apr: 10am–2pm Tue–Sun.
svendborgmuseum.dk

Kattesund, a scenic alley in Svendborg

An elegant apartment in Valdemars Slot, Tåsinge

9 Tåsinge

Road map: D6. 2,500.

The island of Tåsinge is linked by bridge to Funen and Langeland. The major local attraction is **Valdemars Slot**, built by Christian IV for his favourite son Valdemar and completed in 1644.

The castle's architect was Hans van Steenwinckel, who was also responsible for Rosenborg Slot in Copenhagen *(see pp64–5)*. In 1670s the king gave the castle to Admiral Niels Juel in recognition of his successful command of the Danish fleet during the Battle of Køge Bay *(see p175)*. The castle has remained in the hands of the Juel family ever since. The royal apartments, the reception rooms and the kitchens are open to the public. In the attic there is a collection of items including trophies from African safaris. The domestic quarters, arranged around a lake, house a small museum.

Environs
Near the castle, heading for Svendborg, is the fishing port of **Troense**. Its most attractive street, Grønnegade, is lined with half-timbered houses. In Bregninge, the **Tåsinge Museum** illustrates life at sea; it also tells of the ill-fated love affair between circus performer Elvira Madigan and Swedish lieutenant Sixten Sparre.

Valdemars Slot
Slotsalleén 100, Troense. **Tel** 62 22 61 06. **Open** Apr–Oct: 10am–5pm, days vary; see website for details.
valdemarsslot.dk

Statue of Hans Christian Ørsted in Rudkøbing

10 Langeland

Road map: D6. 13,000.
Rudkøbing Torvet 5. **Tel** 62 51 35 05. **langeland.dk**

Langeland is located off the southeast coast of Funen and can be reached by bridge or from Lolland by ferry. The island has a number of good beaches and marked cycling paths. Windmills are dotted here and there, along with quaint hamlets and farms.

Rudkøbing is the capital and the island's only sizeable town. Its most famous citizen was Hans Christian Ørsted (1777–1851), a physicist who made major advances in the field of electromagnetism. The house in which the scientist was born is known as **Det Gamle Apotek** (The Old Pharmacy) and has been arranged to re-create an 18th-century pharmacist's shop and herb garden. In front of it stands a statue of Ørsted. From here it is only a short distance to the market square, which contains a 19th-century town hall and a much older church with an inscription giving its year of founding as 1105.

About 10 km (6 miles) north of Rudkøbing is **Tranekær**, whose main attraction is Tranekær Slot, a pink- coloured castle that dates from around 1200. The castle is normally closed to visitors, but there are some guided tours in July, and the grounds can also be visited. Part of the estate now serves as a botanical garden which has a number of rare trees including some Californian sequoias. An open-air gallery exhibits sculptures and installations by Danish and international artists. About 30 km (18 miles) south of Rudkøbing is the **Koldkrigsmuseum** (Cold War Museum), where you can explore a submarine, a mine-sweeper and a bunker.

Det Gamle Apotek
Brogade 15, Rudkøbing. **Tel** 63 51 63 00. **Open** for guided tours (Jul).

Koldkrigsmuseum
Vognsbjergvej 4B, Bagenkop. **Tel** 62 56 27 00. **Open** May–Sep: 10am–5pm daily; Apr & Oct: to 4pm.
langelandsfortet.dk

Colourful façade of Tranekær Slot, Langeland

Picturesque 17th-century houses in Marstal

⓫ Marstal

Road map: D6. Ærø. 1,500.
Havnegade 5. **Tel** 62 52 13 00.
Open mid-Jun–Aug: 9am–3:30pm Mon–Sat.

Marstal is the largest town on the island of Ærø. Its history has long been associated with the sea and in the 18th century it was a busy port with about 300 ships arriving here every year. The **Søfartmuseum** (Maritime Museum) occupies four buildings near the harbour and contains many items connected with the sea including model schooners and seafaring paintings.

The dependence of the local population on the sea is also apparent in the local church on Kirkestræde, which was built in 1738. The altarpiece in the church depicts Christ calming the rough waves, and hanging in several places within the building are votive sailing ships. Outside in the cemetery there are numerous gravestones of local sailors. The church clock was created by Jens Olsen, who also produced the World Clock in the Rådhus in Copenhagen *(see p78)*.

Exhibit from Marstal's Søfartmuseum

Søfartmuseum
Prinsensgade 1. **Tel** 62 53 23 31.
Open 16 Apr–31 May: 10am–4pm daily; Jun–Aug: 9am–5pm daily; Sep & Oct: 10am–4pm daily; 1 Nov–15 Apr: 11am–3pm Mon–Sat.

⓬ Ærøskøbing

Road map: D6. Ærø. 800.
Havnen 4. **Tel** 62 52 13 00.

Many of the 17th-century houses lining the cobbled streets are a reminder of a time when Ærøskøbing was a prosperous merchant town. The oldest house dates from 1645 and can be found at Søndergade 36. The town's most picturesque dwelling is Dukkehuset (Dolls' House) at Smedegade 37. Also in Smedegade is **Flaske-Peters Samling**, a museum devoted to Peter Jacobsen, who first went to sea at the age of 16. Known as "Bottle Peter", he created about 1,700 ships-in-a-bottle before he died in 1960. Also in the museum is a cross he made for his own grave. **Ærø Museum** has displays on the history of the island and its people, including a collection of 19th-century paintings.

Flaske-Peters Samling
Smedegade 22. **Tel** 62 52 29 50.
Open early Apr–mid-Jun & mid-Aug–mid-Oct: 10am–4pm daily; mid-Jun–mid-Aug: 10am–5pm daily; mid-Oct–early Apr: 1–3pm Tue–Fri, 10am–noon Sat.

Ærø Museum
Brogade 3–5. **Tel** 62 52 29 50.
Open early Apr–mid-Jun: 11am–3pm daily; mid-Jun–mid-Sep: 10am–4pm daily; mid-Oct–early Apr: 10am–1pm Mon–Fri & Sun, noon–3pm Sat.

SOUTHERN AND CENTRAL JUTLAND

As well as the scenic lowlands and undulating hills and meadows found on the eastern side of central Jutland, this region has much to recommend it. Attractions include beautifully preserved medieval towns, traditional hamlets, parks, castles and ancient Viking burial grounds. In addition, no one travelling with children should miss a trip to LEGOLAND®.

Jutland derives its name from the Jutes, a Germanic tribe that once inhabited this peninsula. When the Vikings, who occupied the islands to the east, began to encroach on this territory, the mixing of the two tribes gave rise to the Danes as a distinct people.

After Denmark's defeat during the Schleswig Wars in 1864, Jutland was occupied by Prussia, and subsequently, as part of Schleswig, remained under German control. It was not until a plebiscite in 1920 that it once more became part of the kingdom of Denmark. After the final resolution of this Danish-German border dispute, many families decided to remain on the "other" side. The expatriate minorities are still active on both sides of the border.

On the islands of Fanø and Rømø the influence of the nearby Netherlands can be seen in the tiles decorating some of the houses. The Wadden Sea around these islands is well worth exploring on a seal or oyster safari. The milder east coast features wealthy borough towns with fine museums.

The top attraction for families with children is LEGOLAND®, where millions of plastic LEGO® bricks are used to create Denmark's best-known amusement park. The cities of Aarhus and Silkeborg offer a more cultural option.

Carved Viking figures and replica Viking ship in Vejle Fjord

◀ Terrace café at the Glass Museum (Glasmuseet), Ebeltoft

Exploring Southern and Central Jutland

Jutland is the only part of Denmark that is not an island. The bottom section of the peninsula is cut across by a 69-km- (43-mile-) long national border with Germany. The most popular attraction of southern and central Jutland is LEGOLAND®. However, this region has much more to offer, including four national parks; several historically significant centres – such as Ribe, Denmark's oldest town, and Jelling, which is famous for its ancient burial mounds; and the delightfully arty town of Silkeborg, splendidly located in the heart of a Lake District. Aarhus, Denmark's second city, is famous for its nightlife, fuelled by the students at its university.

Getting Around

Jutland is almost three times larger than the rest of Denmark put together and distances between towns can be significant. The E45 runs from the German border all the way to northern Jutland along the eastern coast of the peninsula, connecting to Esbjerg from Kolding, and to Silkeborg and Herning from Aarhus. The fastest route from Copenhagen is the E20, which joins with the E45 at Fredericia. It is also possible to take a ferry to either Aarhus or Ebeltoft from Copenhagen. Esbjerg's harbour handles ferry traffic from the UK.

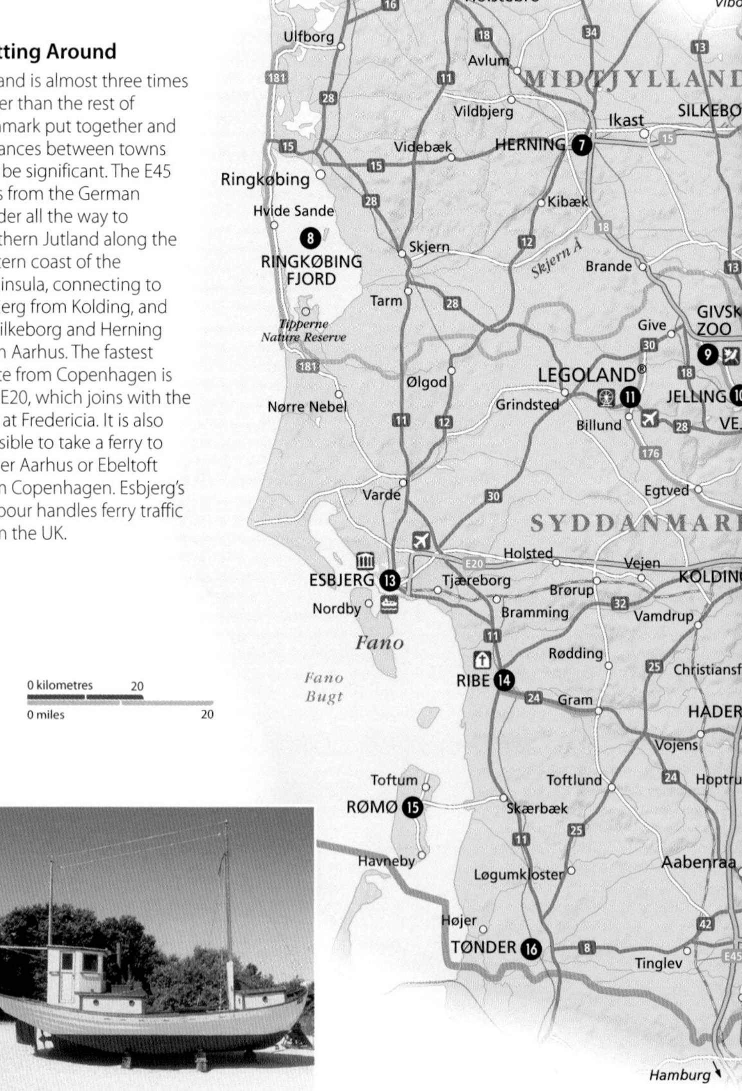

Restored cutter in front of Esbjerg's maritime museum

For hotels and restaurants see pp248–55 and pp262–77

Ramparts around the town of Fredericia in central Jutland

Key

- Motorway
- Motorway under construction
- Major road
- Minor road
- Scenic route
- Main railway
- Minor railway
- International border
- Regional border
- Summit

The 15th-century Koldinghus in Kolding

Sights at a Glance

1. Ebeltoft
2. *Aarhus pp192–3*
3. Moesgård
4. Horsens
5. Silkeborg Lake District
6. Silkeborg
7. Herning
8. Ringkøbing Fjord
9. Givskud Zoo
10. Jelling
11. *LEGOLAND® pp196–7*
12. Vejle
13. Esbjerg
14. Ribe
15. Rømø
16. Tønder
17. Sønderborg
18. Haderslev
19. Kolding
20. Fredericia

For keys to symbols *see back flap*

Fregatten Jylland in Ebeltoft, now serving as a museum

❶ Ebeltoft

Road map: D3. 7,500. S.A. Jensens Vej 3. **Tel** 86 34 14 00.

Boasting the smallest rådhus (town hall) in Denmark, Ebeltoft, part of the Mols Bjerge national park, is over 700 years old. Many of the town's cobbled streets, including Adelgade, are lined with half-timbered houses from the 17th century.

In the harbour is **Fregatten Jylland**, a large restored wooden ship that took part in the Battle of Helgoland in 1864. Groups of visitors can arrange over-night stays on board, sleeping in a hammock and experiencing the life of a sailor. A large museum annex focuses on maritime history and will interest all ages.

Bell from Fregatten Jylland

The nearby **Glasmuseet** has many items of contemporary glass art on display, including pieces by Dale Chihuly and Harvey Littleton.

Fregatten Jylland
S.A. Jensen Vej 2–4. **Tel** 86 34 10 99. **Open** Jan–Mar, Nov & Dec: 11am–3pm daily; Apr–Aug: 10am–5pm daily; Sep & Oct: 11am–4pm daily; during school holidays: 10am–6pm.
fregatten-jylland.dk

Glasmuseet
Strandvejen 8. **Tel** 86 34 17 99. **Open** Jan–Mar, Nov & Dec: 10am–4pm Tue–Sun; Apr–Jun, Sep & Oct: 10am–5pm Tue–Sun; Jul & Aug: 10am–6pm Tue–Sun. **glasmuseet.dk**

❷ Aarhus

See pp192–3.

❸ Moesgård

Road map: D4. 7 km (4 miles) south of Aarhus. **Tel** 87 16 10 16. Vikingetræf (Jul). **moesmus.dk**

Formerly located in a manor house, Moesgård is a large prehistoric museum that is due to reopen to the public in purpose-built premises in 2014–15. Situated on a hill known as Hill of the Elves, a short drive south of Aarhus, the museum has several highlights, ranging from its collection of runic stones, the largest in Scandinavia, to a hoard of votive offerings – swords, axes, shields and other items – found at Illerup Ådal, near Skanderborg, and dating to about 200 AD. Its star exhibit, however, is the Grauballe Man. This mummified body, discovered in 1952 in a bog, had been preserved thanks to a combination of acids and iron in the soil. He is believed to have been about 40 years old when he died in 80 BC. A slash across his throat indicates that he was probably murdered.

Each year in late July, Moesgård becomes the venue for a lively and entertaining Viking festival, Vikingtræf, which features battles, a Viking marketplace and performing Icelandic horses.

Lichtenberg Palace, Horsens, once a residence for the tsar's family

❹ Horsens

Road map: C4. 38 km (24 miles) south of Aarhus. 55,000. Fussingsvej 8. **Tel** 75 60 21 20. Medieval Festival (late Aug). **visithorsens.dk**

Horsens is the birthplace of Vitus Bering (1681–1741), the explorer who discovered Alaska and the straits that separate it from Siberia (these were subsequently named after him). The guns from Bering's ship now stand in the town's main park. Mementos from his expeditions are on display in **Horsens Museum**.

The Danish Romanesque Vor Frelsers Kirke (Our Saviour's Church) is 13th century. Nearby, Lichtenberg Palace was used by the tsar's family after they fled Russia. The **Horsens Kunst Museum** has contemporary Danish art.

Horsens Museum
Sundvej 1A. **Tel** 76 29 23 50. **Open** Jul–Aug: 10am–4pm daily; Sep–Jun: 11am–4pm Tue–Sun.

Horsens Kunst Museum
Carolinelundsvej 2. **Tel** 76 29 23 70. **Open** Jul & Aug: 10am–4pm daily (to 5pm Sat & Sun); Sep–Jun: 11am– 4pm Tue–Sun (to 5pm Sat & Sun).
horsenskunstmuseum.dk

Reconstructed burial chamber at Moesgård

Silkeborg harbour, in Denmark's Lake District

❺ Silkeborg Lake District

Road map: C4.

The stretch between Silkeborg and Skanderborg and the area slightly to the north of it is a land of lakes and hills known as Søhøjlandet. Here, visitors find Jutland's largest lake – the Mossø, as well as Denmark's longest river, the Gudenå (176 km/ 109 miles). The Lake District also has some of the country's highest peaks. In summer it is a favourite destination for canoeists and cyclists, as well as hikers, all of whom make the most of the lakeland scenery.

Gjern has a vintage car museum (with about 70 models, the oldest dating from the early 20th century), while Tange Sø boasts **Elmuseet**, an electricity museum situated next to the country's largest power station.

Other places worth visiting include the church in Veng, which was built around 1100 and is thought to be the oldest monastery in Denmark, and, on the shores of Mossø, the ruins of Øm Kloster, the best-preserved Cistercian monastery in Denmark.

❻ Silkeborg

Road map: C4. 42,000.
Torvet 2A. **Tel** 86 82 19 11.
Jazz Festival (Jun), Country Music Festival (Aug). silkeborg.com

Silkeborg owes much of its past prosperity to the paper factory, built in 1846, that was at one time powered by the local river. Silkeborg's **Culture Museum** occupies a former manor built in 1767. Most visitors head straight for the Tollund Man, one of the best-preserved prehistoric bodies in the world.

The city is also famous for its art galleries, such as **Silkeborg Bad**, which focuses on contemporary art, and **Museum Jorn**, with works by the Danish artist Asger Jorn and other members of the CoBrA movement.

Tollund Man

In summer a 19th-century paddle steamer travels the 15 km (9 miles) to Himmelbjerget, where a 25-m- (82-ft-) high tower offers great views.

Culture Museum
Hovedgårdsvej 7. **Tel** 86 82 14 99.
Open 10am–5pm daily.

Museum Jorn
Gudenåvej 7–9. **Tel** 86 82 53 88. **Open** 11am–5pm Tue–Fri, 10am–5pm Sat & Sun. **museumjorn.dk**

Silkeborg Bad
Gjessøvej 40. **Tel** 86 81 63 29.
Open noon–4pm Tue–Fri, 11am–5pm Sat & Sun (May–Sep: 10am–5pm Tue–Sun). **silkeborgbad.dk**

❼ Herning

Road map: C4. 30,000.
Østergade 21. **Tel** 96 27 22 22.
visitherning.dk

The town of Herning was established in the late 19th century following the arrival of the railway. Herning has twice been named Denmark's 'city of the year' due to its economic importance to the country. The **Herning Museum** tells the story of the town as well as the history and archaeology of the region. **HEART Herning Museum of Contemporary Art** exhibits works by artists such as Carl-Henning Pedersen, a representative of the CoBrA movement. Housed in a building designed by the US architect Steven Holl, **HEART** is a museum of Danish and international contemporary art. The **Danmarks Fotomuseum** has an extensive collection of cameras and interesting photographic displays.

Herning Museum
Museumgade 32. **Tel** 96 26 19 00.
Open 10am–4:30pm Tue–Fri, 11am–4:30pm Sat & Sun (Jul: also Mon).

HEART Herning Museum of Contemporary Art
Birk Centerpark 8. **Tel** 97 12 10 33.
Open 10am–5pm Tue–Sun.
heartmus.dk

Danmarks Fotomuseum
Museumsgade 28. **Tel** 97 22 53 22.
Open noon–4:30pm Tue–Sun (Jul & Aug: 11am–4:30pm daily).

One of Herning's tranquil streets

❷ Aarhus

Denmark's second-largest city dates back to Viking times. It was originally named Aros, meaning "at the mouth of the river", and due to its location on Jutland's eastern coast it became a major seaport. After the Reformation Aarhus grew into an important trading centre, and the 19th century saw the development of the harbour. A university was founded here in 1928, and today Aarhus boasts a vibrant cultural life, with some fine museums and venues, as well as lively cafés and bars. The city is also a major centre for wind energy and the home of many wind turbine manufacturers.

City panorama from the Rådhus tower

Exploring Aarhus

Most of the town's attractions are concentrated within a fairly small area; the only site located more than 1 km (0.6 mile) away is Den Gamle By. Sightseeing is made easier by the Aarhus Card, which gives free admission to some museums and free use of public transport.

Musikhuset

Thomas Jensens Allé 2. **Tel** 89 40 40 40. **Open** 11am–6pm daily. **musikhusetaarhus.dk**

The city's concert hall opened in 1982 and is one of Denmark's foremost cultural centres. The glass-fronted building is home to the prestigious Jutland Opera Company and Aarhus Symphony Orchestra, which holds concerts most Thursday evenings. The building is worth visiting if only to see its vast glazed hall, planted with luxuriant palm trees. The centre features its own café, which often has concerts, and a restaurant, the Richter, named after Johan Richter, the main architect of the building.

Rådhus

Rådhuspladsen. **Tel** 87 31 50 10.

The modern city hall was designed by Arne Jacobsen and Erik Møller and completed in 1941. The building is a prime example of Danish Modernism. It is clad on the outside with dark Norwegian marble and topped with a rectangular clock tower, which affords a good view of the city. The interior has a lighter feel. The large council chamber and Civic Room are worth seeking out.

The modernist Rådhus, designed by Arne Jacobsen

ARoS Kunstmuseum

Aros Allé 2. **Tel** 87 30 66 00. **Open** 10am–5pm Tue, Thu–Sun, 10am–10pm Wed. **aros.dk**

This gallery is housed in a ten-storey building topped by a circular rainbow-coloured walkway; designed by Olafur Eliasson, called *Your Rainbow Panorama* it offers breathtaking views of the city. The art collection presents works spanning from the Danish Golden Age to the present day.

Vikingemuseet

Sankt Clemens Torv. **Open** 10am–4pm Mon–Wed, Fri, 10am–5pm Thu. **vikingemuseet.dk**

In a building across from the cathedral, next to the Nordea Bank, is a museum devoted to the Viking era. The prime exhibit is a section of archaeological excavation that was carried out in Clemens Torv. Fragments of the original Viking ramparts, discovered in 1964, are on display along with items dating from 900 to 1400 including a skeleton, a reconstructed house, wood-working tools, pottery, and runic stones. Similar discoveries at nearby Store Torv have confirmed the importance of Aarhus as a major centre of Viking culture.

Domkirke

Store Torv. **Tel** 86 20 54 00. **Open** May–Sep: 9:30am–4pm Mon–Fri; Oct–Dec: 10am–3pm Mon–Sat (10:30am–2pm Tue). **aarhus-domkirke.dk**

Aarhus's main place of worship is at the heart of the city's oldest district. The cathedral was built in 1201 but destroyed by fire in the 14th century. It was rebuilt in the late 15th century in a Gothic style, and is easily Denmark's longest cathedral with a nave that spans nearly 100 m (328 ft). Until the end of the 16th century most of the cathedral walls were covered with frescoes. During the Reformation these were whitewashed over, but many have since been restored. The five-panel altarpiece dates from 1479 and is the work of Bernt Notke of Lübeck. The Baroque pipe organ dates from 1730.

For hotels and restaurants see pp248–55 and pp262–77

Kvindemuseet

Domkirkeplads 5. **Tel** 86 18 64 70. **Open** 10am–4pm daily (to 8pm Wed). **kvindemuseet.dk**

The Women's Museum has made a name for itself with its imaginative temporary exhibitions relating to women's issues – past and present. Since 1984 the museum has been collecting objects, photographs and documents illustrating the many changes that have taken place over the centuries in the lives of women in Danish society.

Figure from Bernt Notke's altarpiece

Vor Frue Kirke

Frue Kirkeplads. **Tel** 86 12 12 43. **Open** May–Sep: 10am–4pm Mon–Fri; Oct–Apr: 10am–2pm Mon–Fri, 10am–noon Sat. **aarhusvorfrue.dk**

Vor Frue Kirke is a complex of three churches in a former Dominican monastery. The oldest section of this complex is the 11th-century Romanesque stone crypt. The highlight here is a replica of an early crucifix featuring a Christ with Viking plaits. The star adornment inside the church is a 16th-century wooden altarpiece carved by Claus Berg.

VISITORS' CHECKLIST

Practical Information

Road map: D4. 325,000. Banegårdspladsen 20, 8000 Aarhus C. **Tel** 87 31 50 10. Aarhus International Jazz Festival (2nd half of Jul), Aarhus Festuge/Cultural Week (1st week Sep). **visitaarhus.com**

Transport

Aarhus H.

The 11th-century crypt of Vor Frue Kirke

Den Gamle By

Viborgvej 2. **Tel** 86 12 31 88. **Open** year-round opening but check website for current times prior to your visit. **dengamleby.dk**

This open-air museum has exhibits from the 17th, 18th and 19th centuries, as well as from 1927 and 1974. One exhibit is a typical Danish town the way it would have looked in the 19th century, at the time of Hans Christian Andersen. The atmosphere is especially vibrant during the Living History season (Easter–Dec), when actors play key characters in the town, such as the vicar and the town crier.

Aarhus City Centre

1. Musikhuset
2. Rådhus
3. ARoS Kunstmuseum
4. Vikingemuseet
5. Domkirke
6. Kvindemuseet
7. Vor Frue Kirke
8. Den Gamle By

Harbour with Ringkøbing Fjord in the background

8 Ringkøbing Fjord

Road map: B4. Ringkøbing, Torvet 22; Hvide Sande, Nørregade 2B. **Tel** 70 22 70 01. Sand Sculpture Festival (Søndervig, mid-Jun–Nov).
visitvest.dk

A thin strip of land some 35 km (22 miles) long separates Ringkøbing Fjord from the North Sea. This sandy spit is about 1 km (half a mile) wide and has many summer cottages tucked among the dunes. The only water access between the sea and Ringkøbing Fjord is through a channel and lock in the town of Hvide Sande. Ringkøbing Fjord is popular with windsurfers and the calm waters of the bay are suitable for novices; the North Sea, on the other side of the spit, offers more challenging conditions.

On the bay's northern shore is **Ringkøbing**, the largest town in this region. Ringkøbing was once a seaport but over the centuries the entrance from the bay to the sea shifted southwards and the town became an inland harbour. Standing in Torvet, the town's main square, are some of the most historic buildings including Hotel Ringkøbing, a timbered building that dates from 1600. The local **museum** has alternating exhibitions.

The locality includes many attractions. **Fiskeriets Hus** (House of Fisheries) at Hvide Sande contains an aquarium with fish and shellfish from the North Sea and fjord waters as well as displays on the area's fishing industry. A paved footpath, suitable for wheelchair users, leads from the museum to **Troldbjerg**, Hvide Sande's main viewpoint. The mast at the top was once used by sailors to warn them about water levels. Another good view is from the 60-m- (197-ft-) high lighthouse on the Nørre Lyngvig dune, 5 km (3 miles) north of Hvide Sande.

A different kind of scenery can be found on the southern shores of Ringkøbing Fjord, where the marshes form **Tipperne Nature Reserve**, one of Denmark's most important sites for waterfowl. Access is restricted to a few hours on Friday or Sunday mornings so as not to disturb the migrating birds. The reserve contains an observation tower.

Ringkøbing Museum
Herningvej 4. **Tel** 97 32 16 15. **Open** 11am–5pm Mon–Fri, 10am–3pm Sat & Sun.
levendehistorie.dk

Fiskeriets Hus
Nørregade 2B, Hvide Sande. **Tel** 97 31 26 10. **Open** 10am–5pm daily (Nov–Easter: to 4pm). **fiskerietshus.dk**

9 Givskud Zoo

Road map: C4. Løveparken Givskud Zoo: **Tel** 75 73 02 22. **Open** late Apr–mid-Oct: from 10am daily. Closing times vary; check the website for details. **givskudzoo.dk**

A short way north of Jelling is Givskud Zoo (sometimes referred to as Løveparken), home to the largest pride of lions in Scandinavia. When the park was established in 1969 the pride had 29 members; today it has over 40. In addition to the lions, Givskud has about 700 other animals representing 70 species. Givskud is part-zoo, part-safari park, and many of the animals are left to wander freely within their allocated areas. Car drivers can travel along marked routes. Visitors on foot can enjoy a safari by bus.

Bust of Jacob Hansen, Givskud Zoo's founder

The lions are the most popular sight, but there is no denying the appeal of the giraffes, zebras, buffalos, ostriches and other species that inhabit the park. One of the zoo's other attractions is the Western Lowland gorillas enclosure; the family of apes was brought over from Copenhagen's zoo in 2001.

Fenced-off areas provide children with the opportunity to stroke some of the park's more domesticated animals or have fun feeding the camels.

Small herd of zebra wandering freely in Givskud Zoo

For hotels and restaurants see pp248–55 and pp262–77

Ancient burial mound in Jelling

Givskud Zoo is not only a family attraction but also a major scientific establishment. A third of the species at the park are endangered. One of Givskud's programmes resulted in deer and antelope reared at the park being re-introduced into the wilds of Pakistan in the late 1980s.

⑩ Jelling

Road map: C4. 2,500. Gormsgade 23. **Tel** 75 87 23 50. Viking Fair (Aug). **visitvejle.com**

For the Danes Jelling is a special place: this unassuming village served as the royal seat of Gorm the Old, a 10th-century Viking who conquered Jutland and then Funen and Zealand to create a new state. The dynasty he established has ruled Denmark continuously to this day.

Although few traces are left of the old royal castle, **Jelling Kirke** and the two burial mounds beyond it have revealed much of Denmark's ancient history. The church was built in about 1100, but it is now known that the site was occupied far earlier than this by at least three wooden churches. The first of these was, according to legend, built by Gorm's son, Harald Bluetooth, who came to the throne around 958 and adopted Christianity a short time afterwards. For a long time it was believed that the two knolls outside the church contained the remains of Denmark's first ruler, but when they were excavated in the 19th century nothing was found. In the late 1970s, however, archaeologists began a series of digs inside Jelling Kirke and found the remains of the three earlier wooden churches, along with Viking jewellery and human bones. Forensic examinations, conducted at Copenhagen's Nationalmuseet, concluded that the bones could indeed be those of Gorm and in the year 2000, in the presence of the current royal family, the remains were reburied under the floor of Jelling Kirke. Today the place is marked with a silver sign. Close to the church are two runic stones. The larger one, known as the "Danes' baptism certificate", was erected in 965 by Harald in memory of his parents – Gorm and Thyra. Still visible on the stone is a picture of Christ – the oldest representation of Christ in Scandinavia. The stone's inscription proclaims that "Harald king ordered this monument to be erected to Gorm his father and Thyra his mother for the glory of Denmark", and that he converted the Danes to Christianity. This inscription is considered to be the first written record in which the word "Denmark" appears. In 1994 the entire complex was declared a UNESCO World Heritage Site. The landscape is undergoing renovation to display future archaeological finds in as authentic a setting as possible.

Runic stone in Jelling

Kongernes Jelling, an exhibition centre opposite the church is devoted to the history of the Vikings and the establishment of the Danish monarchy.

The atmosphere of Jelling can best be enjoyed during the annual Viking Fair. This weekend-long event is popular with many Danes, some of whom take it as an opportunity to dress up as Vikings and parade through the streets of the town. Another reminder of Denmark's past can be found at Fårup lake where a full-scale replica of a Viking ship takes visitors on cruises of the lake.

Jelling Kirke
Open 8am–5pm Mon–Sat (to 8pm May–Aug), noon–5pm Sun.
jellingkirke.dk

Kongernes Jelling
Gormsgade 23. **Tel** 41 20 63 31.
Open 10am–3pm Mon–Fri.
natmus.dk

Runic writing including the oldest record of the name "Denmark"

⓫ LEGOLAND®

LEGO® bricks, known and loved by children throughout the world, were invented in the 1930s by Danish toymaker Ole Kirk Christiansen. This popular amusement park was opened in 1968. Its attractions include amazingly detailed miniature versions of cities, as well as famous landmarks, constructed entirely from plastic LEGO® bricks. In addition there are thrilling rides, miniature trains and water chutes.

★ Toyota Traffic School
Children aged 7 to 13 can learn to dr here. This is one of the park's most popular attractions, so book ahead.

Atlantis by SEA LIFE ™
At this underwater attraction, visitors are able to get up close and personal with sharks and tropical fish. There are also submarines and shipwrecks.

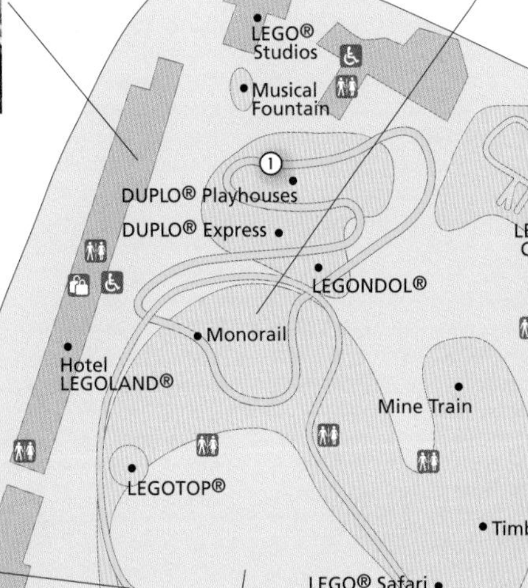

LEGO® Train
Miniland can be explored aboard a train or viewed from a revolving platform that gradually ascends to the top of a tower.

Entrance

★ Miniland
Over 20 million LEGO® bricks were used to construct famous buildings, airports, trains and even entire cities.

The Dragon
Shaped like its namesake, this roller coaster hurtles through the majestic King's Castle and is great fun for children and adults alike.

VISITORS' CHECKLIST

Practical Information
Nordmarksvej 9, 7190 Billund.
Road map C4. **Tel** 75 33 13 33
Open opening days and times vary, but usually: early Apr–Aug: from 10am daily; Sep, Oct: from 10am Fri–Tue. Always consult the website before visiting. Please note that rides close 1 to 2 hours before the park.
LEGOLAND.dk

★ Polar Land
Hop aboard the hair-raising Polar X-plorer, a roller coaster that travels through a frozen polar landscape filled with LEGO® animals.

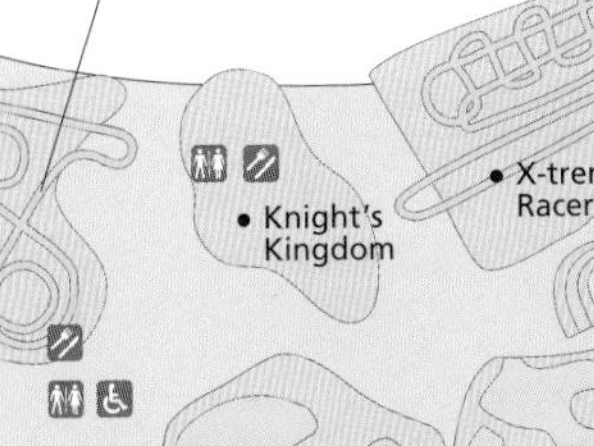

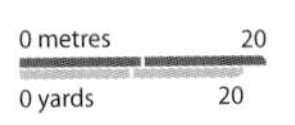

The Temple
Re-creating a large Egyptian archaeological dig, The Temple allows young visitors to go on an exciting treasure hunt.

Pirate Splash Battle
Board a pirate ship and take your position behind a water cannon. See how long you can stay dry in this playful re-creation of a sea battle.

KEY

① **DUPLO® Land** is for the youngest children.

② **Vikings River Splash** is an aquatic roller coaster ride sending rafts splashing down wild water rapids and waterfalls through a world of dragons and Vikings.

Vindmølle, a Vejle landmark with a flour-milling museum

⑫ Vejle

Road map: C4. 53,000. Banegårdspladsen 6. **Tel** 75 81 19 25. **visitvejle.com**

The fjord town of Vejle is famous for being the place where the beech trees (Denmark's national tree) are first to burst into leaf and announce the arrival of spring. Vejle makes a good base for visiting LEGOLAND® *(see pp196–7)* and the burial mounds at Jelling *(see p195)*. Its main point of interest is Sankt Nicolai Kirke, a Gothic church dating from the 13th century. A curiosity of the church, though they can't be seen, are the 23 skulls hidden in its walls, which belonged to 23 robbers executed in 1630.

Rådhustorvet, Vejle's main square, contains the town hall. It stands on the site of a Dominican monastery and its medieval bell can be heard ringing each day from the tower. The **Vejle Museum** is spread over a number of locations in town. A modern interactive venue displays the mummified body of a woman known as Queen Gunhild. The body was found in 1835 in a peat bog; forensic tests have revealed that the woman lived during the Iron Age, around 450 BC. The exhibition in Den Smidtske Gard, an early 19th-century burgher's residence, covers 800 years of Vejle's history. On the edge of town, Vejle Vindmølle is also part of the museum. Built in 1890 and operational until 1960, the windmill houses an exhibition devoted to flour milling.

While in Vejle it is also possible to visit the Ecolarium, a centre that aims to raise awareness of environmental issues and the potential of alternative energy, and Ravninge Broen, a Viking-era bridge in Ravninge Enge (Meadows) exhibition centre.

Vejle Museum
Tel 76 81 31 00. **Open** see the website. **vejleegnensmuseer.dk**

⑬ Esbjerg

Road map: B5. 83,000. Skolegade 33. **Tel** 75 12 55 99. Rock Festival (mid-Jun); Esbjerg Festival Week (mid-Aug), Chamber Music (Aug). **visitesbjerg.dk**

In 1868, the former fishing village of Esbjerg began to develop into a harbour from which Jutland's farmers and producers could export goods. Today it is one of Denmark's largest commercial ports and a centre for North Sea oil operations.

Seals, a favourite sight at Esbjerg's aquarium

Despite lacking a medieval district, Esbjerg has several places worth visiting. For years the town's main symbol was its **Vandtårnet** (Water Tower), which was erected in 1897. Today, it serves as an observation platform, from which there is a panoramic view of the town. Close to the tower is the Musikhuset (Concert Hall) designed by Jørn Utzon and built in 1997.

Esbjerg Art Museum contains one of Denmark's finest collections of contemporary Danish art. The **Fiskeri-og Søfartsmuseet** (The Fisheries and Maritime Museum), 4 km (2 miles) northwest of Esbjerg's centre, contains a large aquarium and various marine-related displays. Most of the sea life in the aquarium comes from the North Sea. Its most popular inhabitants are the seals. This vast museum complex also features a collection of navigation instruments and model vessels, a number of fishing boats placed outside the building and a reconstructed coastal lifeboat station. Outside the museum grounds, on the seashore, are four 9-m- (30-ft-) tall snow-white stylised figures of seated men, which are entitled *Man Meets the Sea* and were created by Svend Wiig Hansen to mark the city's centennial in 1995.

The maritime theme continues in Esbjerg harbour where the 20th-century **Horns Rev Lightship** is moored.

Exhibition room in Esbjerg's Fiskeri-og Søfartsmuseet

For hotels and restaurants see pp248–55 and pp262–77

Vandtårnet
Havnegade 22. **Tel** 76 16 39 39. **Open** Jun–mid-Sep: 10am–4pm Tue–Sun.

Esbjerg Art Museum
Havnegade 20. **Tel** 75 13 02 11. **Open** 10am–4pm daily.

Fiskeri-og Søfartsmuseet
Saltvandsakvariet Tarphagevej 2–6. **Tel** 76 12 20 00. **Open** Sep–Jun: 10am–5pm daily; Jul–Aug: 10am–6pm daily.

Horns Rev Lightship
Tel 21 62 11 04. **Open** May–Aug: 11am–4pm Mon–Fri.

Nave of Ribe Domkirke

⓮ Ribe

Road map: B5. 18,000. Torvet 3, 75 42 15 00. **visitribe.com**

Scandinavia's oldest town is also one of the best preserved and contains many fine buildings including a medieval cathedral and a 16th-century schoolhouse. The medieval centre features a maze of cobbled streets lined with crooked, half-timbered houses with beautifully painted and ornamented doors.

Ribe was once a seaport. With the passage of time the mouth of the river that flows through it became silted up, and now the town is quite a way from the seashore.

In 856 the missionary Ansgar, known locally as the Apostle of Scandinavia, built a small wooden church here. In the 10th century Ribe became a bishopric, and in the mid-12th century it acquired an impressive cathedral, which still stands today. **Ribe Domkirke** is built of a soft porous rock called tufa that was quarried near Cologne. The most prominent entrance, used by the bishops, is on the south side of the church. This entrance features a 13th-century "Cat's Head" doorway that got its name from the knocker made in the shape of a lion's head. Another feature of the portal is the pediment portraying Jesus and Mary – positioned at their feet are the images of Valdemar II and his wife Dagmar, who died in childbirth in 1212. To this day at noon and 3pm the cathedral bells chime the tune of a folk song dedicated to the queen. The most notable features of the church's interior are the 16th-century frescoes and the modern mosaics by Carl-Henning Pedersen. The left wing of the transept contains a marble floor slab from the tomb of Christoffer I, who died in 1259 and is laid in the adjacent sarcophagus. It is thought to be the oldest royal tombstone in Scandinavia. Stunning views of the flat lands and the Wadden Sea can be had from the top of the 14th-century tower.

The night watchman in Ribe

Det Gamle Rådhus, opposite the cathedral's southeast corner, was built in 1496. The town hall's museum has a small collection of torture instruments and executioners' swords. From here it is not far to the river, where the Stormflods-søjlen (Flood Column) indicates the floods that have submerged the town.

Ribe has two Viking museums. Standing opposite the railway station on Odin square is **Ribes Vikinger**, where the market town atmosphere of late 8th-century Ribe is re-created. The **Vikingecenter**, 3 km (2 miles) south of the town centre, is an open-air museum that offers a portrait of Ribe in the Viking era.

Ribe Kunstmuseum, the local art gallery, houses a collection of Danish art from 1750 until 1950, including examples from the Skagen School and the Danish Golden Age.

Environs

At the **Vadehavscentret** (Wadden Sea Centre), you can learn more about the Wadden Sea and arrange safari tours.

Ribe Domkirke
Torvet. **Tel** 75 42 06 19. **Open** daily. Oct–Apr: 11am–3pm (Apr & Oct: to 4pm); May–Sep: 10am–5pm (Jul–mid-Aug: to 5:30pm).

Det Gamle Rådhus
Von Støckens Plads. **Tel** 76 16 88 10. **Open** check webiste for times. **detgamleraadhusiribe.dk**

Ribes Vikinger
Odin Plads 1. **Tel** 76 16 39 60. **Open** Jul–Aug: 10am–6pm (until 9pm Wed) daily; Sep, Oct & Apr–Jun: 10am–4pm daily; Nov–Mar: 10am–4pm Tue–Sun.

Ribe Vikingecenter
Lustrupvej 4. **Tel** 75 41 16 11. **Open** May–mid-Oct; see website for times. **ribevikingecenter.dk**

Ribe Kunstmuseum
Sankt Nicolaigade 10. **Tel** 75 42 03 62. **Open** Jul & Aug: 11am–5pm daily (to 8pm Wed); Sep–Jun: 11am–4pm Tue–Sun.

Vadehavscentret
Okholmvej 5, Vester Vedsted. **Tel** 75 44 61 61. **Open** mid-Feb–Nov: 10am–4pm daily (May–Sep: to 5pm).

Half-timbered houses, adding to the charm of Ribe

Palisade by Rømø dyke

⓯ Rømø

Road map: B5. 750. *i* Nørre Frankel 1. **Tel** 74 75 51 30. **romo.dk**

The largest Danish island in the North Sea, Rømø was a prosperous whaling base in the 18th century. Its western shores are fringed with wide stretches of beach. The island is connected to Jutland by a causeway that passes through marshland rich in birdlife.

In the village of **Toftum** is the Kommandørgården (Captain's House), which dates from 1748. The house, which now serves as a museum, has a thatched roof and some original interior decor, including wall coverings consisting of 4,000 Dutch tiles. Close by is an 18th-century school. A short distance further north, in the hamlet of **Juvre**, is a whale jawbone fence constructed in 1772. In **Kirkeby**, next to the walls that surround the Late-Gothic church, are whalers' gravestones that were brought back from Greenland. The histories of captains and their families have been carved by local artists.

The main point of interest at the south end of the island is **Havneby**, which has a labyrinth park. A ferry goes from here to the tranquil island of Sylt, in Germany, just to the southwest.

⓰ Tønder

Road map: B6. 8,200. *i* Torvet 1. **Tel** 74 72 12 20. Tønder Festival (Aug). **visittonder.dk**

In the Middle Ages Tønder was a major fishing port. During subsequent centuries it became the centre of a lace-making industry, which is now commemorated by a lace-makers' festival held every three years. Examples of fine lace and the sophisticated tools used in its production are on display in the **Tønder Museum**. In the 17th and 18th centuries Tønder also produced ceramics that were used as wall tiles, some of which can be seen in the museum. The Tønder Museum is part of the **Museum of Southern Jutland**, which shows a collection of modern art, including chairs by Danish designer Hans J. Wegner.

Tønder's town centre is a pleasant place to explore and the narrow streets contain many houses with decorative doorways and picturesque gables and window shutters. The best-known house is Det Gamle Apotek (The Old Pharmacy), at Østergade 1, which has a Baroque doorway dating from 1671. The market square contains a 16th-century Rådhus (town hall). Also in the square is the 16th-century Kristkirken, which has some fine paintings and carvings.

Doorway of a house in Østergade, Tønder

Tønder Museum & Museum of Southern Jutland
Kongevejen 51. **Tel** 74 72 89 89.
Open Jun–Aug: 10am–5pm daily; Sep–May: 10am–5pm Tue–Sun.
museum-sonderjylland.dk

Font in Haderslev Domkirke

⓱ Sønderborg

Road map: C6. Als. 30,000. *i* Rådhustorvet 7. **Tel** 74 42 35 55. **visitsonderborg.com**

Sønderborg, meaning "South Castle", is on the island of Als. It owes its name to a **castle** fortress built by Valdemar I in 1170. Over the centuries the castle served a variety of purposes. Christian II was held prisoner here for 17 years in the early 16th century. Later on it was used in turns as a warehouse, a hospital, a prison and military barracks.

The town's turbulent history is brought to life at the **Historie-center Dybbøl Banke**, situated near Sønderborg, close to the village of Dybbøl. In the spring of 1864 this area was the scene of a fierce battle between Danish and Prussian forces. Dybbøl Mølle, a windmill that was damaged during the fighting, is now regarded as a national symbol. As a result of Denmark's defeat, Sønderborg was nearly destroyed and southern Jutland incorporated into Prussia and later into Germany (the territory was returned in 1920).

Environs

About 16 km (10 miles) to the west is the royal castle of **Gråsten**; the garden can be visited when the queen is not in residence.

Sønderborg Castle
Sønderbro 1. **Tel** 74 42 25 39.
Open Apr, May & Oct: 10am–4pm Tue–Sun; Jun–Sep: 10am–5pm daily; Nov–Mar: 1–4pm Tue–Sun.

Historiecenter Dybbøl Banke
Dybbøl Banke 16. **Tel** 74 48 90 00.
Open early Apr–mid-Oct: 10am–5pm daily.

18 Haderslev

Road map: C5. 21,000.
Nørregade 52, 73 54 56 30.
visithaderslev.dk

The present-day capital of southern Jutland is situated between a narrow fjord and a lake that was formed by the construction of a dam. A market town in the 13th century, Haderslev contains many period buildings.

During the Reformation Haderslev was a major centre of Protestantism and in 1526 it became the site of the first Protestant theological college. The town's main place of worship, Haderslev Domkirke, was built in the 13th century but has been remodelled many times. It boasts a magnificent altarpiece featuring a 14th-century crucifix and alabaster statues of the apostles.

Interior of the 13th-century cathedral in Haderslev

Interior courtyard with a fountain at Koldinghus castle

The most enchanting of the town's buildings are found on Torvet, a square flanked by half-timbered houses. The nearby **Haderslev Museum** has exhibits on the archaeological history of the area, a local-history collection and its own mini open-air museum.

Haderslev Museum
Dalgade 7. **Tel** 74 52 75 66. **Open** Jun–Aug: 10am–4pm Tue–Sun; Sep–May: 1–4pm Tue–Sun.

19 Kolding

Road map: C5. 56,000.
Akseltorv 8. **Tel** 76 33 21 00.
visitkolding.dk

Kolding's most important historic building is Koldinghus – a mighty castle that has a distinctive square tower with a flat roof (called the Heroes' Tower). The first fortress on this site was built in 1268, but the oldest surviving walls date from about 1440. More of the castle's history can be learned at the **Museet på Koldinghus**, which also hosts temporary exhibitions on decorative art and design. Kolding's main square is Akseltorv, which contains the beautiful Renaissance Borchs Gård dating from 1595. The **Kunstmuseet Trapholt** on the town's eastern outskirts has a large collection of Danish modern art.

Every August, an outdoor concert by the National Opera Ensemble draws large crowds to the hill of Skamlingsbanken.

Museet på Koldinghus
Markdanersgade 11. **Tel** 76 33 81 00.
Open 10am–5pm daily.
koldinghus.dk

Kunstmuseet Trapholt
Æblehaven 23. **Tel** 76 30 05 30. **Open** 10am–5pm daily (to 8pm Wed).

20 Fredericia

Road map: C5. 40,000.
Vendersgade 30D. **Tel** 72 11 35 11.
visitfredericia.dk

Frederik III decided to build Fredericia on this strategic section of the Lille Bælt (Little Belt) – the narrowest point between Jutland and Funen – in 1650. In 1657 the fortress town was captured by the Swedes who slaughtered the entire garrison stationed here. In 1849, during the Schleswig conflict, it was the scene of a battle between the Danes and the Prussian army. The Landsoldaten monument by the Prince's Gate commemorates that event. The town ramparts remain from the original fortress. The best section is by Danmarksgade, where the grassy embankments reach 15 m (49 ft) in height. The nearby water tower dates from 1909 and provides the best view of the surrounding area. **Fredericia Museum** has displays relating to the town's military and civilian history. Madsby Park, a short way outside the old town, contains a miniature version of Fredericia.

Coat of arms on gate in Fredericia

Fredericia Museum
Jernbanegade 10. **Tel** 72 10 69 70.
Open noon–4pm Tue–Sun (mid-Jun–mid-Aug: daily). **Closed** Jan.
fredericiahistorie.dk

View across the river towards the historic town of Ribe ▶

NORTHERN JUTLAND

Visitors to northern Jutland can enjoy beautiful, pristine scenery and peace in this region of farmland and fields, heathland and dunes. The university town of Aalborg is the area's only large city, but in the summer months, the seaside resorts of Skagen and Lokken-Blokhus can also get very busy. There are a number of places to visit, including a Viking burial ground at Lindholm Høje.

The least populated and the wildest part of this region is its northern end, which is shaped by its proximity to the sea. This area provides excellent nesting grounds for a variety of birds. On the northwestern side, facing Skagerrak, the scenery is dominated by dunes, which display the clear effects of frequent sea breezes that shift the sand by up to 10 m (33 ft) each year.

Many visitors embark on trips to Grenen, Denmark's northernmost point, which is washed over by the waters of the Baltic and the North Sea. This area is sometimes referred to as the "Land of Light" and enjoys more hours of sunshine than anywhere else in Denmark. The extraordinary light has long been appreciated by artists, who came here in search of inspiration in the 19th century. Many settled around Skagen, which became a magnet for prominent painters and writers who formed the Skagen School.

Another distinct feature of northern Jutland's landscape are its heathlands. As recently as the mid-19th century they covered one third of this region; now they can be seen only here and there. Northern Jutland also boasts Rold Skov, Denmark's largest forest. Numerous coves make up the Limfjord straits, where you can find traditional inns and little wooden ferries.

The most important of the area's historic sights are the Lindholm Høje prehistoric burial ground and the 1,000-year-old Viking fortress at Fyrkat, which includes a replica Viking farmstead.

Some of Denmark's best beaches can also be found in northern Jutland and there are many holiday cottages and camp sites in the area.

Renaissance manor in Voergård

◀ Boat-shaped grave at Lindholm Høje – the largest Viking burial ground in Scandinavia

Exploring Northern Jutland

Aalborg makes a good base for exploring this part of the country, while smaller towns such as Thisted, Løgstør, Mariager or Skagen can also serve as good jumping-off points. When heading north, it is best to travel by car, since many of the most attractive areas are some distance from each other, and there may be problems with finding suitable public transport. Even when travelling by car it pays to allow plenty of time as many roads are fairly minor and pass through villages. The advantage of travelling on these minor routes is that the scenery is varied and offers a portrait of Denmark quite different from any seen from motorways.

Viking enthusiast sharpening a blade in the village of Fyrkat

View of the cathedral from the shore of the lake in Viborg

Sights at a Glance

1. Fårup
2. Hirtshals
3. Grenen
4. Frederikshavn
5. Sæby
6. Voergård Slot
7. Lindholm Høje
8. *Aalborg pp212–13*
9. *Limfjorden pp214–15*
10. Holstebro
11. Hjerl Hedes Frilandsmuseum
12. Kongenshus Mindepark
13. Mønsted
14. Viborg
15. Rebild Bakker
16. Mariager
17. Fyrkat
18. Randers
19. Gammel Estrup

For keys to symbols *see back flap*

Getting Around

The major transport artery of the region is the E45 motorway, running from the German border to Frederikshavn. The larger towns of the region are all accessible by train. The main ferry harbours are in Frederikshavn and Hirtshals.

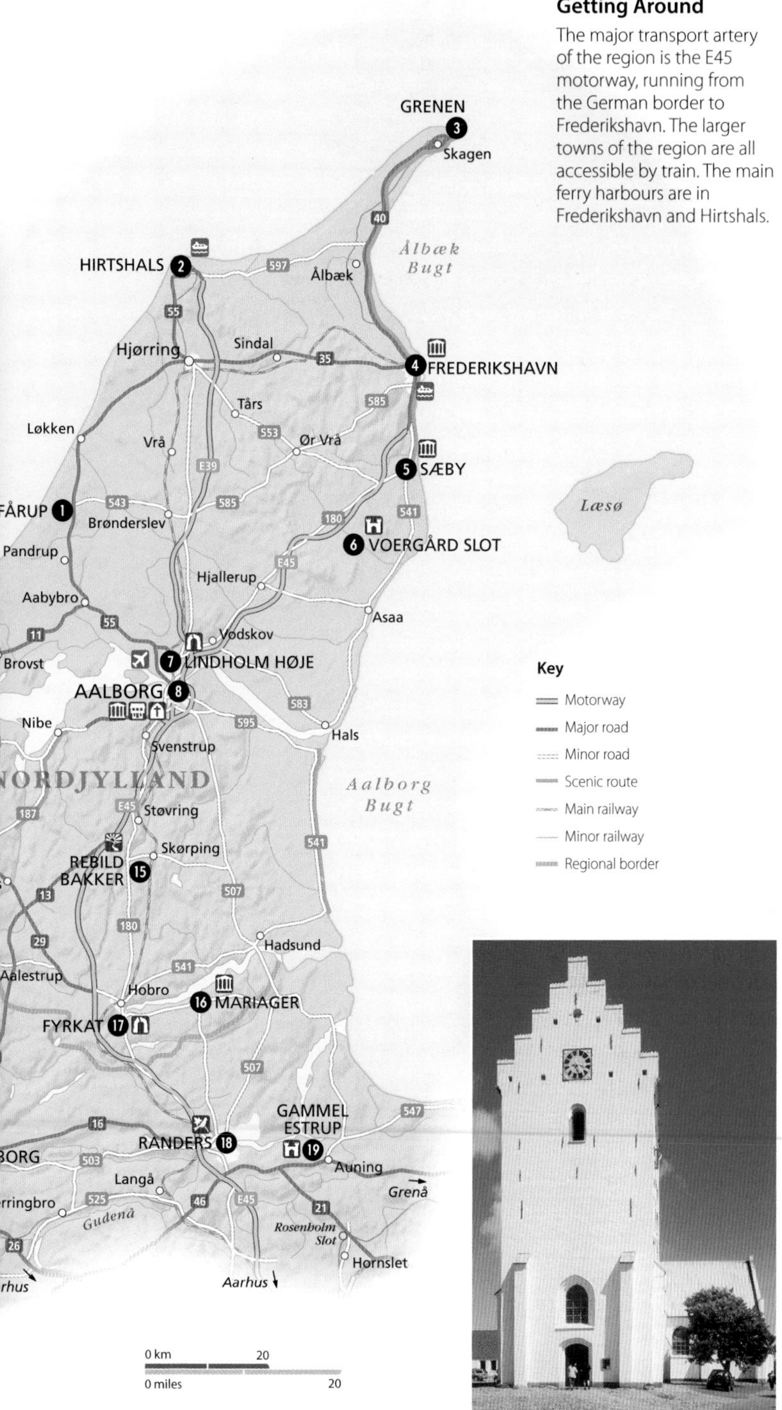

Former Carmelite monastery in Sæby

One of the rides at Fårup Sommerland, a vast amusement park

❶ Fårup

Road map: C2. Pirupvejen 147. **Tel** 98 88 16 00. **Open** May & early Sep: from 10am Sat & Sun; early Jun–late Aug: from 10am daily. Always consult the website before visiting. **W faarup sommerland.dk**

Fårup Sommerland is an amusement park set deep in the forest close to the beach, between Saltum and Blokhus. Among the thrills and spills on offer are wild roller coasters and Denmark's largest and wettest water world. There are also gentler attractions for younger visitors in the children's theme park. Once the splashing is over, visitors can cook a meal in the grill area, jump on the trampolines or take in a film at the 4-D cinema.

❷ Hirtshals

Road map: C1. 15,000. Dalsagervej 1. **Tel** 98 94 22 20. **W visithirtshals.dk**

Towards the end of the 19th century Hirtshals was no more than a small fishing hamlet; now it is one of Jutland's major ports. Regular ferry links with the Norwegian towns of Kristiansand, Oslo and Moss make this small town an important bridge with Denmark's Scandinavian neighbours on the other side of Kattegat. The town has a thriving fishing harbour and every day, at 7am, it becomes the venue for auctioning the night's catch.

The greatest attraction is the **Nordsøen Oceanarium**, a sea-life centre that is situated about 1 km (half a mile) east of the town centre. Since it opened in 1984, the oceanarium has attracted thousands of visitors every year. Its vast tank contains 4.5 million litres (990,000 gallons) of sea water, making it one of Europe's biggest aquariums. The aquarium includes an amphitheatre that looks onto a huge glass pane that is 8 m (26 ft) high and 41 cm (16 in) thick. The fish include schools of herring and mackerel as well as sharks. A diver enters the tank every day at 1pm (and also at 4pm in summer) to feed the fish.

As well as the aquarium, the Nordsøen Oceanarium has numerous displays that explain about the issues surrounding fishing in the North Sea and the ecology of the region. Outside is a seal pool, which has regular feed times at 11am and 3pm.

Hirtshals also offers an extensive network of walking and cycling trails, including one leading to a 57-m- (187-ft-) tall lighthouse and also to Husmoderstrand – a beach with many safe places for children to play and swim.

Hirtshals Museum is in a former fishermen's cottage that dates from 1880. This has an exhibition of everyday objects illustrating the significance of the sea to the local population in the early 20th century.

Aquarium at Nordsøen Oceanarium, Hirtshals

Nordsøen Oceanarium
Willemoesvej. **Tel** 98 94 41 88. **Open** Jan–Mar & Nov: 9am–4pm daily (to 5pm Sat, Sun & hols); Apr–Jun, Sep & Oct: 10am–5pm daily; Jul & Aug: 9am–6pm daily. **W nordsoenoceanarium.dk**

Grenen, where the Baltic meets the North Sea

❸ Grenen

Road map: D1. Vestre Strandvej 10, Skagen. **Tel** 98 44 13 77. **W skagen-tourist.dk**

Grenen is the northernmost point of Denmark. Standing by the car park, from which a 2-km (1-mile) trail leads to the point, is the Skagen Odde Naturcenter. Designed by the Danish architect Jørn Utzon, the centre aims to enable visitors to appreciate the natural environment of this region through a series of imaginative displays utilizing sand, water, wind and light.

The environs of Grenen consist of vast sand dunes, here and there overgrown with heather. This wild landscape captivated the Danish writer Holger Drachmann (1846–1908) to such an extent that he made it his wish to be buried in the sands of Grenen. His grave can be found on one of the nearby dunes.

For hotels and restaurants see pp248–55 and pp262–77

Skagen Artists

The former fishing port of Skagen is now a fashionable resort, full of brightly painted yellow houses and a good number of restaurants and shops. The town's character is accurately represented by its coat of arms, which features a painter's palette in the shape of a flounder. In the late 19th century many artists flocked here in order to "paint the light" and formed what is now known as the Skagen School. Its members included the writer Holger Drachmann, and painters Anna and Michael Ancher, Peder Severin Krøyer, Lautitz Tuxen, Carl Locher, Christian Krogh and Oskar Bjørck. The Skagens Museum exhibits many of their works and it is also possible to visit the former home of the Anchers and that of Drachmann.

The extraordinary light, produced by the reflection of the sun's rays in the waters surrounding Skagen and the dunes, was the inspiration for the 19th-century artists arriving here from all over Denmark, as well as from Sweden and Norway.

The Skagens Museum houses a huge collection of works. Most of the paintings are of local scenes and all of the Skagen School of artists are well represented.

The fishing harbour is crowded with cutters as Skagen is still one of the major centres of fishing in northern Denmark, although much of the town's income now derives from tourism.

Brøndums Hotel, founded by Erik Brøndum in 1859, is charmingly old-fashioned. The hotel was popular with artists, who often met in the bar at night. The Skagens Museum is located in the grounds.

The Skagen artists' work is often characterized by vibrant seascapes and naturalistic portraits. The painting above, by P.S. Krøyer, depicts Anna Ancher and the artist's wife, Marie.

Michael Ancher lived for four years in Brøndums Hotel. Ancher married Anna Brøndum, step-sister of the hotel's owner, who was herself a talented artist. This 1886 portrait of Ancher is by P.S. Krøyer.

❹ Frederikshavn

Road map: D1. 23,000.
Skandiatorv 1. **Tel** 98 42 32 66.
Tordenskiold Festival (Jun).
visitfrederikshavn.dk

The main international ferry port of Jutland has a number of historical sights. The Krudttårnet (Gunpowder Tower) is all that remains of a 17th-century citadel that once guarded the port. Today the tower houses a small military museum. Frederikshavn Kirke dates from the 19th century and contains a painting by Michael Ancher, one of the best-known of the Skagen School *(see p209)*. The **Bangsbo-Museet** is about 3 km (2 miles) south of the centre. This 18th-century manor house has an eclectic collection that includes objects relating to the town's history and the Danish Resistance during World War II. There is also a display of artefacts made from human hair. Perhaps the best exhibit is a reconstructed 12th-century Viking merchant ship.

Bangsbo-Museet
Dronning Margrethes Vej 6. **Tel** 98 42 31 11. **Open** check website for times.
kystmuseet.dk

❺ Sæby

Road map: D1. 18,000.
Algade 14. **Tel** 98 46 12 44.
visitsaeby.dk

The town skyline is dominated by the tower of Vor Frue Kirke (Church of Our Lady), which once formed part of a 15th-century Carmelite monastery. The church is richly decorated with frescoes. Its beautiful Late-Gothic altarpiece dates from around 1520. Next to the church is the grave of Peter Jakob Larssøn, a 19th-century buccaneer who went on to become Sæby's mayor.

Sæby has a compact centre with half-timbered houses and an attractive harbour. In summer a trumpeter heralds the end of each day, which is followed by the ceremonial lowering of a flag. **Sæby Museum**, housed in the 17th-century Ørums Consul's House, contains a 1920s schoolroom and a violinmaker's workshop.

Environs

A short distance north of town is **Sæbygård**, a beautifully preserved 16th-century manor house set in a small beech forest.

Sæby Museum
Algade 1–3. **Tel** 98 46 10 77. **Open** see website for times. **kyst museet.dk /saeby-saebygaard**

Opulent dining room in Voesgård Slot

❻ Voergård Slot

Road map: D2. Voergård 6, Dronningelund. **Tel** 98 86 71 08. **Open** 11am–4pm on certain days from Easter to Oct; variable times so check website for latest information before visiting. compulsory.
voergaardslot.dk

This Renaissance castle is one of Denmark's most stylish buildings. Its splendid portal was intended originally for the royal castle of Fredensborg. Initially the estate was part of a religious complex, but after the Reformation it passed into private hands. The main wing has a large collection of paintings that includes works by Raphael, Goya, Rubens and Fragonard. Also on display are many fine pieces of furniture and porcelain (including a dinner set made for Napoleon I).

❼ Lindholm Høje

Road map: C2. Burial ground: **Open** until dusk. Museum: Vendilavej 11. **Tel** 99 31 74 40. **Open** Apr–Oct: 10am–5pm daily; Nov–Mar: 10am–4pm Tue–Sun. **nordjyllands historiskemuseum.dk**

Denmark's largest Iron Age and Viking burial ground has survived so well due to a thick layer of sand that blew over it. The sand deposit kept the site hidden until 1952, when archaeologists unearthed nearly 700 graves. The oldest ones are triangular; others are circular. The Viking-era graves have been made to resemble ships. Other finds discovered in the vicinity

Half-timbered house in one of Sæby's picturesque streets

indicate that between the 7th and 11th centuries this was an important Viking trading centre. Lindholm Høje comes to life each year during the last week of June, when a Viking festival is held here. Throughout the rest of the year it is possible to visit a museum and try Viking-era food in its restaurant.

8 Aalborg

See pp212–13.

9 Limfjorden

See pp214–15.

10 Holstebro

Road map: B3. 31,000. Jeppe Schous Gade 14. **Tel** 96 11 70 86. **visitholstebro.dk**

The earliest records of Holstebro can be found in 13th-century documents. The town was often plagued by fire, however, and has few historic sights. Continuing a centuries-old tradition the town bells chime every day at 10pm reminding citizens to put out fires for the night.

In front of the mid-19th-century town hall in the centre of town is a sculpture by Alberto Giacometti. The nearby Neo-Gothic church is 20th century and contains the remains of a 16th-century altar.

The **Holstebro Kunstmuseum** has a sizeable collection of paintings (including works by Picasso and Matisse), as well as sculpture and ceramics, mainly by contemporary Danish artists. It also houses interesting temporary exhibitions.

Façade of the Holstebro Kunstmuseum

Village house in Hjerl Hedes Frilandsmuseum

Environs

The **Strandingsmuseet St George**, 45 km (28 miles) to the west of Holstebro, tells the story of a shipwreck that took place in 1811.

Holstebro Kunstmuseum
Museumsvej 2. **Tel** 97 42 45 18. **Open** Jul–Aug: 11am–5pm Tue–Sun; Sep–Jun: noon–4pm Tue–Fri, 11am–5pm Sat–Sun.

Strandingsmuseet St George
Vesterhausgade 1E, Thorsminde. **Tel** 97 49 33 66. **Open** Jan–Mar: 11am–4pm daily; Apr–Oct: 10am–5pm daily; Nov: 11am–3pm daily.

11 Hjerl Hede Frilandsmuseum

Road map: B3. Hjerl Hedevej 14. **Tel** 97 44 80 60. **Open** Opening hours vary; consult the website for details. **hjerlhede.dk**

A short distance northeast of Holstebro is an open-air museum that re-creates the development of a Danish village from 1500 to 1900. The collection of buildings includes an inn, a school, a smithy and a dairy. In summer, men and women wear period clothes and demonstrate traditional skills such as weaving and bread-making.

Kongenshus Mindepark heathland reserve

12 Kongenshus Mindepark

Road map: C3. Vestre Skivevej 142, Daugbjerg, Viborg. **Tel** 86 66 13 78. **Open** all year round. **kongenshus.dk**

A small section of Denmark's uncultivated heathland, of which just 800 sq km (309 sq miles) remains, can be explored at Kongenhus Mindepark. For many years early pioneers attempted to cultivate this windswept and inhospitable area. In the 18th century an army officer from Mecklenburg leased the land from Frederik V, intending it for cultivation. Assisted by the king's generosity, he built a house, which he named Kongenshus (King's House). However, after 12 years the officer abandoned the project and returned to Germany. Today the scenery of Kongenshus Mindepark can be experienced from a tower.

❽ Aalborg

North Jutland's capital city is situated on the south bank of the Limfjorden. It was founded by the Vikings in the 10th century and rapidly acquired a strategic significance as a hub of trade and transport. It prospered in the 17th century thanks to a thriving herring industry and many of its finest buildings date from this time. Aalborg remains a commercial centre and is the seat of the regional government and a university town. The local industry includes the country's leading producer of Danish schnapps, *akvavit*.

Panoramic view of Aalborg, capital of northern Jutland

Coat of arms from Jens Bangs Stenhus

Exploring Aalborg

Most of the historic buildings in Aalborg are clustered around the compact medieval quarter. Jomfru Ane Gade has restaurants and bars and is the centre of the city's nightlife.

Vor Frue Kirke

Niels Ebbesens Gade. **Open** 9am–2pm Mon–Fri, 9am–noon Sat.
W vorfrue.dk

The Church of Our Lady dates back to the 12th century. In the 16th and 17th centuries it was the main place of Christian worship in Aalborg. The west portal deserves a closer look.

Aalborghus Slot

Slotspladsen 1. **Open** 8am–9pm daily. Dungeons: **Open** May–Sep: 8am–3pm Mon–Fri. Underground passages: **Open** 8am–9pm daily.

This modestly sized half-timbered castle was built on the orders of Christian III and completed in 1555. The dank castle dungeons and underground passages leading off them make for an eerie walk.

Utzon Center

Slotspladsen 4. ***Tel*** 76 90 50 00.
Open 10am–5pm Tue–Sun.
W utzoncenter.dk

The Utzon Center, a powerhouse of architectural and design exhibitions, was created by the late Jørn Utzon, in collaboration with his son Kim. Utzon, the man responsible for the Sydney Opera House, grew up in Aalborg. The centre also features a library and an auditorium. It is located by the waterfront, next to the harbour pool, where you can go for a swim.

Jens Bangs Stenhus

Østerågade 9. **Closed** to the public.

A Dutch Renaissance-style house, this five-storey edifice, decorated with gargoyles and floral ornaments, was built in 1624 for Jens Bang, a wealthy merchant. Its façade facing the Rådhus (city hall) includes a stone figure of a satyr sticking its tongue out – this was intended to symbolize the owner's attitude towards the city's councillors who refused to admit him into their ranks. The cellars house a wine bar that also serves traditional Danish food.

Rådhuset

Gammel Torv 2. **Closed** to the public.

The yellow-painted Baroque city hall was completed in 1762 and stands on the site of a demolished Gothic town hall. The motto written above the main door translates as "Wisdom and Determination" and was used by Frederik V, who was on the throne when the city hall was built.

Soldiers preparing for a parade, Aalborghus Slot

For hotels and restaurants see pp248–55 and pp262–77

Budolfi Domkirke

Algade 40. **Tel** 98 12 46 70. **Open** Jun–Aug: 9am–4pm Mon–Fri, 9am–2pm Sat; Sep–May: 9am–3pm Mon–Fri, 9am–noon Sat.

With a distinctive Baroque cupola, this white-plastered Gothic cathedral from around 1400 is an important Aalborg landmark. Among the notable interior features are portraits of wealthy merchants, a gilded Baroque altarpiece and 16th-century frescoes. The church's patron, St Budolfi, is the patron saint of sailors whose cult was propagated by English missionaries.

Delightfully simple interior of Budolfi Domkirke

Historiske Museum

Algade 48. **Tel** 99 31 74 00. **Open** 10am–5pm Tue–Sun. **nordjyllandshistoriskemuseum.dk**

Just west of the cathedral is the local history museum. Its varied collection includes archaeological finds from Lindholm Høje *(see pp210–11)* and rare glassware and ancient coins. The museum's star exhibits include a reconstructed drawing room from an early 17th-century merchant's house. Most interesting of all, perhaps, is the skeleton of a 40-year-old female discovered in a peat bog who died around AD 400.

Helligåndsklostret

Kloster Jordet 1, C.W. Obels Plads. **Tel** 98 12 02 05. late Jun–mid-Aug: 2pm Mon–Fri.

This convent was founded in 1431 and is one of the best-preserved buildings of its type in Scandinavia. The only original part is the west wing; the north and the east wings are 16th century. Guided tours allow visitors to look at the frescoes in the hospital chapel, step into the refectory with its starry vault and listen to the story of a nun who was buried alive for having a relationship with a monk.

VISITORS' CHECKLIST

Practical Information
Road map: C2. 201,000. Nordkraft, Kjellerups Torv 5. **Tel** 99 31 75 00. Aalborg Carnival and Regatta (May). **visitaalborg.com**

Transport
Aalborg.

Helligåndsklostret

Kunsten Museum of Modern Art Aalborg

Kong Christians Allé 50. **Tel** 99 82 41 00. **Closed** for renovation to Oct 2015. **nordjyllandskunstmuseum.dk**

Designed by Alvar Aalto in conjunction with Danish architect Jean-Jacques Baruël, this striking museum has a great collection of Danish and European modern art.

Aalborg Historic Centre

1. Vor Frue Kirke
2. Aalborghus Slot
3. Utzon Center
4. Jens Bangs Stenhus
5. Rådhuset
6. Budolfi Domkirke
7. Historiske Museum
8. Helligåndsklostret

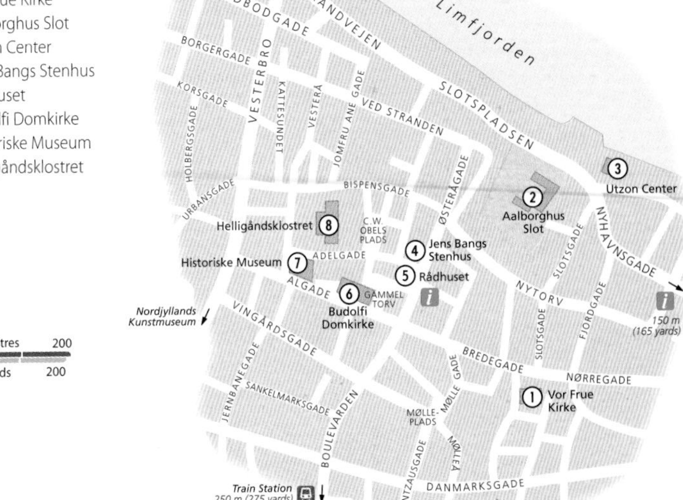

For keys to symbols *see back flap*

❾ Limfjorden

Limfjorden is Denmark's largest body of inland water. Although narrow inlets connect it to both the Kattegat and the North Sea, Limfjorden resembles a lake. In summer, ferries offer trips to the smaller islands and other areas. Just how significant this area was at one time can be deduced from the many Bronze Age burial mounds, churches and castles. The shape of the island of Mors resembles Jutland. According to legend, when God created Jutland he first built a model. It was so good that he placed it at the centre of Limfjorden. The Hanklit Cliffs on the northern tip of Mors have particularly stunning views.

★ Jesperhus Park
This park is planted with half a million flowers. Some are planted to form figures of animals found in the park zoo, such as a crocodile.

Spit
A narrow 10-km (6-mile) spit leads from Thyborøn to Harboøre. The east side is flanked by the fjord, the western side by the North Sea.

★ Spøttrup Borg
Protected against attack by a moat and high ramparts, this medieval castle has changed little since it was built in 1500.

Hjerl Hede Frilandsmuseum
Among the many historic buildings at this open-air museum are an inn, a smithy, a dairy, a school, a vicarage and a grocer's shop *(see p211)*.

Fjerritslev
Situated between the fjord and the North Sea, Fjerritslev is surrounded by beautiful scenery. The town brewery, a red-brick building, has been preserved as a museum.

VISITORS' CHECKLIST

Practical Information
Road map: B2–C2. Thisted.
Store Torv 6. **Tel** 97 92 56 04.
Havnen 4. **Tel** 97 72 04 88.
visitmors.dk **visitthy.dk**
visitskive.dk

Transport
Thisted:
Nykøbing Mors:

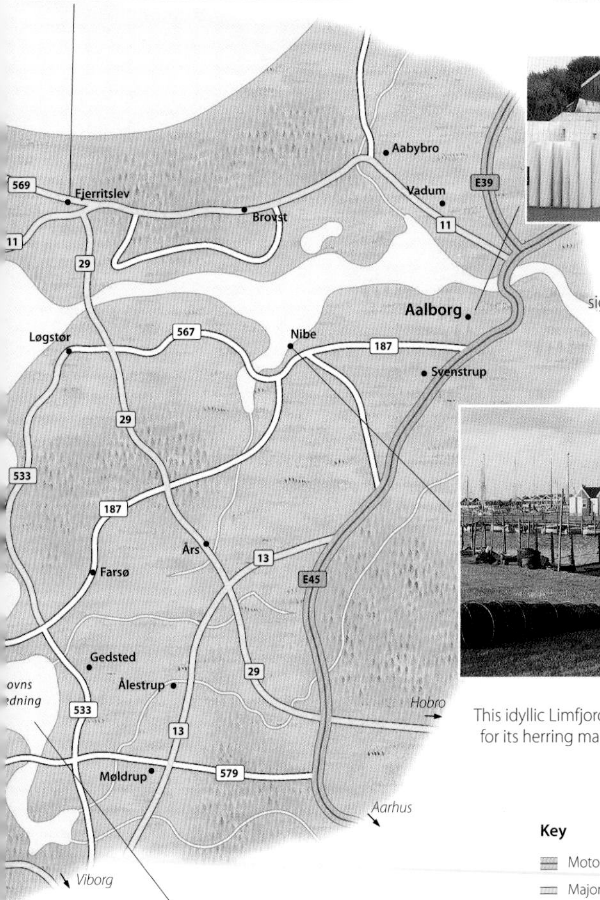

Aalborg
Northern Jutland's capital city has many interesting sights, including the superb Kunsten Museum of Modern Art *(see p213)*.

Nibe
This idyllic Limfjord town used to be famous for its herring markets, which would supply fish for the royal table.

Key

Motorway
Major road
Other road

Lovns Bredning
This section of Limfjorden, which has some enchanting coves, is a protected area because of the rich diversity of birdlife found here.

Mønsted's limestone mine

⓭ Mønsted

Road map: C3. Mønsted Kalkgruber, Kalkværksvej 8. **Tel** 86 64 60 11.
Open Apr–Oct: 10am–5pm daily.
W **monsted-kalkgruber.dk**

As far back as the 10th century the area around Mønsted was famous as a centre of limestone mining. The mine, which was still in operation in the 20th century, is now an unusual local attraction. Although only 2 km (1 mile) of the entire 60 km (37 miles) of its tunnels are open, a walk through the underground maze is an unforgettable experience. Visitors can wander at their own pace through the galleries, but they must wear safety helmets. For those who prefer more comfort, there is a mine train, which travels into the pit, past limestone columns and underground lakes. In view of the mine's steady humidity and temperature, which stays at 8° C (46° C), some of the caves situated 35 m (115 ft) below the surface are used for ripening cheese.

⓮ Viborg

Road map: C3. 35,000.
Nytorv 9. **Tel** 87 87 88 88.
Marching Festival (Jun).
W **visitviborg.dk**

Viborg is scenically located on the shores of two lakes. Its history dates back to the 8th century and it became one of Denmark's bishoprics in 1060. The 12th-century cathedral was used for coronation ceremonies by the Danish monarchy until the 17th century. The present twin-towered **Domkirke** (cathedral) was completed in 1876. This huge granite building has some valuable relics as well as a crypt dating from 1130, which is all that remains of the original cathedral. Other features include a gilded altarpiece and a vast 15th-century candelabra. The cathedral's frescoes form an illustrated Bible and were created by the Danish artist Joakim Skovgaard (1901–06). Other works by the artist can be seen in the **Skovgaard Museet**, which is next to the cathedral. The **Viborg Museum** contains a variety of exhibits relating to the town's history, including some items that date from the Viking era. Viborg's city hall, located on the outskirts of the town, in the middle of a park, is a modern and fully sustainable building designed by the architect Henning Larsen.

Figures from Viborg's Domkirke

Domkirke
Domkirkepladsen, Sankt Mogensgade 4. **Tel** 87 25 52 50. **Open** opening hours vary so see website for latest information befor visiting.
W **viborgdomkirke.dk**

Skovgaard Museet
Domkirkstræde 4. **Tel** 86 62 39 75.
Open Jun–Aug: 10am–5pm Tue–Sun; Sep–May: 11am–4pm Tue–Sun.

Viborg Museum
Hjultorvet 4. **Tel** 87 87 38 38.
Open Jul–mid-Aug: 11am–5pm Tue–Sun; mid-Aug–Jun: 1–4pm Tue–Fri, 11am–5pm Sat & Sun.

⓯ Rebild Bakker

Map C2. VisitRebild – RebildPorten, Rebildvej 25A, Rebild.
Tel 99 88 90 00. **W** **visitrebild.dk**

Rebild Bakker is part of Rold Skov, the largest forest in Denmark. In 1912, after fund-raising among the Danish expatriate community in the USA, a section of it was purchased and turned into this park. Covering 77 sq km (30 sq miles), an array of wildlife lives in the park, including foxes, deer, squirrels, martens, badgers and numerous birds. Close to Rebild Bakker is the **Fiddlers Museum**, where every Sunday afternoon visitors are encouraged to participate in a lively square dance. The museum also explores the way in which the surrounding forest has shaped the economy of the area and the lives of the local people by looking at various forest trades, including hunting and poaching.

Fiddlers Museum
Cimbrervej 2. **Tel** 98 39 16 04.
Open Oct–Apr: 1–5pm Sun; May–Aug: 10am–5pm daily; Sep: 11am–4pm daily.

⓰ Mariager

Road map: D3. 2,500.
Torvet 1B, 70 27 13 77.
W **visitmariager.dk**

In the Middle Ages Mariager was a major centre of pilgrimages, owing to the nunnery that was established here in 1410. Today, it is a quiet fjord town, with cobbled streets and picturesque houses engulfed in roses. The main reminder of the convent is the church standing on a wooded hill. Though it is much smaller than the original

◄ Rubjerg Knude Lighthouse at the end of the dunes in Hjørring, overlooking the North Sea

Banks of Limfjorden, near Mariager

14th-century building it is possible to imagine what the convent would have been like from a scale model in **Mariager Museum**, which is housed in an 18th-century merchant's house.

At **Mariager Saltcenter** visitors can learn about methods of salt production, make their own crystals and take a bath in Denmark's version of the Dead Sea, which has pools filled with warm water so salty that it's quite impossible to dive beneath the surface. Bring a swimsuit.

Small bag of salt from Mariager Saltcenter

Mariager Museum
Kirkegade 4A. **Tel** 99 31 74 60. **Open** mid-May–mid-Sep: noon–4pm daily.

Mariager Saltcenter
Ny Havnevej 6. **Tel** 98 54 18 16. **Open** 10am–4pm daily (to 5pm Sat, Sun & hols). **saltcenter.com**

17 Fyrkat

Road map: C3. Fyrkatvej 37B, Hobro. **Tel** 99 82 41 75. **Open** May: 10am–4pm daily; Jun–Aug: 10am–5pm daily; Sep: 10am–3pm daily. **nordmus.dk**

In 1950 the remains of a Viking settlement dating from around AD 980 were discovered in fields 3 km (2 miles) from the town of Hobro. A modern visitor centre has since been built around the site.

The entire settlement was surrounded by ramparts 120 m (394 ft) in diameter. The entry gates to the fortress, aligned strictly with the points of the compass, were linked with each other by two intersecting streets. An ancient burial site containing 30 graves was discovered outside the main camp. A Viking-style farmstead north of the settlement re-creates many aspects of Viking life. Visitors can try on a Viking tunic and bake bread over an open fire.

18 Randers

Road map: D3. 60,000. Rådhustorvet 4. **Tel** 86 42 44 77. **visitranders.com**

Jutland's fourth largest city was already a major market town in the Middle Ages. Its most important historic sight is the 15th-century Sankt Morten's Kirke. Hanging inside is a model of a ship dating from 1632. The three-storey Paaskesønnernes Gård nearby is late 15th century and one of the city's oldest houses. The most popular attraction is **Randers Regnskov**, an unusual tropical zoo that houses 200 animal species and 450 species of plants in a tropical rain forest environment. Here, regardless of the time of the year, the temperature remains at a constant 25° C (77° F), accompanied by very high humidity. Among the many animals kept at the zoo are crocodiles, gibbons, colourful butterflies, tapirs and snakes. There is also an area focusing on old breeds of Danish farm animals.

Randers Regnskov
Tørvebryggen 11. **Tel** 87 10 99 99. **Open** 10am–4pm Mon–Fri, 10am–5pm Sat & Sun. **regnskoven.dk**

19 Gammel Estrup

Road map: D3. Randersvej 2–4. **Tel** 86 48 30 01. **Open** Opening hours vary; check the website prior to your visit. **gammelestrup.dk**

One of the region's major attractions is the Gammel Estrup estate, near the village of Auning on the Djursland peninsula. The estate's 15th-century manor house is partially surrounded by a moat and now houses a museum. Its interiors, complete with period furniture, paintings and tapestries, include reception rooms, bedrooms, a chapel and an alchemist's cellar. An agricultural museum, the Dansk Landbrugs-museum, focuses on Denmark's agricultural past and includes farm machinery and tools.

Environs
Rosenholm Slot, near Hornslet, is a 16th-century castle built on a small island in the middle of a lake. It was here that Count Rosenkrantz, immortalized in Shakespeare's *Hamlet*, lived.

Façade of Gammel Estrup's manor house

For hotels and restaurants see pp248–55 and pp262–77

BORNHOLM

Far out in the Baltic, the idyllic island of Bornholm has an atmosphere all of its own. For years it remained relatively unknown to outsiders but the beauty of the island's sprawling beaches, its rugged coastal cliffs and distinctive architecture have made it a popular holiday destination. Tourism remains a low-key affair, however, and the villages and towns have changed little over the years.

Bornholmers are proud of their ancestry and have their own flag and, among the older generation, a distinctive dialect that is as unique to the island as the *rundkirke* (round churches) that are found here.

The discovery of ancient burial mounds and engravings suggest that the island was inhabited by 3000 BC. At one time Bornholm was an important centre for trade, and coins have been unearthed from as far afield as Rome and the Near East. The name "Bornholm" appeared for the first time in AD 890 at a time when the island was inhabited by the Vikings.

From the mid-12th century much of Bornholm became the property of the Archbishop of the city of Lund, which at that time belonged to Denmark. For a period in the 17th century it was controlled by Sweden but the islanders' strong allegiance to Denmark resulted in a rapid withdrawal of Swedish forces. Following the surrender of Germany in May 1945 Bornholm was occupied by the Soviets until the Danish army established a permanent garrison.

Today, Bornholm has a thriving fishing industry and no visitor should leave without sampling its smoked herring, known as *røget bornholmer.*

A wide variety of natural habitats is found here ranging from secluded forests and pasture land to rugged cliffs and long, sandy beaches. Another of the island's assets is its climate, with mild winters and Denmark's highest percentage of sunny days. The local flora features many species typical of the Mediterranean, including orchids, figs, grapes and mulberry trees.

Svaneke's yacht marina

◀ Myreagre Molle windmill on the island of Bornholm

Exploring Bornholm

Bornholm has some good cycle paths and exploring by bicycle is both convenient and enjoyable. The northern shore is marked by steep cliffs while sandy beaches are the main feature of the south and southeast coasts. Bornholm is known for its round churches and for the atmospheric ruins at Hammershus Slot. Rønne, the island's main town, has some well-preserved quarters, as do many of the smaller harbour ports. Children will enjoy a visit to Joboland Park, which includes an aquapark and a small zoo, and Østerlars' history centre where they can see what life was like in a medieval village.

Modern power-generating windmills north of Hasle

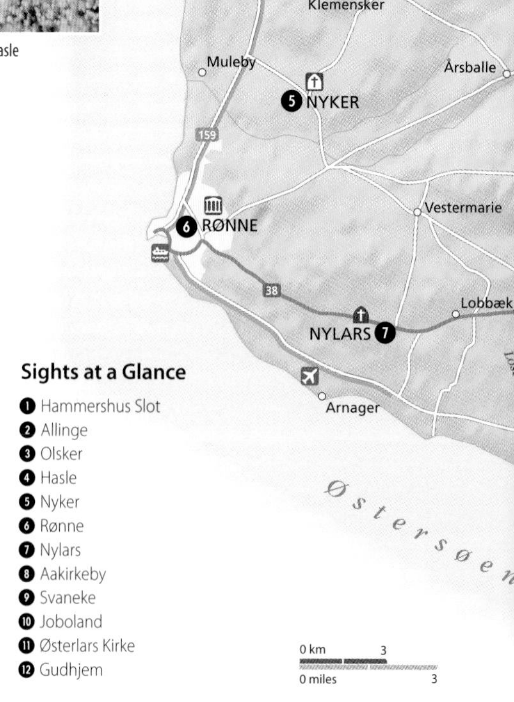

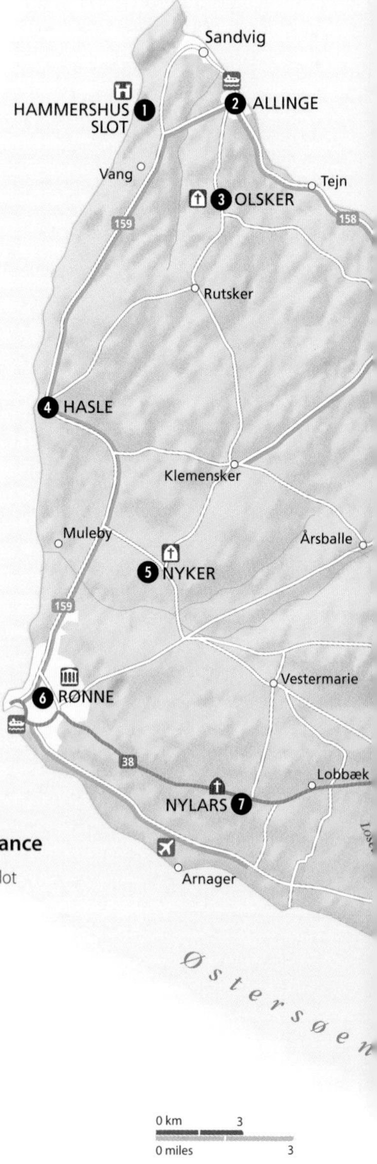

One of Bornholm's fortified 12th-century round churches

Sights at a Glance

1. Hammershus Slot
2. Allinge
3. Olsker
4. Hasle
5. Nyker
6. Rønne
7. Nylars
8. Aakirkeby
9. Svaneke
10. Joboland
11. Østerlars Kirke
12. Gudhjem

For keys to symbols *see back flap*

Key

- Major road
- Minor road
- Scenic route

The scenic coast of Bornholm

Getting There

Bornholm's airport is 5 km (3 miles) southeast of Rønne. A flight from Copenhagen takes half an hour. Many visitors arrive by ferry. The journey from Køge takes six to seven hours (overnight ferries are an option). As an alternative, visitors can take a three-hour journey by train to Ystad in Sweden, and pick up a ferry from there to Rønne. Buses are also available from Copenhagen to Ystad and cost a little less.

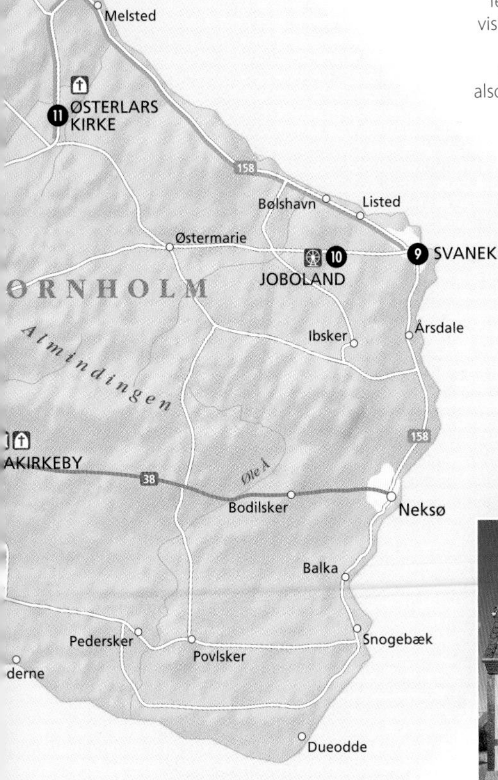

One of Rønne's many colourful half-timbered houses

Picturesque ruins of Hammershus Slot

❶ Hammershus Slot

Castle: **Open** all year round. Hammershus Exhibition: Langebjergvej 128, Allinge. **Open** mid-Apr–mid-Oct: 10am–4pm daily; (Jun–Aug: 10am–5pm daily).

The atmospheric ruins of Hammershus Slot are the largest in northern Europe and stand on a 70-m- (230-ft-) high cliff. The castle was built in the 13th century on the orders of the Archbishop of Lund. Legend has it that Hammershus was originally to be built at a different site, but the walls erected during the day vanished each night. A change of location was thought necessary and horses were let loose; the spot where they finally stopped was chosen as the new site.

The entrance to the castle leads over a stone bridge that was once a drawbridge. The ruins also include what remains of a brewery, a granary and a bakery.

The impressive square tower, Manteltårnet, was used in the Middle Ages for storing the country's tax records and later served as the quarters of the castle commander and also as a prison. In 1660 Leonora Christina, daughter of Christian IV, and her husband were imprisoned in the tower, accused of collaboration with the Swedes. Technological improvements in artillery eventually diminished the castle's defensive capabilities as its walls became vulnerable to attack from powerful cannons. It was abandoned in 1743 and much of the castle was used as building material for local homes. An exhibition includes a model of Hammershus Slot as it was at the peak of its might.

❷ Allinge

2,000. Kirkegade 4. **Tel** 56 48 64 48.

Allinge and nearby Sandvig, 2 km (1 mile) to the northwest, are treated as one town though the two have slightly different characters. Allinge has the majority of commercial facilities while Sandvig is quieter, with walking trails and neatly-tended gardens. Allinge's church is mostly 19th century, although the church itself grew out of a chapel erected five centuries earlier. Inside is a painting that once adorned the chapel in Hammershus Slot as well as tombstones of the castle's past commanders. On the outskirts of Allinge there is a well-kept cemetery for Russian soldiers, with a granite obelisk proudly displaying the Soviet star at the top. This is a reminder of the Red Army, who occupied Bornholm from the end of World War II until March 1946.

Granite obelisk at Allinge Cemetery

On the outskirts of Allinge is Madsebakke Helleristininger – the biggest and the most precious set of rock carvings to be found in the whole of Denmark. These simple enigmatic Bronze Age drawings, depicting ships, boats and the outlines of feet, are thought to be 4,000 years old. Another local curiosity is the Moseløkken quarry, where between May and September visitors can learn all about the excavation of granite on Bornholm and even have a go at splitting a piece themselves.

12th-century three-storey round church in Olsker

❸ Olsker

1,700.

The village of Olsker, south of Allinge, has one of the best known of Bornholm's distinctive round churches. Historians once believed they were of pagan origin. This hypothesis has now been discarded and the current theory is that they were intended for defensive purposes, as well as being used for storage. This three-storey granite building is the slenderest of Bornholm's four round churches and has nine windows. It was erected in the mid-12th century in honour of St Olaf, a Norwegian king who died in 1031, and who is revered in Denmark. The hill on which the church stands affords a beautiful view of the surrounding countryside.

For hotels and restaurants see pp248–55 and pp262–77

Round Churches

Bornholm's four sparkling-white *rundkirke* (round churches) are each dedicated to a different saint. They were built between 1150 and 1200 at a time when pirate attacks were a constant threat to the island and have 2-m (7-ft) thick granite walls. Apart from the one at Nyker, all are three-storey buildings. The bottom level was used mainly for worship. The first floor served as a supply warehouse and also stored the church's valuables and donations received from the faithful. In times of danger the first floor also provided shelter for women and children, while the third, top level was used for surveillance and was an ideal place from which to shoot and throw stones at the advancing enemy below.

Østerlars rundkirke has a central pillar 6 m (20 ft) in diameter. It is adorned with a 14th-century frieze depicting scenes from the life of Christ.

The churches are decorated with paintings dating from the 13th and 14th centuries. The most popular themes are biblical.

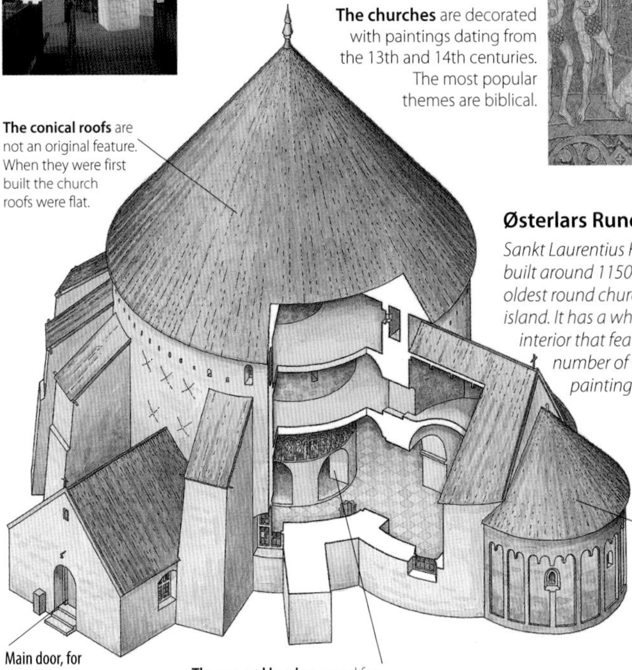

The conical roofs are not an original feature. When they were first built the church roofs were flat.

Østerlars Rundkirke

Sankt Laurentius Kirke was built around 1150 and is the oldest round church on the island. It has a whitewashed interior that features a number of Gothic wall paintings *(see p230)**.*

Apses

Main door, for men only

The ground level was used for worship. Women came in through a separate entrance.

Many elements of furnishing are not as old as the churches themselves. A notable feature of Olsker's church is its richly ornamented 16th-century pulpit.

Top floors were accessed by a stairway leading through narrow passages knocked out of the thick walls.

❹ Hasle

1,800. Havnegade 1. **Tel** 56 96 44 81. **hasleroegeri.dk**

One of Bornholm's oldest towns, Hasle is mentioned in records as early as 1149. The herring industry has long been the town's main source of revenue although many locals were once also employed in excavating brown coal until the mine closed in 1946. The town is popular with visitors, many of whom come to sample the smoked herring. Hasle Smokehouse is the last smokehouse in Bornholm where smoking takes place in the traditional way in open chimneys with alder fire wood. There are smoking sessions every day from May to October and it is possible to follow the smoking process from early morning to about 10:30pm, when the herring and other fish products are finished and ready to be eaten.

In the centre of town stands an interesting 15th-century church with a lovely two-winged altarpiece made in Lübeck in 1520. According to one local story the altar was a gift from a sailor who miraculously escaped from a sinking ship.

A monument in the town square commemorates Peder Olsen, Jens Kofoed and Poul Anker who became the local heroes of an uprising against the Swedes that erupted in Bornholm in 1658.

On the outskirts of the town, on the road leading towards Rønne, is a huge runic stone – the largest one on the island.

Nykirke's pillar with scenes from the Stations of the Cross

❺ Nyker

800.

The smallest of Bornholm's historic round churches *(see p225)* is in Nyker. It is only two storeys high and lacks external buttresses. In keeping with its name (Nykirke or New Church) it is also the most recently built of the churches. A Latin inscription found on the Late-Gothic chalice kept in the church proclaims that the church is dedicated to All Saints. Other items to look out for include the frescoes that decorate the main pillar of the church, which depict the Stations of the Cross, and a stone laid in the portico with a Resurrection scene that dates from 1648. Another interesting object is an 18th-century tablet carved with the names of the local inhabitants who died in two plagues that devastated the area in 1618 and 1654.

❻ Rønne

14,000. Nordre Kystvej 3. **Tel** 56 95 95 00. Wed, Sat. **bornholm.info**

One third of Bornholm's population live in Rønne. The town has grown up around a natural harbour and two of the first buildings that can be seen when approaching from the sea are the 19th-century lighthouse and Sankt Nicolai Kirke.

Rønne has two main squares – Store Torv and Lille Torv (Big Market and Little Market). Store Torv was originally used for military parades but is now the venue for a twice-weekly market.

The Tinghus at Store Torv 1 dates from 1834 and was once used as the town hall, court-house and jail. A number of picturesque cobbled streets lead off from Store Torv and many of the early 19th-century houses are still standing, despite a series of bombing raids carried out by the Soviets in May 1945. One of Rønne's most unusual buildings is in Vimmelskaftet – its width allows for one window only. Standing at the corner of Østergade and Theaterstræde is the restored Rønne Theatre, one of the oldest theatres in Denmark, dating from 1823. **Bornholms Museum** has a good local-history section that includes archaeological finds, a small collection of paintings and a selection of 6th-century golden tablets known as *goldgubber*. Over 2,000 of these tablets engraved with small figures have been found on the island. The **Forsvarsmuseet**

Distinctive white chimneys of a smokehouse in Hasle

Harbourside smithy in Rønne

(Military Museum) is housed in a citadel south of the town centre that was built around 1650. The defensive tower houses a large collection of weapons, ammunition, uniforms and one of the oldest cannons in Denmark.

Bornholms Museum
Sankt Mortensgade 29. **Tel** 56 95 07 35. **Open** Jan–mid-May & mid-Oct–Dec: 1–4pm Mon–Fri, 11am–3pm Sat; mid-May–Jun & Sep–mid-Oct: 10am–5pm Mon–Sat; Jul & Aug: 10am–5pm daily.

Forsvarsmuseet
Arsenalvej 8. **Tel** 56 95 65 83. **Open** mid-May–Sep: 10am–4pm Tue–Sat.

7 Nylars

Situated some 7 km (4 miles) east of Rønne, Nylars Rundkirke is one of Bornholm's four well-preserved round churches *(see p225)*. It was built in 1150 and is dedicated to St Nicholas, the patron saint of sailors. To climb the stairs to the upper levels it is necessary to squeeze through narrow passages knocked through thick walls. For invaders trying to reach the upper floor this presented a big obstacle. The frescoes that adorn the distinctive pillar that rises through all three levels of the building depict biblical scenes including Adam and Eve's expulsion from the Garden of Eden.

8 Aakirkeby

2,000. Torvet 30. **Tel** 56 97 37 20.

During the Middle Ages this was the most important town on the island and the seat of Bornholm's church and the lay authorities. As a result, the 12th-century Aekirke is Bornholm's largest church. The Romanesque building contains a number of treasures including a 13th-century baptismal font and an early 17th-century pulpit. Climbing to the top of the church's high bell tower affords great views of the town. Aakirkeby's latest attraction is **NaturBornholm**, a state-of-the-art natural history museum situated on the southern outskirts of town. A trip to the museum takes visitors back 2,000 years and provides an entertaining and informative way to learn about the flora and fauna of the island. Behind this centre is a gigantic natural fault in the bedrock created some 400 million years ago, which marks the geological boundary between the continental plates of Europe and Scandinavia.

Denmark's national emblem, Åkirke

NaturBornholm
Grønningen 30. **Tel** 56 94 04 00. **Open** Apr–Oct: 10am–5pm.
naturbornholm.dk

9 Svaneke

1,200. Havnebryggen 2. **Tel** 56 49 70 79. Sat.

In the 1970s this appealing town won the European Gold Medal preservation award and Svaneke continues to maintain its unspoilt historic character. A short distance south of the town centre is Svaneke Kirke. A majestic swan adorns the spire of this 14th-century church (Svaneke translates as "Swan Corner"), and the image of a swan is also included in the town emblem.

In the local glass factory, Pernille Bulow, visitors can watch as skilled workers produce glassware. As well as being known as one of the most photogenic towns on Bornholm, Svaneke is also famous for its windmills. These can be seen standing by each of the town's exit roads. The best preserved is the Årsdale Mølle (1877) on the road leading to Nexø. The mill is open to visitors and also sells its own flour.

Horse-drawn tram in Svaneke, a popular way to see the town

⑩ Joboland

3 km (2 miles) from Svaneke, Højevejen 4. **Tel** 56 49 60 76. **Open** early May–Jun & mid-Aug–mid-Sep: 11am–5pm Tue–Thu, Sat & Sun; Jul–early Aug: 10am–6:30pm daily; early Aug–mid-Aug: 11am–5pm daily. **joboland.dk**

This amusement park has enough entertainment to last an entire day. Its greatest attraction is the aquapark with pools of water kept at a constant 25° C (77° F). The aquapark contains five water slides and a 125-m-(410-ft-) long Wild River, which adventurous visitors can ride on a rubber tyre. It is also possible to sail a boat, whizz down a "death slide" and walk across a rope bridge. During high season the park lays on additional shows and games for children, such as treasure hunts. Joboland also has its own small zoo with a variety of animals including peacocks, goats, monkeys and exotic birds.

Climbing frames at Joboland amusement park

Østerlars Kirke, the largest of the island's round churches

⑪ Østerlars Kirke

Vietsvej 25. **Tel** 56 49 82 64. **Open** mid-Apr–mid-Oct: 9am–5pm Mon–Sat (Jul & Aug: 1–5pm Sun).

The largest of Bornholm's round churches *(see p225)* is Østerlars Kirke, which is scenically located in the middle of wheat fields. The church dates from 1150 and is dedicated to Sankt Laurentius (St Laurence). The sturdy buttresses and conical roof are later additions. Inside, the central pillar is decorated with 14th-century frescoes. A rune stone at the entrance dates from 1070 and bears the inscription: "Edmund and his brother erected this stone to the memory of their father Sigmund. May Christ, St Michael and St Mary help his soul."

Near the church is Middelaldercenter, a re-created village where staff in medieval dress work in the smithy, grind corn and tend sheep. There are daily demonstrations of medieval skills such as making clay pots and archery.

Middelaldercenter
Stangevej 1. **Tel** 56 49 83 19. **Open** May & Sep: 11am–3pm Mon–Fri; Jun & Aug: 10am–5pm Mon–Fri; Jul: 10am–4pm Mon–Sat. **bornholmsmiddelaldercenter.dk**

⑫ Gudhjem

700. Ejnar Mikkelsens Vej 17. **Tel** 56 48 64 48.

The village of Gudhjem ("God's Home") is built on a steep hill overlooking the sea. The picturesque harbour, cobbled streets and brightly painted half-timbered houses with red-tiled roofs make it a popular spot with visitors in summer.

The village has long been associated with the fishing industry and in 1893 Gudhjem acquired the first proper smokehouse in Bornholm. The famous "Sun over Gudhjem", a herring smoked in its skin and served with egg yolk, is well worth trying.

In the centre of the village is a late 19th-century church. Close by are the remains of a much older chapel dating from the 13th century. The **Oluf Høst Museet** has a large selection of paintings by the Bornholm artist Oluf Høst who died in 1966. The collection is housed in the artist's home, which he built in 1929. An old railway station houses the **Gudhjem Museum**, which has displays on local history.

Oluf Høst Museet
Løkkegade 35. **Tel** 56 48 50 38. **Open** early May–end Sep: 11am–5pm daily. **Closed** early May–mid-Jun: Mon.

Gudhjem Museum
Stationsvej 1. **Tel** 61 22 33 65. **Open** 10am–5pm Mon–Sat, 2–5pm Sun.

Half-timbered houses in Gudhejm

◀ Rock formations leading into the sea at Bornholm

Cycling on Bornholm

The best way to explore Bornholm is by bicycle and cycle groups are a common sight. The island has 235 km (146 miles) of well signposted cycling routes, many of which connect to the main towns. The routes provide an ideal way to enjoy Bornholm's meadows, fields and forests. Most are far away from busy roads. Rønne, Allinge, and Gudhjem are good places to start. An English language brochure entitled *Bicycle Routes on Bornholm* is available at tourist information centres. Be aware that cycling on Bornholm requires a reasonable level of fitness as there are numerous hills.

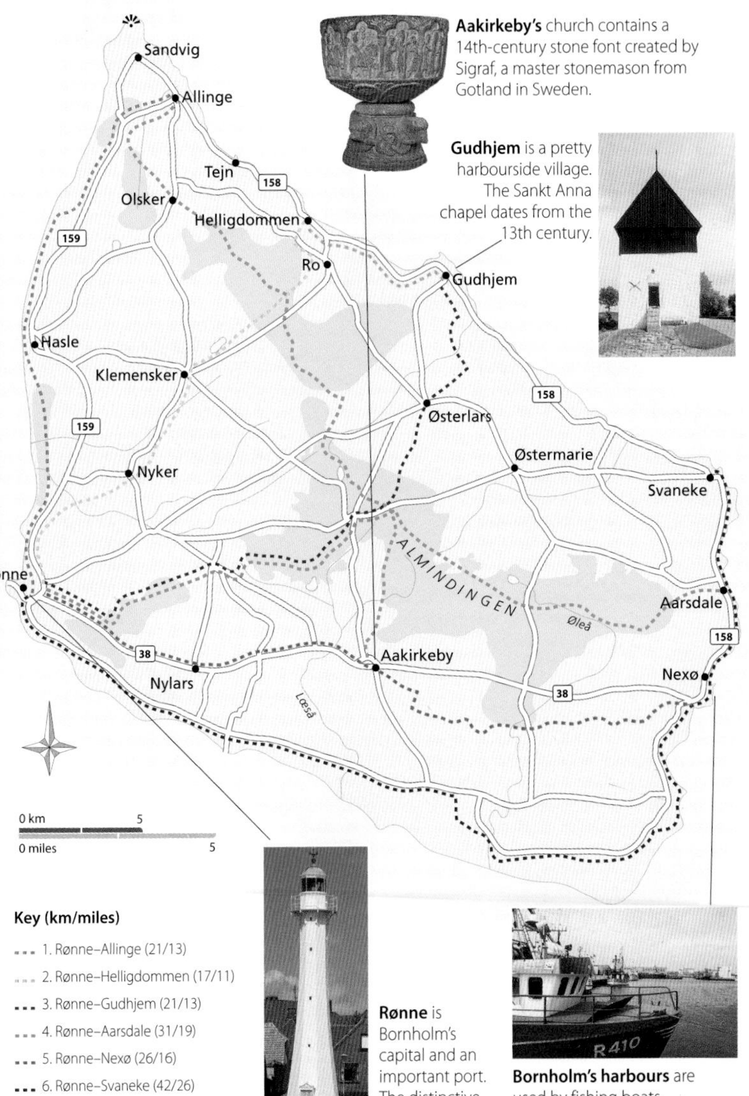

Aakirkeby's church contains a 14th-century stone font created by Sigraf, a master stonemason from Gotland in Sweden.

Gudhjem is a pretty harbourside village. The Sankt Anna chapel dates from the 13th century.

Key (km/miles)

1. Rønne–Allinge (21/13)
2. Rønne–Helligdommen (17/11)
3. Rønne–Gudhjem (21/13)
4. Rønne–Aarsdale (31/19)
5. Rønne–Nexø (26/16)
6. Rønne–Svaneke (42/26)
7. Allinge–Aakirkeby (28/17)
8. Gudhjem–Helligdommen (7/4)

Rønne is Bornholm's capital and an important port. The distinctive lighthouse is 19th century.

Bornholm's harbours are used by fishing boats throughout the year and by visiting yachts in summer.

GREENLAND AND THE FAROE ISLANDS

These two far-flung territories of Denmark offer spectacular adventure and some of the world's most stunning scenery. Greenland's vast frozen glaciers and wondrous northern lights, and the remote settlements and varied birdlife on the Faroe Islands, are ideal for visitors attracted by solitude and natural beauty.

Denmark's two distant island territories enjoy a particular status. Greenland was granted home rule in 1979; the Faroe Islands in 1948. Both have their own government but due to the fact that Denmark retains responsibility for matters such as defence, both are represented in the Danish parliament.

Native Greenlanders share a common heritage with the Inuit of Alaska and northern Canada. Denmark's links with the island began in the 10th century when Viking settlers arrived here and began trading with the Greenlanders. The island was named by Erik the Red, a Viking chief who reached the southern end of Greenland around AD 985.

Early settlers on the Faroe Islands were from Norway. When Norway came under Danish rule in the 14th century the islands also became part of Denmark. Denmark ceded Norway to Sweden in 1814 under the Treaty of Kiel but the Faroes continued under the Danish crown until demands for independence led to eventual home rule. The local name for the Faroes is Føroyar, which translates as "sheep island". The Faroes are aptly named and there are currently almost twice as many sheep as people.

Both Greenland and the Faroe Islands are perfect for nature lovers. A boat tour through parts of Greenland, for instance, takes visitors through crystal-clear waters teeming with marine life including seals and whales. Dog-sled tours across frozen lakes are possible during the winter. The Faroe Islands are a paradise for hikers and ramblers and have a huge variety of birdlife.

Typical Faroe Islands scenery with rocky islets jutting out into the sea

◀ Atlantic puffins on Mykines, the Faroe Islands

Exploring Greenland

Greenland is the world's largest island (assuming Australia is a continent) and has a total area of 2,175,600 sq km (840,000 sq miles) and 40,000 km (25,000 miles) of coast. About 80 per cent of the land mass is covered by a huge ice-sheet that is up to 3 km (2 miles) thick. Despite its great size, the island has a population of just 56,000, who are primarily from Inuit and European backgrounds. For much of the year Greenland is a snow-covered wilderness, though Greenlanders live there, and tourists visit, year round. During spring and summer, the coastal regions thaw and the temperature can rise to as much as 21° C (70° F) in some towns. Many towns and villages have had both Greenlandic and Danish names since the 1980s.

Greenlanders in colourful national costumes

Midnight sun during summer months above the Artic Circle

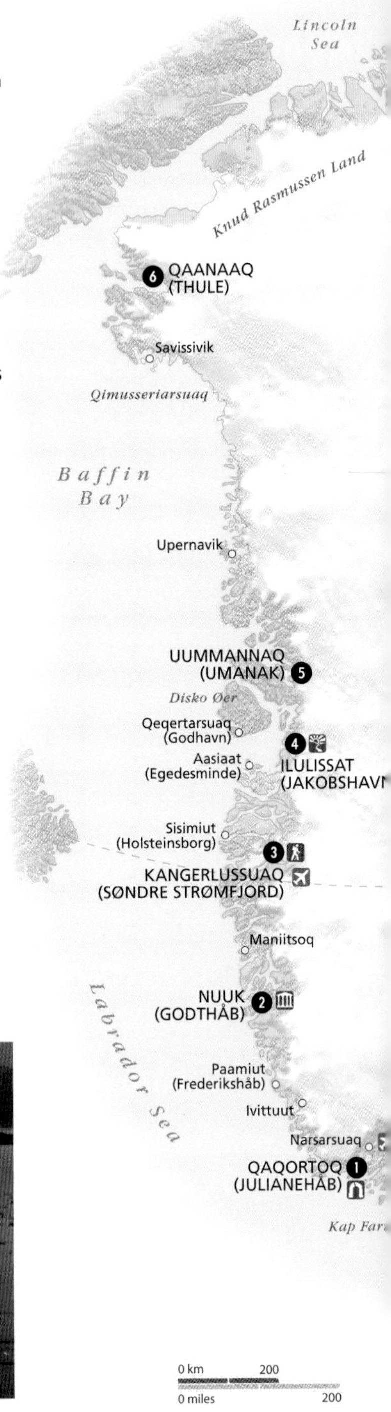

For keys to symbols *see back flap*

Lincoln Sea
Knud Rasmussen Land
6 QAANAAQ (THULE)
Savissivik
Qimusseriarsuaq
Baffin Bay
Upernavik
UUMMANNAQ (UMANAK) 5
Disko Øer
Qeqertarsuaq (Godhavn)
4 ILULISSAT (JAKOBSHAVN)
Aasiaat (Egedesminde)
Sisimiut (Holsteinsborg)
3 KANGERLUSSUAQ (SØNDRE STRØMFJORD)
Maniitsoq
NUUK (GODTHÅB) 2
Labrador Sea
Paamiut (Frederikshåb)
Ivittuut
Narsarsuaq
QAQORTOQ (JULIANEHÅB) 1
Kap Far
0 km 200
0 miles 200

Greenland huskies, sled dogs north of the Arctic Circle and in East Greenland

Getting There & Around

Kangerlussuaq, just north of the Arctic Circle, has Greenland's main airport. It lies 370 km (230 miles) north of Nuuk and serves international traffic from Denmark, as does Narsarsuaq in South Greenland. Ilulisaat, Kulusuk, Naarsarsuaq, Nerlerit Inaat and Nuuk serve international traffic from Iceland. Nuuk also serves international traffic from Canada. All domestic inland services are handled by Air Greenland. These flights tend to be expensive. Domestic travel by coastal ferry is possible, and all are handled by Artic Umiaq Line. Sailing times are vulnerable to adverse weather conditions.

Key

- Ice-free areas
- Permafrost

Sights at a Glance

1. Qaqortoq (Julianehåb)
2. Nuuk (Godthåb)
3. Kangerlussuaq (Søndre Strømfjord)
4. Ilulissat (Jakobshavn)
5. Uummannaq
6. Qaanaaq (Thule)
7. Tasiilaq (Ammassalik)

Ilulissat Icefjord, part of the UNESCO World Heritage site near Ilulissat

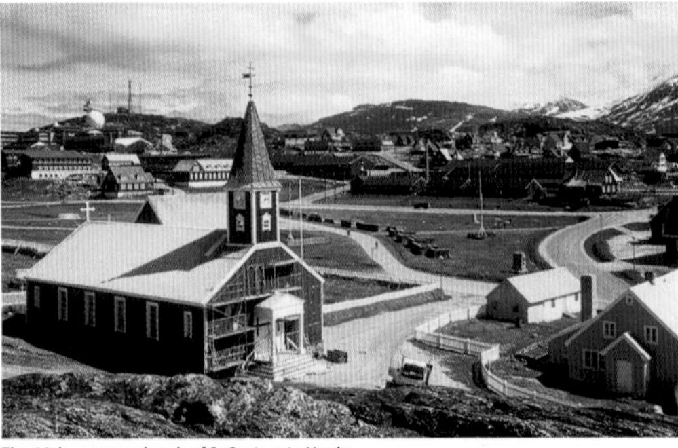

The 19th-century church of St Saviour in Nuuk

❶ Qaqortoq (Julianehåb)

3,300. **Tel** (+299) 64 24 44.
sagalands.com

The town of Qaqortoq was established in 1775. Traces of earlier, 10th-century Viking settlers can be seen in nearby Hvalsey where the remains of a local settlement and church are the best-preserved Nordic ruins in Greenland.

Other local attractions include the hot springs in Uunartoq and the research station in Upernaviarsuk which grows the only apple trees in Greenland.

Qaqortoq participates in Greenland's Stone and Man programme, an open-air sculpture project that uses natural rock formations as base material for a variety of abstract shapes and figures.

❷ Nuuk (Godthåb)

14,800. Ilivinnguaq 1, Postbox 2291. **Tel** (+299) 31 32 18.
tupilaktravel.gl

Greenland's capital was founded in 1728 by Hans Egede, a Danish missionary who established a year-round trading post here. Nuuk is the largest and oldest town on the island and the seat of Greenland's government. Egede's monument is on a hill, close to the cathedral.

More information about the history of Nuuk can be found at the **National Museum**, which has a collection of Inuit costumes as well as other Greenland artefacts.

According to some traditions Santa Claus lives in Nuuk and even has his own post box number (Box 785, 3952 Ilulissat). Next to the post office is a huge letterbox for Santa's letters.

The best time to visit is summer – in June humpback whales can be seen in the bay.

National Museum
Hans Egedesvej 8. **Tel** (+299) 32 26 11. **Open** mid-Jun–mid-Sep: 10am– 4pm daily; mid-Sep–mid-Jun: 10am– 4pm Tue–Sun. **natmus.gl**

❸ Kangerlussuaq (Søndre Strømfjord)

600. World of Greenland – Arctic Circle, P.O. Box 1009. **Tel** (+299) 84 16 48. **wogac.com**

Situated near the fjord of the same name, Kanger-lussuaq was until 1992 home to Blue West 8, a US base. A museum, located in the former HQ building, contains memorabilia from the base's history including a replica of the commander's hut.

This area is an excellent venue for hiking, biking, camping and fishing and is inhabited by large herds of reindeer as well as musk ox, arctic foxes and polar hares. A popular day-trip is to Russells Glacier, part of the Greenland ice sheet some 25 km (16 miles) away. Rising about 10 km (6 miles) from Kanger-lussuaq is Sugarloaf Mountain, which has a wonderful view of the Greenland ice sheet from its peak.

Gently sloping green coastline near Kangerlussuaq

❹ Ilulissat (Jakobshavn)

4,500. Destination Avannaa, Fredericap aqq 7A. **Tel** (+299) 94 33 37. **northgreenland.com**

The town of Ilulissat looks out over Disko Bay, which is full of floating icebergs. It has been calculated that almost 10 per cent of the icebergs floating on Greenland's waters come from the nearby 40-km (25-mile) long glacial fjord, where the ice can be up to 1,100 m (3,600 ft) thick. The glacier can be reached by boat from Ilulissat.

The most famous inhabitant of Ilulissat was the polar explorer Knud Rasmussen. His former house contains objects associated with Inuit art and the everyday life of Greenlanders.

Other museums include the Museum of Hunting and Fishing and the so-called Cold Museum (it has no heating), which has a selection of tools and machinery from a former trading settlement.

❺ Uummannaq

1,300. c/o Hotel Uummannaq Box 202. **Tel** (+299) 95 15 18. **icecaphotels.gl**

Despite its location 600 km (373 miles) north of the Arctic Circle, this place enjoys more days of summer sunshine than anywhere else in Greenland. Such favourable conditions have for a long time been a magnet for hunters and whalers. The charm of this town, situated on a small island, is due in part to its colourful houses set on a rocky shore against the backdrop of the 1,175-m (3,855-ft) high Hjertetjeldet ("Heart Shaped") mountain. The old stone cottages with turf roofs date from 1925. The nearby museum, housed in a late 19th-century hospital, contains hunting implements, kayaks and a display devoted to German scientist Alfred Wegener's expedition across the inland ice in 1930 on propeller-driven sledges. Nearby is the Inuit village of

Children dressed in colourful Greenlandic national costumes

Qilakitsoq, where some mummified bodies were discovered in a cave in 1972. The mummies can be seen in Nuuk's National Museum.

In winter it is possible to take an exhilarating dog-sled trip across the frozen fjord.

❻ Qaanaaq (Thule)

700. P.O. Box 75. **Tel** (+299) 97 14 73. **turistqaanaaq.gl**

Greenland's northernmost town was built in the 1950s. Its inhabitants follow a traditional way of life hunting for seals, walruses and polar bears. Visitors can participate in hunts, which involve sleeping in igloos and travelling by sled. Hunts such as these are an important means of survival in this area and not for the squeamish.

About 500 km (311 miles) from Qaanaaq is the vast North and East Greenland National Park. The park is mostly covered by an inland ice cap and contains musk ox, polar bears and, in summer, walruses. Permission to enter must be obtained from the Expedition Office of the Government of Greenland *(exp@nanoq.gl)*.

❼ Tasiilaq (Ammassalik)

1,900. P.O. Box 506, Skæven Ujuaap Aqqutaa B 48. **Tel** (+299) 98 12 43 or 98 15 43. **eastgreenland.com**

Situated on the shores of a fjord, surrounded by high mountains, Tasiilaq is one of eastern Greenland's larger towns. The first Europeans arrived here about 100 years ago, and tourism is becoming increasingly important. From here, visitors can go whale watching, visit the nearby "Valley of Flowers" (in summer this is a splendid opportunity to enjoy the Arctic flora) or climb the mound that towers over the town (it was raised in 1944 to celebrate the 50th anniversary of Tasiilaq), from which there are some stunning views.

The town's other points of interest include a modern church dating from 1985 and decorated with Greenland artefacts. The oldest of Tasiilaq's houses dates from 1894 and was built by a Danish missionary.

Uummannaq, built on the rocks of a small island

Exploring the Faroe Islands

This cluster of 18 islands, sandwiched between the Atlantic and the Norwegian Sea, is home to about 48,000 people, almost half of whom live in the capital Tórshavn on Streymoy. The Faroes have a total area of 1,399 sq km (540 sq miles) and are 450 km (280 miles) from the Shetland Islands and 1,500 km (900 miles) from Copenhagen. Many of the islands are interlinked by a network of tunnels and causeways. The Faroes are perfect for ramblers, and marked trails cover many routes. This is rough terrain and the right equipment, including maps and a compass, should always be carried. The island's seafaring past is evident in the busy harbours, while the town museums have displays on island customs and folklore. Sea cruises are an ideal way to explore the Faroes.

Garden gate made from a ship's wheel

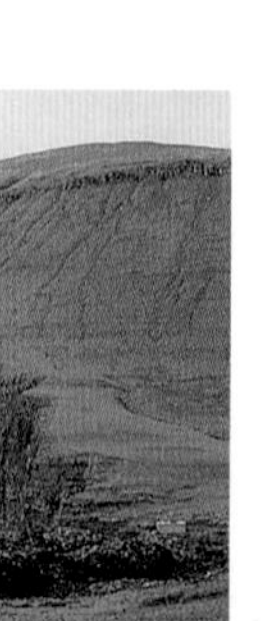

Rugged cliffs on the tiny island of Koltur

Key

Minor road

Tunnel

For keys to symbols *see back flap*

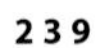

Steel sheep sculpture in Tórshavn

Getting There & Around

The Faroe Islands Smyril Line ferry service operates regularly between Tórshavn, the island's capital, and Hanstholm in northern Jutland. In summer there are additional services from Seyđisfjörđur in Iceland. Atlantic Airways serves routes from Copenhagen in Denmark, Oslo in Norway, the UK, Spain and Italy. The Faroe Islands' international airport is near the town of Sørvágur, on the island of Vágar, about 70 km (43 miles) from Tórshavn. A bus connects the airport with Tórshavn. Most of the towns and villages are connected by road, while local ferries cater for the more outlying settlements.

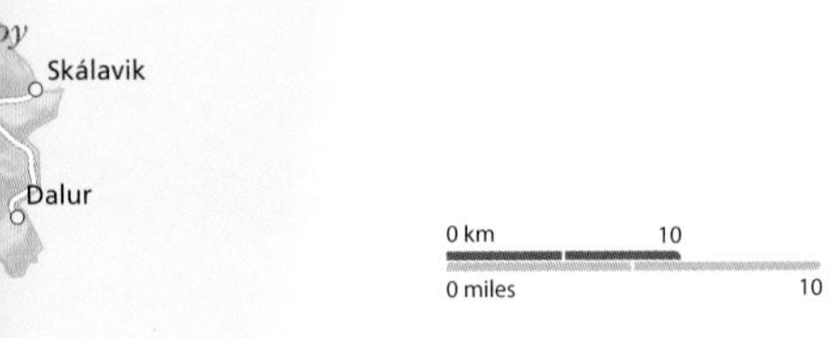

Sights at a Glance

1. Tórshavn
2. Streymoy
3. Vágar
4. Mykines
5. Suđuroy
6. Eysturoy
7. Kalsoy

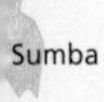

Fishing boats in Klaksvík's harbour

Brightly coloured houses lining Tórshavn harbour

❶ Tórshavn

19,000. Vaglið 4, Tórshavn. **Tel** (+298) 30 24 25.

The Faroe Islands' capital is a lively and picturesque place with a well-preserved old centre, although much of the town is fairly modern. Tórshavn was granted municipal status in 1909, but its history stretches back much further.

In the 11th century Tórshavn became a venue for annual Viking gatherings known as the Althings, an early form of the Faroese parliament. The meetings were held in summer and were used to settle quarrels and as an opportunity to trade. A permanent settlement developed around the annual event, and eventually became Tórshavn.

Some of the Faroes' earliest inhabitants were Irish friars, and Tórshavn's oldest building is the 15th-century Munkastovan, or Monks' House, which is one of the few buildings to survive a fire in 1673.

The ruins of Skansin Fort, which was built in 1580 to defend the village from pirates, can still be seen. The fort acquired its present shape in 1780 and was used by British troops during World War II. Today, it provides a good viewpoint for surveying the town's busy harbour, which is crammed with fishing boats, ferries and pleasure craft.

Søvn Landsins (Historical Museum) has a wide-ranging collection tracing the Faroes' seafaring history, including boats and fishing equipment, as well as some religious artefacts and items dating back to the Viking era.

Søvn Landsins
Brekkutún 6, Hoyvík. **Tel** (+298) 34 05 00. **Open** mid-May–mid-Sep: 10am–5pm daily (from 2pm Sat & Sun); mid-Sep–mid-May: 2–5pm Thu & Sun. **savn.fo**

❷ Streymoy

22,000. Vaglið 4, Tórshavn. **Tel** (+298) 30 24 25.

The largest of the Faroe Islands has a varied terrain and is criss-crossed by ancient paths that were once used to travel between settlements.

Saksun is a small village on the shores of an inlet that leads into Pollur lake – a fine spot to fish for trout and salmon. The **Dúvugarðar Museum**, located in an old turf-roofed farmhouse, has exhibits on island life from medieval times to the 1800s.

Traces of a group of 8th-century Irish friars have been found in the village of Kirkjubøur, at the south end of Streymoy. Written records show that Kirkjubøur was a busy place in medieval times. A reminder of those days is the 12th-century church of St Olaf, the archipelago's oldest historic site.

Southwest from Tórshavn are the Vestmannabjørgini (Bird Cliffs) where hundreds of sea birds inhabit the 640-m- (2,100-ft-) high cliff face.

Dúvugarðar Museum
FO436, Saksun. **Tel** (+298) 34 05 00. **Open** 2–5pm daily during the summer.

❸ Vágar

2,800. Flogvøllurin 2, Sørvágur. **Tel** (+298) 33 34 55.

The Faroe Islands' modern airport is on Vágar and was originally used as a landing strip by the RAF. This mountainous island has some of the region's most stunning sights including the 313-m (1,027-ft) tall needle rock called "Trollukonufingur" ("Troll Woman's Finger"). Lake Sorvagsvatn is a little way from Midvagur, Vágar's largest town, and is a great place for fishing. Sandavagur, a nearby village, is the birthplace of Venceslaus Ulricus Hammershaimb (b. 1819), creator of the Faroese alphabet.

House hugging the cliff on Streymoy

Lighthouse standing on the cliffs of Mykines

❹ Mykines

20. Flogvøllurin 2, Sørvágur. **Tel** (+298) 33 34 55.

On this tiny island of only 10 sq km (4 sq miles), the inhabitants are vastly outnumbered by the birds, including thousands of puffins. All the islanders live in the same village, which is a pretty place with colourful houses topped by turf roofs. This is one of the hardest islands to reach but the trip is worth it, especially for keen hikers. Mykineshólmur, a tiny islet, is a good spot from which to view gannets, as well as large colonies of puffins. It is connected to the island by a footbridge that has been built 24-m (79-ft) above the sea.

❺ Suðuroy

5,000. Tvørávegur 37, Tvøroyri. **Tel** (+298) 61 10 80.
visitsuduroy.fo

The largest town on Suðuroy, the Faroes' southernmost island, is Tvøroyri, which has a population of 1,800. The little village of Famjin, on the west coast, is more historically important, however, as its church contains the original Faroe Islands' flag. The red-and-blue cross on a white background was designed by two students and accepted as the national ensign in 1940. A short hike above the village is Kirkjuvatn ("Church Lake"), one of the Faroes' largest lakes.

The village of Sandvik, at the northern end of the island, has an isolated and expansive beach. In AD 1000 Sigmund Bresterson, an early Norwegian settler and hero of the Faroe Sagas, was murdered here while preaching Christianity. On the way from Sandvik to Hvalba are two stones that, according to legend, were brought here by Bresterson. Passing between them is believed to be unlucky and can spell misfortune or even death.

Goat on one of the islands' rural smallholdings

❻ Eysturoy

11,000. Heiðavegur 26, Runavík. **Tel** (+298) 41 70 60.
visiteysturoy.fo

The second largest island of the archipelago is connected to Streymoy by a road bridge, which is often jokingly described by locals as the only bridge across the Atlantic.

Eysturoy has a number of unique features. At 882 m (2,894 ft), Slættaratindur is the Faroes' highest point. The summit can easily be reached by climbing the mountain's eastern ridge – the views from the peak are breathtaking.

Close to Fuglafjørður are the Varmakelda hot springs. Their water remains at a constant 18° C (64.4° F) and is believed to have medicinal properties. Further north is the village of Oynadarfjordur. Just beyond its shore are the Rinkusteinar, or rocking stones, two huge blocks that constantly rock, moved by the motion of the sea.

At nearby Gjógv there is a 200-m- (656-ft-) long gorge that with time has eroded to become a sea-filled bay.

❼ Kalsoy

140. Tingstøðin, Klaksvík. **Tel** (+298) 45 69 39.

Nicknamed the "flute" because of its elongated shape, this rugged island is ideal for hikes. Many walkers head towards Kap Kallur, at the island's northern tip, where the lighthouse makes an excellent point from which to view the cliffs. Puffins are a frequent sight. The sea stacks at Eysturoy's northern tip can be seen on a clear day.

Faroe Islands website: www.faroeislands.com; www.visit-faroeislands.com

HEP

TRAVELLERS' NEEDS

WHERE TO STAY

Holiday accommodation in Denmark is of a high standard and provides visitors with plenty of options. The choice ranges from luxury boutique hotels and quality chain hotels to roadside inns, budget hotels, family-friendly hostels, self-catering apartments, private homes and camp sites. Information is readily available from tourist offices and via the Internet. More unusual accommodation is also becoming widely available, from old-fashioned beachfront bathing hotels to inner-city boutique hotels with unique design features and organic breakfast buffets. For those on a tight budget, however, staying on a camp site or in one of the country's well-run hostels provides the cheapest alternative. Those seeking something a little different might choose to stay in an historic manor house or on one of the farms taking part in Denmark's agritourism scheme.

Main entrance to a hotel in Sandvig, Bornholm

Choosing a Hotel

Travellers in Denmark have a wide choice of hotel accommodation. Information is readily available and details of hotels found in brochures and on websites is generally both up to date and accurate. Most of Denmark's hotels are of 3-star standard or higher, and are aimed at holiday-makers as well as business travellers. The majority offer rooms with a private bathroom, telephone and TV.

Be clear when booking a room if a bath is specifically required, as most hotels have showers rather than baths in rooms. Visitors should be able to use their laptops as rooms usually have Internet access, but it is wise to check.

Cheaper hotels tend to be rather plain, but even these are generally clean and well run. An all-you-can-eat breakfast, consisting of pastries, bread, cereal, coffee/tea and fruit, is often included in the price of a room, although bigger city hotels may offer breakfast for an additional cost (usually around 100 Dkr).

When planning a journey to Denmark by car, take into account the cost of parking in town centres. It is worth finding out in advance whether the hotel has its own car park or off-street parking.

Hotels on Greenland and the Faroe Islands tend to be rather spartan in design and costly, particularly outside the capital cities, although ecotourism is growing in popularity.

How to Book

During peak season, hotels are often booked up in Denmark so it pays to reserve a room in advance. Prices vary immensely according to both demand and season, and pre-booking on the Internet offers the best rates, often directly via the hotel's own website. Information on hotels in the area, as well as links for booking, can be found at www.dkhotellist.com or www.visitdenmark.com. Alternatively, bookings can be made by telephone or e-mail. Local tourist offices can also provide accommodation lists for their towns.

Hotel Prices

Hotel prices in Denmark can be rather high. There are many hotels at the lower end of the scale, however, which charge about 600 to 700 Dkr per night; the most expensive ones may quote up to 10,000 Dkr for a luxury suite. The majority of room prices fall into the 900–1,400 Dkr bracket. Many hotels offer discounted rates at weekends, while those that cater for tourists rather than business travellers may offer special reduced winter rates.

Chain Hotels

Many hotels in Denmark belong to large hotel chains including First & Clarion, Hilton, Radisson and Scandic. Some chains, such as Best Western, have their own schemes whereby visitors can get discounted rooms at weekends or during the holiday period. It is best to book in advance for these, though deals can sometimes be struck on the spot.

Historic Houses

A number of Denmark's manor houses offer accommodation, especially in connection with conferences and weddings. These historic buildings, while

◀ Sailing boats in the harbour at Sønderborg, Southern Jutland

A guest room in the Admiral Hotel, Copenhagen *(see p248)*

privately managed, are typically affiliated with the **Danske Slotte & Herregaarde** (The Danish Association of Castles and Manor Houses). They are usually located in the countryside, surrounded by nature, and having a car is essential for guests. The venues are undeniably romantic, but they can be rather expensive.

Inns

Outside larger towns, it is possible to stop for a night in an inn, known as *kro* in Denmark. The variety on offer ranges from modern roadside inns to meticulously restored period houses and *badehoteller* – traditional beachside inns offering old-fashioned seaside relaxation. Some country inns have retained much of their 18th or 19th-century rusticity; others are downright luxurious. Many *kro* offer a family atmosphere, and it is not unusual for inns to be used for family gatherings and big occasions such as weddings. **Danske Kroer & Hoteller** is an association of country inns that manages over 100 inns, castles and manor houses.

Camp Sites

Denmark has hundreds of camp sites, 460 of them approved by the **Danish Camping Union**. Of these, around 100 are open all year round, providing relatively inexpensive accommodation, often in areas of outstanding natural beauty. Campsites are rated by the Dansk Camping Union using a system of stars from one to five. Prices depend on the number of stars, which reflect not only comfort and a site's attractiveness, but also specific facilities, such as whether the site has a playground and the distance to the nearest grocery store. The cost per night generally includes a charge for pitching a tent or parking a caravan, plus a charge for each occupant. One-star sites will have little more than basic facilities, such as fresh drinking water and toilets. Sites rated three stars and above will have a TV room, on-site shop and a café or restaurant. Whatever the rating and the amenities on offer, it is rare to find a Danish camp site that is not efficiently run.

Most of Denmark's camp sites also feature chalet accommodation, or cabins that can sleep four to six. Many cabins have cooking facilities, but visitors usually have to supply their own linen, including towels. Most cabins do not have private washing or toilet facilities.

A comprehensive database available at www.danskecampingpladser.dk allows a search according to location and facilities.

Anyone wishing to camp in Denmark will need a Visitor's Pass. These annual permits are readily available and can be purchased on the spot at any of the official camp sites.

Denmark also offers the chance to pitch a tent, at "primitive nature camp sites". These are designated areas with basic facilities such a public toilet, running water and sometimes a place to make a fire. About one-third of the sites also have a primitive shelter to use for overnight sleeping. Details of these sites can be obtained from www.visitdenmark.com. Cars, caravans and other motor vehicles are not permitted on these sites.

Wild camping, while not actually encouraged, should be done with respect for both nature and neighbours. Guidelines and regulations for wild camping in Denmark can be obtained at the website of the **Danish Nature Agency**.

A traditional furnished room in the historic Dragsholm Slot, Hørve *(see p250)*

Historic hotel room in Liselund Ny Slot, Møn

Hostels

Most of Denmark's 95 or so hostels or *vandrehjem* are incorporated into the **Danhostel** association, which registers its hostels in five categories marked by stars. Along with communal dormitories, most hostels have private "family" rooms, which usually sleep four to six and must be booked in advance. Blankets and pillows are usually provided, but it is generally the case that visitors supply their own bed linen and towels (though these are available for a fee). In all hostels it is possible to buy breakfast; many also offer dinner or even packed lunches, and charge half-price for children up to the age of 12.

The prices of family rooms can vary, but the maximum price of a bed in a communal dormitory is fixed each year for the entire country. Prices vary between high and low seasons. From September until May a place in a provincial hostel must be booked at least three days ahead. During peak season all hostels should be booked as early as possible.

It is not necessary to have a Youth Hostel Association (YHA) card to stay at a hostel, but card-holders enjoy reduced rates. For visits that exceed five days it is worth buying membership.

Danhostel's website has telephone numbers and website addresses for all of its hostels, where additional information can be found.

In the cities, independent hostels offer more specialised lodging, such as Generator Hostel Copenhagen, for a more luxurious hostel experience.

Bed & Breakfasts

Denmark's bed and breakfasts offer good quality and value, and usually charge about 600 Dkr for a double room per night. B&Bs can usually be booked from local tourist offices. Alternatively, a list is available from **Dansk Bed & Breakfast**. Some Danish B&Bs quote a price that only includes accommodation. Breakfast usually costs extra, or it may not be available at all.

Disabled Travellers

Many hotels can accommodate disabled guests, especially the newer and larger ones, although it is best to check when booking. The majority of multi-storey hotels have lifts. The **God Adgang** scheme, which also provides classification for restaurants, provides a list of hotels with disabled access.

Travelling with Children

Taking children on holiday to Denmark is not a problem. Many hotels and hostels, particularly establishments aimed at holiday-makers, offer family rooms for three to four people. Hotels belonging to the Scandic group are also ready to receive young guests; many of these have playrooms. Hotel restaurants provide high chairs for babies and toddlers and also offer special menus that will satisfy all but the most picky children.

Cottages and Holiday Centres

Cottages are available to rent – usually on a weekly basis (from Saturday to Saturday). Weekend mini-breaks are also possible out of high season (which runs from July through to mid-August). Many places are let out by private owners but managed by professional rental agencies. Others are run purely as commercial ventures. Either way, a cottage must be booked well in advance.

Holiday centres, which have purpose-built accommodation, children's playgrounds, swimming pools and other family-friendly amenities, have lots of space for children to play. Prices vary widely.

Farm Holidays and Home Exchanges

Spending time on a farm is becoming an increasingly popular activity in Denmark. There are now more than 100 Danish farms where a stay is possible, and most are far away from busy resorts. Such rural retreats provide a chance to relax in

Entrance to one of Denmark's converted manor houses

Stylish hostel family accommodation at Danhostel Copenhagen City *(see p249)*

pastoral surroundings and, in some cases, to muck in with the chores. Farm stays can be booked via **Landsforeningen for Landboturisme**. A holiday of this sort can be arranged in several ways. You can choose B&B or full-board accommodation. Cottages, a simple apartment with a kitchen, or a room can be rented. Alternatively, visitors can pitch a tent or park a caravan on farm land.

Regardless of what type of vacation is on offer, visitors can be sure of a clean room and warm rural atmosphere. Prices start from 200 Dkr per adult (for bed and breakfast).

A home exchange allows participants to swap their home with that of a family in Denmark, offering an authentic Danish experience. Visit **Home Link** for information.

Recommended Hotels

The hotels in this book have been carefully selected and are among the best in the country. A wide variety of accommodation options are covered, from classic city hotels, country inns and even renovated castles, to ultra-modern design hotels. The list also includes youth hostels, family-friendly guesthouses and budget accommodation.

Entries labelled as DK Choice draw attention to establishments that stand out in some way. This might be the exceptional surroundings, historic building, excellent service, friendly hosts or in-house restaurant on offer.

DIRECTORY

Information on Accommodation & Reservations

W hotel.dk
W visitdenmark.com

Information on Accommodation & Reservations in Copenhagen

Copenhagen Right Now Information and Booking Service
Vesterbrogade 4A.
Tel 70 22 24 42.
Fax 70 22 24 52.
W visitcopenhagen.com

Historic Houses

Danske Slotte & Herregaarde
L. Sct. Mikkelsgade 7, 1, 8800 Viborg.
Tel 86 60 38 44.
W slotte-herregaarde.dk

Inns

Danske Kroer & Hoteller
Vejlevej 16, 8700 Horsens.
Tel 75 64 87 00.
W smalldanishhotels.com

Camp Sites

Campingrådet
Mosedalvej 15, DK-2500 Valby.
Tel 39 27 88 44.
Fax 39 27 80 44.
W campingraadet.dk

Danish Nature Agency
Haraldsgade 53, 2100 Copenhagen Ø.
Tel 72 54 30 00.
W naturstyrelsen.dk

Dansk Camping Union
Korsdalsvej 135, 2605 Brøndby.
Tel 33 21 06 00.
W dcu.dk

DK-CAMP 2002
Industrivej 5, Bredballe, 7120 Vejle Ø.
Tel 75 71 29 62.
Fax 75 71 29 66.
W dk-camp.dk

FDM Camping
Firskovvej 32. 2800 Kgs. Lyngby.
Tel 45 27 07 07.
W fdmcamping.dk

Hostels

Danhostel Danmarks Vandrehjem
Vesterbrogade 39, 1620 Copenhagen V.
Tel 33 31 36 12.
W danhostel.dk

B&Bs

Dansk B&B
Sankt Peders Stræde 41, 1453 Copenhagen K.
Tel 39 61 04 05.
W bedandbreakfast.dk

Disabled Travellers

God Adgang
W godadgang.dk

Holiday Centres

Danland & DanCenter
Lyngbyvej 20, 2100 Copenhagen Ø.
Tel 33 63 02 00.
Fax 70 13 70 71.
W danland.dk

Dansk Folkeferie
Hedegaardsvej 88, 2300 Copenhagen.
W folkeferie.dk

Cottages

Dansommer
Voldbjergvej 16, 8240 Risskov.
Tel 86 17 61 22.
Fax 86 17 68 55.
W dansommer.dk

Novasol
Rygårds Alle 104, 2900 Hellerup.
Tel 70 42 44 24.
W novasol.co.uk

Sol & Strand
Ilsigvej 21, Hune, 9492 Blokhus.
Tel 99 44 44 44.
Fax 99 44 44 45.
W sologstrand.com

Farm Holidays and Home Exchanges

Home Link
W homelink.org

Landsforeningen for Landboturisme
Føllevej 5, 8410 Ronde.
W bonde gaardsferie.dk

Where to Stay

Copenhagen

North Copenhagen

DK Choice

Babette Guldsmeden ⓚⓚ
Boutique **Map** 2 E4
Bredgade 78, 1260 Cph K
Tel *33 14 15 00*
W guldsmedenhotels.com/Home/GuldsmedenHotels.aspx
Formerly the Hotel Esplanden, Babette Guldsmeden opened in 2014 and is centrally situated yet enjoys green and leafy surroundings as it is directly opposite Churchillparken. An eco-friendly boutique hotel, guests can enjoy Balinese-style furnishings, four-poster beds and original artwork in their rooms. In addition the hotel offers luxurious, organic breakfasts.

Generator Copenhagen ⓚⓚ
Hostel **Map** 2 D5
Adelgade 5–7, 1304 Cph K
Tel *78 7 754 00*
W generatorhostels.com/en/destinations/copenhagen
A six-storey design hostel placed a short walk from Kongens Nytorv square. The chain caters for luxury-seeking backpackers, with private rooms and modern features as well as dorms.

Wakeup Copenhagen – Borgergade ⓚⓚ
Family **Map** 2 D5
Borgergade 9, 1300 Cph K
Tel *44 80 00 00*
W wakeupcopenhagen.com/the-hotels/copenhagen/borgergade
The second Wakeup Copenhagen hotel provides budget accommodation that rises in price the higher up the building you stay. Modern features include air conditioning and Wi-Fi.

71 Nyhavn ⓚⓚⓚ
Historic **Map** 4 E1
Nyhavn 71, 1051 Cph K
Tel *33 43 62 00*
W 71nyhavnhotel.com
Part of the citywide Arp Hansen Group, and located in a renovated 1880s warehouse, this hotel overlooks the waterfront. Rooms are rather small but charming.

Admiral Hotel ⓚⓚⓚ
Designer **Map** 2 E4
Toldbodgade 24–28, 1253 Cph K
Tel *33 74 14 14*
W admiralhotel.dk
An 18th-century granary, this expansive waterfront hotel has been carefully restored with a maritime theme, and features exposed beams and uniquely designed rooms. There is also an excellent restaurant, SALT.

Central Copenhagen

Hostel Downtown ⓚ
Hostel **Map** 3 B2
Vandkunsten 5, 1467 Cph K
Tel *70 23 21 10*
W copenhagendowntown.com
This lively, central hostel on one of the city's most attractive streets offers typical dorm accommodation as well as doubles and triples. Guests can eat in the cafeteria or cook in the communal kitchen.

Sømandshjemmet Bethel ⓚ
Character **Map** 4 D1
Nyhavn 22, 1051 Cph K
Tel *33 13 03 70*
W hotel-bethel.dk
The old seaman's hostel on Nyhavn's quieter side operates as a budget hotel with basic, but clean and friendly accommodation. Free tea and coffee as well as a breakfast buffet.

Hotel Opera ⓚ
Historic **Map** 4 D1
Tordenskjoldsgade 15, 1055 Cph K
Tel *33 47 83 00*
W hotelopera.dk
Friendly three-star hotel located under the arches on a quiet side street behind the Royal Theatre. While the rooms are rather small, there is plenty of theatrical atmosphere and charm.

Chill out area at the stylish hostel Generator Copenhagen

Price Guide
Prices are based on one night's stay in high season for a standard double room, inclusive of service charges and taxes.

ⓚ	up to 850 Dkr
ⓚⓚ	850–1,500 Dkr
ⓚⓚⓚ	over 1,500 Dkr

First Hotel Kong Frederik ⓚⓚ
Historic **Map** 3 A1
Vester Voldgade 25, 1552 Cph K
Tel *33 12 59 02*
W firsthotels.com
A short walk from the Rådhuspladsen, this elegant 19th-century townhouse has been refurbished in classic English style, with plenty of dark wood.

The Square ⓚⓚ
Designer **Map** 3 A2
Rådhuspladsen 14, 1550 Cph V
Tel *33 38 12 00*
W thesquarecopenhagen.com
A trendy, modern six-storey hotel in a central location overlooking Rådhuspladsen, the Square boasts stylish design features and modern facilities in all rooms as well as its expansive lobby.

Ascot Hotel & Apartments ⓚⓚⓚ
Historic **Map** 3 A1
Studiestræde 61, 1554 Cph K
Tel *33 12 60 00*
W ascot-hotel.dk
A former public baths, this 4-star hotel has retained many original features. Guests can choose to stay in hotel or apartment accommodation, and there are spa and fitness facilities.

Hotel Alexandra ⓚⓚⓚ
Designer **Map** 3 A1
H.C. Andersens Boulevard 8, 1553 Cph V
Tel *33 74 44 44*
W hotelalexandra.dk/
Situated close to the town hall, this classic building dates from the early 19th century and is furnished by notable 20th-century Danish designers, including Finn Juhl and Vernor Panton. Eco-friendly.

Hotel D'Angleterre ⓚⓚⓚ
Luxury **Map** 4 D1
Kongens Nytorv 34, 1050 Cph K
Tel *33 12 00 95*
W dangleterre.dk
A landmark on Kongens Nytorv since 1755, the D'Angleterre remains synonymous with luxury, its celebrity guests ranging from Winston Churchill to Robbie Williams. It underwent extensive refurbishment in 2013.

Hotel Sankt Petri ®®®
Designer **Map** 3 B1
Krystalgade 22, 1172 Cph K
Tel *33 45 91 00*
W sktpetri.com
In a former department store, this modern design hotel has a rooftop terrace, trendy wine bar and air conditioning in all rooms, plus a fantastic location in the historic Latin Quarter.

Nimb Hotel ®®®
Luxury **Map** 3 A3
Bernstorffsgade 5, 1577 Cph K
Tel *88 70 00 00*
W hotel.nimb.dk/en/
An expensive, luxury boutique hotel in the Moorish Nimb building with views over Tivoli Gardens. No two rooms are the same, and the attention to detail is exquisite.

DK Choice

Palace Hotel ®®®
Historic **Map** 3 B2
Rådhuspladsen 57, 1550 Cph K
Tel *33 14 40 50*
W palacehotel copenhagen.com
Declared a historic landmark in 1985, the Palace overlooks Rådhuspladsen almost as majestically as the adjacent Town Hall. It was built in 1910 by Anton Rosen as one of the city's grandest hotels, though its reputation had faded. Following extensive refurbishment, the Palace is returning to its former glory.

Radisson Blu Royal ®®®
Designer **Map** 3 A2
Hammerichsgade 1, 1611 Cph K
Tel *33 42 60 00*
W radissonblu.com/royalhotel-copenhagen
Designed by Danish architect Arne Jacobsen in the 1950s, the 20-storey Royal was the world's first design hotel; today, only room 606 remains as Jacobsen left it.

South Copenhagen

Danhostel Copenhagen City ®
Designer **Map** 3 C3
H.C. Andersens Boulevard 50, 1553 Cph V
Tel *33 11 85 85*
W danhostelcopenhagencity.dk
Huge design hostel with 192 modern rooms that is as popular with families as it is with young groups. Includes a playroom and private rooms for four, six and eight people.

Riverside deck on the floating Hotel CPH Living

Hotel Amager ®
Family **Map** 4 F4
Amagerbrogade 29, 2300 Cph S
Tel *32 54 40 08*
W hotelamager.dk
Small, independent hotel in a residential building in the suburb of Amager, with good transport connections into the centre. Cheap four-bed rooms are available for families and there's a ground floor café.

Hotel Copenhagen ®
Family **Map** 3 C4
Egilsgade 33, 2300 Cph S
Tel *32 96 27 27*
W hotelcopenhagen.dk
Family-friendly, budget hotel in the rejuvenated waterfront Islands Brygge district. Options include basic rooms sleeping up to four in bunks, as well as studio apartments.

Hotel CPH Living ®®
Boutique **Map** 3 C3
Langebrogade 1C, 1411 Cph K
Tel *61 60 85 46*
W cphliving.com
Copenhagen's floating boutique hotel offers designer double rooms on a boat moored in Copenhagen's harbour, overlooking Slotsholmen and Den Sorte Diamant. The price includes breakfast and use of the sundeck.

Radisson Blu Scandinavia ®®
Modern **Map** 4 D4
Amager Boulevard 70, | 2300 Cph S
Tel *33 96 50 00*
W radissonblu.com/ scandinaviahotel-copenhagen
With 26 storeys, this hotel rises high above Copenhagen's skyline. A modern hotel with spotless rooms, it offers impeccable service, upmarket restaurants and a casino. It is popular with business guests.

DK Choice

STAY Apartment Hotel Copenhagen ®®®
Designer
Islands Brygge 79, 2300 Cph S
Tel *72 44 44 34*
W staycopenhagen.dk
STAY Apartment Hotel opened in 2010 after the conversion of a 1960s office building by renowned architectural firm HAY into spacious designer apartments with up to 3 bedrooms. Facilities include a gym, bakery, grocery shop, washing machines, balconies and waterfront views. STAY makes a great (though not cheap) alternative to traditional hotel accommodation.

Further Afield

Woodah Hostel ®
Hostel **Road Map** F4
Abel Cathrinesgade 1–3, 1654 Cph V
Tel *23 90 55 63*
W woodah-hostel.com
Small, independent hostel in Vesterbro with focus on eco-accommodation in bunks in 8- and 12-bed dorms and private doubles. Provides organic breakfast, bedding, vegetarian snacks and morning yoga sessions.

Andersen Boutique Hotel ®®
Boutique **Map** 3 A3
Helgolandsgade 12, 1653 Cph V
Tel *33 31 46 10*
W andersen-hotel.dk
Andersen offers personal service and bright, designer rooms in various colour schemes in an old building full of character. Located close to the Central train station.

For more information on types of hotels *see pages 244–5*

Bella Sky Comwell Kr Kr
Designer **Road Map** F4
Center Boulevard 5, 2300 Cph S
Tel *32 47 30 00*
W bellaskycomwell.dk
Architecturally noteworthy and 23 floors high, Bella Sky is located in Ørestad, near the airport. Its modern facilities include a wellness centre and shops. Pet-friendly hotel.

Hotel Tiffany Kr Kr
Family **Map** 3 A3
Colbjørnsensgade 28, 1652 Cph V
Tel *33 21 80 50*
W hoteltiffany.dk
Small, family-run hotel close to Central Station. Rooms feature a kitchenette with a fridge, microwave and toaster; breakfast is delivered to your room at the time you choose.

Savoy Hotel Kr Kr
Historic **Road Map** F4
Vesterbrogade 34, 1620 Cph V
Tel *33 26 75 00*
W savoyhotel.dk/
Independent, family-run hotel in the Art Nouveau "Løvenborg" building that dates from 1905 on bustling Vesterbrogade. Wide range of room sizes available, all facing the rear courtyard.

Axel Guldsmeden Kr Kr Kr
Boutique **Map** 3 A3
Helgolandsgade 11, 1653 Cph V
Tel *33 31 32 66*
W guldsmedenhotels.com/
Part of the Guldsmeden chain, Vesterbro's Axel Guldsmeden offers luxurious boutique accommodation focusing on eco-friendly products. The courtyard garden and spa are pleasant surprises in the urban setting.

Hotel Kong Arthur Kr Kr Kr
Character **Map** 1 A5
Nørre Søgade 11, 1370 Cph K
Tel *33 45 77 77*
W arthurhotels.dk/hotel-kong-arthur
Built in 1882, this historic hotel is surprisingly quiet for its central location, facing the lakes and with a secluded inner courtyard. Includes Copenhagen's oldest spa, Ni'mat.

Northwestern Zealand

CHARLOTTENLUND: Skovshoved Hotel Kr Kr Kr
Historic **Road Map** F4
Strandvejen 267, 2920 Charlottenlund
Tel *39 64 00 28*
W skovshovedhotel.com
A coaching inn with old world atmosphere dating from 1660. Located on the Øresund coastal road, it features an upmarket restaurant and offers sea views from many of the bedrooms.

GILLELEJE: Gilleleje Badehotel Kr Kr
Luxury **Road Map** F4
Hulsøvej 15, 3250 Gilleleje
Tel *48 30 13 47*
W gillelejebadehotel.dk
A nostalgic spa hotel, this classic white and blue painted establishment dates back to 1895 and is set high on a cliff with views over to Sweden.

HELSINGØR: Hotel Skandia Kr
Character **Road Map** F4
Bramstræde 1, 3000 Helsingør
Tel *49 21 09 02*
W hotelskandia.dk
Rather basic, old-fashioned hotel with personal service and a handy location within walking distance of all Helsingør's attractions. Breakfast is included in the price.

HOLBÆK: Holbæk Vandrerhjem Kr
Hostel **Road Map** E4
Ahlgade 1B, 4300 Holbæk
Tel *59 44 29 19*
W sidesporet.dk/vandrerhjem/
Holbæk's 5-star hostel is located on the harbour. Offering bright and modern en suite rooms, its own Turkish baths and an excellent restaurant, guests will forget they are in a hostel.

DK Choice

HORNBÆK: Hotel Hornbækhus Kr Kr
Character **Road Map** F4
Skovvej 7, 3100 Hornbæk
Tel *49 70 01 69*
W hornbaekhus.com
Unashamedly romantic, Hornbækhus was a popular retreat for wealthy Copenhageners in the1920s and 1930s. Tastefully modernised and furnished in Swedish 18th-century Gustavian style, many of the rooms have balconies. Guests can relax in the hotel's elegant living room, which opens onto a large garden.

HØRVE: Dragsholm Slot Kr Kr Kr
Historic **Road Map** E4
Dragsholm Alle, 4534 Hørve
Tel *69 65 33 00*
W dragsholm-slot.dk
One of Denmark's oldest castles, 13th century Dragholm oozes historical atmosphere. Its luxurious, period-furnished rooms look out onto the moat or the grounds; the restaurant meanwhile is world class.

Traditional decor at Dragsholm Slot in Himmelseng

KALUNDBORG: Debbie's Bed and Breakfast Kr
B&B **Road Map** E4
Hovvejen 114, 4400 Kalundborg
Tel *29 92 29 28*
W debbiesbedandbreakfast.dk
In a building dating from 1886, Debbie's B&B is a working farm 3 km (2 miles) from Kalundborg centre. It offers rooms with and without en suite bathrooms, and a small kitchen is available for guests to use.

LEJRE: Gammel Lejre Guesthouse Kr
Family **Road Map** F4
Orehøjvej 3A, 4320 Lejre
Tel *23 93 97 93*
W gammellejrebb.dk
This small, self-service style guesthouse located in beautiful countryside is close to Lejre's Land of Legends. The pleasant doubles have their own entrance, kitchen facilities and bathroom.

ROSKILDE: Hotel Prindsen Kr Kr
Historic **Road Map** F4
Algade 13, 4000 Roskilde
Tel *46 30 91 00*
W hotelprindsen.dk
This inn on Roskilde's central walking street is close to everything, combining modern facilities and traditional elegance. Note the street can be noisy at weekends; courtyard-facing rooms are quieter.

SORØ: Hotel Postgården Kr Kr
Historic **Road Map** E5
Storgade 25, 4180 Sorø
Tel *57 83 22 22*
W hotelpostgaarden.dk

Key to Price Guide *see page 248*

Housed in an over 300 year-old building on Sorø's main shopping street, this small, historic hotel offers friendly service and elegant rooms. It makes a great base from which to explore the local attractions.

South Zealand

DK Choice

BANDHOLM: Bandholm Hotel ⓀⓇ
Historic **Road Map** E6
Havnegade 37, 4941 Bandholm
Tel *54 75 54 76*
W bandholmhotel.dk
This privately owned hotel is not only handy for visiting the nearby Knuthenborg Safari Park, but also a luxurious place in its own right, with elegantly furnished rooms and apartments, a seaside beach location, a Danish restaurant and a wellness centre. Ferries to tiny Askø and Lilleø depart from near the hotel.

KØGE: Centralhotellet ⓀⓇⓀⓇ
Historic **Road Map** F5
Vestergade 3, 4600 Køge
Tel *56 65 06 96*
W centralhotellet.dk
Inexpensive accommodation at Køge's oldest hotel, which dates from the 1800s and has a good central location. Rooms are clean though fairly basic, with a choice of en suite or shared bathrooms.

MØN: Liselund Ny Slot ⓀⓇⓀⓇ
Historic **Road Map** F6
Langebjergvej 6, 4791 Borre, Møn
Tel *55 81 20 81*
W liselundslot.dk
A romantic atmosphere is assured at this doll-sized castle built in 1887 and located some 5 km (3 miles) from Møns Klint. The tastefully decorated rooms are named after H.C. Andersen's fairy tales.

NÆSTVED: Hotel Kirstine ⓀⓇⓀⓇ
Character **Road Map** E5
Købmagergade 20, 4700 Næstved
Tel *55 77 47 00*
W hotelkirstine.dk
Privately owned hotel in a quaint, half-timbered farmhouse from 1745 that was once a mayoral residence, with upmarket restaurant and antique furnished rooms. A popular venue for wedding parties.

NYKØBING F: Ny Kirstineberg Bed & Breakfast ⓀⓇ
B&B **Road Map** F6
Ny Kirstinebergvej 7, 4800 Nykøbing Falster
Tel *22 57 39 00*
W bedbreakfast-nykøbingfalster.dk
This 19th-century country villa just north of Nykøbing Falster is more manor house than B&B. It offers elegantly furnished singles, doubles and triples, plus a shared kitchen and large garden for guests to use.

RINGSTED: Sørup Herregaard ⓀⓇⓀⓇ
Luxury **Road Map** E5
Sørupvej 26, 4100 Ringsted
Tel *57 64 30 02*
W sorup.dk
Relax in 4-star comfort at this 14th-century manor house located a short drive south of Ringsted. It sits in 400 hectares (990 acres) of land and features a lake plus facilities for crazy golf, petanque and swimming.

SAKSKØBING: Hotel Sakskjøbing ⓀⓇⓀⓇ
Historic **Road Map** E6
Torvet 9, 4990 Sakskøbing
Tel *54 70 40 39*
W hotel-saxkjobing.dk
Dating from 1835, this hotel on Sakskøbing town square is co-owned by culinary guru Claus Meyer, who has injected new life into both the restaurant and rooms.

VORDINGBORG: Hotel Kong Valdmar ⓀⓇ
Character **Road Map** F6
Algade 101, 4760 Vordingborg
Tel *55 31 12 10*
W hotelkongvaldemar.dk
Ideal for visiting Vordingborg Slot, the hotel's most immediate neighbour, this hotel is friendly enough if rather lacking in character. Doubles and triples are available, and there's a small petanque terrain in the garden.

Funen

ÆREØSKØBING: Pension Vestergade 44 ⓀⓇⓀⓇ
Historic **Road Map** D6
Vestergade 44, 5970 Ærøskøbing
Tel *62 52 22 98*
W vestergade44.com
Built in 1784, this charming guesthouse's beautifully furnished rooms have a romantic feel. It has a lovely garden and cosy sitting room.

FAABORG: Danhostel Faaborg ⓀⓇ
Hostel **Road Map** D5
Grønnegade 71, 5600 Faaborg
Tel *62 61 12 03*
W danhostelfaaborg.dk
This atmospheric hostel is located in a 19th-century former poorhouse in central Faaborg, 10 minutes' walk from a sandy beach. Guests have access to a garden courtyard and a shared kitchen.

FAABORG: Hotel Faergegaarden ⓀⓇⓀⓇ
Historic **Road Map** D5
Chr IX's Vej 31, 5600 Faaborg
Tel *62 61 11 15*
W hotelfg.dk
Close to the harbour, this small hotel dates back to the late 19th century. There are sea views from many rooms and a traditional Danish restaurant on the premises.

KERTEMINDE: Tornøes Hotel ⓀⓇⓀⓇ
Historic **Road Map** D5
Strandgade 2, 5300 Kerteminde
Tel *65 32 16 05*
W tornoeshotel.dk
Inexpensive, spacious rooms are available at this classic seaside hotel, which dates back to the 1600s and has offered lodging since 1865. Centrally located, most rooms feature fjord or harbour views.

Outdoor seating and garden at the luxurious Bandholm Hotel, Bandholm

NYBORG: Hotel Villa Gule Ⓚ
Historic **Road Map** D5
Østervoldgade 44, 5800 Nyborg
Tel *65 30 11 88*
W villa-gule.dk
This small hotel – dating from the 1800s and located in the centre of medieval Nyborg – offers sea views from many of the rooms, good breakfasts and friendly service. Two apartments are also available in an adjacent building.

ODENSE: Hotel Domir Ⓚ
Character **Road Map** D5
Hans Tausens Gade 19, 5000 Odense C
Tel *66 12 14 27*
W domir.dk
A good budget option close to the Kongens Have park and central train station, this small, privately owned hotel offers comfortable, clean rooms, friendly 24-hour reception and a breakfast buffet.

DK Choice

SVENDBORG: Stella Maris ⓀⓀ
Luxury **Road Map** D5
Kogtvedvænget 3, 5700 Svendborg
Tel *62 21 25 25*
W stellamaris.dk
Stella Maris opened in 2014, in a building dating from 1904 that has had many purposes – originally a stately home, it was a Christian retreat for years. Now a luxurious seafront boutique hotel with a cocktail lounge, smart bistro and bright, simply decorated rooms. There is also a farm shop in the grounds.

TRANEKÆR, LANGELAND: Damgaarden Økologisk B&B Ⓚ
B&B **Road Map** D6
Emmerbøllevej 5, 5953 Tranekær
Tel *62 59 16 45*
W damgaarden.dk
A sprawling, child-friendly farmhouse that has been run as an organic B&B since the 1990s. Enjoy breakfast in the garden in summer. Shared kitchen facilities and a TV/games room are available to guests.

South and Central Jutland

AARHUS: Simple Bed Hostel Ⓚ
Hostel **Road Map** D4
Åboulevarden 86, 8000 Aarhus C
Tel *53 23 21 89*
W simplebedhostel.com
Independent, self service hostel with two dorms in a handy riverside location. There's no reception but the owners live in the flat above. There's a shared bathroom, kitchen and TV room.

DK Choice

AARHUS: Villa Provence ⓀⓀ
Boutique **Road Map** D4
Fredens Torv 12,8000 Aarhus
Tel *86 18 24 00*
W villaprovence.dk
Many guests have fallen in love with this small, intimate hotel tucked away in a quiet corner of central Aarhus. Despite its nostalgic, guesthouse feel, Villa Provence's modern facilities include charging facilities for electric cars. The Provence-style rooms are spacious and romantic; many have four-posters and clawfoot tubs.

EBELTOFT: Hotel Ebeltoft Strand ⓀⓀ
Family **Road Map** D3
Ndr. Strandvej 3, 8400 Ebeltoft
Tel *86 34 33 00*
W ebeltoftstrand.dk
This modern seafront hotel complex offers apartments and double/family rooms, with panoramic bay views and a smart gourmet restaurant. Family-friendly facilities include loan of Nintendos and a kids' playroom.

ESBJERG: Hotel Ansgar ⓀⓀ
Character **Road Map** B5
Skolegade 36, 6700 Esbjerg
Tel *75 12 82 44*
W hotelansgar.dk
A family-owned hotel for more than a century, centrally-located Ansgar prides itself on providing personal service. Rooms are clean and spacious, and both ferries and trains are within walking distance.

Stylish guest room at the intimate Villa Provence in Aarhus

FREDERICIA: Hotel Postgaarden Ⓚ
Historic **Road Map** C5
Oldenborggade 4, 7000 Fredericia
Tel *75 92 18 55*
W postgaarden.dk
This renovated older hotel just outside Fredericia's town ramparts offers rooms in both a modern wing and an older one, allowing guests to choose between modern comforts or old-world atmosphere.

HERNING: Best Western Hotel Eyde ⓀⓀ
Historic **Road Map** C4
Torvet 1, 7400 Herning
Tel *97 22 18 00*
W eyde.dk
On the town square in the centre of Herning, this elegant hotel has been thoroughly updated with modern facilities including a gym and a sauna. Breakfast is included.

HORSENS: Scandic Bygholm Park ⓀⓀ
Family **Road Map** C4
Schüttesvej 6, 8700 Horsens
Tel *75 62 23 33*
W scandichotels.com/Hotels/Denmark/Horsens
This former stately home on the outskirts of Horsens is now run by the family-friendly Scandic chain. In addition to enjoying the modern facilities, guests are free to wander around the vast park.

KOLDING: Hotel Koldingfjord ⓀⓀ
Luxury **Road Map** C5
Fjordvej 154, 6000 Kolding
Tel *75 51 00 00*
W koldingfjord.dk
A stately house, ringed by forest and fjord, which was a children's sanatorium until 1960. The elegant 1911 building has been a luxury spa hotel since 1990.

RIBE: Weis Stue Ⓚ
Historic **Road Map** B5
Torvet 2, 6760 Ribe
Tel *75 42 07 00*
W weis-stue.dk
One of Denmark's oldest inns - established 1600 - this half-timbered house on Ribe town square has retained many early 18th-century features. Upstairs, the quaint, antique rooms (shared bath) breathe history.

RINGKØBING: Fjordgården Ⓚ
Family **Road Map** B4
Vester Kær 28, 6950 Ringkøbing
Tel *97 32 14 00*
W hotelfjordgaarden.dk
Despite its rather uninspiring-looking building, Fjordgården is

Key to Price Guide *see page 248*

located amidst beautiful countryside and a short walk into town is pleasant. Rooms are clean and functional.

SILKEBORG: Radisson Blu Papirfabrikken ⓀⓀ
Modern **Road Map** C4
Papirfabrikken 12, 8600 Silkeborg
Tel *88 82 22 22*
W radissonblu.com/hotel-silkeborg
This former paper mill has been transformed into a modern design hotel with restaurant, riverside terrace and sleekly furnished rooms. Surrounded by woodland and water, but close to local attractions.

SØNDERBORG: Comwell Hotel Sønderborg ⓀⓀ
Luxury **Road Map** C6
Rosengade 2, 6400 Sønderborg
Tel *74 42 19 00*
W comwellsonderborg.dk
In a great location looking out over the Alssund, next door to Sønderborg Slot and within walking distance of Sønderborg centre, this hotel's four-star luxuries include a pool, gym and massage treatments.

VEJLE: Hotel Australia ⓀⓀ
Modern **Road Map** C4
Dæmningen 6, 7100 Vejle
Tel *76 40 60 00*
W hotelaustralia.dk
An inexpensive hotel in Vejle overlooking the fjord, with friendly reception and air conditioning in the rooms. It is well placed for the bus and train stations, as well as the town's pedestrian street.

North Jutland

DK Choice

AALBORG: Hotel Krogen Ⓚ
Character **Road Map** C2
Skibstedsvej 4, 9000 Aalborg
Tel *98 12 17 05*
W krogen.dk
Small, family-owned hotel-guesthouse in a palatial villa from 1872. Aalborg's bustling centre seems far away from its peaceful location in residential Hasseris, though the city's main sights are within walking distance. Aside from the romantically furnished rooms, the hotel's unique feature is its large miniature railway encircling the garden.

Mongolian yurt at Bunken Strand Camping in Skagen

FREDERIKSHAVN: Hotel Scandic The Reef ⓀⓀ
Family **Road Map** D1
Tordenskjoldsgade 14, 9900 Frederikshavn
Tel *98 43 32 33*
W scandichotels.com
Keep the kids happy with the tropical water park and family-friendly restaurant at this modern hotel with functional rooms.

HIRTSHALS: Hotel Montra Skaga ⓀⓀ
Modern **Road Map** C1
Willemoesvej 1, 9850 Hirtshals
Tel *98 94 55 00*
W skagahotel.dk
Located just steps from Nordsøen Oceanarium, the exterior of this modern hotel block may not excite as much as the beauty of its windswept surroundings, between an orchard and the sea.

HJØRRING: Hjørring Kro Ⓚ
Inn **Road Map** D1
Birthesvej 2, 9800 Hjørring
Tel *98 92 53 29*
W hjoerringkro.dk
Hjørring Kro inn is known for its friedly staff. Rooms are plain but clean and comfortable, and the restaurant serves traditional fare.

HOBRO: Hotel Amerika ⓀⓀ
Luxury **Road Map** C3
Amerikavej 48, 9500 Hobro
Tel *98 54 42 00*
W hotelamerika.dk
This country estate is surrounded by forest; a footpath from the 4-star hotel leads directly to Mariager Fjord. There is a spa, wellness centre and restaurant on site.

HOLSTEBRO: Centrum Bed & Breakfast Ⓚ
B&B **Road Map** B3
Sønderlandsgade 21, 7500 Holstebro
Tel *25 33 90 34*
W aas.dk
Close to the town centre, this well-equipped B&B offers breakfast from the adjoining Café Aas, as well as access to a communal kitchen. There are shared bathroom facilities and a pleasant outdoor terrace.

RANDERS: Best Western Hotel Kronjylland ⓀⓀ
Character **Road Map** D3
Vestergade 51–53, 8900 Randers
Tel *86 41 43 33*
W bestwestern.dk
Centrally located 300 m (328 yds) from the station, Kronjylland dates from the early 1900s, although its modern rooms are decorated in clean Scandinavian style. Breakfast is included and there's Wi-Fi in the public areas.

SKAGEN: Bunken Strand Camping Ⓚ
Campsite **Road Map** D1
Ålbækvej 288, 9980 Aalbæk
Tel *98 48 71 80*
W bunkenstrandcamping.dk
This well-equipped campsite a few miles south of Skagen offers direct access to a sandy beach. In addition to rental cabins and caravans, the campsite has two yurts imported from Mongolia.

SKAGEN: Hotel Plesner ⓀⓀ
Boutique **Road Map** D1
Holstvej 8, 9990 Skagen
Tel *98 44 68 44*
W hotelplesner.dk
This historic seaside hotel dates from 1907 and is close to Skagen's beautiful beaches and reknowned art galleries. Renovations have accentuated the boutique qualities at Hotel Plesner, with individually decorated rooms and a pristine, landscaped garden.

For more information on types of hotels *see pages 244–5*

SKAGEN: Ruth's Hotel (Kr)(Kr)(Kr)
Luxury **Road Map** D1
Hans Ruths Vej 1, 9990 Skagen
Tel *98 44 11 24*
W ruths-hotel.dk
This legendary seaside hotel opened as a small guesthouse in 1904. Several generations of the Ruth family later, the place is known for 5-star luxury, spa treatments and its gourmet restaurant.

THISTED: Hotel Thisted (Kr)(Kr)
Character **Road Map** B2
Frederiksgade 16, 7700 Thisted
Tel *97 92 52 00*
W hotelthisted.dk
In the centre of historic Thisted, this small, family-owned hotel has been well-maintained throughout its long tenure as a town inn. Its French-Danish restaurant famed for homemade schnapps.

VIBORG: Oasen (Kr)
B&B **Road Map** C3
Nørregade 9, 8800 Viborg
Tel *86621425*
W oasenviborg.dk
This inexpensive guesthouse in central Viborg offers quaintly decorated rooms and self-catering apartments with breakfast. There is a pleasant closed-in garden patio and a coin-operated laundry for guests.

Bornholm

ALLINGE: Hotel Friheden (Kr)(Kr)
Luxury
Tejnvej 80, 3770 Allinge
Tel *56 48 04 25*
W hotelfriheden.dk
Modern, family-run resort hotel with seaside location in Sandkås, a holiday area south of Allinge. The spacious, well-equipped rooms have either a balcony or terrace and a kitchenette; many also offer sea views.

ALLINGE: Pension Næsgaarden (Kr)(Kr)
Guesthouse
Løsebækgade 20, 3770 Allinge
Tel *56 48 02 18*
W naesgaarden.dk
An old-fashioned guesthouse from the early 1800s, with a beach on its doorstep, delightful cobbled yard and fruit trees in the garden. There's a small kitchen for guests; breakfasts are homemade and organic.

GUDHJEM: Hotel Klippen (Kr)(Kr)
Character
Grevens Dal 50, 3760 Gudhjem
Tel *56 44 32 22*
W hotelklippen.dk
A sprawling villa above Gudhjem overlooking the sea, Klippen offers a variety of rooms in different annexes, with either a terrace or a balcony. Weekly rates are available. Nice café-bar on the premises.

DK Choice

GUDHJEM: Stammershalle Badehotel (Kr)(Kr)
Historic
Sdr. Strandvej 128, 3760 Gudhjem
Tel *56 48 42 10*
W stammershalle-badehotel.dk
Historic seaside hotel established in 1911 perched on the cliffs between Allinge and Gudhjem, offering dramatic Baltic views from most of its bright, airy rooms. It features an award-winning gourmet restaurant, Lassens; full board is available. Behind the hotel, traces of the small zoo built by the original owner can still be seen.

HASLE: Hotel Herold (Kr)
Guesthouse
Vestergade 65, 3790 Hasle
Tel *56 96 40 24*
W hotelherold.dk
A charming, friendly little hotel on Hasle's renovated harbour front. There are sea views from many rooms, which offer the opportunity to enjoy a perfect Bornholm sunset. Good breakfasts are included in the room rate.

NEXØ: Hotel Balka Strand (Kr)(Kr)
Family
Boulevarden 9A, Balka, 3730 Nexø
Tel *56 49 49 49*
W hotelbalkastrand.dk
Just 150 metres (164 yds) from one of Bornholm's best sandy beaches, this modern complex comprises several buildings. All rooms have furnished terraces. The self-catering apartments can sleep up to five guests.

RØNNE: Hotel Griffen (Kr)(Kr)
Modern
Nordre Kystvej 34, 3700 Rønne
Tel *56 90 42 44*
W bornholmhotels.dk/?Id=1215
This resort is the largest hotel on Bornholm. It's placed right on the seafront a short walk from the ferry, with extensive spa and bathing facilities.

RØNNE: Radisson Blu Fredensborg Hotel (Kr)(Kr)
Family
Strandvejen 116, 3700 Rønne
Tel *56 90 44 44*
W radissonblu.com/hotel-bornholm

Historic seaside hotel Stammershalle Badehotel at Gudhjem

Large, modern hotel complex situated just south of Rønne. Equipped to a very high standard, it offers exceptional service and sea views from the balcony/terrace of all rooms.

SANDVIG: Hotel Hammersø (Kr)
Luxury
Hammershusvej 86, Sandvig, 3770 Allinge
Tel *56480364*
W hotel-hammersoe.dk
Located on the edge of Bornholm's largest lake, this adults-only half-board hotel offers old-fashioned resort pastimes with a billiards room and deckchairs to relax around the solar-heated swimming pool.

SVANEKE: Hotel Siemsens Gaard (Kr)(Kr)
Historic
Havnebryggen 5, 3740 Svaneke
Tel *56 49 61 49*
W siemsens.dk
Situated behind the harbour in a 17th-century merchant's house, Siemsens Gaard was rebuilt as a hotel in the 1930s. Some rooms have a kitchenette and a terrace opening onto the peaceful rear courtyard.

Greenland

ILULISSAT: Hotel Avannaa (Kr)(Kr)
Character
Nuussuattaap Aqq. 2, 3952 Ilulissat
Tel *29 99 44 002*
W hotelavannaa.gl
Breathtaking views of Ilulissiat Ice Fiord are reason enough to visit this small hotel/B&B. All rooms have a balcony and Internet access (fees may be charged); some have a kitchenette. Triples are available.

Key to Price Guide *see page 248*

DK Choice

ILULISSAT: Hotel Arctic ®®®
Luxury
Mittarfimmut Aqq. B-1128, 3952 Ilulissat
Tel *29 99 44 153*
W hotel-arctic.gl
As the world's most northerly luxury hotel situated right on the edge of the UNESCO-listed Ilulissiat Ice Fiord, finding more stunning views from a hotel room would be a challenge. Ilulissiat town is situated on the other side of the fiord to the south. The hotel offers two high-standard restaurants.

KANGERLUSSUAQ: Polar Lodge ®®
Hostel
Mittafeqarfiit Aqq. 1009, 3910 Kangerlussuaq
Tel *29 98 41 648*
W wogac.com/accommodation/polar-lodge
This hostel is housed in a former US airbase, with Mount Hassel as its backdrop. Kitchen facilities, Wi-Fi and bike rental are available.

NUUK: Hotel Apartments Nordbo ®®
Apartments
Vandsøvej 13, 3900 Nuuk
Tel *29 93 26 644*
W hotelnordbo.gl
Centrally-located, Nordbo offers a range of reasonably priced, simply furnished apartments with kitchen and laundry facilities, available for long- and short-term rentals.

NUUK: Hans Egede Hotel ®®®
Modern
Aqqusinersuaq, 3900 Nuuk
Tel *29 93 24 222*
W hhe.gl
The Greenland government uses this hotel for all of its conferences. Behind the unappealing façade is a well-equipped hotel housing one of Nuuk's best restaurants.

SISIMIUT: Hotel Sisimiut ®®
Modern
Aqqusinersuaq 86, 3911 Sisimiut
Tel *29 98 64 840*
W hotelsisimiut.com
Located just north of the Arctic Circle in the Sisimiut settlement, this hotel offers rooms and suites. Its upmarket restaurant is one of the best in town.

TASIILAQ: Hotel Angmagssalik ®®
Modern
PO Box 511, 3913 Tasiilaq
W arcticwonder.com/hotels/hotel-angmagssalik
This pleasant hotel overlooks Tasiilaq settlement and is well equipped. Budget dorm lodgings are available in an annexe.

Faroe Islands

DK Choice

GJOGV, EYUSTUROY: Gjaargardur Guesthouse Gjogv ®®
Eco
Dalavegur 20, 476 Gjogv
Tel *29 84 23 171*
W gjaargardur.fo/
An hours' drive from Tórshavn, amidst spectacular scenery, this eco-friendly guesthouse has a grass roof that blends into the surrounding hillside. It offers modern facilities, friendly service and will even make packed lunches on request. The attic rooms are cheaper with a shared bathroom, but offer spectacular views.

KLAKSVIK: Hotel Klaksvik ®®
Modern
Víkavegur 38, 700 Klaksvík
Tel *298455333*
W hotelklaksvik.fo
Great views from the rooms of Klaksvik's sole 3-star hotel, all but three of which are en suite. Note that although the hotel has two restaurants, both have a strictly no alcohol policy.

RUNAVIK, EYUSTUROY: Hotel Runavik ®®
Modern
Heiðavegur 6, 620 Runavík
Tel *298663333*
W hotelrunavik.fo
The only hotel in this part of the Faroes is located in a renovated former seaman's mission from the 1950s on Runavik's main street. Rooms are brightly furnished and well-equipped.

TÓRSHAVN: Bladypi Guesthouse ®
Hostel
Doktara Jakobsens gøta, 100 Tórshavn
Tel *29 85 00 600*
W hostel.fo/
One of the cheapest options in Tórshavn, this basic guesthouse is centrally located and offers both private rooms and hostel-style dorm accommodation. There are shared kitchen facilities as well.

TÓRSHAVN: Hotel Tórshavn ®®
Modern
Tórsgøta 4, 100 Tórshavn
Tel *29 83 50 000*
W hoteltorshavn.fo
A 3-star hotel with brightly decorated rooms and a fancy brasserie restaurant. Centrally located near the harbour, some rooms at Tórshavn have sea views, though you'll pay a little extra for the privilege.

TÓRSHAVN: Hotel Føroyar ®®®
Designer
Oyggjarvegur 45, 100 Tórshavn
Tel *29 83 17 500*
W hotelforoyar.com
This architecturally fascinating hotel is characterised by the way it blends into the surrounding landscape, with a grass roof, and light rooms. The hotel restaurant is equally innovative.

TVØROYRI, SUDUROY: Guesthouse Undir Heygnum ®
Guesthouse
800 Tvøroyri
Tel *298372046*
W guest-house.dk
Remotely situated on Suduroy's northeastern shore, "Under the Hill" is a wood-framed 1920s villa. Guests can use the shared kitchen, enjoy the garden and, in summertime, go out on a boat.

Simple accommodation and spectacular scenery at Gjaargardur Guesthouse, Gjogv

For more information on types of hotels *see pages 244–5*

WHERE TO EAT AND DRINK

Denmark's restaurant scene is fashionable like never before. The global trend for "New Nordic Cuisine" and the international fame of Copenhagen restaurant Noma, which bases its menu exclusively on locally produced, seasonal ingredients, has filtered down into all regions of Denmark. Even smaller, provincial eateries now offer a version of Nordic cuisine, with regional specialties such as horseradish and beetroot, and rye bread making a comeback. It's not only the big cities such as Copenhagen and Aarhus where diners can be assured a high culinary standard; the island of Bornholm, for example, has developed a reputation for its regional specialties and exceptional restaurants, while Greenland and the Faroes have their own gourmet restaurants that showcase local ingredients and take an innovative approach to traditional dishes. Travellers looking for more modest meals will find cafés in most small towns serving snacks, pastries and drinks, but traditional street stands offering the Danish hot dog *pølser* are becoming less and less visible.

Light-filled dining room at New Nordic restaurant, Orangeriet *(see p262)*

When to Eat

Danish breakfast tends to be a fairly modest affair, though this is changing, especially in Copenhagen, where many cafés open from 7am. At weekends, hearty and wholesome brunches are popular, and cafés known for their brunches often fill up fast. As an alternative, many bakeries sell bread, pastries and coffee and occasionally provide a table at which to sit.

Frokost (lunch) is consumed between 11:30am and 2pm. It can take various forms, from a light meal to a large banquet of open sandwiches and salads. At lunchtime many restaurants also serve hot main courses such as meatballs, but the helpings are smaller and prices lower than the same meal at dinnertime. *Aftensmad* (dinner) is from 6pm onwards, with many restaurants closing their kitchens by 9pm. Evening dining can be expensive: it's not unusual for prices to rise between lunch and dinner at the same establishment. Late-night snacks are generally limited to fast food, such as noodles, pizza or kebabs.

Opening Hours

Bakeries open early, usually around 6am. Fast-food restaurants that serve breakfast open at around 8 or 9am. Restaurants that cater for the lunchtime trade generally open around 11am and often close around 3pm, and traditionally serve *smørrebrød* (open sandwiches) with a selection of toppings. Restaurants generally finish serving by 10pm, and restaurants that are not licensed to remain open all night close at 1am. Cafés tend to stay open all day and often late into the night.

Menu

Many restaurants have menus written in English. In addition to the full menu, some offer a specially priced *dagens ret*, or "dish of the day", which is often written up on a board. Some restaurants serve good value fixed-price two-, three- or four-course lunches and evening meals. Seasonal changing set menus have become especially popular in "New Nordic" eateries,

Outside tables at coffee microroastery, Kaffehuset Møn *(see p269)*

Sea views from the terrace at Kadeau Bornholm, Aakirkeby

where a limited choice keeps prices down and the quality of ingredients high.

Children

Most restaurants in Denmark offer high chairs and special "child-friendly" menus and activity packs. The best time to take children to a restaurant is late afternoon. Eating at this time of day is quieter, less stressful and generally means that no one need wait long to be served.

Prices and Tips

Prices in restaurants vary enormously. Many cheaper Danish establishments offer set-price all-you-can-eat buffets at lunchtime, as do some of the Thai and Middle-Eastern restaurants. Some hostels also serve good value lunch and evening meals for about 100 Dkr. A three-course meal in a mid-priced restaurant will cost between 250–400 Dkr not including alcohol, while at an upmarket restaurant, diners should be prepared to pay in excess of 800 Dkr.

Soft drinks, beer and *akvavit* (a kind of schnapps) cost about the same in most places; however, prices for wines and liqueurs vary greatly and tend to be steep in some of the upmarket restaurants.

In Denmark, a service charge and tax are automatically included in the price. Leaving no tip is not considered bad manners; however, it is customary to round up the bill.

Most restaurants accept credit cards and display the appropriate signs at their entrance.

Reservations

Guests are generally required to book well in advance at the most popular restaurants. Even in quieter restaurants it is advisable to book at the weekend.

If it is too late to book, then the best option is to head to an area where there are clusters of restaurants.

Vegetarians

The diet in Denmark is heavily based on meat and fish. However, most restaurants should offer at least one vegetarian dish. Restaurants that serve only vegetarian food are a rarity.

Disabled Guests

As elsewhere in Europe, restaurants providing facilities for disabled people cannot be taken for granted. Especially in the bigger towns, older establishments are often located in basements, while more modern premises (such as restaurants attached to hotels and museums) are more likely to be accessible to all. It is best to check when booking. Local tourist offices should be able to help visitors locate accessible restaurants in the area. Another useful source for tourists is the Accessibility Label Scheme website (www.godadgang.dk), which lists establishments that have joined the scheme and are accessible to those with special needs.

Recommended Restaurants

The restaurants listed here have been carefully selected to offer a cross-section of options for every region. In addition to Copenhagen's best Michelin-starred restaurants, we have provided an alternative to suit all budgets and tastes, whether you are on a culinary tour or looking for a place to take the family for lunch. Danish cuisine is regarded among the world's best, and the "New Nordic" kitchen is heavily featured here, both in fine-dining and in more down-to-earth establishments.

The DK choice entries focus on those eateries that are exceptional and innovative in their use of raw ingredients, often produced locally at the restaurant's own farms. At many of them, advance booking is needed.

Selection of cakes on display at La Glace *(see p262)*

The Flavours of Denmark

Denmark's cuisine, like that of other Scandinavian countries, has always been rich in meat and fish dishes. Specialities from the sea include smoked salmon, pickled herring, eel and haddock. Cod is served baked, steamed, fried or dried *(klipfisk)*. The *kolde bord*, a lunchtime buffet, is a good way to try out various local dishes, with a selection of *smørrebrød*, cold cuts and hearty pork dishes. Most Danes have a sweet tooth and *wienerbrød* (Danish pastries) are eaten at any time of day. Berries appear in many desserts, and Danish ice cream is among the best in the world.

Danish pastries

Punnets of ripe strawberries, freshly harvested on Samsø Island

Smørrebrød

The classic *smørrebrød* (open sandwich) is as popular as ever with the Danes. Preparation is easy enough: buttered slices of *rugbrød* (unleavened rye bread) are topped with any number of sliced meats, fish or cheeses, such as prawns, smoked eel, ham, lamb and beef. They are then garnished with dill, cucumber, tomato or lemon, a remoulade (mayonnaise-based sauce), caviar, or even a raw egg yolk served in its shell. Among national favourites are *Sol over Gudhjem* and *Bornholmer*, both variations on smoked herring fillets topped with an egg yolk, raw onion, chives and radishes. *Marineredesild* (vinegar-cured herring with onions and capers) and *Stjerneskud* ("shooting star", fried fish fillet with prawns, lemon and dill) are also popular. Meat varieties include *dyrlægens natmad*, a towering creation laden with liver pâté, salt beef, flavoured lard, onion rings and watercress; *roastbeefmad*, rare roast beef with fried onions and grated horseradish; and *rullepølsemad*, slices of pork belly seasoned with raw onions, herbs, horseradish and watercress.

Selection of typical Danish *smørrebrød*

Danish Dishes and Specialities

To this day, Danish cuisine retains a flavour of pre-industrial times, when the diet centred around rye bread, salted pork and herring – basically whatever could be grown and harvested in a short summer or pulled from the sea and preserved. This type of cuisine is enjoying quite a resurgence. Typical are dishes such as *øllebrød* (barley porridge), *æbleflæsk* (slices of pork with apples fried in the fat) and *grønlangkål* (thick kale stew with sausages and mustard). Many dishes are served with new potatoes and root vegetables. Cucumber salad, pickled beetroot, and peas and carrots in white sauce also appear. Desserts include Apple Charlotte with whipped cream, breadcrumbs and almonds, and *rødgrød med fløde*, a jellied fruit juice served with thick cream.

Dill

Frikadeller meatballs made of pork and veal are fried in Danish butter and served with boiled new potatoes.

Herrings hanging in a Bornholm smokery

Fish & Seafood

With its 406 islands, Denmark abounds with seafood. Herring is the most caught, cooked and consumed fish in the country. It is eaten fresh or preserved by salting, drying and smoking, and is served with sauces including curry, garlic, mustard and tomato. Salmon also features prominently, smoked, roasted, poached or cured in a salt-sugar-dill mixture, as do smoked eel, roe, mackerel and plaice. Fish fillets are often fried in butter and served with new potatoes and a buttery parsley sauce, washed down with lager or *akvavit* (Danish schnapps). Seafood is best enjoyed in the distinctive *røgeri* (smokehouses) found in harbours and pier restaurants all over the country.

Meat

Pork is the most common meat; there are four times as many pigs as people in Denmark, and Danish bacon is famous throughout the world. Traditional preparations include *stegt flæsk med persillesovs,* fried slices of pork with parsley sauce, served with potatoes; and *medisterpølse*, a thick and spicy pork sausage.

Sausages are popular, no more so than the ubiquitous *pølse*, a hotdog that is sold in kiosks everywhere and flavoured with any number of toppings. Though it is hardly haute cuisine, it is still a must for any visitor.

Beef, veal and lamb appear widely on menus, often in stews or minced to make rissoles and *frikadeller* (meatballs). In season, there are also game birds such as pheasant or duck, and venison and red deer.

Snegl (literally "snail") pastries in a baker's window

DANISH PASTRIES

The "Danish" was introduced to Denmark in the 1870s, when striking breadmakers were replaced by Viennese immigrant bakers, with their repertoire of sweet breads, cakes and puff pastries. Pastries come in all shapes and sizes, and are filled with raisins, fruit compotes and custards, then topped with nuts and sweet icing. Some of the best examples are *spandauer*, a flat twist of dough filled with vanilla custard, and the almond-filled *hanekam*. Moist and light, all are perfect with a coffee. Note that the same cakes and buns will have different names in different regions.

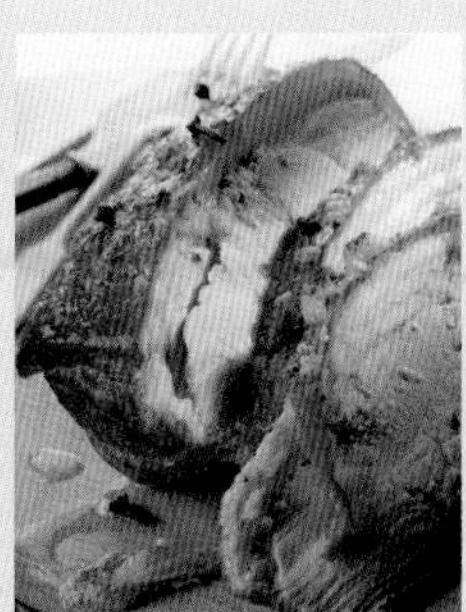

Flæskesteg is a joint of roasted pork with crackling. It is usually served with cabbage and gravy.

Rødbeder is a side dish that consists of sliced pickled beetroot (beets). Horseradish sauce is also popular.

Risalamande is a Christmas rice pudding with almonds. It is served cold, topped with a rich, fruity cherry sauce.

What to Drink in Denmark

As far as drinks are concerned the Danes have two passions – coffee and beer. People over 60 are also very attached to their liqueurs, which come in a variety of flavours and appear under the common name of *akvavit*. The beer market is dominated by a handful of companies, of which Carlsberg is the best known, but there are also many micro-breweries, such as Mikkeler in Copenhagen. Danish beer comes in a variety of strengths and colours, from fairly tame draught Pilsner through to stout with an alcohol content of about 10 per cent. Wine was not always so popular but is readily available in supermarkets and restaurants. Non-alcoholic drinks include mineral water and numerous soft drinks.

Drinkers enjoying the sun outside one of Denmark's extremely popular bars

Lager

Faxe Royal lager

Lager is the most popular Danish beverage. Most Danish beers are of the Pilsner type with an alcohol content of about 4.5 per cent. They include brands such as Carlsberg, Grøn Tuborg, Faxe and Star. Before Christmas and Easter the shops sell Julebryg and Påskebryg in standard and strong varieties. These beers are slightly sweet and make perfect additions to *akvavit*. Bars and restaurants serve both draught beer *(fadøl)* and bottled beers. Sometimes draught beer is ordered in a jug. Beer is most often sold in bottles rather than cans.

Beer is consumed throughout the day. It is not uncommon, and perfectly respectable, for Danes to drink beer in the park at lunchtime. It is rare to see drunkenness and drink-driving is not tolerated.

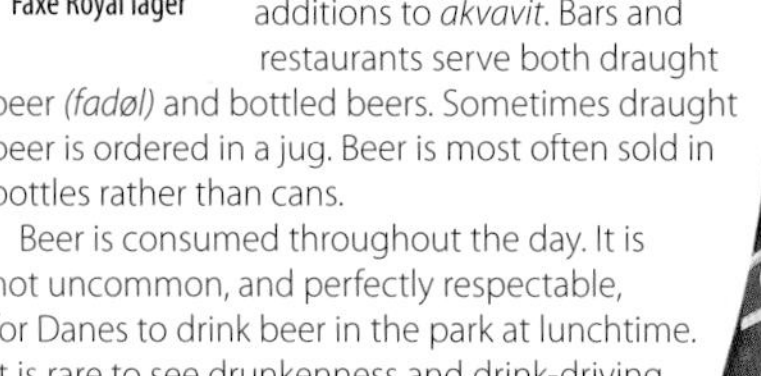

Logo of the Carlsberg brewery

Carlsberg Pilsner

Tuborg lager

Faxe Classic

Carlsberg stout

Carlsberg Elephant

Brown Ale

There are over 400 varieties of beer produced in Denmark, including many fine brown ales. These generally have more flavour and are often stronger than Pilsner beers, with an alcoholic content of about 8 per cent or above. Some cafés and bars specialize in these beers, which tend to be slightly sweeter and less fizzy than lager. Among the popular brown ales are Carlsberg's Elephant and Sort Guld from the Tuborg brewery. The darkest beers are stouts and porters; these often have a higher percentage of alcohol. Organic microbrews, such as Thy Bryghus, also have a slice of the market.

Wine

The Danish climate does not allow for the cultivation of grapes, although a few enthusiasts are trying to introduce the hardier varieties to southern Scandinavia. So far their efforts have not yielded any commercially viable vintages, and Danes, who are increasingly swapping a tankard of beer for a glass of wine, have to settle for imported wines. White wine is referred to as *hvidvin*, red wine is *rødvin* and sparkling wine is *mousserende-vin*. Hot mulled wine, or *gløgg*, is served with almonds and raisins in the run–up to Christmas.

Gløgg – mulled wine

Hot Drinks

An aromatic herbal tea

The Danes are coffee connoisseurs and coffee is the most popular drink in the country. Roasted beans are freshly ground on café premises and brewed in special jugs. Strong Italian espressos are also available, as are cappuccinos and increasingly popular lattes. Caffeine-free coffee is rarely found, but a delicious hot chocolate served with whipped cream is a fine alternative. Tea is not as popular in Denmark as coffee and consists of no more than a tea bag placed in a cup. Herbal teas are available in most cafés.

A cup of black coffee

Liqueurs

The traditional Christmas feast is often accompanied in Denmark by chilled *akvavit*. This schnapps-like beverage comes in a variety of herbal flavours and often bears the name *akvavit* on the label. It is usually drunk in a single shot and is followed by a glass of beer. As well as schnapps, the Danes drink other strong alcoholic herb infusions. The most popular of these is Gammel Dansk, which is traditionally drunk early in the morning. Danes used to regard a small glass of this bitter herbal preparation as a preventative medicine. Another local drink is Peter Heering, a sweet liqueur made from cherries, which is sipped after meals.

Herb-flavoured Gammel Dansk

Akvavit –Danish schnapps

Sparkling mineral water

Fizzy soft drink

Soft Drinks

When ordering a meal it is customary to ask for a bottle or jug of water. Danish tap water *(postevand)* is perfectly safe. Still bottled water is *minaralvand;* the sparkling variety bears the proud name of *danskvand* (Danish carbonated water). All restaurants, bars and pubs also serve low-alcohol beer, known as *let øl*. Soft drinks such as Coca-Cola go by the name of *sodavand*; bottled fruit juices are known as *saft*. Drinking chocolate – both hot *(varm chokolade)* and cold *(chokolademælk)* – is popular.

Bottle of chocolate milk

Where to Eat and Drink

Copenhagen

North Copenhagen

Mormors (Kr)
Café **Map** 2 E5
Bredgade 45, 1260 Cph
Tel *33 16 0 70*
A charming, nostalgic café with friendly service and bar seating next to the large street window. Mormors serves tasty home-made sandwiches and cakes – food like "*mormor*" (grandma) would make. Gluten- and lactose-free options are available.

Café Petersborg (Kr)(Kr)
Danish **Map** 2 E4
Bredgade 76, 1260 Cph
Tel *33 12 50 16* **Closed** *Sat dinner, Sun*
One of Copenhagen's oldest restaurants, its name comes from the visitors from the Russian Consulate that was once above it. The basement locale serves traditional Danish fare in hearty portions, for lunch and dinner.

Ida Davidsen (Kr)(Kr)
Smørrebrød **Map** 2 D5
Store Kongensgade 70, 1264 Cph
Tel *33 91 36 55* **Closed** *Sat, Sun; Jul*
This famed, lunch-only *smørrebrød* café has been run by the Davidsen family for five generations, and in its present location since 1974. With more than 170 variations, the smørrebrød list is record-breaking; some are named after royalty and celebrities.

Madklubben Bistro De-Luxe (Kr)(Kr)
New Nordic **Map** 2 D5
Store Kongensgade 66, 1264 Cph
Tel *33 32 32 34* **Closed** *Sun*
The original restaurant in what is now a string of Copenhagen eateries, Madklubben is all about serving simple, yet high-quality traditional dishes such as soups, fish and prime ribs cheaply and informally. Vegetarian options too.

The Red Box (Kr)(Kr)
Chinese Fusion **Map** 2 D5
Store Kongensgade 42, 1264 Cph
Tel *43 33 43 33* **Closed** *Sun*
A fresh, modern take on Chinese food, fusing traditional Asian dishes with the contemporary European kitchen for meals that are light and healthy. The decor is similarly modern and minimalist, the atmosphere relaxed.

Ché Fè (Kr)(Kr)(Kr)
Italian **Map** 2 D5
Borgergade 17A, 1300 Cph
Tel *33 11 17 21* **Closed** *Sun*
Organic trattoria Ché Fè (meaning "What's up?" in Italian) is run by the same team as Christianshavn's Era Ora. The food is not cheap, but the level of quality and authenticity is high.

Koefoed (Kr)(Kr)(Kr)
New Nordic **Map** 2 D5
Landgreven 3, 1301 Cph
Tel *56 48 22 24* **Closed** *Sun, Mon*
In basement premises on a side street near Store Kongensgade, this simply decorated restaurant in a former coal cellar specialises in cuisine from the Danish island of Bornholm. Free-range meat is sourced from individual farms to produce simple, seasonal dishes. Large selection of Bordeaux wines to chose from.

DK Choice

Lumskebugten (Kr)(Kr)(Kr)
Danish **Map** 2 F4
Esplanaden 21, 1263 Cph
Tel *33 15 60 29* **Closed** *Sun (lunch & dinner); Mon & Tue (dinners)*
A former sailor's tavern situated between the cruise ports and Kastellet, *"Lumskebugten"* is what Danes call a place to run aground. The food is a modern take on traditional Danish dishes; open sandwiches and fried fish are served simply with delicious lightness. The setting is cosy, with seating for around 30 diners, but as it's an old building, the acoustics aren't always perfect.

Serving counter at traditional Copenhagen patisserie La Glace

Price Guide
Prices are based on a two-course meal for one without alcohol or a tip, but including tax.

(Kr)	up to 200 Dkr
(Kr)(Kr)	200–350 Dkr
(Kr)(Kr)(Kr)	over 350 Dkr

Orangeriet (Kr)(Kr)(Kr)
New Nordic **Map** 1 C5
Kronprinsessegade 13, 1306 Cph
Tel *33 11 13 07* **Closed** *Sun dinner*
Located in beautiful green surroundings in a glass-fronted conservatory in Kongens Have, Orangeriet serves simple, seasonal dinners and lunchtime open sandwiches. There's also a mouth-watering cake table on Sunday afternoons.

Central Copenhagen

Atlas Bar (Kr)
International **Map** 3 B1
Larsbjørnsstræde 18, 1454 Cph
Tel *33 15 03 52* **Closed** *Sun*
A long-standing favourite with the area's students, this casual, inexpensive basement café serves dishes from around the globe with one of the best vegetarian selections in the city.

Café Retro (Kr)
Café **Map** 3 B1
Knabrostræde 26, 1210 Cph
Tel *41 83 35 35* **Closed** *Mon*
A non-profit café with a pleasant atmosphere run by a team of international volunteers, with lots of sofas and armchairs and an upstairs room. There are no main meals, but soups, cakes and nachos are served.

La Glace (Kr)
Café **Map** 3 B1
Skoubogade 3, 1158 Cph
Tel *33 14 46 46* **Closed** *Sun (Easter–Sep)*
An old-fashioned, rather genteel patisserie dating from 1870. Six generations later, La Glace is much the same, with an incredible selection of elaborately decorated cakes.

Makke Kaffe (Kr)
Café **Map** 3 C2
Nybrogade 18–20, 1203 Cph
Tel *52 40 01 84* **Closed** *Sun*
Run by a smiling Italian woman, this family-friendly basement café on the canal side, not far from the Nationalmuseet, has sofas, books and toys. It serves cheap and healthy cakes, tapas and sandwiches.

Riz Raz Sticks 'n' Veggies Ⓚ
Mediterranean **Map** 3 B2
Kompagnistræde 20, 1208 Cph
Tel *33 15 05 75*
One of two Riz Raz eateries in the city, the affordable and filling all-you-can-eat Mediterranean buffets served for both lunch and dinner (lunch is cheaper) have long been popular with backpackers and students.

Royal Smushi Café Ⓚ
Café **Map** 3 C1
Amagertorv 6, 1160 Cph
Tel *33 12 11 22*
The café of the Royal Copenhagen store is a quirkily decorated, pastel-toned place, where *smørrebrød* is served in dolls' sizes dubbed "smushi", along with cakes and coffee – all on blue fluted porcelain.

Slotskælderen hos Gitte Kik Ⓚ
Smørrebrød **Map** 3 C1
Fortunstræde 4, 1065 Cph
Tel *33 11 15 37* **Closed** *Sun, Mon*
This classic *smørrebrød* lunch restaurant dates from 1910 and still looks much the same now as it did then. Traditional open sandwich toppings are served with a lunchtime schnapps and an old-fashioned atmosphere.

Aamanns Etablissement ⓀⓀ
Smørrebrød **Map** 1 B3
Øster Farimagsgade 10–12, 2100 Cph Ø
Tel *35 55 33 44* **Closed** *Mon, Tue dinner*
Reinterpreting traditional *smørrebrød* for a contemporary audience, Aamanns is both take-away deli and eat-in restaurant (Etablissement), serving open sandwiches and evening meals.

Café Europa 1989 ⓀⓀ
Café **Map** 3 C1
Amagertorv 1, 1160 Cph
Tel *33 14 28 89*
On one side of busy Amagertorv Square, this café is a popular meeting place and it can be hard to get a seat. The cosmopolitan decor and menu are both influenced by the best of European café traditions.

Café Norden ⓀⓀ
Café **Map** 3 C1
Østergade 61, 1100 Cph
Tel *33 11 77 91*
A popular meeting spot over-looking Storkespringvandet in the middle of Strøget. In summer, tables tumble out onto the street from the two-storey Art Deco building. Enjoy coffee and cake, brunch or various hot dishes.

Café Europa1989 on Amargertorv Square

Cap Horn ⓀⓀ
Organic **Map** 4 E1
Nyhavn 21, 1051 Cph
Tel *33 12 85 04*
Dine outside on picturesque Nyhavn's jetty or inside the charming old building, which has retained many original fixtures. The seasonal, organic menu offers a varied selection of fish, meat and vegetarian dishes.

Geist ⓀⓀ
Danish fusion **Map** 4 D1
Kongens Nytorv 8, 1050 Cph
Tel *33 13 37 13*
Located amongst upmarket restaurants on Kongens Nytorv, Geist ("pleasure") is a stylishly informal eatery where the menu comprises many smaller dishes – mix and match as you like.

Krogs ⓀⓀ
Seafood **Map** 3 C1
Gammel Strand 38, 1202 Cph
Tel *33 15 89 15*
Krogs has been known as Copenhagen's most exclusive fish restaurant since 1910. In 2014 a change of ownership led to a more informal, bistro atmosphere (and lower prices), but with the same quality.

Uformel ⓀⓀ
Danish-French **Map** 3 A2
Studiestræde 69, 1609 Cph
Tel *70 99 91 11* **Closed** *Sat lunch & Sun*
Located around the corner from Palads cinema, this cool eatery, furnished with dark wood and decor, is run by the team behind Formel B. This is their cheaper, casual option, serving a pick and choose menu of starter-sized gourmet dishes.

Bror ⓀⓀⓀ
New Nordic **Map** 3 A1
Sankt Peders Stræde 24A, 1453 Cph
Tel *32 17 59 99* **Closed** *Mon, Tue*
The breakaway restaurant of a couple of ex-Noma chefs, Bror is similar in spirit, championing seasonal, New Nordic dishes and innovative taste pairings. It's far easier to get a table here though.

Krebsegaarden ⓀⓀⓀ
International **Map** 3B1
Studiestræde 17, 1455 Cph
Tel *20 12 40 15* **Closed** *Sun, Mon*
This small restaurant has built up a following with a unique concept – the menu is inspired by exhibitors in the adjoining gallery (through the courtyard), so may feature specialities from their region or country.

DK Choice

Marv & Ben ⓀⓀⓀ
Gastro pub **Map** 3 C1
Snaregade 4, 1205 Cph
Tel *33 91 01 91* **Closed** *Sun, Mon*
This New Nordic gastro pub has a charming setting, in an old apartment building down a narrow cobbled street. It spans two floors (upstairs is more intimate, downstairs has the energy of the open kitchen) and offers two- to five-course set menus only; much of the produce is sourced from the restaurant's own gardens.

The Standard ⓀⓀⓀ
New Nordic/Indian **Map** 4 E1
Havnegade 44, 1058 Cph
Tel *72 14 88 08* **Closed** *Mon (Studio and Verandah)*
Actually three restaurants (plus jazz club) combined in an Art Deco, ex-customs building on the harbour. Open for breakfast, lunch and dinner, at either Verandah (contemporary Indian cuisine); Almanak (modern Danish); or Michelin-starred Studio (New Nordic).

For more information on types of restaurants *see pages 256–7*

South Copenhagen

Rabes Have (Kr)
Smørrebrød **Map** 4 D3
Langebrogade 8, 1411 Cph
Tel *32 57 34 17* **Closed** *Mon, Tue*
Dating back to 1678, this traditional Danish lunch restaurant serves *smørrebrød* and schnapps in an authentic setting. Dine in the charming courtyard in summer. It can get very busy.

Restaurant Julian, Nationalmuseet (Kr)(Kr)
Café **Map** 3 B2
Ny Vestergade 10,1471 Cph
Tel *33 93 07 60* **Closed** *Mon*
The museum café focuses on Nordic cuisine and the Danish culinary heritage. It also produces "climate-friendly" menus where the carbon footprint is minimal. The weekend brunch buffets are very popular so arrive early.

Spiseloppen (Kr)(Kr)
International **Map** 4 F3
Bådmandsstræde 43, 1407 Cph
Tel *32 57 95 58* **Closed** *Mon*
A fixture in Christiania for decades, this restaurant offers fine dining and great cooking in premises that are never snobbish or exclusive. The international kitchen staff serve a global selection, and always offer vegetarian options.

Amass (Kr)(Kr)(Kr)
New Nordic
Refshalevej 153, 1432 Cph
Tel *43 58 43 30* **Closed** *Sun, Mon, Tue–Thu (lunch)*
In a former shipyard, quite a buzz surrounds Amass, an upscale but informal New Nordic eatery led by ex-Noma chefs. Communal dining is encouraged but not mandatory. Reservations are advised, with only six seats saved for walk-in diners.

Bastionen & Løven (Kr)(Kr)(Kr)
Danish-European **Map** 4 E3
Christianshavns Voldgade 50, 1424 Cph
Tel *31 34 09 40* **Closed** *Sun, Mon*
This former windmill – it lost its blades sometime in the 19th century – on the city ramparts is a lovely setting for a weekend brunch or evening meal, especially in the garden during the summer months.

Era Ora (Kr)(Kr)(Kr)
Italian **Map** 4 E2
Overgaden Neden Vandet 33B, 1414 Cph
Tel *32 54 06 93* **Closed** *Sun*
One of Copenhagen's best – and most expensive – Italian restaurants, Michelin-starred Era Ora concentrates on the cuisine of Italy's northern regions, flying in fresh ingredients especially. Lunchtime dining is somewhat cheaper.

Kadeau København (Kr)(Kr)(Kr)
New Nordic **Map** 4 E3
Wildersgade 10A, 1408 Cph
Tel *33 25 22 23* **Closed** *Sun, Mon, Tue lunch, Wed lunch*
This Michelin-starred, rustic Christianshavn eatery was one of the forerunners of the New Nordic movement. Together with its namesake in Aakirkeby, Kadeau has elevated regional specialities from Bornholm to a higher gastronomic level, serving gourmet-quality set menus inspired and dominated by Bornholm produce.

DK Choice

Noma (Kr)(Kr)(Kr)
New Nordic **Map** 4 F1
Strandgade 93, 1401 Cph
Tel *32 96 32 97* **Closed** *Sun, Mon*
Pioneer of the New Nordic food movement, two Michelin-starred Noma was named the world's best restaurant from 2010–12 and again in 2014. In a converted 19th-century warehouse in Christianshavn, it utilises only ingredients indigenous to Scandinavia – head chef Rene Redzepi having coined the culinary concept of "foraging". Reservations should be made at least three months in advance.

Restaurant Kanalen (Kr)(Kr)(Kr)
Danish-French **Map** 4 E2
Wilders Plads 2, 1403 Cph
Tel *32 95 13 30* **Closed** *Sun*
Upmarket Kanalen exploits its canalside location to the fullest, with al fresco dining in summer and cosy, candlelit dinners by the fire in winter. Its classic menus are Danish-French inspired and use fresh local ingredients.

Further Afield

Kaffesalonen (Kr)
Café
Peblinge Dossering 6, 2200 Cph N
Tel *35 35 12 19*
A popular, long-established café with a fairly standard menu that is notable for its location on the lakes and terrace of outdoor tables, as well as its nostalgic, American diner vibe.

The rustic yet chic dining room at Kadeau København

Kates Joint (Kr)
International
Blågårdsgade 12, 2200 Cph N
Tel *35 37 44 96*
A small, cheap café that is one of the Nørrebro locals' best-kept secrets. Kate's menu travels the globe, changing continents daily, always with plenty of vegetarian options available. It is popular with the ex-pat crowd.

Mother (Kr)
Italian
Høkerboderne 9–15, 1712 Cph V
Tel *22 27 58 98*
This trendy Kødbyen pizzeria serves top-quality, sourdough pizzas made with ingredients direct from Italy and cooked in a wood-fired oven. Delicious Italian antipasti and desserts are available too. The weekend brunches and weekday break-fasts are popular.

Bankeråt (Kr)(Kr)
Café **Map** 1 A5
Ahlefeldtsgade 27–29, 1359 Cph
Tel *33 93 69 88*
Though its name means "bankrupt", this is one of the area's most long-standing cafés. It is famed for its display of stuffed animals in home-made outfits and the local atmosphere. There's a good range of European newspapers to enjoy.

B'india (Kr)(Kr)
Indian **Map** 1 B1
Blegdamsvej 130, 2100 Cph Ø
Tel *35 43 88 38*
A smart and stylish Indian restaurant where the focus is on healthy, delicious dishes and subtlety of flavour. Vegetarian and children's menus are available, as well as changing weekly specials.

Key to Price Guide *see page 262*

BioMio
Organic
Halmtorvet 19, 1700 Cph V
Tel *33 31 20 00*
The ultimate organic restaurant, a self-styled "people's kitchen" where guests dine communally at long tables in a renovated Bosch warehouse (the neon sign outside has been kept for posterity). There are plenty of vegetarian options.

Carte Blanche
French **Map** 2 D3
Dag Hammarskjolds Alle 1B, 2100 Cph1 Ø
Tel *35 43 31 25*
This well-established, rather low-key French restaurant in the diplomatic district of Østerbro is ideal for a romantic dinner. The decor is charmingly old-fashioned and the menu majors on classic French dishes.

Cofoco
Danish-European
Abel Cathrines Gade 7, 1654 Cph V
Tel *33 13 60 60* **Closed** *Sun*
The first restaurant of what is now a citywide chain, Cofoco radicalised Copenhagen's dining scene in 2004 by offering simple, quality dining at affordable prices. The menu consists of a variety of starter-sized dishes.

Granola
Café
Værnedamsvej 5, 1819 Frederiksberg
Tel *33 25 00 80* **Closed** *Sun (dinner).*
Entering this café is like walking through a time warp – the nostalgic diner has faithfully recreated a kitsch 1930s universe open for breakfast, lunch and dinner. Dishes on offer range from breakfast prridge to steak Parisienne.

Höst
New Nordic **Map** 1 A5
Nørre Farimagsgade 41, 1364 Cph
Tel *89 93 84 09*
A New Nordic restaurant aimed at appealing to a broader audience with raw wooden furnishings and a seasonally changing set menu as well as à la carte. It is over two levels – street and basement.

Kødbyens Fiskebar 
Seafood
Flæsketorvet 100, 1711 Cph V
Tel *32 15 56 56*
This casual seafod joint in one of Kødbyen's typical white and blue buildings, serves freshly caught fish, shellfish (and meat/vegetarian options) of very high quality. It serves perhaps the best fish and chips in the city.

Nam Nam
Singaporean
Vesterbrogade 39, 1620 Cph V
Tel *41 91 98 98* **Closed** *Sun*
This is a brightly furnished, casual Singapore street kitchen that hopes to introduce Danes and visitors to the vibrant tastes, smells and colours of the Paranakan kitchen – considered a melting pot of Asian cuisine – in a shared dining experience.

Nose2Tail
Organic
Flæsketorvet 13A, 1711 Cph V
Tel *33 93 50 45* **Closed** *Sun*
Inspired by similar ventures in the UK, this white-tiled, basement restaurant in the meat-packing district is surprisingly warm and inviting. Every part of the free-range, locally sourced meat is used, "from nose to tail".

Pony
New Nordic
Vesterbrogade 135, 1620 Cph V
Tel *33 22 10 00* **Closed** *Mon*
A more relaxed, bistro edition of Kadeau Copenhagen, which has moved out to Christianshavn. Pony offers simple dishes from the New Nordic kitchen with the focus – though not exclusively – on Bornholm produce.

Radio
New Nordic
Julius Thomsens Gade 12, 1632 Cph
Tel *25 10 27 33* **Closed** *Sun, Mon, lunch) Tue–Thu*
An informal New Nordic restaurant that won't leave you out of pocket. Radio offers seasonal, locally grown produce in innovative but simple vegetable, fish and meat dishes. The wooden decor is minimalist but inviting.

Spicylicious
Thai/Vietnamese
Halmtorvet 10, 1700 Copenhagen V
Tel *33 31 13 11*
This brightly coloured, youthful Asian eatery has merged with Wokbaren in premises on Halmtorvet Square. The menu is a mixture of Thai and Vietnamese cuisine, prepared as vibrantly as the restaurant decor.

DK Choice

Enomania 
Italian
Vesterbrogade 187, 1800 Frederiksberg C
Tel *33 23 60 80* **Closed** *Sat–Mon; dinners Tue & Wed*
Located at the far end of Vesterbro, this cosy Italian restaurant and wine bar seats just 25, and is characterised by a passion for both food and wine. With its excellent reputation, reservations are advised.

Frederiks Have
Danish-French
Smallegade 41, 2000 Frederiksberg
Tel *38 88 33 35* **Closed** *Sun*
A pleasant restaurant near Frederiksberg Runddel that's ideal for a romantic dinner, especially on a warm summer evening when the covered courtyard is open. It is pleasantly formal, with the focus on the Scandinavian kitchen.

Romantic courtyard dining at Frederiks Have

For more information on types of restaurants *see pages 256–7*

Mêlée KrKrKr
French
Martensens Allé 16, 1828 Frederiksberg
Tel *35 13 11 34* **Closed** *Sun, Mon*
A French bistro restaurant on a side street of Gammel Kongevej that honours the classic French kitchen with simple dishes, desserts and fine wines. It focuses on offering quality yet relaxed dining.

Relæ KrKrKr
New Nordic
Jægersborggade 41, 2200 Cph N
Tel *36 96 66 09* **Closed** *Sun–Tue*
Ex-Noma chef Christian Pugsili's Michelin-starred gourmet restaurant attracts discerning diners, despite its offbeat location in Nørrebro. Organic and seasonal set menus only are served in the tiny basement premises. There is always a vegetarian and a meat option.

North Zealand

Charlottenlund: Café Jorden Rundt KrKr
Café **Road Map** F4
Standvejen 152, 2920 Charlottenlund
Tel *39 63 73 81*
In a carousel-shaped building from the 1930s that was once the public toilets, this eatery serves typical, though mostly organic, café fare, but its real draw are the sea views from its glass façade.

Charlottenlund: MASH Skovridderkroen KrKrKr
Steakhouse **Road Map** F4
Strandvejen 235, 2920 Charlottenlund
Tel *33 13 93 00*
A countryside edition of the popular Copenhagen steakhouse chain (MASH stands for Modern American Steakhouse). In an old inn between forest and sea, the decor here is stylish and modern, with lots of red leather.

Fredensborg: Asminderød Kro KrKr
Danish **Road Map** F4
Asminderødgade 53, 3480 Fredensborg
Tel *48 48 00 02* **Closed** *Sun–Wed*
Traditional lunch and evening restaurant in the historic setting of a 17th-century coaching inn. Renovated and modernised, the inn offers classic Danish dishes and friendly service.

Frederikssund: Chefs Café KrKr
Café **Road Map** F4
Jernbanegade 10A, 3600 Frederikssund
Tel *87 10 01 00* **Closed** *Sun*
This organic café is centrally situated on Frederikssund's pedestrian street. A range of healthy lunches are offered, as well as a vegetarian option and a daily special in the early evening. Service is friendly and takeaways are available.

Frederiksværk: Restaurant Tinggården KrKrKr
French **Road Map** F4
Frederiksværkvej 182, 3300 Frederiksværk
Tel *48 71 22 35* **Closed** *Mon, Tue; Wed (Nov–Apr); open daily mid-Jul–mid-Aug*
Dine in an old (1702) farmhouse between Helsinge and Frederiksværk that divides its tables between three small rooms and, in summer, the cobbled yard. Seasonal dishes are inspired by the rustic French kitchen.

Gilleleje: Restaurant Gilleleje Havn KrKrKr
Danish **Road Map** F4
Havnevej 14, 3250 Gilleleje
Tel *48 30 30 39* **Closed** *Mon–Thu*
A traditional Danish eatery with two dining areas: the *krostue* or bar room and the more formal and lighter furnished restaurant. The focus is on *smørrebrød* at lunchtime and freshly caught fish for dinner.

Gilleleje: Brasseriet Gilleleje Havn KrKrKr
Danish-French **Road Map** F4
Nordre Havnevej 3, 3250 Gilleleje
Tel *48 30 21 30*
Modern-looking eatery with great views over the harbour serving *smørrebrød* and other Danish classics from its first floor or outdoor terrace. There's no shortage of fresh fish as the place is owned by a fishmonger.

Spartan interior at New Nordic restaurant Relæ

Helsingør: Spisehuset Kulturværftet Kr
New Nordic Café **Road Map** F4
Allegade 2, 3000 Helsingør
Tel *49 28 37 51*
The café of the "Culture Yard", an initiative in Helsingør's former shipyard, boasts innovative architecture and a seasonal, New Nordic-inspired menu. Organic and tasty burgers are on offer, alongside sandwiches, cakes and great fish and chips.

Helsingør: Amici Miei KrKr
Italian **Road Map** F4
Stengade 15, 3000 Helsingør
Tel *49 26 26 71*
A long-standing and popular Italian restaurant in one of Helsingør's oldest streets. The café serves an excellent lunchtime brunch menu, while the evening menu focuses on classic Italian pasta, pizza, meat and fish dishes.

Helsingør: Madame Sprunck KrKrKr
Southern European **Road Map** F4
Bramstræde 5, 3000 Helsingør
Tel *49 26 48 49*
There is both a café and a restaurant in this centrally located, combined hotel-eatery-nightclub with casual dining in the café and a formal setting in the restaurant of this historic building.

Hillerød: Spisestedet Leonora Kr
Danish **Road Map** F4
Frederiksborg Slot, Møntportvej 2, 3400 Hillerød
Tel *48 26 75 16*
Frederiksborg Slot's restaurant is located in what was once the castle stables. The views over the lake from the terrace in summer are especially enjoyable over a traditional *smørrebrød* lunch.

Hillerød: Saffran KrKr
Indian **Road Map** F4
Slotsgade 59C, 3400 Hillerød
Tel *48 22 12 21*
A reliable and authentic Indian restaurant not far from Frederiksborg Slot, with a fresh, modern approach and a range of colourful, lightly spiced dishes to eat in or take away.

Holbæk: SuRi KrKrKr
Seafood **Road Map** E4
Havnevej 5, 4300 Holbæk
Tel *59 44 06 10* **Closed** *Sun*
Situated directly on the rejuvenated Holbæk harbour in an eye-catching wood and glass building, SuRi is both a fishmongers and a gourmet seafood restaurant with high ambitions on the culinary front.

Key to Price Guide *see page 262*

Hornbæk: Restaurant Olivia (Kr)(Kr)(Kr)
European **Road Map** F4
Havnevej 1, 3100 Hornbæk
Tel *49 76 11 77* **Closed** *Sun dinner, Mon*
Romantic, seaside eatery in the centre of resort town Hornbæk, inspired by Provençal cooking and decor. The patio garden is an especially pleasant spot for dining, while indoors, the decor is bright and airy.

Hornbæk: Søstrene Olsen (Kr)(Kr)(Kr)
Danish-French **Road Map** F4
Øresundsvej 10, 3100 Hornbæk
Tel *49 70 05 50* **Closed** *Mon–Wed*
The thatched blue-and-white cottage by the harbour, secluded back garden and choice of delicate, seasonal dishes paint an idyllic backdrop. Run by a husband-and-wife team, it has many loyal customers. Reservations are advised.

DK Choice

Hørve: Dragsholm Slot (Kr)(Kr)(Kr) **((Kr)(Kr) in eatery)**
Danish-European **Road Map** E4
Dragsholm Alle, 4534 Hørve
Tel *59 65 33 00* **Closed** *Sun, Mon, Tue (Sep–Jun), Wed (Sep–May), Thu (Nov–Mar)*
The gourmet Castle Kitchen at Dragsholm (also a hotel) attracts some of Denmark's best chefs and has lofty ambitions, not only culinary but also in highlighting its history and location, in a 17th-century castle, with atmospheric decor and locally-produced cuisine. Reservations are necessary.

Humlebæk: Bolettes Gæstebud (Kr)(Kr)
Danish-French **Road Map** F4
Gl. Strandvej 7, 3050 Humlebæk
Tel *49 19 45 00* **Closed** *Sun, Mon*
Traditional *kro* restaurant serving classic Danish and French dishes with fresh fish and a daily menu. Enjoy a typical *smørrebrød* lunch on the pleasant terrace in summer, or a candlelit evening meal in cooler seasons.

Humlebæk: Restaurant Sletten (Kr)(Kr)(Kr)
Danish-European **Road Map** F4
Gl. Strandvej 137, 3050 Humlebæk
Tel *49 19 13 21* **Closed** *Sun, Mon*
Sletten is run by the same team as gourmet restaurant Formel B in Copenhagen, but with an à la carte menu and cheaper prices. The restaurant has direct views of the Øresund and the dishes are exquisite.

Snekken restaurant in the harbour that overlooks Roskilde Fjord

Jægerspris: Gerlev Kro (Kr)(Kr)
Danish **Road Map** F4
Bygaden 4, 3630 Jægerspris
Tel *47 52 21 74*
This charming, thatched country inn close to Frederikssund golf club might not actually have the historic heritage it suggests, but more than makes up for it in its warm welcome and traditional home-cooked meals.

Kalundborg: Hotel Ole Lunds Gaard (Kr)(Kr)
Danish **Road Map** E4
Kordilgade 1–3, 4000 Kalundborg
Tel *59 51 01 65* **Closed** *Sun*
A popular hotel restaurant close to Kalundborg's harbour that serves generous portions of classic Danish dishes and holds regular "family nights" on Fridays. The hotel courtyard is opened to diners in summer.

Klampenborg: Den Gule Cottage (Kr)(Kr)
Danish-European **Road Map** F4
Strandvejen 506, 2930 Klampenborg
Tel *39 64 06 91* **Closed** *Mon–Wed (Nov–Apr); 22 Dec–17 Feb.*
On the coastal road north of Copenhagen are two delightful country cottages, both restaurants. This – the yellow one – is the least formal of the two, offering upmarket yet relaxed dining in a romantic setting.

Kongens Lyngby: Brede Spisehus (Kr)(Kr)(Kr)
Danish-French **Road Map** F4
I.C. Modewegs Vej, 2800 Kgns. Lyngby
Tel *45 85 54 57* **Closed** *dinner Mon & Sun*
Lake views and a historic setting combine in a former canteen for local factory workers, which has been restored by the Nationalmuseet and is now part of Frilandsmuseet. The kitchen is surprisingly upmarket, and its dishes delicate and refined.

Korsør: Madam Bagger (Kr)(Kr)
Danish-French **Road Map** E5
Havnegade 17B, 4220 Korsør
Tel *58 37 01 49* **Closed** *Sun*
This traditional, historic restaurant is named after Korsør's beloved innkeeper, who fed its hungry residents during the 1700s and 1800s. Lunches are traditionally Danish, while in the evening, the focus is on the French-Danish kitchen.

Roskilde: Café Satchmo (Kr)
Café **Road Map** F4
Rosenhavestræde 2, 4000 Roskilde
Tel *46 35 03 15* **Closed** *Sun (except 1st Sun of month, and in Dec)*
Down a side street from Roskilde's main walking street, Café Satchmo is a pleasant café with a quiet back courtyard open in summer. It serves sandwiches, snacks and cakes, as well as a lunchtime brunch.

Roskilde: Kaffekilden (Kr)
Café **Road Map** F4
Hestetorvet 7, 4000 Roskilde
Tel *32 14 60 30*
This small café across the road from Roskilde station makes a great place to enjoy a coffee and a slice of cake while waiting for your train; it also has Wi-Fi.

Roskilde: Snekken (Kr)(Kr)(Kr)
New Nordic **Road Map** F4
Vindeboder 16, 4000 Roskilde
Tel *46 35 98 16*
Next to the Vikingeskibsmuseet, Snekken has teamed up with the museum on a menu of contemporary "Viking" cuisine, prepared only with those ingredients available to Vikings but using modern methods for a different yet delicious meal.

For more information on types of restaurants *see pages 256–7*

Søllerød: Søllerød Kro ⓀⓀⓀ
French-European **Road Map** F4
Søllerødvej 35, 2840 Holte
Tel *45 80 25 05* **Closed** *Mon, Tue*
Michelin-starred Søllerød Kro offers gourmet dining experiences in the idyllic surroundings of this refurbished, 17th-century inn next to the village pond and parish church, with woods behind. Set meals only; reservation necessary.

Sorø: Støvlet Katrines Hus ⓀⓀⓀ
Danish-European **Map** E5
Slagelsevej 63, 4180 Sorø
Tel *57 83 50 80* **Closed** *Sun; middle 2 weeks in Jul*
Named after a distinguished resident of the house, Støvlet Katrine (1745–1805). The decor is simple yet romantic and the gourmet French-Danish kitchen offers both set and à la carte menus.

Tisvildeleje: Den Røde Tomat Ⓚ
Pizza **Map** F4
Hovedgaden 45, 3220 Tisvildeleje
Tel *48 70 45 46* **Closed** *Mon*
An informal pizzeria in what has become a rather exclusive seaside resort. Offers delicately baked pizzas and sandwiches, as well as selected wines and other Italian imports from its deli counter.

South Zealand

Køge: Café T Ⓚ
Café **Map** F5
Nyportsstræde 17, 4600 Køge
Tel *60 17 27 65* **Closed** *Sun*
Cosy, nostalgic coffee shop and tea rooms serving home-made cakes and waffles as well as breakfasts. If you like the look of the antique chair you're sitting on, you can buy that too.

Køge: Christians Minde Ⓚ
Chinese/Danish **Map** F5
Brogade 7, 4600 Køge
Tel *56 63 68 56*
An interesting mix of traditional Danish dishes and Chinese food is served in this well-established eatery in the centre of Køge. At lunchtime enjoy open sandwiches outside on the cobbled square.

Køge: Vallø Slotskro ⓀⓀⓀ
Contemporary Scandinavian **Map** F5
Slotsgade 1, 4600 Køge
Tel *56 26 62 66* **Closed** *Sun–Tue*
The gourmet kitchen of this elegant castle restaurant serves monthly changing menus based on seasonal local produce. All dishes are starter-sized; order as many as you feel like. Reservations are advised.

Maribo: Restaurant B ⓀⓀ
European **Map** E6
Vesterbrogade 23, 4930 Maribo
Tel *54 78 10 08* **Closed** *Sun*
The nearest Maribo is likely to get to a gourmet restaurant, "B" offers good quality steaks as well as more adventurous seasonal set menus in pleasant and spacious surroundings.

Næstved: Rådhuskroen ⓀⓀ
Danish **Map** E5
Skomagerrækken 8, 4700 Næstved
Tel *55 72 01 56* **Closed** *Sun*
One of Næstved's oldest restaurants, this historic inn by the town hall has retained its atmosphere and tradition. It offers an overwhelmingly Danish menu, but with vegetarian options available. There's pleasant courtyard dining in summer.

Næstved: Restaurant Ronni ⓀⓀ
Thai **Map** E5
Østergade 4, 4700 Næstved
Tel *55 73 45 64*
With vibrant red walls and plenty of gold-coloured Buddhas, Ronni offers inexpensive and authentic Thai restaurant cuisine in the centre of town. The service is efficient and friendly.

Nakskov: Hotel Skovriddergaarden ⓀⓀ
Danish-European **Map** E6
Svingelen 4, 4900 Nakskov
Tel *54 92 03 55* **Closed** *Sun*
A hotel and restaurant surrounded by woodland on the outskirts of Nakskov, with an outdoor terrace in summer and an open fire in winter. The menu fairly traditional but reliable, the service friendly and efficient.

Nykøbing F: La Comida ⓀⓀ
European Map F6
Slotsgade 22, 4800 Nykøbing F.
Tel *54 85 09 10* **Closed** *Sun, Mon*
In basement premises in central Nykøbing, this stylishly furnished gourmet restaurant is a hidden gem. Both set and à la carte menus use seasonal, locally-sourced produce to create exciting pan-European dishes.

Nysted: The Cottage ⓀⓀ
Danish **Map** E6
Skansevej 19, 4880 Nysted
Tel *54 87 18 87* **Closed** *Sun–Tue*
This charmingly romantic hotel restaurant dating from 1908 is located in an idyllic woodland setting not far from the town beach. The seasonal menus are freshly prepared using locally sourced produce.

Den Røde Tomat, in the seaside resort of Tisvildeleje

Ringsted: Restaurant Mango ⓀⓀ
Asian fusion **Map** E5
Sct. Bendtsgade 10, 4100 Ringsted
Tel *61 73 90 58* **Closed** *Mon*
Ringsted isn't overflowing with innovative modern restaurants, so this Asian-inspired kitchen with a Danish twist is a nice surprise. The prices are reasonable and there's also a buffet and a kids' menu.

Ringsted: Raadhuskroen ⓀⓀⓀ
Danish **Map** E5
Sct. Bendtsgade 8, 4100 Ringsted
Tel *57 61 68 97*
This very traditional Danish restaurant inn serves *smørrebrød* lunches, juicy dinnertime fish plates and a wide variety of steaks (six different kinds). It's a popular choice with locals.

Sakskøbing: Hotel Saxkjøbing ⓀⓀⓀ
New Nordic **Map** E6
Torvet 9, 4990 Sakskøbing
Tel *54 70 40 39*
Run by New Nordic food pioneer Claus Meyer, the kitchen of this hotel restaurant creates innovative and exciting menus using produce sourced from Lolland-Falster and the surrounding islands.

Stege: David's Ⓚ
French-Danish Café **Map** F6
Storegade 11, 4780 Stege
Tel *33 13 80 57*
In a striking glass house on Stege's high street, this lunchtime café serves tasty dishes made with fresh local produce, in a pleasant setting with views of the old church tower from its cosy courtyard.

Key to Price Guide *see page 262*

Stege: Kaffehuset Møn (Kr)
Café **Map** F6
Storegade 48, 4780 Stege
Tel *31 44 49 14*
Primarily a micro-roastery that sells its own gourmet coffee and tea blends, this excellent coffee shop also serves tasty breakfasts, lunches and a small selection of hot dishes after 5pm.

DK Choice

Vordingborg: Babettes (Kr)(Kr)(Kr)
Danish-French **Map** F6
Kildemarksvej 5, 4760 Vordingborg
Tel *55 34 30 30* **Closed** *Sun–Tue; last 2 weeks Jul; Dec–early Jan*
This well-established, award-winning gourmet restaurant is known and respected as one of the country's best eateries. With the same kitchen team since 1991, its solid reputation is based on quality seasonal and locally sourced produce, predominantly organic, deliciously refined dishes and the simple yet elegant surroundings.

Funen

Ærøskøbing: Restaurant Mumm (Kr)(Kr)
Danish **Map** D6
Søndergade 12, 5970 Ærøskøbing
Tel *62 52 12 12* **Closed** *Sun, Mon*
A popular restaurant in an atmospheric old building next to Ærøskøbing's town square. The garden courtyard is especially pleasant in summer. House specialities include freshly caught plaice and teriyaki steak.

Kerteminde: Rudolf Mathis (Kr)(Kr)(Kr)
Seafood **Map** D5
Dosseringen 13, 5300 Kerteminde
Tel *65 32 32 33* **Closed** *Sun, Mon*
The two white-painted smokehouses of this gourmet fish restaurant are a landmark in the small town of Kerteminde. It's a long-standing fixture directly on the harbour offering fresh and delicious seafood.

Millinge: Falsled Kro (Kr)(Kr)(Kr)
Danish-French **Map** D5
Assensvej 513, 5642 Millinge
Tel *62 68 11 11* **Closed** *Mon (Sep–Apr); Tue (Jan–Feb)*
This romantic country idyll up the coast north of Faaborg attracts some of Denmark's top chefs. Menus are planned around the culinary calendar using local produce; the brasserie lunch is considerably cheaper.

Munkebo: Munkebo Kro (Kr)(Kr)
Danish **Map** D5
Fjordvej 56, 5330 Munkebo
Tel *65 97 40 30* **Closed** *Mon, Tue*
Set in a historic, half-timbered inn overlooking the fjord, this restaurant has a long-standing gourmet reputation, though the menu respects the traditional Danish kitchen over innovative experimentation.

Nyborg: Lieffroy (Kr)(Kr)(Kr)
Danish-French **Map** D5
Skræddergyden 34, 5800 Nyborg
Tel *65 31 24 48* **Closed** *Sun, Mon; last 2 weeks in Jul*
One of Funen's best restaurants is situated right on the waterfront in an idyllic rural setting. The gourmet kitchen is rooted in French cuisine but the ingredients are primarily locally sourced.

Odense: No. 61 (Kr)(Kr)
Danish-European **Map** D5
Kongensgade 61, 5000 Odense C
Tel *61 69 10 35* **Closed** *Sun, Mon*
Beautifully simple brasserie-style restaurant in a lovely old building with exposed beams and raw wooden tables. Seasonal menus take the best of Danish produce and French culinary tradition without charging the earth.

Odense: Sieu (Kr)(Kr)
Asian fusion **Map** D5
Østre Stationsvej 40, 5000 Odense C
Tel *66 12 88 89* **Closed** *Sun, Mon*
Exciting contemporary Asian restaurant with stylish decor, where the Thai, Japanese, Chinese and Vietnamese cuisines form the basis of elaborately arranged dishes served on spotlessly white oval dinnerware.

Odense: Den Gamle Kro (Kr)(Kr)(Kr)
Danish-French **Map** D5
Overgade 23, 5000 Odense C
Tel *66 12 14 33*
Situated in a 17th-century half-timbered house in Odense's historic centre, the premises are an attraction in themselves (check out the courtyard, with its rolling glass roof). The food, however, is top-notch.

Odense: Goma (Kr)(Kr)(Kr)
Japanese **Map** D5
Kongensgade 66–68, 5000 Odense C
Tel *66 14 45 00* **Closed** *Sun*
This stylish and sophisticated restaurant inspired by the Kaiseki style is considered to be the "haute cuisine" of Japanese cooking. The attached cocktail lounge is equally adventurous in its drinks menu.

Odense: Restaurant Nordatlanten (Kr)(Kr)(Kr)
New Nordic **Map** D5
Nordatlantiske Promenade 1, 5000 Odense C
Tel *22 39 76 00* **Closed** *Sun dinner*
A contemporary Scandinavian restaurant that takes its standards from gourmet French cooking, applying them to ingredients sourced in the North Atlantic region. Enjoy harbour views from the panoramic windows.

DK Choice

Odense: Under Lindetræet (Kr)(Kr)(Kr)
French-Italian **Map** D5
Ramsherred 2, 5000 Odense C
Tel *66 12 92 86* **Closed** *Sun dinner, Mon,*
Neighbour to H.C. Andersens Hus, this gourmet restaurant in Odense's oldest quarter is located in an atmospheric building from the 1700s. Aside from the luxurious and delicate five- and seven-course evening menus, a four-course weekend brunch is also served. Reservations are advised.

Traditional setting at micro-roastery Kaffehuset Møn, Stege

For more information on types of restaurants *see pages 256–7*

Odense: Sortebro Kro ⓀⓀⓀ
Contemporary Danish **Map** D5
Sejerskovvej 20, 5260 Odense S
Tel *66 13 28 26*
Out in "Den Fynske Landsby", south of central Odense, this historic coaching inn, with its half-timbered exterior and thatched roof, exudes atmosphere. Ingredients are sourced locally.

Svendborg: Restaurant Svendborgsund ⓀⓀⓀ
Danish **Map** D5
Havnepladsen 5, 5700 Svendborg
Tel *62 21 07 19*
Traditional Danish lunches and evening meals are served in historic surroundings, not far from Svendborg harbour. This eatery dates back more than 300 years and remains popular with local residents.

South & Central Jutland

Aarhus: Café Gaya Ⓚ
Organic **Map** D4
Vestergade 43, 8000 Aarhus C
Tel *86 18 14 15* **Closed** *Sun*
At this organic café the majority of dishes are vegan/vegetarian and the focus is on healthy eating. Salads, soups, hot dishes and burgers are served, plus brunch on Saturday and live music every Friday.

Aarhus: Forlæns og Baglæns ⓀⓀ
Tapas **Map** D4
Jægersgårdsgade 23, 8000 Aarhus C
Tel *86 76 00 70* **Closed** *Sun–Tue; Wed (Jan–Feb)*
Cosy tapas bar with lively atmosphere serving great-tasting dishes to suit both large and small appetites. Guests are packed together and communal dining is encouraged. Cocktails are served at weekends.

Aarhus: Kähler Spisesalon ⓀⓀ
Danish-European **Map** D4
M.P. Bruuns Gade 33, 8000 Aarhus C
Tel *86 12 20 53*
Stylish café-bistro that's designed to perfection – Kähler is a world-renowned ceramics manufacturer. The *smørrebrød* is especially rated, but the menu also offers weekend brunch and hot meals.

Aarhus: Pinden ⓀⓀ
Danish **Map** D4
Skolegade 29, 8000 Aarhus C
Tel *86 12 11 02* **Closed** *Sun*
A good, old-fashioned Danish lunch and dinner restaurant that serves traditional and classic dishes in generous servings. The decor shows a similar respect for the long-standing traditions of the Danish kitchen.

Aarhus: Frederikshøj ⓀⓀⓀ
New Nordic **Map** D4
Oddervej 19, 8000 Aarhus C
Tel *86 14 22 80* **Closed** *Sun–Tue*
One of Denmark's top restaurants, Frederikshøj's head chef, Wassim Hallal, is uncompromising in his search for the ultimate gastronomic experience. Beautifully located in woodland in Aarhus' Mindeparken. Book ahead.

Aarhus: Mefisto ⓀⓀⓀ
Seafood **Map** D4
Volden 28, 8000 Aarhus C
Tel *86 13 18 13*
In an old building in Aarhus' Latin Quarter, this informal seafood restaurant serves high quality lobster, mussels and fish, always beautifully presented. An outside courtyard opens in summer. The daily brunch is also popular.

Aarhus: Nordisk Spisehus ⓀⓀⓀ
New Nordic **Map** D4
M.P. Bruuns Gade 31, 8000 Aarhus C
Tel *86 17 70 99* **Closed** *Sun*
An innovative and adventurous contemporary restaurant that takes up a new theme each month. It is inspired by the world's best gourmet restaurants, but uses New Nordic ingredients and ideals.

Aarhus: Restaurant Miro ⓀⓀⓀ
French-International **Map** D4
Marstrandgade 2, 8000 Aarhus C
Tel *86 13 87 00* **Closed** *Sun, Mon*
This is the oldest gourmet restaurant in Aarhus, still with the same owner. Rooted in the classic French kitchen, inspiration for the changing set menus is global. The aim is a total experience of food, wine and service.

Decor reflecting a regularly-changing theme at Nordisk Spisehus

Aarhus: Sechzehn ⓀⓀⓀ
International **Map** D4
Europaplads 16, 8000 Aarhus C
Tel *86 20 88 00* **Closed** *Sun–Tue*
A trendy "concept" restaurant and wine bar where guests arrive at the same time to enjoy an identical four-course gourmet surprise menu. It offers modern, minimalist decor, and views out across the harbour.

Åbenrå: Knapp ⓀⓀⓀ
Danish **Map** C6
Stennevej 79, Stollig, 6200 Aabenraa
Tel *74 62 00 92* **Closed** *Mon*
In a 19th-century watermill that was restored in the 1980s as a restaurant and hotel, Knapp is surrounded by parkland and is a popular retreat for wedding parties. It serves gourmet Danish three- to six-course dinners and is filled with antique furnishings.

Ebeltoft: Molskroen ⓀⓀⓀ
French-Danish **Map** D3
Hovedgaden 16, Femmøller Strand, 8400 Ebeltoft
Tel *86 36 22 00* **Closed** *Sun*
This gourmet restaurant with a strong reputation for exquisite French-Danish dishes attracts some of the country's best chefs. Reservations are essential. For less formal dining, check out the adjacent Strandhotel Brasserie.

Esbjerg: Café Le Chi Ⓚ
Asian **Map** B5
Englandsgade 23, 6700 Esbjerg
Tel *75 12 02 38*
Casual and friendly Asian café/takeaway that also serves breakfasts and sandwiches as well as a variety of more exotic dishes, mostly Vietnamese. All are fresh, tasty and reasonably priced. There's an Asian kids' menu too.

Esbjerg: Restaurant Gammelhavn ⓀⓀ
Danish-European **Map** B5
Britanniavej 3, 6700 Esbjerg
Tel *76 11 90 00* **Closed** *Sun*
Located in an historic port building from 1900, this beautifully renovated restaurant overlooks Esbjerg harbour, with sea views from its glass-panelled veranda. It features both a café and an elegant dinner venue.

Fredericia: Ti Trin Ned ⓀⓀⓀ
Modern Scandinavian **Map** C5
Norgesgade 3, 7000 Fredericia
Tel *75 93 33 55* **Closed** *Sun, Mon*

Key to Price Guide *see page 262*

In the basement of a former distillery, gourmet restaurant Ti Trin Ned (Ten Steps Down) is imbued with calm and simplicity. While the kitchen refuses to be labelled as "Nordic", local produce is definitely in focus.

Haderslev: LMNT ⓚⓚ
Café **Map** C5
Apotekergade 1, 6100 Haderslev
Tel *74 52 00 82*
Trendy café and cocktail lounge near Haderslev town square, pronounced "Element". It is open for snacks, drinks and hot meals at all times of the day including tapas, burgers and a daily brunch.

DK Choice

Henne: Henne Kirkeby Kro ⓚⓚⓚ
European **Map** B4
Strandvejen 234, 6854 Henne
Tel *75 25 54 00* **Closed** *Sun–Tue; Wed dinner*
Michelin-starred chef Paul Cunningham, formerly of The Paul in Tivoli, is head chef in this gourmet idyll in the heart of the Jutland countryside. Seasonally-changing set menus are stunning in their simplicity, locally sourced – often from the vast kitchen garden – and inspired by the global kitchen. Booking ahead is necessary.

Herning: Restaurant Baghuset ⓚⓚ
Tapas **Map** C4
Bredgade 12, 7400 Herning
Tel *97 21 71 74* **Closed** *Sun dinner*
This family-friendly tapas bar is simply decorated with a stone tiled floor and rough brick walls. The menu features vegetarian, fish and meat dishes, and there is also a tapas buffet on weekends.

Herning: Mad Donna ⓚⓚ
Italian **Map** C4
Østergade 30, 7400 Herning
Tel *97 26 90 89*
A casual dining restaurant that is very family friendly and popular for local parties and celebrations. The cuisine is Italian and there's a Saturday brunch buffet.

Horsens: Café Dolly ⓚⓚ
Danish **Map** C4
Havnen 15, 8700 Horsens
Tel *75 62 34 81* **Closed** *Sun*
Cosy and traditional Danish café-restaurant in a 100 year-old red brick building by Horsens harbour. It is known for its green-and-white checked tablecloths and house speciality, *stegt flæsk* (fried bacon with parsley sauce).

Pale wood decor at Jutland restaurant Henne Kirkeby Kro

Horsens: Mackie's ⓚⓚ
American **Map** C4
Graven 2, 8700 Horsens
Tel *75 60 16 22*
American diner complete with red leather bar stools and Americana collectibles hanging from the walls. It is a popular meeting place for the town's younger residents, with live music several times a month.

Kolding: Den Gyldne Hane ⓚⓚ
Danish-French **Map** C5
Christian 4 Vej 23, 6000 Kolding
Tel *75 52 97 20* **Closed** *Mon & Tue dinners*
This idyllic Danish *kro* in a thatched house is one of Kolding's oldest, surrounded by parkland yet minutes from the town centre. The old-fashioned kitchen respects both Danish and French culinary traditions.

Kolding: Nicolai Biograf & Café ⓚⓚ
Italian Café **Map** C5
Skolegade 2A, 6000 Kolding
Tel *75 50 03 02*
A combined café and cinema with a mostly Italian menu and wide selection of tasty pizzas to eat in or take away. There's a popular weekend brunch and an all-you-can-eat buffet on Sunday evenings. Very family friendly.

Ribe: Kolvig ⓚⓚ
Danish **Map** B5
Mellemdammen 13, 6760 Ribe
Tel *75 41 04 88* **Closed** *Sun*
Both lunchtime café and evening restaurant, this former chicory factory from the 1600s overlooks Ribe river; the outside tables have lovely riverside views. The good-quality, seasonal menus are based on locally sourced produce.

Ribe: Sælhunden ⓚⓚⓚ
Danish **Map** B5
Skibbroen 13, 6760 Ribe
Tel *75 42 09 46*
Historically placed in a half-timbered listed building that's over 400 years old, with lovely views of the river, especially from the small courtyard. The food is unmistakably Danish, generously served.

Silkeborg: Gastronomisk Institut ⓚⓚⓚ
European **Map** C4
Søndergade 20, 8600 Silkeborg
Tel *86 82 40 97* **Closed** *Sun, Mon; last 2 weeks in Jul*
A gourmet restaurant in Silkeborg's centre offering both a changing seasonal menu and a more fixed à la carte menu. Rooted in the classic French culinary tradition, both the cuisine and decor are European in outlook.

Silkeborg: Piaf ⓚⓚⓚ
European **Map** C4
Nygade 31, 8600 Silkeborg
Tel *86 81 12 55* **Closed** *Sun, Mon; Jul*
This small, rather understated gourmet restaurant in Silkeborg's Latin Quarter features simple, romantic decor. Rooted in the classic French kitchen, locally sourced dishes take inspiration from across southern Europe.

Silkeborg: Traktørstedet Ludvigslyst ⓚⓚⓚ
Danish **Map** C4
Julsøvej 248, Svejbæk, 8600 Silkeborg
Tel *86 88 80 40* **Closed** *Mon, Tue (except in summer), Sun dinner*
Located in a lovely rural setting close to Himmelbjerget peak, the rustic surroundings and decor of this out-of-town retreat complement the organic, locally sourced menu.

For more information on types of restaurants *see pages 256–7*

Vejle: Tortilla Flats (Kr)(Kr)
Mexican **Map** C4
Dæmningen 44, 7100 Vejle
Tel *75 72 42 22*
This centrally located Mexican restaurant is especially popular for local family parties. The extensive menu offers a wide variety of Mexican dishes, including starters, desserts and vegetarian dishes.

North Jutland

Aalborg: Penny Lane (Kr)
Café **Map** C2
Boulevarden 1, 9000 Aalborg
Tel *98 12 58 00* **Closed** *Sun*
Cute, nostalgic café, bakery and shop with a reputation for baking some of the best bread in town. It is popular with locals, who enjoy the cosy atmosphere over coffee or breakfast. Lunch-time salads are also served.

Aalborg: Mumbai (Kr)(Kr)
Indian **Map** C2
Kjellerups Torv 1, 9000 Aalborg
Tel *98 16 41 22*
Aalborg's only Indian restaurant and café, Mumbai is located in the modern culture house, Nordkraft. It serves authentic and spicy Indian cuisine, including a very cheap lunch menu and many vegetarian options.

Aalborg: Duus Vinkælder (Kr)(Kr)
Danish **Map** C2
Østergade 9, 9000 Aalborg
Tel *98 12 50 56* **Closed** *Sun*
The basement premises of this historic restaurant date from 1624, making "Jens Bangs Stenhus" one of the city's oldest buildings. Traditional Danish dishes are served in truly medieval surroundings.

Aalborg: Pingvin (Kr)(Kr)
Tapas **Map** C2
Adelgade 12, 9000 Aalborg
Tel *98 11 11 66* **Closed** *Sun*
Café Pingvin calls itself a tapas bar having redefined the term to mean tapas-sized dishes from anywhere in the world. This casual, lively eatery also boasts an incredible selection of wines.

Aalborg: Prinses Juliana (Kr)(Kr)
Seafood **Map** C2
Vestre Havnepromenade 2, 9000 Aalborg
Tel *98 11 55 66* **Closed** *Sun*
Dine in Aalborg's harbour – literally – on this floating gourmet seafood restaurant on a former Dutch training ship that has been serving dinner guests for over 30 years. Upmarket Danish-French kitchen.

Aalborg: Restaurant Sans (Kr)(Kr)
French-Nordic **Map** C2
Sankelmarksgade 1, 9000 Aalborg
Tel *72 30 20 22* **Closed** *Sun, Mon*
The basic concept of this innovative French-Danish restaurant is to serve healthy dishes of exceptional quality at everyday prices. It also offers a complete three-course vegan menu, all served in simple yet elegant surroundings.

Aalborg: Fusion (Kr)(Kr)(Kr)
Japanese-Danish fusion **Map** C2
Strandvejen 4, 9000 Aalborg
Tel *35 12 33 31* **Closed** *Sun*
Enjoy exceptional views across the Limfjord and the city's waterfront from this stylish modern restaurant that fuses European and Asian cuisine in a healthy and flavoursome combination. There is also a takeaway sushi bar.

DK Choice

Aalborg: Mortens Kro (Kr)(Kr)(Kr)
Danish-International **Map** C2
Mølleå 4, 9000 Aalborg
Tel *98 12 48 60* **Closed** *Sun*
This stylish gourmet restaurant is one of the most exclusive in Aalborg, and hardly what you would call a *kro*: its luxurious designer decor is more metropolitan than historic, its clientele international and its flamboyant owner an award-winning chef. The innovative kitchen is contemporary Danish with a global outlook.

Aalborg: Søgaards Bryhus (Kr)(Kr)(Kr)
Danish **Map** C2
C.W. Obels Plads 1A, 9000 Aalborg
Tel *98 16 11 14*
This micro-brewery restaurant serves classic lunches and main meals from the modern Danish kitchen in light and informal surroundings. There's also a tasty daily brunch.

Aalborg: Sangiovanni La Cantina (Kr)(Kr)(Kr)
Italian **Map** C2
Vingårdsgade 25A, 9000 Aalborg
Tel *98 11 37 55* **Closed** *Sun, Mon*
A gourmet Italian restaurant located in a wine cellar that has been run by the Volpi family since opening in 1988. Champions of "slow food", dishes made from scratch with the very best ingredients.

Valuted-ceiling dining room at Sangiovanni La Cantina, Aalborg

Frederikshavn: Frida by Jensen (Kr)(Kr)
Danish **Map** D1
Havnegade 5, 9900 Frederikshavn
Tel *70 70 74 88* **Closed** *Sun–Tue*
This stylish-looking restaurant opened in 2014. Visit in daytime for a light lunch, or after 5:30pm when a buffet served directly from the grill includes a large choice of different fish and meats.

Frederikshavn: Katfizk (Kr)(Kr)
Seafood **Map** D1
Søsportsvej 12, 9900 Frederikshavn
Tel *33 21 88 88* **Closed** *Mon, Tue*
This marina café-restaurant serves a huge seafood buffet for both lunch and dinner, much of it freshly caught. Dine directly on the terrace or indoors in bright, fresh surroundings.

Hjørring: Restaurant Kamii (Kr)(Kr)
Japanese **Map** D1
Springvandspladsen 2, 9800 Hjørring
Tel *98 93 11 11*
Centrally placed Japanese restaurant and sushi bar that serves high quality, authentic dishes at very reasonable prices, especially Tuesday's 200 Dkr sushi menu, both to eat in and take away. Kids' sushi menu too.

Hjørring: Bryghuset Vendia (Kr)(Kr)(Kr)
Danish-French **Map** D1
Markedsgade 9, 9800 Hjørring
Tel *98 92 22 29* **Closed** *Sun*
This upmarket restaurant in a micro-brewery is positioned in the centre of Hjørring. The restaurant has two sections: gourmet and brasserie, offering formal evening dining and casual walk-in visits respectively.

Key to Price Guide *see page 262*

Hobro: Theater Restauranten ⓀⓀ
Steakhouse **Map** C3
Theatertorvet 1, 9500 Hobro
Tel *98 52 17 00*
Despite its Vietnamese head chef and owner, this traditional restaurant and steakhouse prepares classic old school Danish lunches and evening meals from the carvery at very reasonable prices.

Holstebro: Borbjerg Mølle Kro ⓀⓀⓀ
Danish international **Map** B3
Borbjerg Møllevej 3, 7500 Holstebro
Tel *97 46 10 10*
This historic lakeside inn about 8 km (5 miles) northeast of Holstebro sits next to a working water mill. The restaurant offers quality, locally sourced dishes, from the Danish and global kitchens. Very family friendly.

Holstebro: Under Klippen ⓀⓀⓀ
Danish-French **Map** B3
Lille Østergade 3, 7500 Holstebro
Tel *97 40 66 55* **Closed** *Sun*
Shadowed by a huge artificial rock – Holstebro's modern art folly – between a glass-panelled office block and car park is this gourmet restaurant, where seasonal Danish produce is cooked to perfection.

Lønstrup: Villa Vest ⓀⓀⓀ
Scandinavian **Map** C1
Strandvejen 138, 9800 Hjørring
Tel *98 96 05 66* **Closed** *Sun–Tue (spring & autumn); lunch Wed & Thu (except summer); Oct–Mar*
At this gourmet restaurant located directly overlooking the North Sea at Lønstrup Strand, exquisite three- to five-course set menus only are carefully prepared with locally sourced produce. Advance booking only; seasonal opening.

Mariager: Hotel Postgaarden ⓀⓀⓀ
Danish **Map** D3
Torvet 6, 9550 Mariager
Tel *98 54 10 12*
In a half-timbered, listed building from 1710, this coaching inn is found on a cobbled street in the centre of Mariager village. The restaurant is open for lunch and dinner and serves classic, traditional Danish dishes.

Randers: Fladbro Kro ⓀⓀⓀ
Danish-French-International **Map** D3
Randersvej 75, 8920 Randers NV
Tel *86 42 02 10* **Closed** *Mon, Tue, Sun dinner*
This gourmet restaurant in a historic inn situated near the bridge over the river Nørreå offers an innovative seasonal menu that includes everything from locally sourced vegetables to kangaroo fillet. It is inspired by the "slow food" movement.

Randers: Fru Larsen ⓀⓀⓀ
New Nordic **Map** D3
Østergade 1, 8870 Langå
Tel *86 46 83 88* **Closed** *Sun, Mon*
In a village 16 km (10 miles) southwest of Randers, the award-winning head chef of hotel and restaurant Fru Larsen creates gourmet dishes with Nordic ingredients. Four- or five-course gourmet menus or a simpler à la carte option are available.

Randers: Østergade 1 ⓀⓀⓀ
French **Map** D3
Østergade 1, 8900 Randers
Tel *86 43 02 55* **Closed** *Sun, Mon*
Stylishly decorated, French-inspired gourmet restaurant with both à la carte and all-inclusive menus. Dining is fancy yet casual. Very centrally-located and with high gastronomic ambitions.

Skagen: Skagen Bryghus ⓀⓀ
Danish **Map** D1
Kirkevej 10, 9990 Skagen
Tel *98 45 00 50*
This brewery-restaurant serves a variety of classic fish and meat dishes chosen to complement the selection of beer. It also serves a Sunday lunch buffet, holds live concerts and offers guided brewery tours.

Skagen: Kokkenes ⓀⓀⓀ
Danish **Map** D1
Havneplads 20, 9990 Skagen
Tel *98 44 48 48* **Closed** *Sun–Tue (Sep–Apr); also Wed (Oct–Feb)*
A traditional and romantic evening restaurant serving high quality French-Danish dishes with a prime location right on the harbour. It has many loyal return guests.

Skagen: Nordens Folkekøkken ⓀⓀⓀ
New Nordic **Map** D1
Havnevej 11, 9990 Skagen
Tel *53 53 82 50* **Closed** *Sun–Tue; Sep–early Apr*
Skagen's branch of the New Nordic "people's kitchen" in Aarhus is open in the summer season only. Seasonally changing menus are chalked across the blackboard wall. Diners here enjoy top quality Nordic produce and relaxed gourmet dining.

Skagen: Ruth's Hotel ⓀⓀⓀ
Danish-French **Map** D1
Hans Ruths Vej 1, 9990 Skagen
Tel *98 44 11 24* **Closed** *Sun, Mon; Tue & Wed (May, Jun & Sep); Tue–Thu (Oct–Apr)*
This legendary seaside hotel has an equally renowned gourmet restaurant that prides itself on regional cuisine of the highest quality. More casual is its classic French brasserie, where you can dine on the large terrace.

Viborg: Latinerly ⓀⓀ
Steakhouse **Map** C3
Sct. Mathiasgade 78, 8800 Viborg
Tel *86 62 08 81* **Closed** *Sun*
Despite its historic cellar locale, Latinerly – one of Viborg's oldest restaurants – is a modern steakhouse and café-bar-nightclub that attracts plenty of the town's younger residents. There's live music every Friday.

Viborg: For Enden af Gaden ⓀⓀ
Danish **Map** C3
Sct. Mathiasgade 9, 8800 Viborg
Tel *86 60 05 00*
"At the End of the Street" is a lively café-restaurant in a lovely old townhouse spanning three storeys and serving everything from snacks and cakes to top-notch three-course dinners. Kids' and vegetarian options too.

Fru Larsen, an historic restaurant in Randers

For more information on types of restaurants *see pages 256–7*

Viborg: Niels Bugges Kro (Kr)(Kr)(Kr)
Nordic **Map** C3
Ravnsbjergvej 69, 8800 Viborg
Tel *86 63 80 11*
Historic inn overlooking Hald Sø a few miles south of Viborg, where walking and cycling routes abound. Top quality Nordic dishes are made with regional produce, in either the inn or the adjacent Restaurant Skov.

Bornholm

Aakirkeby: Christianshøjkroen (Kr)(Kr)
New Nordic
Segensvej 48, 3720 Aakirkeby
Tel *56 97 40 13* **Closed** *Mon*
Partly a training project for mentally handicapped adults, this gourmet restaurant offers lunchtime *smørrebrød* and delicate set menus that change daily, made with organic and regional produce, in an idyllic woodland setting.

DK Choice

Aakirkeby: Kadeau Bornholm (Kr)(Kr)(Kr)
New Nordic
Baunevej 18, Vestre Sømark, Pedersker, 3720 Aakirkeby
Tel *56 97 82 50* **Closed** *Mon–Wed (in low season); Oct–Apr*
Located in a renovated beach pavilion on the very south of the island, this gourmet restaurant is surrounded by sea, beach and forest. Its white furnishings are as fresh as the food, which is exclusively regional, exciting and innovative. The restaurant is open from spring to autumn only; booking ahead is advised.

Allinge: Nordbornholms Røgeri (Kr)
Fish
Kæmpestranden 2, 3770 Allinge
Tel *56 48 07 30*
One of two smokehouses in Allinge, NRK is located south of the harbour on the cliffs. Various types of smoked fish are available, as well as an extensive buffet. There are open grounds and great sea views.

Allinge: Det Gamle Posthus (Kr)(Kr)
Regional Danish
Kirkegade 8, 3770 Allinge
Tel *56 48 10 42*
This historic building has been many things as well as a post office, including a sweet makers and a book store. The ambience and decor are welcoming, and the quality food is prepared with respect for Bornholm cuisine.

Allinge: Margeritten (Kr)(Kr)
Steakhouse
Kirkeplads 1B, 3770 Allinge
Tel *56 48 22 09*
Family-owned steakhouse and restaurant that serves classic meat and seafood dishes at reasonable prices, in the centre of Allinge. There are lots of kid-friendly options.

Allinge: No.9 (Kr)(Kr)
Danish-French
Havnegade 9, 3770 Allinge
Tel *56 48 11 08* **Closed** *Oct–Mar*
A pleasant summertime gourmet restaurant on the seafront in Allinge with a limited but considered menu. Regional Bornholm produce, inspired by both French and Danish kitchens, is combined with great service.

Christiansø: Christiansø Kro og Gæstgiveri (Kr)(Kr)
Danish-French
Christiansø 10, 3760 Gudhjem
Tel *56 46 20 15* **Closed** *Nov–Mar*
The sole restaurant on tiny Christiansø (as well as its shop and inn) serves generous portions of classic Danish dishes for lunch and dinner daily in high season. During other months, it's wise to call ahead.

Gudjem: Pandekagehuset (Kr)
Café
Brøddegade 15, 3700 Gudhjem
Tel *56 48 55 17*
The pancake house sells exactly that, and has done for over 20 years. These are not just for the kids, either, as both savoury filled pancakes and dessert versions are available at all times of the day. Omelettes are available too.

Lassen's Restaurant located in Stammershalle Badehotel, Gudjem

Gudhjem: Café Provianten (Kr)
Café
Ejnar Mikkelsensvej 28, 3760 Gudhjem
Tel *40 76 81 96*
Harbour-placed café serving hot and cold drinks, large sandwiches and tapas plates during summer, when it opens in the evenings. On summer mornings, people gather outside to sing to the Christiansø ferry as it sets sail.

Gudhjem: Lassen's Restaurant (Kr)(Kr)(Kr)
New Nordic
Strandvej 128, Stammershalle, 3760 Gudhjem
Tel *56 48 42 10* **Closed** *Mon (Oct–Jun); Sun & Tue (Oct–Apr); Wed (Apr)*
Stammershalle Badehotel's restaurant, perched on the cliffs between Allinge and Gudhjem, attracts some of Denmark's top chefs. Simple, Nordic dishes are made to perfection from regional produce. Reservation advised.

Hasle: Hasle Røgeri (Kr)
Seafood
Søndre Bæk 20, 3790 Hasle
Tel *56 92 20 02* **Closed** *Oct–Mar*
Smoking is still done here using traditional methods in open stacks. Come early and you can watch the herring being smoked before eating it. The fish buffet lets you try some of everything.

Hasle: Le Port (Kr)(Kr)(Kr)
Danish-French
Vang 81, 3790 Hasle
Tel *56 96 92 01* **Closed** *Sun, Mon; Tue–Wed (in low season)*
One of Bornholm's most established gourmet restaurants, Le Port specialises in Danish and French classics. The popular summer terrace enjoys lovely sea views and fantastic sunsets.

Nexø: BendixenMAD (Kr)(Kr)
New Nordic
Havnen 11, 3730 Nexø
Tel *56 49 37 30* **Closed** *Mon–Wed; Sun dinner*
Opened in 2014, but already developing a reputation as one of the best in the area for its regional take on Nordic cuisine. The restaurant remains casual and informal, and even does a Nordic kids' menu.

Nexø: Restaurant Culinarium (Kr)(Kr)
European
Havnen 4A, 3730 Nexø
Tel *56 44 33 61* **Closed** *Sat lunch*
This fairly traditional restaurant on Nexø's harbour is open for both lunch and dinner, serving an assortment of *schnitzels*, steaks and fish dishes alongside German wines and beers.

Key to Price Guide *see page 262*

Østermarie: Hallegård Gårdbutik ⓚ
Café-deli
Aspevej 3, 3751 Østermarie
Tel *56 47 02 47* **Closed** *Sat, Sun*
Enjoy tapas and other handmade delicacies from this farm shop that makes its own organic hot dogs on the premises with locally sourced pork. Guaranteed fresh produce out in the countryside.

Østermarie: Fru Petersens Café ⓚ
Danish
Almindingensvej 31, 3751 Østermarie
Tel *56 47 06 18* **Closed** *Mon–Tue (Jun & Sep–Oct); Wed (Oct); also Nov–May*
A charming café-restaurant in a fabulous half-timbered house serving classic Danish cuisine "like grandma used to make". Furnished like a private home from a century ago, both the menus and decor aim at historical accuracy.

Rønne: Selma's Home Cooking ⓚ
International
Tornegade 6, 3700 Rønne
Tel *56 95 34 75* **Closed** *Sun–Tue*
This small, rather hard to find restaurant is a good budget option, with both buffet and hot dishes inspired by the global kitchen. It is family friendly, with a big focus on vegetarian dishes.

Rønne: Restaurant Texas ⓚⓚ
American
Store Torvegade 14, 3700 Rønne
Tel *56 91 10 09*
At this American-inspired café-restaurant, centrally placed in Rønne's pedestrian street, steaks, pizzas, burgers and chicken wings are on the menu, all reasonably priced. It can get lively at weekends and in the evenings.

Rønne: Restaurant Di 5 Stauerna ⓚⓚⓚ
Danish-French
Strandvejen 116, 3700 Rønne
Tel *56 90 44 44*
Radisson Blu Fredensborg Hotel's gourmet restaurant comprises five interconnected rooms (hence the name), and offers an intimate, romantic dining experience. The regionally-sourced dishes are inspired by French and Danish cuisine.

Rønne: Poul P ⓚⓚⓚ
Café
Store Torvegade 29, 3700 Rønne
Tel *28 77 60 40*
A lively café run by artist Poul Pava (his paintings adorn the walls) in Rønne's Laksetorvet square. It offers a good selection of light lunches and mains, all originally titled. There are regular live concerts from local talent.

Diners enjoying meals outside smokehouse Røgeriet, Svaneke

Rønne: Restaurant Victoria ⓚⓚⓚ
New Nordic
Nordre Kystvej 34, 3700 Rønne
Tel *56 90 42 44* **Closed** *in summer; selected days in winter, call first*
A window table is highly recommended at Hotel Griffen's smart restaurant, where the sea views are a big draw. The restaurant's signature "Sunset Menu" makes use of regional produce and Nordic inspiration.

Snogebæk: Æblehaven ⓚⓚⓚ
Danish
Hovedgade 15, Snogebæk, 3730 Nexø
Tel *56 48 88 85* **Closed** *Mon; Tue & Wed (Oct–May)*
A cosy, family-run evening restaurant with a small but select menu, on the harbour of the quaint fishing village Snogebæk. The Danish-French kitchen is given an Asian twist thanks to chef Sophia's Thai heritage.

Svaneke: Aarsdale Silde Røgeri ⓚ
Seafood
Gaden 2, 3740 Svaneke
Tel *56 49 65 08* **Closed** *Mon (May); Sun & Mon (Oct); Nov–Apr*
Traditional smokehouse south of Svaneke near Paradisbakkerne that's been smoking locally caught herring for over a century. Individual portions are served with potato salad or you can order the large fish platter.

Svaneke: Røgeriet ⓚ
Seafood
Fiskergade 12, 3740 Svaneke
Tel *56 49 63 24* **Closed** *late Oct–early Apr*
The smokehouse in the centre of Svaneke sells smoked fish of all varieties as well as fish cakes to eat on the wooden tables outside, with views out to Christiansø, or to take away.

Svaneke: Svaneke Ismejeri ⓚ
Ice cream parlour
Svaneke Torv 3, 3740 Svaneke
Tel *40 74 65 35*
Svaneke's ice cream is considered one of Denmark's best, made from local and organic ingredients. Take a tour of the production area or sit in the café and choose from the range of daily flavours.

Svaneke: Syd-Øst for Paradis ⓚ
Beach Café
Skovgade 34, 3740 Svaneke
Tel *50 70 42 48* **Closed** *Sep–May or in bad weather*
This former ice cream stand, now a thriving summer café, calls itself "chirinquito", which is Spanish for "beach café with tapas". The café's speciality is a grill-it-yourself paella.

Svaneke: Louisekroen ⓚⓚ
Danish
Bølshavn 22, 3740 Svaneke
Tel *56 49 62 03* **Closed** *Oct–Apr*
Traditional, half-timbered inn situated on the coast between Svaneke and Gudhjem. The decor is retro and many of the guests have been coming every year for decades. It is known for its good Danish steaks.

Svaneke: Bryghuset Svaneke ⓚⓚ
Nordic
Svaneke Torv 5, 3740 Svaneke
Tel *56 49 73 21*
In an 18th-century merchant's house on Svaneke's town square, this award-winning micro-brewery has an excellent restaurant with an extensive à la carte menu. Dining can be combined with a guided tour of the brewery.

For more information on types of restaurants *see pages 256–7*

Greenland

Ilulissat: Restaurant Icefiord ⓀⓀ
European/Thai
Jørgen Sverdrupip Aqq. 10, 3952 Ilulissat
Tel *29 99 44 480*
The restaurant of Hotel Icefiord serves both a seasonal menu dominated by steak and fish (although it includes regional specialities like home-smoked musk ox) and a Thai menu.

Ilulissat: Marmartut ⓀⓀⓀ
Greenlandic
Sermermiut Aqq. 4, 3952 Iulissat
Tel *29 99 45 100* **Closed** *Sun*
This small, wood-framed restaurant seats 40 and offers views over Disko Bay. Add a head chef with an impressive, lengthy CV and lots of local specialities like freshly caught ammassak fish, a staple of the Greenlandic diet.

Ilulissat: Restaurant Ulo ⓀⓀⓀ
Scandinavian
Aaron Mathiesenip Aqquserna B-1128, 3952 Ilulissat
Tel *299944153*
Hotel Arctic's gourmet restaurant has great views and an ambitious kitchen, headed by a chef formerly of Nuuk's Nipisa. Try the five-course set evening menu of locally sourced, tapas-sized dishes or a simpler lunch menu.

Kangerluusuaq: Restaurant Roklubben ⓀⓀⓀ
Greenlandic
P.O. Box 49, 3910 Kangerlussuaq
Tel *29 95 24 526*
A few miles from its nearest settlement Kangerluusuaq, this established restaurant on the shore of Lake Ferguson may look like a hut from outside, but it serves good, nourishing Greenlandic specialities. Book ahead.

Narsaq: Restaurant Klara ⓀⓀ
European
Sarquanguaqvej B-819, 3921 Narsaq
Tel *29 96 61 290*
This is the restaurant of Hotel Narsaq and pretty much the only place to eat in town. The menu can be rather limited depending on what's available in the kitchen that day, but staff are helpful and eager to please.

Narsarsuaq: Restauant Narsarsuaq ⓀⓀ
International/Greenlandic
Hotel Narsarsuaq, 3923 Narsarsuaq
Tel *29 96 65 253*
The à la carte restaurant of Hotel Narsarsuaq in southern Greenland serves both international standards and regional specialities, along with various imported wines and Greenlandic coffee.

Nuuk: Café Katuaq Ⓚ
Café
Imaneq 21, 3900 Nuuk
Tel *29 93 63 770*
The pleasant in-house café of Nuuk's cultural centre serves quality dishes with regional specialities such as snowcrab at good rates, as well as good brunch.

Nuuk: Café Esmeralda ⓀⓀ
Café
Aqqusinersuaq 6, 1st floor, 3900 Nuuk
Tel *29 93 29 005*
This modern-looking, inviting café is one of few places in Nuuk where you can get a fairly standard green and healthy breakfast, brunch or lunch, most of it homemade with freshly flown-in vegetables. Cocktails are served later in the evening.

Nuuk: Charoen Porn ⓀⓀ
Thai
Aqqusinersuaq 5, 3900 Nuuk
Tel *29 93 25 759*
A Thai restaurant and takeaway that is surprisingly authentic, though not overly spicy, considering its polar location. It also offers some regional specialities, including the Greenlandic coffee ritual and a popular local version of sashimi.

Nuuk: Godthåb Bryghus ⓀⓀ
Danish
Imaneq 30, 3900 Nuuk
Tel *29 93 48 080* **Closed** *Sun*
This decent brewery restaurant in the centre of Nuuk serves juicy steaks and burgers and pub-style snacks, as well as Greenlandic specialities, all washed down with one of the brewery's many ales and lagers.

Nuuk: Hereford Beefstouw ⓀⓀⓀ
Steak
Hotel Hans Egede, Aqqusinersuaq 1, 3900 Nuuk
Tel *29 93 24 222*
Hotel Hans Egede's other restaurant is one of a Danish-wide chain of reliable steakhouses. This one surely has the best views of all of them, overlooking the fiord on the hotel's fifth floor.

Nuuk: Nipisa ⓀⓀⓀ
Nordic
Kolonihavnen, Hans Egedesvej 29, 3900 Nuuk
Tel *29 93 21 210* **Closed** *Mon, Tue*

Restaurant Icefiord offers regional and Thai cuisine as well as a view of fjords, Ilulissat

Gourmet restaurant Nipisa, which means "lumpfish" in Greenlandic, offers a jaw-dropping 15-course regional menu and innovative Sunday brunch, plus amazing views; there's potential for whale watching from your table. Book ahead.

DK Choice

Nuuk: Sarfalik ⓀⓀⓀ
Nordic
Hotel Hans Egede, Aqqusinersuaq1, 3900 Nuuk
Tel *29 93 24 222* **Closed** *Sun dinner*
The gourmet "gathering place" in Hotel Hans Egede is a world-class, innovative restaurant that has put Greenlandic cuisine on the culinary map. More adventurous guests can try the local menu, where delicacies include indigenous flora as well as reindeer and musk ox, or the (slightly) safer global menu. Book ahead.

Qaqortoq: Steakhouse Nanoq ⓀⓀⓀ
Steakhouse
P.O. Box 509, 3920 Qaqortoq
Tel *29 96 42 282*
The steak restaurant in Hotel Qaortoq serves a wide range of meats as well as Greenlandic beer made with water from melted icebergs. Diners can enjoy excellent views over the town's harbour.

Qarqortoq: Ban Thai ⓀⓀ
Thai
Torvevej B 67, 3920 Qaqortoq
Tel *29 96 43 222*
A beautifully decorated Thai restaurant in a cottage on the town square that fuses

Key to Price Guide *see page 262*

pleasant though rather bland Thai cuisine with a traditional Greenlandic buffet. There's always plenty of fresh fish and Greenland-style sushi on offer.

Faroe Islands

Eyusturoy: Gjaargardur Kr Kr
Scandinavian
Dalvegur 20, 476 Gjogv
Tel *29 84 23 171* **Closed** *Mar; open for light lunches only to hotel guests in Oct; Nov–Feb by arrangement only*
Situated in an isolated but beautiful landscape, it's advisable to call the house restaurant of this eco hotel ahead of arrival to avoid disappointment, particularly on Sundays, when a hearty three-course lunch is served.

Klaksvik: Roykstovan Kr
Pub
Klaksviksvegur 41, 700 Klaksvik
Tel *29 84 56 125*
Together with the parish church, this red-and-blue painted pub overlooking the fjord is one of the town's landmarks and popular with locals. It serves bar snacks and pub food such as soups and burgers.

Klaksvik: Restaurant Hereford Kr Kr Kr
Steakhouse
Klaksvikvegur 45, 700 Klaksvik
Tel *29 84 56 434* **Closed** *Mon*
On the town's main street looking directly out onto the fjord, this wood-panelled restaurant is furnished with cosy booths. The menu ranges from steaks and fresh lamb to puffin and chateaubriand.

Tórshavn: Etika Kr
Sushi
Áarvegur 3, 100 Tórshavn
Tel *29 83 19 319*
This trendy and stylish sushi bar with a cool, colourful interior, offers sushi boxes to eat in or take away. Fresh fish is a must for good sushi, and the salmon here comes fresh from Faroese waters.

Tórshavn: Irish Pub Kr
Pub
Grims Kambansgøta 13, 110 Tórshavn
Tel *29 83 19 091*
Generous portions of traditional but inexpensive pub dinners and lunches are served in this casual Irish pub, as well as a wide range of Faroese beer.

Tórshavn: Barbara Fish House Kr Kr
Seafood
Gongin 4–6, 100 Tórshavn
Tel *29 83 31 010*
A charming seafood restaurant in Tórshavn's old quarter with historic atmosphere and nostalgic decor. Fish dishes are served in tapas-sized portions to be shared by all at the table.

Tórshavn: Carello Kr Kr
Italian
Havnargøta 1, 100 Tórshavn
Tel *29 83 20 360*
This Italian café and restaurant serves standard pizza and pasta dishes from an à la carte evening menu or lunch buffet. Wash it down with an Italian wine or a cold local beer.

Tórshavn: Hvonn Brasserie Kr Kr
Italian-American
Tórsgøta 4, 100 Tórshavn
Tel *29 83 50 035*
The first floor restaurant of the Hotel Tórshavn has an international kitchen and a massive choice. It is open all day for steaks, burgers, sandwiches, pasta, pizza and curries.

Tórshavn: Restaurant 11 Kr Kr Kr
Scandinavian
Tórsgøta 11, 100 Tórshavn
Tel *29 83 11 611* **Closed** *Sat lunch*
A centrally located, quality restaurant serving both Faroese and European dishes, all well presented. The lamb is especially recommended. It doesn't tend to get crowded, so the service is very attentive.

Tórshavn: Aarstova Kr Kr Kr
New Nordic
Gongin 1, 100 Tórshavn
Tel *29 83 33 000*
This innovative gourmet restaurant in a charming, listed building in Tórshavn's old town specialises in local produce and regional specialities, with three-course, five-course and à la carte menus. Book ahead.

DK Choice

Tórshavn: Koks Kr Kr Kr
New Nordic
Oyggjarvegur 45, 100 Tórshavn
Tel *29 83 33 999* **Closed** *Sun, Mon*
It's been dubbed the Faroese Noma; an innovative gourmet restaurant that invites its diners to experience the changing seasons of the Faroes through its local produce. With its newer "Roots and Branches" menus, Koks even collaborates with local biologists in finding new Faroese fauna and flora to use. Book ahead.

Tórshavn: Restaurant Hafnia Kr Kr Kr
Scandinavian
Áarvegur 4–10, 100 Tórshavn
Tel *29 83 88 000* **Closed** *Sat lunch*
On the first floor of the Hotel Hafnia overlooking the main street, this quality restaurant makes good and original use of Faroese produce. A traditional roast dinner is served on Sunday afternoons and holidays.

Vidareidi: Matstivan hja Elisabeth (Elisabeth's Restaurant) Kr Kr
Scandinavian
Eggjarvegur 13, Vidareidi, 750 Vidoy
Tel *29 84 51 275*
Seating just 30, Elisabeth serves local specialities such as fresh fish, puffin and the national dessert, rhubarb trifle. The traditional Faroese knits on display are for sale in the shop next door. Reservation required.

An atttractive display of Faroese dishes at Restaurant Hafnia, Tórshavn

SHOPPING IN DENMARK

Most major towns in Denmark have large, shopping centres and department stores such as the country-wide chain Magasin du Nord. Prices can be high, however, especially in the more exclusive shops such as those found along Strøget in Copenhagen. Many bargains on clothes can be found, especially during the post-seasonal sales. Flea markets are widespread in Denmark. Much of what is on sale is junk, but persistence and a keen eye can sometimes uncover real treasures. The many independently run shops selling beautiful household goods satisfy the Danes' love of good design. Jewellery made from Danish amber is also popular and relatively cheap. Danish herb-flavoured *akvavit* (a kind of schnapps) comes in a variety of flavours and colours and makes a good present.

Busy Saturday market in Svaneke, popular with Danes and visitors

Opening Hours

In Denmark shopping days and opening hours are regulated due to union demands for reasonable working hours. The regulated hours are, for the most part, rigorously adhered to, although during the Christmas season and around busy tourist resorts longer openings are usual. Most shops open at 10am and remain open until 6pm Monday to Thursday. On Fridays many shops are open until 7 or 8pm. On Saturdays most shops close at about 2pm; some larger shops and department stores remain open until 4pm. Most shops now also open on Sundays, though opening times vary from store to store.

Some smaller, independent shops keep longer opening hours. Stores attached to petrol stations and kiosks found in town centres remain open 24 hours but offer a limited choice of goods.

In the run-up to Christmas and other festivals many shops and department stores in the capital and in larger towns extend their opening hours and often trade on Sundays.

Markets

Produce markets are very popular in Denmark, often held twice weekly in most towns; one of the best is the upscale Torvehallerne market in Copenhagen *(see p104)*. The Danes also relish their flea markets, which are held periodically in many towns. Genuine antiques are mixed up with piles of bric-à-brac. A morning spent at a flea market offers a trip down memory lane for many Danes and also provides a good opportunity to munch on a hot sausage from one of the many snack bars. Pre-Christmas fairs are also common. Seasonal fairs sell a variety of festive decorations including handmade wooden or knitted items, candles and colourful elves and gnomes fashioned from balls of bright wool.

Sign in Ærøskøbing

Vat

The rate of VAT (known as MOMS) is 25 per cent in Denmark; this is always already included in the selling price quoted. Some goods, such as alcohol, tobacco and petrochemical products, carry an additional excise.

Visitors from outside the EU can claim a tax refund of between 13 and 19 per cent of the total price of an item on purchases over 300 Dkr. Shops operating this scheme carry a Tax Free logo. When making

12th-century cellars being used for wine storage

Hvide Hus – a handicraft shop in Gudhjem on Bornholm

a purchase ask for a Global Refund certificate. The shopkeeper may ask to see a passport. On leaving the country the certificate must be stamped by a customs officer, who will need to see that the product is intact in its original packaging. The stamped certificate may be used when reclaiming VAT in allocated banks or border agencies. For more information, visit *www.taxfreeworldwide.com*.

Seasonal Reductions

Reductions on many items can be obtained by shopping during the sales, which are known locally as "Udsalg". In Denmark, the traditional months for sales are January and June/July, although many stores shift their dates by one or two weeks either way. Sales are also held to mark the anniversary of a shop's opening or even the founding of a chain. As with most promotions, it pays to be cautious, however, as reductions can often be quite insignificant or apply only to a limited number of goods.

Methods of Payment

Cash is the easiest form of payment but for larger sums it is safer to use credit cards, which are widely accepted throughout the country. Cards can be used in many shops, restaurants, hotels and museums. This method of payment carries a small surcharge.

Contemporary Design

Denmark is famous for its cutting edge design of ceramics, contemporary furniture and home accessories. Copenhagen has a wealth of independent outlets, but many brands are available throughout the country. The price of such merchandise can be high, especially for items by major designers, but smaller, more affordable items are available such as glasses by Bodum, silver Christmas tree decorations by Georg Jensen, cheese cutters or small porcelain items.

Food Products

Many types of cheese are produced in Denmark so there is no excuse for sticking to a simple Danish blue. Those who like sharp-tasting cheeses should go for "Gamle Ole". This strongly flavoured cheese goes particularly well with Danish rye bread, a dense and healthy loaf made with seeds and grains.

For those with a sweet tooth, chocolates and sweets are also well worth seeking out. Often these are handmade, beautifully presented and far superior to the mass-produced variety. Hand-made boiled sweets are also good quality.

One of the Danes' favourite foodstuffs is pickled herring, which is served on its own and often on bread as *smørrebrød*. Many different recipes are used when marinating the fish to produce a wide range of tastes. Smoked fish, especially from Bornholm, is also popular.

The southern region of Jutland is famous for its meat products, which include salamis of various flavours and seasonings, all of which are delicious.

Assorted coffee-related gadgets such as grinders and percolators are often on sale in coffee shops, which sell a bewildering range of roasted beans from around the world.

Alcoholic Drinks

While in Denmark it is worth sampling *akvavit* (a form of schnapps). Many regions, and even individual restaurants, have their own special recipes for these flavoursome drinks, which are then sold as *husets snaps*. Visitors can, for instance, savour an Aalborg Porse flavoured with Jutland herbs. As well as *akvavit*, Denmark produces some excellent beers *(see p260)*. Some of the lesser known brands and dark beers are worth trying, and make a welcome alternative to the ubiquitous light Pilsners.

An antique shop in Copenhagen

ENTERTAINMENT IN DENMARK

Denmark is a vibrant country with a wide range of culture and entertainment on offer. Clubs and bars promote all kinds of music from mainstream pop and jazz to the latest in alternative sounds, while venues such as Det Kongelige Teater (The Royal Theatre) put on world-class theatre and ballet. Summer time is the season for a number of high-profile festivals such as Roskilde's rock festival in early July. Local festivals include re-creations of Denmark's Viking past. Cinemas can be found in most towns and often screen English language films with Danish subtitles. Sport, too, is popular, and Danish soccer clubs are among the best in Europe. Children are sure to enjoy a visit to one of the country's amusement parks, including LEGOLAND®. For information on entertainment in Copenhagen see pages 106–109.

Columbine, Pierrot and Harlequin at Tivoli

Theatre, Music and Dance

A visit to the theatre is one of the most popular pastimes in Denmark. Cultural life blossoms throughout the country, and university towns, such as Aarhus, Aalborg and Odense, have much to offer.

Aarhus is the biggest cultural centre after Copenhagen and has the **Musikhuset Aarhus**, a modern concert hall with four venues that stages musical and dance performances. It is home to Den Jyske Opera (The Jutland Opera) and the Jutland Symphony. Aalborg, in northern Jutland, has the cultural centre Nordkraft and a resident symphony orchestra, which often gives concerts in the **Aalborg Kongres og Kulturcenter**.

In Odense, the **Odense Koncerthus** has a regular programme of classical music, which includes performances of music by Carl Nielsen (1865–1931), a native of the city.

Most large towns have a large hall for concerts, theatre, ballet and modern dance performances. During the summer, Denmark hosts a number of open-air concerts, often in the grounds of manor houses. People bring along picnics for an evening of opera or classical music. There are also several rock, pop and folk music festivals. Visit *www.visitdenmark.com* for more details of live music in Denmark.

Amusement Parks

Denmark's amusement parks provide entertainment for children and adults alike. The parks are open mainly in summer, although some of them start their season earlier. One of the most famous is **LEGOLAND®** in central Jutland *(see pp196–7)*, which includes LEGO® sculptures along with high-octane rides. As with many of Denmark's amusement parks, the admission price to LEGOLAND® includes free use of all the attractions. Less high-profile amusement parks are dotted throughout the country and include fairgrounds, water parks and science centres. **BonBon-Land** in southern Zealand *(see p161)*, for instance, is packed with rides and amusements as is **Fårup Sommerland** in northern Jutland *(see p208)*.

In addition to its traditional zoos, Denmark has numerous safari parks and aquariums where visitors can see wild animals and aquatic creatures. Two of the best known are **Knuthenborg Safari Park**

Miniature buildings in LEGOLAND®

Det Kongelige Teater performance in Copenhagen *(see p73)*

(see pp164–5) and Esbjerg's **Fiskeri-og Søfartsmuseet** aquarium *(see p198)*.

Nightlife

Apart from those in Copenhagen, the best clubs are in university towns, such as Aarhus, Aalborg and Odense, where they cater for the exacting demands of the student population. Among the most popular places in Aarhus are **Train**, **VoxHall** and **Musikcaféen**, which play a mixture of rock and techno depending on the night. In Aalborg **Skråen** and **The Irish House** have a lively feel. Two of the best clubs in Odense are **Posten** and **Jazzhus Dexter**. The latter has live jazz at the weekend.

Performances in Danish music venues range from local bands to major acts from abroad. Many concerts are free although prices can be fairly steep for the biggest international names. Nightclubs are also popular and can be found even in some of the smaller towns. Clubwise, nothing really gets going until about 11pm in Denmark. Pubs and clubs usually stay open until 1am on weekdays. At weekends many of them don't close their doors until dawn.

Spectator Sports

Football (soccer) is a passion in Denmark and the Danish national side is one of the top teams in Europe. Watching football is a popular pastime and many games are attended by entire families. Three of the best-known clubs are **FC Midtjylland**, **FC København** and **Aalborg BK**. International matches are played at Parken, Denmark's national stadium and home ground of FC København.

Handball has quite a high profile following the gold-medal success of the women's team at the 2000 Olympics. Other common sports include ice hockey, badminton, dirt-bike racing and cycling. Gymnastics clubs are also popular, and shows and competitions are frequently advertised in smaller towns.

Feeding the seals at the Fiskeri-og Søfartsmuseet, southern Jutland

DIRECTORY

Theatre, Music and Dance

Aalborg Kongres og Kulturcenter
Europaplads 4, 9000 Aalborg. **Tel** 99 35 55 55.

Aarhus Teater
Teatergaden, 8000 Aarhus C. **Tel** 70 21 30 21.
W aarhusteater.dk

Granhøj Dans
Klosterport 6, 8000 Aarhus C. **Tel** 86 19 26 22.
W granhoj.dk

Musikhuset Aarhus
Thomas Jensens Allé, 8000 Aarhus C.
Tel 89 40 40 40.
W musikhusetaarhus.dk

Odense Koncerthus
Claus Bergs Gade 9, Odense C.
Tel 66 14 78 00.

Odense Teater
Jernbanegade 21, 5100 Odense C.
Tel 62 12 00 52.
W odenseteater.dk

Nightlife

The Irish House
Østerågade 25, 9000 Aalborg.

Jazzhus Dexter
Vindegade 65, 5000 Odense C.

Musikcaféen
Mejlgade 53, 8000 Aarhus C.

Posten
Ostre Stationsvej 35, 5000 Odense C.

Skråen
Nordkraft, Kjellerup Torv 5, 9000 Aalborg.

Train
Toldbodgade 6, 8000 Aarhus C.

VoxHall
Vester Allé 15, 8000 Aarhus C.

Spectator Sports

Aalborg BK
Hornevej 2, 9220 Aalborg Øst.
Tel 96 35 59 00.
W aabsport.dk

FC København
Parken, Øster Allé 50, 2110 Copenhagen.
Tel 35 43 74 00.
W fck.dk

FC Midtjylland
Kaj Zartowsvej 5, 7400 Herning.
Tel 96 27 10 40.
W fcm.dk

OUTDOOR ACTIVITIES

The Danes are keen on sport and fitness, and many adults and most children participate in one sport or another. The country's gentle terrain and the many miles of well maintained cycle routes have helped to make cycling an integral part of Danish culture – it is not unusual for entire Danish families to embark on cycling holidays. Golfers are also well catered for and Denmark has over 100 courses, many of which can be found close to hotels and camp sites. With its many fjords, protected waters and tiny islands to explore, Denmark is a good place for sailors. The country is also ideal for water sports such as windsurfing and canoeing. The same sheltered fjords are perfect for novice windsurfers, and there are many companies near Danish holiday resorts that can arrange lessons. Horse riding and fishing are other popular activities.

Horse Riding

Equestrian pursuits are popular in Denmark and the country has a large number of riding stables. Some Danes have their own horses and keep them in community-style stables. Those who are unable to keep their own horses make use of the numerous riding clubs that offer riding lessons and provide horses for individual unsupervised rides. A small number of clubs will accept riders paying an hourly rate. Rides are also on offer in beach resorts such as Rømø, Thy and Løkken.

A good way for beginners to learn about riding and looking after horses is to sign up for a farm holiday *(see p247)*, some of which include riding lessons and accompanied treks through the countryside. Riding holidays on Icelandic horses (the traditional Viking horse) are available in Mols National Park.

Horse riding – a popular pastime in Denmark

Horse and driver on a carriage racetrack

For something a little different, it is possible to travel the country by wagon. Four to six people can usually be carried in the wagons, which are hired complete with horses from companies such as **Prærievognsferie Og Hesteudlejning** on Funen. Training is provided and the wagon is equipped with everything that travellers might need while on the road. A map is supplied marking the route to the camp site, where there is pasture for horses and often a welcoming bonfire. Prairie wagon holidays can be great fun, particularly for children. Contact **Dansk Ride Forbund** (The Danish Equestrian Federation) for details of activities in the area you are visiting.

For those who prefer to spectate, horse races are held in several towns, including Klampenborg, Aarhus, Fyn, Aalborg and Bornholm.

Water Sports

The many Danish lakes and some 7,300 km (4,536 miles) of coastline make Denmark a perfect location for water-sports enthusiasts. Equipment for windsurfing, water-skiing and sea kayaking can be hired in waterside resorts, as can jet skis and other gear. In Silkeborg it is possible to book canoeing holidays.

Visitors intending to take up some form of water sport should check in advance whether the region they plan to visit allows for such pursuits – for example, water-skiing is prohibited in some ecologically sensitive areas.

Fishing

Denmark is an ideal destination for anglers. Its many streams and lakes are well maintained and have healthy stocks of fish including plentiful supplies of pike and trout both for coarse

Windsurfers making the most of Denmark's coastal waters

and fly-fishing. The long coastline is also good for saltwater fishing and anglers can hope to catch sea trout, plaice, mackerel and cod. Anglers between the age of 18 and 67 must carry an appropriate licence. These are sold at post offices, tourist information offices and shops that sell angling equipment; they are also available at *www.fisketegn.dk*. Licences are issued for one day, one week or annually and cost 40, 130 and 185 Dkr respectively. Fishing in lakes and streams requires the permission of the owner, which often is the local angling club. Tourist offices will have details of angling holidays and some camp sites are especially geared for anglers with rooms set aside for gutting and cleaning fish.

Anyone fishing in Denmark will be expected to know the regulations concerning the size and types of species that may be caught. Some clubs may impose restrictions concerning the number or the total weight of the catch.

Those keen on deep-sea fishing can join the crew of a fishing vessel and head out to offshore fishing grounds, such as Gule Rev, in the North Sea off Hanstholm. The cutter **T-248 Skagerak** sails to this reef daily (weather permitting).

Anyone interested in a fishing holiday in Denmark should contact the local tourist office. The website *www.fiskekort.dk* provides maps of good fishing areas.

Motorcycle Tours

Touring around Denmark by motorcycle is a pleasant way to get to know the country. Traffic is reasonably light and many Danes are themselves keen motorcyclists.

Motorcycle rallies, known as *motorcykeltrief*, are organized countrywide. The size of events varies from small weekly meetings to large rallies that feature live music and competitions for the most impressive bikes. Major events can last days and attract locals as well as foreign enthusiasts.

Denmark has a network of scenic roads known as the Marguerite Route, which takes in some of the most beautiful parts of the country. The route consists mostly of secondary and minor roads and is marked on road signs by a white daisy on a brown background *(see p301)*. Maps mark the route with green dots or a green line.

Anyone travelling in Denmark on a motorcycle should take into account the wind, which at times can be very strong and make riding difficult and sometimes even hazardous. When crossing bridges, particularly over some of the long straits, the wind can be especially strong and blow in sudden and unexpected gusts. When strong winds prevail, motorcyclists may be banned from using these bridges.

Motorcyclists in Denmark must adhere to the highway code. Riders and passengers are required by law to wear helmets and carry the necessary documentation at all times.

Bikers and bikes at an annual motorcycle rally

Cyclists on one of the country's many cycling routes

Cycling

Riding a bike is a hugely popular activity in Denmark and the lowland areas especially are excellent regions for a cycling holiday, as is the island of Bornholm *(see p231)*. The whole country is criss-crossed with an extensive network of cycling routes. It is easy to plan a journey and routes take in most of the big towns and cities as well as more rural parts of the country.

Organized cycle races are common in Denmark. Many cover short distances and are open to amateurs. Races for elite riders include the Grand Prix Aalborg and the prestigious CSC Classic, where teams compete to earn points towards the world-ranking list. Races such as the CSC Classic are for serious competitors only.

Playing the green at a golf club near Gilleleje, northwestern Zealand

Cycling Tours

Cycling is an excellent way to tour Denmark, and enthusiasts are very well catered for. Specialist bicycle shops are found throughout the country. Alongside traditional touring bikes, they sell the very latest in cycling equipment. Dedicated maps for cycling make planning a tour fairly straight-forward. Maps are widely available and cover virtually every part of the country. The maps include not only cycle routes but all the major sights along the way such as museums and castles. In addition, they indicate which roads have cycle paths and on which roads it is forbidden or too dangerous to ride. Cycling maps are useful in a number of other ways. They often include details of camp sites and hostels, for instance, as well as grocery stores. Maps can be ordered from **Dansk Cyklist Forbund** (The Danish Cycling Federation) as well as from bookshops and tourist offices.

The Dansk Cyklist Forbund can also provide details of packaged cycling tours. Tours can be expensive but they have the advantage of providing suitable cycles and organizing the accommodation along the route. Tour operators often arrange for luggage to be carried, so that riders need not be weighed down by tents and other items.

Tandem bicycle, popular in Denmark

There are several places in Denmark where visitors can hire a bicycle; the local tourist office will be able to help. Larger towns usually have free city bikes available for short rides.

Finding someone to fix a bike is easy. Most cycling maps include details of cycle workshops where minor repairs such as mending a punctured tyre or fixing a spoke can be carried out quickly and cheaply.

Golf

Denmark has more than 100 golf courses. Most of them will honour the membership card of your own club, and most clubs admit novices as well as experienced players. Green fees vary but are fairly reasonable, averaging around 300 Dkr per day (370 Dkr at weekends). Buying a package golfing holiday that also includes accommodation can work out cheaper. Golf clubs generally hire and sell golfing equipment and also run improvement courses for all levels. The **Dansk Golf Union** can provide information about the country's golf courses.

Sailing

The waters around Denmark are dotted with islands, many of which have harbours in which to moor a boat. The coastline is highly diversified and there is plenty of scope for sailing at all levels of ability. Storms and gales are uncommon in bodies of water such as the sea between Zealand and Lolland as well as many of the fjords and these calm, forgiving conditions are perfect for novices and less experienced sailors.

If you wish to hire a sailing boat in Denmark, local tourist offices will be able to point you in the direction of a reputable company.

Sailing boats, a common sight on Danish waters

Coastal dunes, an ideal area for walks

All craft intended for charter must carry a seaworthiness certificate issued by the State Inspectorate of Shipping. When chartering a boat, it is important to ask to see this certificate before sailing.

Boat Cruises

Boat cruises are popular in Denmark and depart regularly from Nyhavn in Copenhagen, bound for the islands situated in the Øresund (Sound). It is even possible to book a cruise on a reconstructed Viking ship. Stationed in Roskilde harbour are several small ships that are faithful copies of 10th-century wooden Viking boats and these embark on regular cruises. Cruises of the lakes and rivers are another option. One popular jaunt is to jump aboard one of the small ships that depart from Ry harbour on a cruise along the Gudena river. Another alternative is to take a trip back in time on the *Hjejlen*, a paddle steamer that travels daily from Silkeborg to Himmelbjerget. A trip on one of the many ferries that link the various islands can be considered a pleasant cruise too.

Walking

Walking trails in Denmark are clearly signposted, with information boards giving the names of the destination points and the length of the route. In Denmark the public have conditional access to the coast even if the land is privately owned. Many signed walks follow the shoreline and are especially beautiful. The country's forests are also good for walking. Some marked trails lead across private land. When this is the case it is important to stick to the trail, otherwise walkers risk being arrested (although this is highly unlikely). Many routes are through nature reserves and may be marked with the sign of a daisy. Tourist offices and libraries often have brochures listing some of Denmark's best walks. The town of Viborg has a walking festival along old drove and army roads.

Denmark's hostels and inns are used to catering for the needs of walkers, as are the country's camp sites. **Dansk Vandrelaug** (The Danish Ramblers Association) provides maps (in Danish) for visitors.

Swimming

Denmark has many beautiful beaches. Most are ideal for swimming although the temperature can be on the chilly side. Even in summer, the water temperature rarely rises above 17° C (63° F). As an alternative, virtually all cities and major towns have swimming baths, which are well maintained.

Children may enjoy a visit to one of the many water parks, such as **Fårup Sommerland** *(see p208)* and **Joboland** *(see p230)*, which have splash pools and waterslides.

DIRECTORY

VisitDenmark
W **visitdenmark.com**

Sporting Organizations

Dansk Idræt Forbund
Idrættens Hus, Brøndby Stadion 20, 2605 Brøndby.
Tel 43 26 26 26.
W **dif.dk**

Horse Riding

Dansk Ride Forbund
Idrættens Hus, Brøndby Stadion 20, 2605 Brøndby.
Tel 43 26 28 28.
W **rideforbund.dk**

Prærievognsferie Og Hesteudlejning
Holmdrup Huse 3, 5881 Skårup, Funen.
Tel 62 23 18 25.

Fishing

Danmarks Sportsfiskerforbund
Skyltevej 4, Vingsted, 7182 Bredsten.
Tel 75 82 06 99.
W **sportsfiskeren.dk**

T-248 Skagerak
Vorupør Strand, 7700 Thisted.
Tel 97 92 07 41.
W **skagerak-t248.dk**

Cycling Tours

Bornholm Velcomstcenter (Visitors Centre)
Nordre Kystvej 3, 3700 Rønne. **Tel** 56 95 95 00.
W **bornholminfo.dk**

Dansk Cyklist Forbund
Rømersgade 5, 1362 Cph K. **Tel** 33 32 31 21.
W **dcf.dk**

Golf

Dansk Golf Union
Idrættens Hus, Brøndby Stadion 20, 2605 Brøndby.
Tel 43 26 27 00.
W **danskgolfunion.dk**
W **golf.dk**

Walking

Dansk Vandrelaug
Kultorvet 7, DK-1175 Copenhagen K.
Tel 33 12 11 65.
W **dvl.dk**

TOUCAN

SURVIVAL GUIDE

PRACTICAL INFORMATION

Large numbers of holiday-makers travel to Denmark each year, drawn by the wide range of attractions and accommodation on offer. The peak season is relatively short, however, since the winter months are cold and daylight hours few. The country has a good tourism infrastructure, with a network of efficient tourist offices. Information on destinations and attractions is easy to obtain, especially on the Internet, and planning a trip should be a straightforward undertaking, since most hotels and attractions have excellent English websites. Denmark's hotels and inns are welcoming and clean, as are the many good-value camp sites and hostels. The major museums and galleries display world-class collections, accompanied by English-language displays, guidebooks and even digital guides and apps to help visitors get the most from the exhibits.

When to Go

The best time to visit Denmark is during the milder months (mid-April–mid-October) or in December, when most of the country's towns and villages sparkle with festive Christmas decorations. The ideal time for cycling holidays is between mid-June and late August.

Most Danes go on holiday between late June and mid-August, to coincide with school vacations. During this time the camp sites, beaches and resorts tend to be full. A good time to visit, then, is in mid-August, after the schools have reopened – the beaches and attractions are less busy, but the days are still warm.

Visas and Passports

EU citizens do not need a visa to enter Denmark; visitors from other parts of the world should check if their country has reciprocal agreements on waiving visa requirements. Visitors not obliged to have a visa are allowed to stay in Denmark for up to 90 days.

Contact your embassy in an emergency, such as the loss of your passport or a motoring accident. However, it is worth noting that embassies expect you to have your own travel insurance *(see p291)*, and they are not likely to help if you have been jailed or fined for committing a crime. Most embassies are located in Copenhagen, but there are some in other cities too – visit the **Ministry of Foreign Affairs** website for a list.

Customs Information

The customs allowance for EU visitors travelling to Denmark is 800 cigarettes and 10 litres of spirits; for people travelling from non-EU countries, it is 200 cigarettes and 1 litre of spirits. All food articles must be vacuum-packed by the manufacturer. Commercial quantities and presents of a value exceeding 1,350 Dkr are subject to customs duty.

There is no limit – within reason – on how much alcohol or tobacco EU citizens can take out of the country. US citizens are allowed to take home $400 worth of goods before duty must be paid.

Tourist Information

Most Danish towns have tourist information centres with multilingual staff. They can supply maps and information on local sights, festivals and events; they will also hand out free pamphlets containing information on hotels, cycling routes, walking trails and disabled access to various attractions. In smaller towns with no tourist centres, visitors can usually get this type of information from their hotel. The official website of the Danish Tourist Board, **VisitDenmark**, is also very useful.

Aarhus, Denmark's second-largest city, relies heavily on QR tags and the Internet to deliver information to tourists.

Tourist information at the Shopping Street in Aarhus

Admission Prices and Opening Hours

Some museums and historic attractions, especially those in Copenhagen, waive admission charges once a week (usually on Wednesday). In larger cities, visitors can purchase passes that combine reduced entry fees to museums and other attractions with unlimited use of public transport *(see p302)*.

Many museums and galleries are closed on Monday, while some art museums, such as Louisiana and Aarhus' AroS, stay open late on selected days.

Shops are usually open 10am–6pm; on Friday they close at 7 or 8pm, and on Saturday any time between noon and 4pm. Most shops are now open on Sundays too, though the opening hours can vary from store to store. In tourist resorts, shops are generally open seven days a week during July and August.

Sign for a historical site

◀ A dramatic landscape of the southern Greenland fjords, Prince Christian Sound

Danish churches are open only on certain days and between certain hours, so it is wise to check in advance. Note that churches are closed to sightseers during services.

Tourist attractions often make seasonal changes to their opening hours. Some attractions and seaside restaurants close completely in January and February, while many restaurants and cafés in Copenhagen close in July.

Travellers with Special Needs

With a little forward planning, travellers with special needs should find a holiday in Denmark straightforward and enjoyable. Modern holiday centres, hotels, museums and other attractions generally provide wheelchair-accessible ramps and lifts, as well as facilities for the visually and hearing-impaired. However, hotels, museums and restaurants located in older buildings may not have such resources, and so you could find you have to negotiate stairs at street level and face space restrictions. It pays to check well in advance, either online or by phone.

Travelling with Children

Hotels, holiday centres and cottage-letting agencies in Denmark will often provide travel cots, high chairs, and garden toys such as swings. Taking children to a restaurant is perfectly acceptable, though it's best to go before 8pm.

Restaurants generally have children's menus, high chairs and changing facilities.

Most buses and stations on the public transport network are equipped with lifts that allow easy access for buggies.

Travelling on a Budget

Farm holidays and B&Bs offer fairly cheap accommodation, as do camp sites and hostels. YHA hostels have private rooms as well as dorms, and camp sites often offer accommodation in wooden chalets, a cheaper alternative to summer houses. Note that there is a charge at all Danish official camp sites; a free solution is to pitch a tent at a "nature camp" with only basic amenities (running water and a public toilet). See the VisitDenmark website for more information. **CouchSurfing** is free of charge, and is also a fun way to meet local people.

Savings can be made on train travel by booking tickets well in advance at "orange" saver rates *(see p298)*. Alternatively, you can travel around the country by sharing a private car ride. Visit the **GoMore** website for a list of destinations and quotes.

Responsible Tourism

Denmark has always been progressive when it comes to environmental issues. Any bottles marked with the recycling logo can be placed in the machines *(flaskeautomat)* found in supermarket foyers. Press the green button for your receipt, which can then be redeemed inside the shop for cash or goods. Other glass can be placed in the green recycling containers outside.

Many hotels and holiday centres are **Green Key**-certified, meaning they have adopted a number of eco-friendly initiatives. Organic, or *økologisk*, food is widely available, and there are also some organic restaurants. "Klima+" restaurants combine organic food with a policy of reducing carbon emissions.

Certified organic vegetables for sale at a market stall

DIRECTORY

Visas and Passports

Ministry of Foreign Affairs
W **http://um.dk**

Tourist Information

Aalborg Tourist Office
Kjellerup Torv 5, Niveau 13, 9000 Aalborg.
Tel 99 31 75 00.
W **visitaalborg.com**

Bornholms Visitor Centre
Ndr Kystvej 3, 3770 Rønne.
Tel 56 95 95 00.
W **bornholm.info**

Copenhagen Visitor Centre
Vesterbrogade 4A, 1620 Copenhagen V.
Tel 70 22 24 42.
W **visitcopenhagen.com**

Odense Tourist Office
Rådhuset, 5000 Odense C.
Tel 63 75 75 39.
W **visitodense.com**

VisitDenmark
Islands Brygge 43, 2300 Copenhagen S.
Tel 32 88 99 00.
W **visitdenmark.com**

Travelling on a Budget

CouchSurfing
W **couchsurfing.org**

GoMore
W **gomore.dk**

Responsible Tourism

Green Key
W **green-key.org**

Personal Security and Health

Denmark is a safe country with low levels of crime. Even in the larger cities there is little likelihood of visitors encountering problems. The chances of falling victim to crime can be further minimized by not carrying excessive amounts of cash and by keeping credit cards, mobile phones and other valuables hidden away. In the event of a crime or accident, the Danish police and emergency services work very efficiently. It is also worth asking passers-by or witnesses to the event for their help. As a rule, Danes will not refuse such a request.

Ambulance with its lights on, attending to an emergency

White police patrol car parked in front of a shopping centre in Odense

Police

During the summer season the Danish **police** are dressed in blue shirts and black trousers; in winter they also wear black jackets. Road police generally wear all-in-one leather suits and ride large white motorcycles. Ordinary police patrol cars are white with the word "POLITI" in blue lettering, while the cars driven by the criminal division are dark blue. Criminal division police usually wear civilian clothes and will show their ID cards when required.

The majority of Danish policemen and policewomen will have at least a working knowledge of the English language. In most cases they will be able to provide some assistance, such as giving you directions or helping you contact a breakdown service.

Although they are not part of the police force, traffic wardens, are entitled to check if someone has a valid parking ticket and can impose a fine for illegal parking *(see pp301 and 303)*. Traffic wardens in Copenhagen wear dark green jackets.

What to be aware of

The summer months and the run-up to Christmas are the times when thieves are most likely to be operating, especially in busy places. Visitors are advised to be on their guard, particularly in the main train stations, such as Copenhagen's Central Station, as well as in the prime shopping areas. Valuables should be deposited at the hotel reception or kept in the safe in your room; money and documents should be carried under clothing rather than in handbags, backpacks or trouser pockets. Make sure all valuable items are out of sight if left in a car.

In an Emergency

In the event of a road accident, life-threatening situation, fire, attack or any other predicament that requires immediate intervention by the **emergency services**, visitors should call 112. This toll-free line is staffed by qualified operators who are able to speak several foreign languages, including English; they will determine which service should be sent to the scene of the incident.

Emergency telephones installed along the hard shoulders of motorways can be used to report a breakdown or accident. Special telephones found in S-tog railway stations and on metro lines enable passengers to contact railway duty officers when needed.

An accident or mugging should be reported to the police. The victim and any witnesses to the incident are entitled to give evidence in their native language.

Consulates and embassies can help to contact a visitor's family in the event of an incident, and they may also be able to provide financial help or advance the money for a ticket home.

Lost and Stolen Property

Any theft of money, travel documents, credit cards or other valuables, as well as any theft from a car or hotel room, should be reported immediately at the local police station, where an officer will issue a note confirming that the crime has been reported. This note may well be required when filling out an insurance claim or visiting an embassy or consulate to obtain a temporary passport.

If you have lost any personal belongings, enquire at the **lost property office** *(hittegods)* closest to the area where they went missing. There are *hittegods* at all local police stations. Any items left behind on a train, S-tog or metro should be reported to the duty personnel at the station; if lost on a bus, report it to the passenger service office of the appropriate bus company. Lost or stolen credit cards should be reported to the card issuer as soon as possible. Keep the relevant telephone numbers separately from your cards.

The entrance to a hospital in Copenhagen

Hospitals and Pharmacies

Addresses of doctors and hospitals can be obtained from hotel receptionists and camp site managers, or found in a telephone directory. Most Danish doctors speak English.

Note that not all hospitals in Denmark have an emergency department, and that the old word for emergency room, *skadestue*, is being replaced by *akutklinik*.

Pharmacies *(apotek)* are usually open from 9am to 5:30pm on weekdays and until 1pm on Saturdays. In larger towns there is always one pharmacy that is open 24 hours a day; the address will be displayed on the doors or windows of any pharmacy. You will usually have to call or buzz at a side entrance outside of normal opening hours (after 8pm Monday to Friday, after 4pm on Saturday and all day Sunday). A small surcharge is generally added to the cost of non-prescription medicines purchased during these times.

If you require constant medication, be sure to take an adequate supply with you – medicines can be expensive in Denmark. Controlled drugs require a doctor's prescription.

Minor Hazards

Travellers to Denmark do not require any special vaccinations. Mosquitoes can be a problem near large lakes in the summer; spray-on repellents can be bought in any pharmacy. Those on hiking or camping holidays should check regularly for blood-sucking ticks, especially on children; ticks must be removed completely and any subsequent redness treated promptly with antibiotics. Note that antiseptic lotions, such as Savlon, are not available in Denmark, so it is advisable to bring some with you.

It is safe to drink tap water in Denmark, and stomach upsets are uncommon.

Travel and Health Insurance

Anyone with a medical emergency is entitled to free treatment in hospitals and doctor's surgeries in Denmark, provided that the person has not arrived in the country specifically for that treatment and is unfit to return home. EU visitors in possession of a European Health Insurance Card (EHIC) are covered by Danish national health insurance. Greenland and the Faroe Islands are not part of the EHIC scheme. Non-EU citizens must have health insurance.

Travel insurance is advisable for all visitors, as it can make it easier to get treatment and should cover the cost of an ambulance (which the patient is responsible for) or an emergency flight home.

A pharmacy in Copenhagen

DIRECTORY

In an Emergency

Emergency Services
Tel 112 (toll free).

Police
Tel 114 (toll free).

Lost And Stolen Property

Lost Property Office, (Copenhagen)
Copenhagen police station, Slotsherrensvej 113, 2720 Vanløse.
Tel 38 74 88 22.

Hospitals

Aarhus Universitets Hospital
Nørrebrogade 44, 8000 Aarhus C.
Tel 78 45 00 00.

Amager Hospital (Copenhagen)
Italiensvej 1, 2300 Copenhagen S.
Tel 32 34 32 34.

Odense Universitets Hospital
Sønder Blvd 29, 5000 Odense C.
Tel 65 41 22 71.

24-Hour Pharmacies

Aalborg Budolfi Apotek
Algade 60, 9000 Aalborg.
Tel 98 12 06 77.

Aarhus Løve Apotek
Store Torv 5, 8000 Aarhus C.
Tel 86 12 00 22.

Copenhagen Steno Apotek
Vesterbrogade 6C, 1620 Copenhagen V. **Tel** 33 14 82 66.

Copenhagen Sønderbro Apotek
Amagerbrogade 158, 2300 Copenhagen S. **Tel** 32 58 01 40.

Odense Apoteket Ørnen
Filosofhaven 38B, 5000 Odense C.
Tel 66 12 29 70.

Banks and Currency

Visitors arriving in Denmark from outside the EU are obliged to have adequate means to support themselves for the duration of their stay. Immigration authorities are usually satisfied with a verbal assurance regarding a visitor's credit card limit. While credit cards can be used almost anywhere, it's worth having some Danish kroner to hand for buying small treats like ice creams, or to use on public transport and when travelling to the more remote islands.

A branch of Jyske Bank in Copenhagen

Banks and Bureaux de Change

Banks in Denmark are open from 10am until 4pm Monday to Friday, with extended opening hours on Thursday (until 6pm). Banks are closed on Saturday, Sunday and public holidays.

Be aware that banks in Denmark's smaller towns generally do not carry cash and will be able to provide money only from the ATM (Automated Teller Machine).

Foreign currency can be exchanged at many places throughout the country. Exchange booths at Copenhagen Airport are open most of the day. Hotels can also exchange money, though they offer the least favourable rates. Banks and special automatic money-exchange machines offer slightly better rates, but they also charge a commission. The best deals can generally be obtained at branches of **Forex**, since they do not charge a commission. In addition, their opening hours are usually more flexible than those of the banks. Exchange rates are usually displayed by the door.

Anyone who wishes to bring more than 40,000 Dkr into the country or make a deposit of a similar sum must have a certificate confirming the legality of the money's source.

ATMs

All Danish banks have cash machines from which kroner can be withdrawn with a credit or debit card. ATMs are widespread in the towns and cities, and they all provide directions in English, as well as in a number of other European languages.

ATMs are not so readily available in more remote parts of Denmark, including some of its smaller islands, camp sites and summer house areas; anyone planning to visit these parts should have enough Danish kroner to last until they return to a larger town.

Credit and Debit Cards

Visitors to Denmark should have no problem using credit cards such as MasterCard, VISA or Eurocard, though some restaurants may charge a small fee for non-Danish cards. American Express and Diners Club are less readily accepted. Be aware that some shops may refuse to take credit cards as payment for low-cost items, while others accept only a Danish debit card called Dankort.

In many restaurants and shops, staff will use a reader to enter a card's data and ask the customer to sign a receipt or key in the card's PIN code.

In order to ensure your card works overseas, contact your bank or credit card provider before travelling.

If your credit or debit card is lost or stolen, report it to your card issuer immediately.

DIRECTORY

Banks

Danske Bank
Højbro Plads 5, 1200 Copenhagen K. **Map** 3 C1.
Tel 45 12 45 50.
W danskebank.dk

Jyske Bank
Vesterbrogade 9, 1780 Copenhagen V. **Map** 3 A2.
Tel 89 89 00 10.
W jyskebank.dk

Nordea
Kongens Nytorv 28, 1050 Copenhagen K. **Map** 4 D1.
Tel 70 33 33 33. **W nordea.dk**

Sydbank A/S
Kongens Nytorv 30, 1050 Copenhagen K. **Map** 4 D1.
Tel 74 37 78 00. **W sydbank.dk**

Bureaux de Change

Forex Aalborg
Ved Stranden 22.
Tel 98 18 97 00.

Forex Aarhus
Banegårdspladsen 20.
Tel 86 80 03 40.

Forex Copenhagen
Nørre Voldgade 90. **Map** 1 B5.
Tel 33 32 81 03.
Hovedbanegården.
Map 3 A3. **Tel** 33 11 22 25.

Forex Odense
Banegardscentret, Østre Stationsvej 27. **Tel** 66 11 66 18.

Currency

Denmark is one of the few EU countries to reject joining the European monetary union, keeping the krone (plural: kroner) instead. In large towns and tourist resorts, however, prices are often quoted in both kroner and euros. The Danish krone (or crown) is divided into 100 øre. Coins come in denominations of 50 øre, and 1, 2, 5, 10 and 20 kroner. Notes come in denominations of 50, 100, 200, 500 and 1,000 kroner. The Danish krone is written as DKK in most international money markets, but as Dkr in northern Europe and simply as kr in Denmark.

The Faroe Islands have their own version of the Danish krone, known as the Faroese krona, which has exactly the same value as its Danish counterpart. Danish currency is accepted on the Faroe Islands, but the Faroese krona is not accepted in Denmark, so exchange any Faroese krona notes at a bureau de change.

The Danish krone is the official currency in Greenland.

Be aware that while all Scandinavian currencies are called krone or krona, they are not interchangeable. Swedish kronar and Norwegian kroner, for example, are not valid currencies in Denmark.

50 kroner

Bank notes

Danish bank notes differ from each other in terms of size and colour. The lowest denomination bank note in circulation is the violet-blue 50-Dkr note. The largest denomination is the red-and-green 1,000-Dkr note.

100 kroner

200 kroner

500 kroner

Coins

The 10- and most of the 20-Dkr coins are golden in colour, with the queen's image on the reverse. The 1-, 2- and 5-Dkr coins are nickel with a hole in the centre. The 50-øre coin is copper-coloured.

50 øre

1 krone

20 kroner

10 kroner

5 kroner

2 kroner

Communications and Media

Danish postal services are very efficient. Letters and postcards take one to two days to reach their destinations within the country, and about two to four days within Europe. Telephoning abroad is straightforward, although public telephones are becoming increasingly rare due to the popularity of mobile phones. Nevertheless, visitors should be able to find a public telephone at a post office, railway station, camp site reception or hotel lobby. Making calls from your hotel room usually incurs a steep fee, so check in advance.

A public telephone that accepts both coins and phone cards

Dialling Codes

- To make an international call, dial 00, the country code, the area code and the number.
- Calling Denmark from abroad: 0045
- Country codes: UK 44; US/Canada 1.
- Directory enquiries: 118 (inland), 80 60 40 55 (overseas).

International and Local Telephone Calls

Denmark has no area codes, and all numbers consist of eight digits, generally written and read out by Danes in blocks of two. Numbers starting with 20 through to 31 are mobile numbers, while those starting with 32 through to 39 are Copenhagen landline numbers. Numbers starting with 80 are toll-free, while premium rate lines start with 90. Danes refer to land lines as *fastnet*.

Prepaid phone cards for calling overseas are available in many kiosks in the larger cities, and they offer better value for money than a **Lycos** (Denmark's main telecommunications company) phone card. Always state where you're calling for the best rates to that country. Prepaid phone cards can also be used with mobile phones.

Calling from a payphone is more expensive than using a private phone, but cheaper than phoning from a hotel room. The minimum charge for a call from a public phone is 5 Dkr, and denominations of 1, 2, 5 and 10 Dkr are accepted; many payphones also take euros. All calls, including local calls, are charged by the minute. Clear instructions on how to make a call are displayed in English, and a list of dialling codes for other countries is usually available.

Skype is a free alternative to costly international phone calls. Anyone with a computer or phone with Internet access can use Skype, as long as they have registered for an account.

Using a mobile phone while cycling in Denmark

Mobile Phones

Most mobile phone networks provide the facilities for making international calls. Before departure, make sure that your phone will work in Denmark. If not, it is sometimes possible to get an upgrade for the duration of your holiday. When using a prepaid mobile phone in Denmark, you should check whether your package covers international roaming. Danish mobile phone providers include Lycos, **Telia** and **Oister**.

Making calls from Denmark is more expensive than calling from home; incoming calls will also be charged at a higher rate. Receiving texts from abroad is free, but sending them is usually subject to a substantial fee.

Public Telephones

The increase of mobile phones in Denmark means that public telephone boxes are not as common as they used to be. However, those that do remain – usually outside train stations – are well maintained. There are two types of phone booths: those that accept both coins and cards, and those that take cards only. Card phones also accept credit cards. Phone cards are available in about 1,500 outlets, including post offices and many shops.

Internet

Denmark moved swiftly into the broadband era, and free Wi-Fi connections are commonplace – not only in most hotel rooms (even the cheaper ones), but also in cafés and on some public transport, including the high-speed ICE train from Copenhagen to Aarhus, the regional S-tog in Copenhagen and some buses. Wi-Fi is also available throughout Copenhagen Airport. If you plan on using your own laptop, be sure to bring an adaptor suitable for Denmark's plug sockets and 230 voltage.

Most hotels in Danish holiday resorts can provide Internet access at reception. Many youth hostels and camp sites also have computers with Internet access.

The number of Internet cafés has declined, due to Wi-Fi becoming more widespread, but, these can still be found in Danish towns and cities. Free Wi-Fi hotspots are available throughout Denmark. You can search for locations using **openwifi**.

Postal and Courier Services

Danish post offices are indicated by the word "POST" in white letters on a red background. Most post offices are open 10am–5pm Monday to Friday (until 6pm on Thursday) and 10am–noon on Saturday. You can post parcels, send registered letters and collect *poste restante* mail from all of Denmark's post offices.

Stamps can be purchased at post offices, in many souvenir shops and from vending machines. A letter sent to a European country requires a "Europa" tariff postage stamp.

Danish post boxes are painted red. They feature the crown and trumpet insignia of the national postal service and display the time of the next collection. International mail sent from Copenhagen should leave the country within 24 hours.

Danish postal services' logo

When posting something to a Danish address, you should include the name of the recipient, street, house number, town and a four-digit post code. It is important to include the post code, since many Danish towns, as well as many streets in Copenhagen, have the same name. For details of post codes, visit the website of **Post Danmark**, the national postal service provider. The address for an apartment may sometimes include the floor and staircase, as well as the number of the flat within a building. For example, the address may be written as "Bjergvej 20, 3.tv", where "3" stands for 3rd floor and "tv" stands for *til venstre*, meaning "to the left".

Express courier services such as **DHL** and **UPS** usually provide a telephone booking service in English.

Bright-red Danish letterbox, showing collection times

Newspapers and Magazines

Most of the major foreign papers, including US and UK dailies such as *The Times*, *The Guardian* and the *Wall Street Journal*, can be found at train station kiosks and in some of the main newsagents in Copenhagen, and other large towns. Magazines such as *Time* and *The Economist* are also readily available. Libraries often provide free access to international newspapers.

Denmark's own press consists of about 50 regional and national daily newspapers. Of these, *Politiken* and *Jyllandsposten* have the largest circulation. The weekly *Copenhagen Post* has national news and a pull-out listings section in English; it can be found at kiosks and newsagents in Copenhagen, as well as in many cafés, public libraries and tourist offices.

DIRECTORY

International and Local Telephone Calls

Lycos
Tel 70 70 30 30.

Skype
W skype.com

Mobile Phones

Oister
Tel 70 31 30 70.
W oister.dk

Telia
Tel 80 40 40 40.
http://telia.dk

Internet

openwifi
W openwifi.dk

Postal And Courier Services

DHL
Tel 70 34 53 45.
W dhl.dk

Post Danmark
Tel 70 70 70 30.
W postdanmark.dk

UPS
Tel 86 75 29 24 (Aarhus).
Tel 35 25 80 80 (Zealand).
W ups.com

Television and Radio

All television in Denmark is broadcast digitally. There are two public-service channels, DR1 and DR2, screening news and current affairs along with light entertainment. Other channels are more commercial in character, showing a large amount of soap operas and comedies. Many US and British programmes are shown with Danish subtitles. English-language news is often available on cable and satellite TV.

Many summer houses have satellite dishes that receive German, Norwegian and Swedish channels. German channels are largely available in Southern Jutland, while viewers in Northern Jutland should be able to pick up Swedish and Norwegian TV.

TRAVEL INFORMATION

Flights to Denmark from most parts of northern Europe are frequent. Planes from over 100 cities worldwide land at Copenhagen, and the airport receives more than 20 million passengers a year. Frequent connections are available on internal flights. Fewer people arrive by train and ferry, although ferries are popular with visitors from elsewhere in Scandinavia. Ease of travel has increased with the construction of the Storebælt (Great Belt) Bridge, linking Zealand and Funen, and the fixed-link Øresund Bridge between Zealand and Sweden, but many of the smaller Danish islands can be reached only by ferry. Travelling on the mainland and around the major islands is easy, thanks to a network of well-maintained motorways and railways, and an efficient coach service.

Arriving by Air

Most visitors to Denmark arrive at Copenhagen Airport, located 12 km (7 miles) southeast of the city centre. **SAS** connects Copenhagen to most European capitals, and it also has non-stop flights from New York and Chicago. From Australasia the best connections to Denmark are via Bangkok. Other airlines serving Copenhagen include **British Airways**, **Norwegian**, **bmi** (from Edinburgh and Glasgow) and **easyJet** (from London Gatwick, London Stansted and Manchester, as well as other airports in Europe). **Ryanair** has daily flights from London Stansted to Aarhus and Billund, and also to Malmø, in Sweden, with a special connecting coach to Copenhagen.

Jutland can be reached via the international airports of Aarhus, Aalborg and Billund. **Aarhus Airport**, which is 40 km (25 miles) northeast of the city, receives flights from London Stansted and Barcelona among others. Buses link the airport to the city, dropping passengers off at Aarhus's railway station. The journey time is about 45 minutes.

Billund Airport (for LEGOLAND®) is the largest international airport in West Denmark, and it receives flights from many European cities, including London (Stansted and City), Frankfurt and Amsterdam. Bus routes operate from here to Vejle, Horsens, Aarhus, Kolding and Esbjerg.

Aalborg Airport offers easy access to the very north of the country and receives flights from such places as London Gatwick, Berlin and Oslo. An express bus links the airport with the city centre.

Copenhagen Airport

The country's main airport is **Copenhagen Airport** (formerly known as Kastrup), situated on Amager Island, a short way from the city centre. It has four terminals: three for international flights and one for domestic flights. Terminal 4, which is known as CphGo, is used exclusively by easyJet and other low-cost airlines.

Sleek, streamlined interior of Copenhagen Airport

Bilingual information board at Copenhagen Airport

Copenhagen Airport has helpful staff and excellent information services. Facilities include shops and restaurants, cash machines and lockers. Cars can be hired at terminals 1 and 3.

The CPH Advantage programme is available to all passengers and allows free Wi-Fi access through all of Copenhagen Airport. Passengers flying business class can also enjoy the CPH Apartment, located within the transit hall, for free Wi-Fi, printing and recharging facilities, and light meals and drinks at a nominal fee.

Special assistance for passengers with disabilities is provided by **Falck**. However, note that this service should be booked in advance either via the airport website or by calling Falck directly.

A fast and economical train service runs every 10 minutes from the airport's Terminal 3 to Central Station in Copenhagen (a journey of about 12 minutes). Trains run throughout the day, as well as during the night, albeit less frequently. Many trains are listed as running to Helsingør because they continue up the coast

SAS aircraft on the tarmac at Aalborg Airport

after stopping at Copenhagen's Central Station. Passengers should be aware that trains from Copenhagen Airport also run in the other direction, to Sweden, so it's important to find the correct platform.

The metro also runs from the airport to the city centre, taking about 15 minutes and stopping at Kongens Nytorv and Nørreport stations. It's also possible to take the bus, which drops passengers off at Rådhuspladsen. The price of a bus ticket is the same as the train (36 Dkr), however, and the journey time is nearly three times as long.

Visitors with a lot of heavy luggage will find a taxi rank by the exit of Terminal 3. Rates to the city centre start around 250 Dkr and fares can be paid by credit card.

Tickets and Fares

Intense competition, rising airport taxes and CO_2 tariffs mean that airlines vary their prices continuously and it is difficult to be precise about fares. Booking in advance is recommended, as travellers who book at short notice invariably pay higher prices. It is always worth shopping around, and often the best deals can be found online.

It is possible to purchase a one-way, non-refundable ticket on a low-cost airline for as little as €35–45 (including taxes) from London, Berlin and other European capitals. Direct return flights with SAS from New York or Chicago to Copenhagen cost around US$700, with no refunds or flexibility.

Most airlines connecting Denmark to other European destinations charge for light snacks. SAS still allows one piece of 23-kg (50-lb) luggage free of charge, as well as offering discounts to people over 65 and to children and students. Low-cost airlines offer good deals to people who bring only an item of hand luggage.

Internal Flights

Air travel within Denmark is fairly inexpensive, as long as you book your tickets a couple of weeks in advance of your departure date. The major domestic carrier is SAS.

A route that is particularly worth recommending is the one from Copenhagen to Aalborg (a 5-hour journey by car). Connections are frequent, especially on weekdays. Another important domestic hub is **Karup Airport**, which is located in the flatlands around Herning, in Jutland.

On Arrival

All visitors from EU countries must have their passport or ID card ready for exiting the arrivals area; this is usually a fairly quick process. Citizens of many non- EU countries, such as the USA and Australia, do not need a visa to enter Denmark, but they may need to show a return ticket and evidence of sufficient funds to cover the duration of their planned stay in the country.

SAS

Logo of SAS (Scandinavian Airlines)

DIRECTORY

Arriving by Air

Aalborg Airport
Ny Lufthavnsvej 100, 9400 Nørresundby.
Tel 98 17 11 44.
W aal.dk

Aarhus Airport
Ny Lufthavnsvej 24, 8560 Kolind.
Tel 87 75 70 00.
W aar.dk

Billund Airport
Passagerterminalen 10, 7190 Billund. **Tel** 76 50 50 50.
W bll.dk

bmi (British Midland)
Tel 0844 417 2600 (UK).
W flybmi.com

British Airways
Tel 0844 493 0787 (UK).
W britishairways.com

easyJet
Tel 0843 506 9856 (UK).
W easyjet.com

Norwegian
Tel 0843 378 0888 (UK).
W norwegian.com

Ryanair
Tel 0871 246 0000 (UK).
W ryanair.com

SAS
Denmark **Tel** 70 10 20 00.
Ireland **Tel** 01 844 5440.
UK **Tel** 0871 226 7760.
USA/Canada **Tel** 1800 221 2350 (toll free).
W flysas.com

Copenhagen Airport

Copenhagen Airport
Lufthavnsboulevarden 6, 2770 Kastrup.
Tel 32 31 32 31.
W cph.dk

Falck
Tel 70 33 33 11.

Internal Flights

Karup Airport
N.O. Hansens Vej 4, 7470 Karup J.
Tel 97 10 06 10.
W krp.dk

Travelling Around by Train, Coach and Ferry

Danish trains are mostly run by the Danish State Railway (DSB) and Arriva; they are reliable and fast, making it possible to travel between Copenhagen and Aarhus in under 3 hours. Coaches run between the large cities and to other destinations in Europe; they take longer than the train, but they are cheaper. A network of ferries provides a convenient way to travel to some of Denmark's many islands, including the Faroe Islands, as well as between Denmark and countries such as England, Germany, Sweden, Norway and Iceland.

Arriving by Train

The most common railway routes into Denmark are from Germany to Jutland or via the Puttgarden-Rødby ferry from Hamburg to Lolland and up to Zealand. Many people also travel to Zealand by train from Sweden across the Øresund Bridge. Travel from the UK is generally via the Netherlands and through Germany.

Trans-European trains are fast and efficient, particularly the high-speed ICE services between Copenhagen and Gothenburg and Stockholm, in Sweden; and between Copenhagen and Hamburg and Berlin, in Germany.

Copenhagen's Central Station, in the heart of the city, is the main point of arrival for international rail services.

Main Stations

Danish railway stations are clean and well maintained. Facilities often include heated waiting rooms and snack bars. Copenhagen's Central Station has shops, ATMs, cafés, a currency exchange, a post office and a police station. Aarhus's Central Station is set in the middle of a shopping mall.

Domestic Trains

DSB's extensive network covers both local and long-distance lines. Long-distance trains, such as those that run between Copenhagen and Aarhus, are modern, safe and stylish. Seats are arranged in pairs facing each other. Above each seat is a reading light and, often, individual music jacks for headphones and power supply sockets for laptop computers. Many trains have Wi-Fi connections for an additional charge (29 Dkr); trains with Internet access are marked with a white logo on a dark background and the word "Internet". Intercity trains also offer payphones, baby-changing facilities and even children's play areas. Information displayed above each seat indicates whether a seat has been reserved and to which station. In some parts of the train, known as *stille zoner*, silence must be maintained, and the use of mobile phones is prohibited. On many routes, DSB also operates "business class" carriages, which supply passengers with Wi-Fi, free drinks, snacks and papers.

Local trains, many of which have double-decker carriages, tend to be slower and have fewer facilities.

On some routes, such as from Copenhagen to Aarhus, Bornholm and Odden, it's possible to buy a combined train-and-ferry ticket.

Details of the network and main schedules are available from all DSB stations.

Train Tickets and Fares

Tickets can be bought at train stations or by calling the DSB reservation line or logging on to their website. The **Rejseplanen** website offers useful information on train and coach travel.

Train passes such as InterRail (available to European travellers) and Eurail (for visitors from outside Europe) give the holders substantial discounts on travel in Europe and a flexible range of options. There are many other rail concessions within Denmark, so it pays to ask about discounts for off-peak travel, family tickets and return fares. Often the best prices can be obtained by booking early and online. Those travelling between Copenhagen and Jutland and Funen can get the best savings by booking an "orange" ticket well in advance via the DSB website.

Children aged between 10 and 15 travel for half price; adults with valid tickets can take up to two children under 12 for free. Further information can be obtained from DSB ticket offices.

A coach is often the cheapest way to travel around Denmark

Travelling by Coach

Abildskou travels to Aarhus from Berlin via Hamburg Airport. It also operates daily services from Copenhagen to Aarhus and Aalborg. Tickets can be bought on board, but it is wise to reserve a seat in advance. Between Monday and Thursday, discounts are available for students and the over-65s. The bus leaves from outside **Valby Station**, arriving in Jutland via Odden or the Mols-Linien ferry *(see opposite)*.

Eurolines operates coach journeys from the larger Danish cities to various European destinations. In Copenhagen, they depart from Ingerslevsgade, below the Central Station.

A domestic ferry sailing between Denmark's islands

Arriving by Ferry

The major international ferry companies are **DFDS Seaways**, **Stena Line**, **Color Line**, **Fjord Line** and **Scandlines**.

The opening of the bridges spanning the Øresund (Sound) and the Storebælt has greatly reduced the demand for ferries between Zealand and Sweden, and between Zealand and Funen. However, ferry travel remains a popular option with many visitors.

Main Terminals

Most ferry travellers from the UK will arrive at the port of Esbjerg. Other main terminals are located in Copenhagen, just north of the city centre, and Frederikshavn and Hirtshals, in northern Jutland.

There is usually a bus link between the port and the town's train station, as well as a taxi rank and long- and short-stay car parking.

Ferry passengers will often be asked to check in at least 1 hour before departure.

Domestic Ferries

Ferry services, such as those provided by **Færgen**, play a vital role in Denmark's transport infrastructure, linking a number of islands. Some routes are very short, taking a matter of minutes, while the longest route (Køge–Bornholm) takes nearly 7 hours.

Ferries also link different parts of mainland Denmark. The **Mols-Linien**, from Odden in West Zealand to Ebeltoft or Aarhus in Jutland, is a popular alternative to the Storebælt Bridge, as it saves paying the bridge toll charge; the same is true of the **Kattegatruten** (Kalundborg–Aarhus). In the summer, **Smyril Line** runs two weekly ferries from Hirtshals to the Faroe Islands (journey time: a day and a half).

Most ferries take both foot passengers and cars, but there are some small islands where passenger-only ferries operate.

Ferry Tickets and Fares

Tickets for ferry services can usually be reserved online. Fares vary widely, depending on the season and the time of day. Substantial discounts are often available for students and young people with an international rail pass.

There is no need to book in advance on short routes, but it is compulsory to do so for longer journeys. Reservations should also be made when travelling at busy times (like Christmas) or with a vehicle.

International ferry connecting Denmark with Germany and Sweden

DIRECTORY

Domestic Trains

DSB
Tel 70 13 14 15.
W dsb.dk

Rejseplanen
W rejseplanen.dk

Travelling by Coach

Abildskou
Tel 70 21 08 88.
W abildskou.dk

Eurolines
Tel 33 88 70 00.
W eurolines-travel.com

Valby Station
Lyshøjgårdsvej, Cph V.

Arriving by Ferry

Color Line
Tel 99 56 19 00.
W colorline.com

DFDS Seaways
Tel 0871 522 9955 (UK).
W dfdsseaways.co.uk

Fjord Line
Tel 97 96 30 00.
W fjordline.com

Scandlines
Tel 33 15 15 15.
W scandlines.eu

Stena Line
Tel 96 20 02 00.
W stenaline.dk

Domestic Ferries

Aerøfærgenrne
Tel 62 52 40 00.
W aeroe-ferry.com

Færgen
Tel 70 23 15 15.
W faergen.com

Kattegatruten
Tel 38 11 12 22.
W kattegat-ruten.dk

Mols-Linien
Tel 70 10 14 18.
W mols-linien.dk

Smyril Line
Tel (+298) 34 59 00.
W smyrilline.com

Travelling by Car

Although Denmark's public transport network is excellent, a car can still be a convenient way of travelling, especially when visiting out-of-the-way places. For groups of three or four people, a car can also reduce travel costs significantly. Danish motorways are toll-free, but the Storebælt and Øresund bridges are not. The major roads are well signposted and of a good standard, and travelling over one of the bridges, such as the Storebælt Bridge between Zealand and Funen, can be a truly breathtaking experience.

Arriving by Car

Most people driving to Denmark arrive from Germany, the country's only land border, or from Sweden via the Øresund Bridge. Immigration checkpoints between EU countries have been abolished; however, there are still customs checkpoints at sea and land borders with Germany.

The main routes into the country are the E45, running from the German border all the way through Jutland up to Frederikshavn; the E47, which connects Lübeck and Hamburg with Lolland via the car ferry from Puttgarden to Rødby; and the E20, which travels over the Øresund Bridge from Malmø in Sweden. From 2020, the Puttgarden–Rødby ferry will be replaced by the Fehmarn Belt Fixed Link, which will connect the German island of Fehmarn, north of Lübeck, with Lolland.

What You Need

Anyone driving in Denmark must have all the relevant documents, including insurance and an international driver's licence. Check that you have breakdown cover with a company that has reciprocal arrangements with Denmark. **FDM**, the Danish motoring organization, can provide further information.

While it is not compulsory to carry a first-aid kit, it is a good idea to have one in the car, in addition to a car fire extinguisher, a torch and a tow rope. A warning triangle must be kept in the car to be used to warn other motorists in the event of a breakdown.

Motorway road signs

Roads and Tolls

Motorway signs in Denmark are colour-coded and easy to understand. The blue signs indicate the exits, while the green ones indicate the cities that can be reached along the motorway.

Denmark has five trans-European motorways. The E20 runs west–east from Esbjerg through Kolding and Odense, across the Storebælt and on to Køge and Copenhagen; the E29 links Hirtshals to Nørresundby; the E45 crosses the German border and links Kolding, Aarhus, Aalborg and Frederikshavn; the E47 links Helsingør, Copenhagen, Køge, Maribo and Rødby harbour; and the E55 runs between Helsingør, Copenhagen, Køge, Nykøbing F and Gedser.

Danish motorway sign

Part of the E20 consists of bridges over the Storebælt and Øresund (Sound). The toll charged to cross is collected at entry or exit points. The toll stations are equipped with card machines or manned by staff at busier times. The yellow *Manuel* lanes are for payment by credit card or cash.

The toll charge on the **Storebælt Bridge** is 235–370 Dkr, depending on the size and height of your vehicle. Similar toll charges apply for the **Øresund Bridge**. A BroBizz pass – a small transponder that you affix on the windscreen behind the rear-view mirror – can be used on both bridges and offers considerable discounts if you're making regular trips. Visit www.storebaelt.dk for more information.

Other major bridges in Denmark include the Farø Bridges that connect Zealand and Falster; the Lille Bælt Bridge, between Jutland and Funen; the Sallingsund Bridge, between Mors and Salling; and the bridge from Fyn to the island of Langeland. These bridges are toll-free.

A proposal that is likely to become reality within the next decade is the Kattegat Bridge, a bridge and tunnel connecting Kalundborg in Zealand with Aarhus via the island of Samsø.

Rules of the road

As in all continental European countries, the Danes drive on the right. Both cars and motorcycles must have dipped headlights during the day (cars from the UK will need to have their headlights adjusted). Seat belts must be worn at all times, and children under three must be in a child seat. When turning right, drivers must give way to cyclists on the inside.

The speed limit is usually 50 km/h (30 mph) in towns, 80 km/h (50 mph) on most roads and up to 130 km/h (80 mph) on motorways.

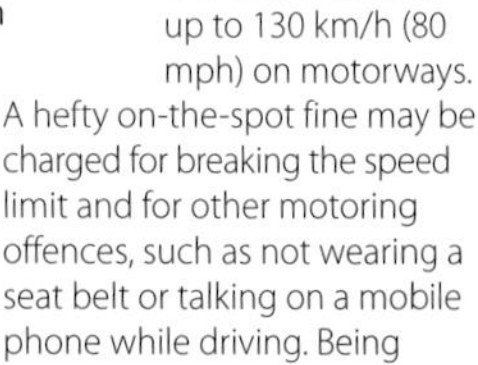

A hefty on-the-spot fine may be charged for breaking the speed limit and for other motoring offences, such as not wearing a seat belt or talking on a mobile phone while driving. Being caught driving under the

A pretty country road next to a rapeseed field

influence of alcohol will incur even stiffer penalties and possibly imprisonment.

Parking

Tickets for parking are obtained from kerbside machines *(billet-automat)*, which accept most coins. In many smaller towns, parking is free and regulated by a parking disk that has an hour hand, which is available from all garages. Different zones are marked with a blue sign with the letter "P". Also on the sign is the time limit for parking; signs marked as *1 time* mean you can stay for an hour; *2 timer* is two hours and so on. When parking within these time zones, set the hour hand on your parking disk to indicate the time when you arrived and leave it on the dashboard, so that the wardens can check whether the limit has been exceeded. In larger towns, parking is often free 6pm–8am on weekdays, after 2pm on Saturday and all day Sunday.

The Danish for "no parking" is *parkering forbudt*. For more information about parking in towns see p303.

Petrol

There is no shortage of petrol stations in Denmark, and most international brands are represented. Pumps are generally self-service, with daily opening hours from 6 or 7am to midnight. At 24-hour petrol stations, payment facilities are automated using Dkr notes, though you are unlikely to find instructions in English. Petrol is expensive, with prices slightly higher than in Britain or Germany. Autogas (LPG) is not widely used and is available only at a few selected petrol stations.

Breakdown Services

In the event of a breakdown, telephone the emergency number supplied by your car hire company or breakdown organization. Phones on motorways are placed at 2-km (1-mile) intervals. For other emergencies, dial 112 and ask for the relevant service. The main breakdown companies in Denmark are **Falck Autohjælp** and **Dansk Autohjælp**.

Car Hire

Representatives of most major car hire firms can be found at airports, upmarket hotels and in city centres.

One of the roads on the scenic Marguerite Route

DIRECTORY

What You Need

FDM
Firskovvej 32, 2800 Lyngby.
Tel 45 27 07 07.
W **fdm.dk**

Roads and Tolls

Øresund Bridge
Tel 70 23 90 60.
W **oresundbron.com**

Store Bælt Bridge
Tel 70 15 10 15.
W **storebaelt.dk**

Breakdown Services

Dansk Autohjælp
Tel 70 10 80 90.
W **dah.dk**

Falck Autohjælp
Tel 70 10 20 30.
W **falck.dk**

Car Hire

Avis
Tel 33 26 80 00.
W **avis.dk**

Europcar
Tel 89 33 11 33.
W **europcar.dk**

Hertz
Tel 33 17 90 00.
W **hertzdk.dk**

Car hire tends to be expensive in Denmark; booking beforehand through an international firm can work out much cheaper. Three of the major firms in Denmark are **Avis**, **Europcar** and **Hertz**.

Great Drives

The Marguerite or Daisy Route (*Margueritruten* in Danish) is a scenic motoring route indicated by a sign showing a daisy on a brown background. It was started in 1991 and named after Queen Margrethe II and Denmark's national flower. The route passes through more than 100 major attractions, including the castles of Egeskov and Kronborg, providing a pleasant alternative to travelling on the main highways.

Getting Around Danish Towns

Most Danish towns and cities can be easily explored on foot or by bicycle. Cycling is popular, and motorists treat cyclists as they would any other legitimate road user. Public transport in most cities is efficient, safe and reasonably priced. Taxis are another good way to get around, and they are especially convenient for anyone who is carrying heavy luggage or large amounts of shopping.

City bus – tickets can be bought on board or in advance

Green Travel

It is possible to travel around Denmark without leaving a massive carbon footprint thanks to the country's great train network and many ferry connections. Electric buses and cars are not as common as in neighbouring Sweden, but they are becoming more popular. The country's first electric taxis operate in Odense, and at least one taxi firm in Copenhagen is working towards making the move by 2020. In Copenhagen, some bus routes, including the sightseeing bus CityCirkel, use electric vehicles.

Cycling is widespread and it has been estimated that Danes cycle, on average, more than 600 km (373 miles) a year. Danish cities make many allowances for cyclists, including cycle paths and favourable laws regarding right of way.

Some small islands are virtually car-free, while some others offer the possibility of hiring a horse-drawn gypsy wagon for an especially green vacation.

Public Transport

Most cities in Denmark have well-run, modern public transport networks, so there is little need for a car. There are also well-maintained bus routes on all Danish islands, even the small ones. Here, bus timetables usually run in conjunction with ferry schedules, and a bus is likely to be waiting at the port as you disembark from the ferry.

Central bus stations in towns and cities are usually situated next to the main train station or by the ferry terminal. Maps and timetables that list the major bus and rail routes, as well as the most important sights, are available from tourist offices.

More information on public transport in Copenhagen can be found on pages 304–305.

Tickets

Multi-ticket clip cards *(klippekort)*, valid on buses and local trains, are readily available in the major cities, such as Copenhagen, Aarhus and Odense. Travel passes bought in Copenhagen are also valid in other towns in the Greater Copenhagen (HT) region, including Roskilde, Helsingør and Hillerød. The Aarhus Pass and Odense City Pass allow unlimited travel on public transport and include discounted or free admission to some city attractions. Reduced-fare travel cards for children up to the age of 16 are also available.

In smaller towns, it is also possible to buy single tickets directly from the driver upon boarding. This is the best option if you are unlikely to be making multiple journeys. On the island of Mors, in the Limfjord, travelling on local buses is free of charge.

Walking

All of Denmark's towns and cities are compact, and most have pedestrianized areas. In addition, many sights tend to be closely grouped together, making getting around on foot a pleasant experience.

Nevertheless, pedestrians should observe the traffic regulations. Take care when crossing the road, although Danish drivers are very attentive towards pedestrians and would never enter a crossing when there are people on it. However, pedestrians who step on to the cycle lanes that run along beside the pavements are strongly frowned upon, especially during rush hour.

Walking tours provide a fun, alternative way to explore the major towns and cities in Denmark. Local tourist offices *(see pp288–9)* will be able to provide details of tours that are available in the area, as well as maps for those who wish to explore the city on foot without a guide.

Pedestrianized street in Aalborg

Visitors enjoying a walking tour

Taxis

Taxis in Danish cities are plentiful, but they can be rather expensive. Taxi ranks can be found in front of all railway stations, airports and ferry terminals, as well as in town centres and major shopping centres. Cabs with a lit sign saying *fri* can be flagged down in the street. Taxis can also be booked on the phone. Fares start around 40–50 Dkr and then increase by the kilometre. A higher rate is levied at night and when booked by phone. Most taxis in Denmark accept credit cards, and there is no need to tip the driver.

Sign for a taxi rank

Driving

Avoid driving in the larger towns if at all possible. As per its environmental policy, the Danish government does its best to discourage people from using their car. Most cities have designated car-free centres, and parking and fuel are very expensive, as is the cost of hiring a car. Cyclists and pedestrians take precedence on city roads, and when turning right, car drivers are obliged to give way to cyclists coming up on the inside and, even if there is a green light, to pedestrians crossing the road.

Parking

A fee is charged for on-street parking in Denmark's city centres between 8am and 6pm Monday to Friday and between 8am and 2pm on Saturday. It can be difficult to find a parking space at any time of day, especially in the centre of towns and cities. It can also be expensive to park a car. Some Danish cities have parking zones, with zones closest to the centre costing the most. High fines are charged for failing to pay parking fees or exceeding the time limit. See page 301 for more on parking in Denmark.

Cycling

Cycling is another popular and practical way to get around: bikes can be hired from hotels or special bike-hire places. In Aarhus, you can use free bikes supplied by the city and available at designated areas in the city centre *(see p305)*. Bicycle lanes exist all over the country, in rural areas as well as in big towns, and you can obtain a map of scenic routes from tourist offices. Many Danes spend their holidays touring an island such as Samsø or Bornholm by bike.

Bikes and accessories such as helmets, child seats and even attachable trailers for transporting kids and heavy bags can be hired in many towns and cities from companies such as **Baisikeli**, **Bikes4rent.dk** and **CSV Cykeludlejning**.

Cycling is a fun way to get around, but a number of factors should be taken into account. Never leave a bike unlocked; expensive bikes, in particular, are highly desirable to thieves. In larger towns, attach the bicycle to a cycle rack. When using cycle lanes, cyclists must observe general traffic regulations, such as not jumping red lights. Buses often stop in areas allocated for cyclists, so beware of people getting off the bus. Bicycles must be equipped with lights after dark and have reflectors fitted at the back and front. Cyclists stopped under the influence of alcohol may not only incur a hefty fine but also lose their driver's licence. Everybody, especially children, should wear safety helmets.

Outside of peak hours, bicycles can be taken onto trains (excluding ICE trains) upon purchase of a special bicycle ticket. This is required on all trains, excluding Copenhagen's S-tog, but the cost is minimal.

Cycling is a popular form of transport in Danish towns

DIRECTORY

Taxis

Aarhus Taxa
Aarhus. **Tel** 89 48 48 48.

Dantaxi
Nationwide. **Tel** 70 25 25 25.

Taxa Fyn
Funen (incl. Odense).
Tel 66 15 44 15.

Cycling

Baisikeli Bike Rental
Copenhagen.
W **cph-bike-rental.dk**

Bikes4rent.dk
Aarhus. **Tel** 20 26 10 20.
W **bikes4rent.dk**

CSV Cykeludlejning
Odense.
Tel 29 29 25 89 (May–Sep); 66 12 12 58 (Oct–Apr).
W **odensecykler.dk**
W **cityhotelodense.dk**

Getting Around Copenhagen

Copenhagen has an excellent round-the-clock public transport system, and you can use the same *klippekort* (clip cards) and travel passes on the buses, metro, S-tog and regional trains. Walking and cycling are also pleasant options. Copenhagen is one of the safest cities in Europe, and there should be no problem travelling alone, even at night.

The platform of a metro station in Copenhagen

Buses

Copenhagen's efficient bus network, run by **Movia**, shares its fare structure with the city's various train networks. Bus stops are marked by a yellow sign with the word "BUS" and display the relevant bus's timetable.

Insert your clip card into the yellow time clock next to the driver. If you don't have a clip card, you can pay the driver with cash; change is given, but be aware that large notes will not be appreciated. The next stop is displayed on a digital screen towards the front of the bus, and disembarking is via the central or back doors.

Buses, like trains, start running at about 5am (6am on Sunday). Less frequent night buses (marked by the prefix "N") operate on special routes.

Metro

Copenhagen's modern underground rail network, the **Metro**, has two lines, one of which links the airport to the city centre. The metro system, which complements the S-tog rail network, stops at Frederiksberg, Forum, Nørreport, Kongens Nytorv and Christianshavn in the city centre. A circle line (due by 2018) will stop at Nørrebro, Østerbro, Vesterbro and the Central Station. Metro stations are marked with the red letter "M" and can be spotted by the 5-m- (16-ft-) high illuminated information posts outside.

Metro trains are fully automated and consist of single driverless carriages that are sleek, bright and rarely feel crowded. The doors open automatically in line with the platform doors, making it impossible for anyone to fall on to the track. Call points by each of the carriage doors can be used in an emergency or by people with mobility issues. Travel cards must be punched into the yellow time clocks on the platform before boarding.

S-Tog

Copenhagen's rail system is known as **S-tog** and is run by the DSB state railway. This fast and convenient service consists of 10 lines that all pass through Central Station and run to the outskirts of the city. The DSB website *(see p299)* has a journey planner that allows you to find the best route around Copenhagen.

All S-tog trains have bright carriages with plenty of space for passengers with bicycles, prams and wheelchairs (outside of peak times). Screens in the carriages show traffic information and news in Danish, and there is also free broadband connectivity.

Tickets can be bought at the station. Travel cards must be punched into one of the yellow time clocks on the platform by inserting it with the magnetic strip facing downwards.

All trains are marked with a red hexagon bearing a white letter "S". Those marked with an "X" are express trains with limited stops. Most of the system has been adapted for disabled passengers, and there are lifts from street level to the platforms.

Trains operate from about 5am until around 1am during the week and on Sundays, and throughout the night on Fridays and Saturdays.

Cyclists boarding a train at Copenhagen's Central Station

Regional Trains

The Greater Copenhagen (HT) transport region stretches as far north as Helsingør and Hornbæk and as far east as Roskilde and Lejre. Many outlying attractions – including the Louisiana art galleries in Humlebæk – can be visited on a day trip using regional trains and a Copenhagen area *klippekort*.

Tickets

Public transport tickets in Copenhagen are valid on trains, buses and the metro, and it is possible to transfer from one mode of transport to another on the same ticket. Tickets are available from ticket offices, vending machines at stations and bus drivers.

The metropolitan area is split into seven zones. The cheapest ticket *(billet)* allows you to travel within two zones. A *klippekort* is valid for 10 trips within two zones; for travel between three or more zones, you will need to buy the correct ticket or clip the appropriate number of *klippekort* tickets. Clipping stamps your travel card with the date, time and the zone from which you are departing. Cards stamped for journeys within the same zone or between two or three zones are valid for 1 hour. Four-, five- and six-zone tickets are valid for 90 minutes, and tickets and stamped 10-trip cards for all zones are valid for 2 hours. Fares on night buses are the same. Travelling without a valid ticket carries a high penalty.

Special tickets that allow for unlimited travel over a 24-hour period are available. Tourist passes like the Copenhagen Card (for dealers, visit the Copenhagen Visitor Centre website, *see p289)* allow unrestricted travel on public transport, as well as reduced entry to many attractions.

Two children up to the age of 12 travel free when accompanied by an adult with the correct ticket. Four children up to the age of 12 can travel on one ticket, or one clip of an adult *klippekort*. Children under 16 pay a child's fare when travelling alone.

Driving

Much of Copenhagen's city centre is car-free, and parking spaces are in high demand and expensive. Driving in central Copenhagen is there fore not recommended.

Taxis

Taxis operate all over the city at all times. To hail a cab in the street, simply wave to any that displays a lit *fri* sign. There are taxi ranks outside the Central Station, Nørreport Station and Kongens Nytorv.

Walking

Copenhagen is the perfect city for walking around. Green spaces and parks provide plenty of places to take a break. The tourist office *(see p289)* runs themed walking tours on subjects such as history, food and design. The more energetic visitor can join a **Running Copenhagen** tour.

Cycling

Copenhagen is one of the most cycle-friendly cities in the world, with cycle lanes over much of it, and cycle- and footbridges crossing the canals. Nørrebrogade is open to bicycles, pedestrians and buses only.

A hire scheme of intelligent City Bikes has been launched in Copenhagen and Frederiksberg. The bikes are available 24/7, 365 days a year. Each city bike has a handlebar-mounted touchscreen tablet used for navigation, payment and to guide users to points of interest. The first time you use the city bike, you enter your credit card information and unlock the bike on the touchscreen. The rental charge is 25 Dkr per hour. The bikes can be returned to any station in the system.

Cycling is a great way to see the city, and bikes can be taken free of charge on the S-tog. Guided tours, like **Bike Copenhagen With Mike**, are also available.

Take care when cycling in the city and obey the rules of the road at all times. Cycle lanes can be quite aggressive, especially at peak times.

DIRECTORY

Buses

Movia
Tel 36 13 14 00.
W moviatrafik.dk

Metro and S-Tog

Metro
Tel 70 15 16 15.
W m.dk

S-tog / Regional Trains
Tel 70 13 14 15.
W dsb.dk

Walking

Running Copenhagen
Tel 20 58 58 77.
W running-copenhagen.dk

Cycling

Bike Copenhagen With Mike
Tel 26 39 56 88.
W newsite.bikecopenhagen withmike.dk

Waterbuses

DFDS Canal Tours
Tel 32 96 30 00.
W canaltours.dk

Waterbuses

A trip on a waterbus is a good way to see Copenhagen, as the city's canals lead past many of the major sights. The trips run by **DFDS Canal Tours** are accompanied by a guide and are particularly appealing to people with children. The yellow harbour buses 991, 992 and 993, operated by Movia and subject to the same fare system as buses and trains, are a cheaper alternative.

Departure point for a waterbus on a canal in Copenhagen

General Index

Page numbers in **bold** refer to main entries. The Danish letters å (aa), æ and ø fall at the end of the alphabet.

H

M

N

O

P

Acknowledgments

Hachette Livre Polska would like to thank the following people whose contribution and assistance have made the preparation of the book possible:

Additional Text Sue Dobson, Roger Norum, Marek Pernal, Jakub Sito, Barbara Sudnik-Wójcikowska, Jennifer Wattam Klit.

Additional Illustrations Dorota Jarymowicz, Paweł Pasternak.

Additional Photographs Oldrich Karasek, Ian O'Leary, Roger Norum, Laura Pilgaard Rasmussen, Jakub Sito, Jon Spaul, Barbara Sudnik-Wójcikowska, Monika Witkowska, Andrzej Zygmuntowicz and Ireneusz Winnicki, Juliusz Żebrowski.

Dorling Kindersley would like to thank the following people whose contribution and assistance have made the preparation of the book possible:

Publisher Douglas Amrine.

Publishing Managers Anna Streiffert, Vicki Ingle.

Managing Art Director Kate Poole.

Senior Editor Kathryn Lane.

Editorial Assistance Sam Fletcher, Anna Freiberger.

Additional Picture Research Rachel Barber, Ellen Root.

Cartography Vinod Harish, Vincent Kurien, Azeem Siddiqui, Casper Morris.

DTP Designers Uma Bhattacharya, Mohammad Hassan, Jasneet Kaur, Alistair Richardson.

Factcheckers Britt Lightbody, Katrine Anker Møller.

Proofreader Stewart J. Wild.

Indexer Helen Peters.

Jacket Design Tessa Bindloss.

Revisions Team

Marta Bescos, Lokesh Bisht, Imogen Corke, Mariana Evmolpidou, Elisabeth Fogh, Jane Graham, Claire Jones, Laura Jones, Sumita Khatwani, Priya Kukadia, Jude Ledger, Delphine Lawrance, Carly Madden, Hayley Maher, Alison McGill, Vikki Nousiainen, Scarlett O'Hara, Catherine Palmi, Laura Pilgaard Rasmussen, Pollyanna Poulter, Lucy Richards, Ellen Root, Simon Ryder, Susie Peachey, Lokamata Sahoo, Sands Publishing Solutions, Susana Smith, Kathleen Sauret, Stuti Tiwari, Dora Whitaker, Conrad van Dyk.

Special Assistance and Permissions

The Publishers also wish to thank all persons and institutions for their permission to reproduce photographs of their property, for allowing us to photograph inside the buildings and to use photographs from their archives:

Amager Youth Hostel; Amalienborg, Copenhagen (S. Haslund-Christensen, Lord Chamberlain and Colonel Jens Greve, Palace Steward); Amber Museum, Copenhagen; Aquarium, Charlottenlund; Arbejdermuseet, Copenhagen (Peter Ludvigsen); Bornholm Tourist Information Centre (Pernille Larsen); Carlsberg Brewery; Ceramics Museum, Rønne; Christiansborg, Copenhagen; Copenhagen Airports A/S (Bente Schmidt – Event- and visitor department); Copenhagen Town Hall (Allan Johansen); Corbis (Łukasz Wyrzykowski); Danish Tourist Board Photo Database (Christian Moritz – Area Sales Manager); Dansk Moebelkunst (Dorte Slot) (Bredgade 32, Copenhagen K) www.dmk.dk; Davids Samling, Copenhagen; Danish Chamber of Tourism & SAS Group PR (Agnieszka Blandzi, Director); Egeskov Castle; Experimentarium, Copenhagen; H. Ch. Andersen Museum, Odense; Holmegaard Glass Factory; Jagna Noren – a guide to Bornholm; Jesper T. Møller and other employees of the National Museum in Copenhagen; Karen Blixen Museum; Knud Rasmussens Haus; Kronborg castle; Legoland, Billund; Lene Henrichsen – assistant to the director of the Louisiana museum; Louisiana – Museum for Modern Kunst (Susanne Hartz); The Museum of Holbæk and Environs, Holbæk; Det Nationalhistoriske Museum på Frederiksborg, Hillerød; Nationalmuseet, Copenhagen (Heidi Lykke Petersen); The Nobel Foundation (Annika Ekdahl); Ny Carlsberg Glyptotek in Copenhagen (Jan Stubbe Østergaard); Palaces and Properties Agency, Denmark (Peder Lind Pedersen); Pritzker Prize (Keith Walker) for making available the photographs of the interiors of Jørn Utzon's house; Ribe VikingeCenter (Bjarne Clement – manager); Rosenborg Castle – The Royal Danish Collection (Peter Kristiansen – curator); Roskilde Cathedral; The Royal Library, Copenhagen (Karsten Bundgaard – photographer); Royal Porcelain Factory, Copenhagen; Skagens Museum (Mette Bøgh Jensen – curator); Scandinavian Airlines SAS (Wanda Brociek i Małgorzata Grążka); Statens Historiska Museum, Stockholm; Statens Museum for Kunst: (Eva Maria Gertung & Marianne Saederup); Stine Møller Jensen (Press coordinator, Copenhagen Metro); Bo Streiffert; Tivoli, Copenhagen – Stine Lolk; Tobaksmuseet, Copenhagen (W.Ø. Larsens); Tycho Brahe Planetarium, Copenhagen; Tønder Tourist Office (Lis Langelund-Larsen – tourist officer); Voergård Slot; Aalborg Symfoniorkester (Jan Bo Rasmussen); Østerlars Kirke, Bornholm (Ernst A Grunwald).

Picture Credits

Key: a-above; b-below/bottom; c-centre; f-far; l-left; r-right; t-top.

Aalborg Opera: 35cra. **Aarhus Kommune:** 298cr. **Agency for Palaces and Cultural Properties:** 131tl. **Alamy Images:** Arcaid Images 186; The Art Archive 168-9; Linn Arvidsson 120; blickwinkel 15bc; Bernie Epstein 80cb; imageBROKER 11br, 19, 94, 156, 242-3; Ionotec/Thierry Lauzun 222bl; John Peter Photography 116-7; OJPHOTOS 161tl, 228-9 ; Robert Harding World Imagery 239br; Niels Poulsen DK 140-1; Niels Quist 14br, 33br; Pep Roig 258cl; Frantisek Staud 241t; vario images GmbH & Co.KG/Stephan Gabriel 259tl; Vikslove 177b; Ken Welsh 258c; Westend61 GmbH 216-7. **Artothek:**209bl. **AWL Images:** Walter Bibikow 152-3; Hemis 54, 84, 176, 204.

Bandholm Hotel: 251br. **Bang & Olufsen Products**: 28cla. **The Bridgeman Art Library**: Bonhams, London, UK/Private Collection *Street Scene* (oil on canvas), Danish School, (19th century) 8-9; Nordiska Museet, Stockholm *Bella and Hanna Nathansson* (1783–1853) Christoffer-Wilhelm Eckersberg 46tr; Skagens Museum, Denmark 13tc; Thorvaldsens Museum, Copenhagen *Shepherd Boy* (1817) Bertel Thorvaldsen 46bl. **Bunken Strand Camping:** 253tr.

CinemaxX Danmark: 107br. **Cisternerne:** 97crb. **Copenhagen Aiports:** Arne V. Petersen 296bl. **Corbis:** © Archivo Iconografico, S. A. 42–3c, 45br; © Bettmann 41bl, 42tr, 47bc, 48crb, 125crb; Francis Dean 291bl, 294tr; © Werner Forman 38cla, 38bl, 40bl; © Hulton–Deutsch Collection 49tl; Robbie Jack 130br; Wolfgang Kaehler 240tl, 240br; © Douglas Kirkland 125bl; © Bob Krist 12tr, 139br, 209cla, 209cr; © Stefan Lindblom 32cla, 49br; © Massimo Listri 31b, © Wally McNamee 49c; © Adam Woolfitt 58br. **CPH Living**: 249tr.

Danhostel Copenhagen City: 247tl. **DanishEVPhotos:** Rasmus 290cla. **Dansk Moebelkunst:** 28clb, 29cla. **Niels Jakob Darger:** 93bl. **Davids Samling:** 62c. **Den Rode Tomat:** 268tr. **Dragsholm Slot:** 245br, 250tr. **Dreamstime.com:** Arnphoto 10cra; Dbjohnston 15tr; Evolove 23t; Fabian Fischer 157b; Gittenielsen13 233b; Isselee 232; Jorisvo 19b; Åsa Larsson 14tr; Laser143 130tr; Christian Mueringer 220; Ohmaymay 12bl; Derek Rogers 11tr; Rolf52 13b; Roza 68; Tupungato 292cl.

Europa1989 Kantiner: 263tr. **Experimentarium City:** 98cr.

FLPA: Imagebroker/NielsDK 50-1; Minden Pictures/Tui De Roy 286-7; Roger Wilmshurst 202-3.**Fredensborg:** 133tr, 135cra. **Frederiksborg:** Ole Haupt 40tl; Lennart Larsen,42cla, 44tl; Hans Petersen 43tc, 44crb, 45tl, 45crb. **Fru Larsen:** 273br. **Færgen:** 299tl.

Tommy H. Galskepr: 150br. **Generators Hostels:** 248bc. **Getty Images:** AFP/Stringer 290clb; Chris Jackson 291tl. **Gjaargardur Guesthouse:** 255br. **La Glace:** 262bc.

Dave Hanlon: 197tr. **Henne Kirkeby Kro http:// hennekirkebykro.dk:** 271tr

Kadeau/Marie Louise Munkegaard: 257tl, 264tr. **Kaffehuset Moen:** 256br, 269br. **Oldrich Karasek:** 52cla, 52bl, 53br, 61br, 234cl, 237tc.

Lalandia A/S: 166br. ©2012 **The LEGO Group:** LEGO, the LEGO logo, the Brick and Knob configurations, the Minifigure and LEGOLAND are trademarks of the LEGO Group. 196cla, 197 all. **Louisiana – Museum for Moderne Kunst:** 127tc; *Dead Drunk Danes* (1960) Asger Jorn © DACS, London 2011 30br; *Big Thumb* (1968) Cesar Baldaccini © ADAGP, Paris and DACS, London 2011 126tr; Poul Buchard/Brøndum & Co 126bl, Poul Buchard/ Strüwing 127bl; *Breakfast on the Grass* (1961) Pablo Picasso © Succession Picasso/DACS, London 2011 126ca; *Venus de Meudon* (1956) Jean Arp © DACS, London 2011 126clb; *Marilyn Monroe* (1967) Andy Warhol © Licensed by the Andy Warhol Foundation for the Visual Arts, Inc/ARS, New York and DACS, London 2011 127cra; Henry Moore, *Two Piece Reclining Figure No.5* (1963–4) © by kind permission of the Henry Moore Foundation 127clb.

Metro Kundeservice: 304cla. **MEPL:** 38clb, 40crb, 41tl, 41crb, 42bl, 47tl, 48tl, 48bcl, 48bcr, 243c. **Munthe plus Simonsen:** 103tr.

Nationalmuseet: 37bl, 88 all, 89cla. **Naturepl.com:** Michael Hutchinson 25tr. **Nikolaj, Copenhagen Contemporary Art Centre:** 74tl. **Nimb Hotel and Restaurant:** 81bl. **Nordisk Spisehus/Kähler Design:** 270bc.

Orangeriet Kongens Have: 256cl. **B. V. Petersen;** 24cb, 24bcl, 24bcr, 24bl, 25clb, 25crb, 25bcr, 25bl, 25br. **Photoshot:** TTL/ Stuart Black 2-3. **POLFOTO:** Hansen Claus 171br.

Relae/Per Anders Jörgensen: 266bc. **Restaurant Era Ora:** 266cl. **Restaurant Frederiks Have ApS:** 265br. **Restaurant Hafnia:** 277br. **Restaurant Icefiord:** 276tr. **Restaurant Snekken:** 267tr. **Ribe Vikinge Center:** 32br. **Røgeriet i Svaneke:** 275tr. **Rosenborg Castle:** 64bc, 65cra, 65br. **Royal Library:** (Karsten Bundgaard) 125br

Safari Park: Finn Brasen164 all, 165cra, 165crb, 165bc. **Sangiovanni La Catina:** 272tr. **Scandlines:** 299bl. **Shutterstock:** 303br. **Jakub Sito:** 26tr, 27tc, 27ca, 31tr, 31cl.**Skagens Museum** P. S. Krøyer, Michael Ancher (1886) phot. Esben Thorning 209br. **Skuespilhuset- Royal Danish Playhouse:**JensMarkus Lindhe 75bl. **Stammershalle Badehotel:** 254tr, 274bc. **Anna and Janusz Starościk:** 5t. **Statens Museum for Kunst (Copenhagen):** SMK Foto 30tr, 30cla, 36, 46cl, 46br, 46–7c, 66cla, 66clb, 67tc, 67cra; *Portrait of Mrs Matisse* (1905) Henry Matisse © Succession H Matisse/DACS, London 2011 66bl; *Last supper* (1909) Emil Nolde 66cal. **Barbara Sudnik-Wójcikowska:** 24clb, 25bcl.

TeliaSonera: 295tc. **Tivoli:** Henrik Stenberg 80cl, 81tl. **Tønder Tourist Office:** 34cra.

Jørn Utzon: 28–9c.

Villa Provence: 252bc. **VisitDenmark:** 35bl, 45c, 63br, 72c, 87cr, 165tl; Aalborg Tourist- og Kongressbureau 215ca; Bent Næsly 33cla, 121b, 209cl; Bob Krist 280cl; Cees van Roeden 150cra,178br, 187b, 214bl, 283cr; Ditte Isager 288cr; Dorte Krogh 279b; Jan Kofoed Winther 100b; Jette Jørs 106cr; John Sommer 42clb, 62clb, 205b, 284c; Jørgen Schytte 260tr, 301tl; Juliusz Żebrowski 238cl, 238bl, 239tr; Kim Wyon 289bl; Lars-Kristian Crone 304cr; Strüwing 29br; Thomas Nykrog 301bl; ukendt 1, 281tl; VisitAalborg/Michael Damsgaard 297tl, 302br, 303tl.

Monika Witkowska: 82cb, 82bl, 83tl, 83clb, 234bl, 235tr, 235br, 236tl, 236b, 237br.

Front Endpaper: Alamy Images: Arcaid Images Ltl; Linn Arvidsson Rtc; imageBROKER Rtc; **AWL Images:** Hemis Ltc, Lbc; Rcra; **Dreamstime.com:** Isselee Lbl; Christian Mueringer Rcrb.

Jacket

Front and spine top - **Corbis:** Marco Cristofori

All other images Dorling Kindersley.
For further information see www.dkimages.com

Phrasebook

In an Emergency

Can you call an ambulance?	**Kan du tilkalde en ambulance?**	*kann do till-kalleh ehn ahm-boo-lang-seh?*
Can you call the police?	**Kan du tilkalde politiet?**	*kann do till-kalleh po-ly-tee'd?*
Can you call the fire brigade?	**Kan du tilkalde brand-væsenet?**	*kann do till-kalleh brahn-vaiys-ned?*
Is there a telephone here?	**Er der en telefon i nærheden?**	*e-ah dah ehn tele--fohn ee neya-hethen?*
Where is the nearest hospital?	**Hvor er det nærmeste hospital?**	*voa e-ah deh neh-meste hoh-spee-tahl*

Useful Phrases

Sorry	**Undskyld**	*ons-gull*
Goodnight	**Godnat**	*goh-nad*
Goodbye	**Farvel**	*fah-vell*
Good evening	**Godaften**	*goh-ahf-tehn*
Good morning	**Godmorgen**	*goh-moh'n*
Good morning (after about 9am)	**Goddag**	*goh-dah*
Yes	**Ja**	*yah*
No	**Nej**	*nye*
Please	**Værsgo/ Velbekomme**	*vehs-goh/ vell-beh-commeh*
Thank you	**Tak**	*tahgg*
How are you?	**Hvordan har du det?/ Hvordan går det?**	*voh-dann hah do deh?/voh-dan go deh?*
Pleased to have met you	**Det var rart at møde dig**	*deh vah rahd add meutheh die*
See you!	**Vi ses!**	*vee sehs!*
I understand	**Jeg forstår**	*yay fuh-stoah*
I don't understand	**Jeg forstår ikke**	*yay fuh-stoah egge*
Does anyone speak English?	**Er der nogen, der kan tale engelsk?**	*e-ah dah noh-enn dah kann tah-leh eng-ellsgg?*
on the left	**til venstre**	*till vehn-streh*
on the right	**til højre**	*till hoy-reh*
open	**åben**	*oh-ben*
closed	**lukket**	*luh-geth*
warm	**varm**	*vahm*
cold	**kold**	*koll*
big	**stor**	*stoah*
little	**lille**	*lee-leh*

Making a Telephone Call

I would like to call...	**Jeg vil gerne ringe til...**	*yay vill geh-neh ring-eh till...*
I will telephone again	**Jeg ringer en gang til**	*yay ring-ah ehn gahng till*

In a Hotel

Do you have double rooms?	**Findes her dobbelt-værelser?**	*feh-ness he-ah dob-belld vah-hel-sah?*
With bathroom	**Med bade-værelse**	*meth bah-the-vah-hel-sah*
With washbasin	**Med hånd-vask**	*meth hohn-vasgg*
key	**nøgle**	*noy-leh*
I have a reservation	**Jeg har en reservation**	*yay hah ehn res-sah-vah-shohn*

Sightseeing

cathedral	**domkirke**	*dom-kia-keh*
church	**kirke**	*kia-keh*
museum	**museum**	*muh-seh-uhm*
railway station	**banegård**	*bah-neh-goh*
airport	**lufthavn**	*luhft-havn*
train	**tog**	*toh*
ferry terminal	**færgehavn**	*fah-veh-havn*
a public toilet	**et offentligt toilet**	*ehd off-end-ligd toa-led*

Shopping

I wish to buy...	**Jeg vil gerne købe...**	*yay vill geh-neh kyh-beh...*
Do you have...?	**Findes der...?**	*feh-ness de-ah...?*
How much does it cost?	**Hvad koster det?**	*vath koh-stah deh*
expensive	**dyr**	*dyh-ah*
cheap	**billig**	*billy*
size	**størrelse**	*stoh-ell-seh*
general store	**købmand**	*keuhb-mann*
greengrocer	**grønthandler**	*grund-handla*
supermarket	**supermarked**	*suh-pah-mah-keth*
market	**marked**	*mah-keth*

Eating Out

Do you have a table for... people?	**Har I et bord til... personer?**	*hah ee ed boah till... peh-soh-nah?*
I wish to order...	**Jeg vil gerne bestille...**	*yay vill geh-neh beh-stilleh...*
I'm a vegetarian	**Jeg er vegetar**	*yay eh-ah veh-gehta*
children's menu	**børnemenu**	*byeh-neh-meh-nye*
starter	**forret**	*foh-red*
main course	**hovedret**	*hoh-veth-red*
dessert	**dessert**	*deh-seh'd*
wine list	**vinkort**	*veen-cod*
May I have the bill?	**Må jeg bede om regningen?**	*moh yay beh-theh uhm rahy-ning-ehn*

Menu Decoder

brød	**bread**	*bruth*
danskvand	**mineral water**	*dansg vann*
fisk	**fish**	*fesgg*
fløde	**cream**	*flu-theh*
grøntsager	**vegetables**	*grunn-saha*
is	**ice cream**	*ees*
kaffe	**coffee**	*kah-feh*
kartofler	**potatoes**	*kah-toff-lah*
kød	**meat**	*kuth*
kylling	**chicken**	*killing*
laks	**salmon**	*lahggs*
lam	**lamb**	*lahm*
leverpostej	**liver paté**	*leh-vah-poh-stie*
mælk	**milk**	*mailgg*
oksekød	**beef**	*ogg-seh-kuth*
ost	**cheese**	*ossd*
pølse	**sausage**	*pill-seh*
rejer	**shrimps**	*rah-yah*
røget fisk	**smoked fish**	*roy-heth fesgg*
saftevand	**squash**	*sah-fteh-vann*
salat	**salad**	*sah-lad*
salt	**salt**	*sald*
sild	**herring**	*sil*
skaldyr	**shellfish**	*sgall-dya*
skinke	**ham**	*sgeng-geh*
smør	**butter**	*smuah*
sodavand	**fizzy drink**	*sodah-vann*
svinekød	**pork**	*svee-neh-kuth*
te	**tea**	*teh*
torsk	**cod**	*tohsgg*
vand	**water**	*vann*
wienerbrød	**Danish pastry**	*vee-nah-bryd*
æg	**egg**	*egg*
øl	**beer**	*uhl*

Numbers

0	**nul**	*noll*
1	**en**	*ehn*
2	**to**	*toh*
3	**tre**	*tray*
4	**fire**	*fee-ah*
5	**fem**	*femm*
6	**seks**	*seggs*
7	**syv**	*siu*
8	**otte**	*oh-deh*
9	**ni**	*nee*
10	**ti**	*tee*
20	**tyve**	*tyh-veh*
30	**tredive**	*traith-veh*
40	**fyrre**	*fyr-reh*
50	**halvtreds**	*hahl-traiths*
60	**tres**	*traiths*
70	**halvfjerds**	*hahl-fyads*
80	**firs**	*fee-ahs*
90	**halvfems**	*hahl-femms*
100	**hundrede**	*hoon-dreh-the*
200	**tohundrede**	*toh-hoon-dreh-the*
1,000	**tusind**	*tooh-sin-deh*
2,000	**totusinde**	*toh-tooh-sin-deh*

Road Map of Denmark
A
B
C
1
2
3
4
5
6
Kristiansand, Stavanger, Bergen, Tórshavn, Seydisfjordur
Larvik, Langesund
Hirtshals
Lønstrup
Hjørring
Løkken
Fårup
Blokhus
Brønderslev
Hanstholm
Brovst
Fjerritslev
Lindholm Høje
Aalborg
Thisted
Løgstør
Limfjorden
Støvring
Rebild Bakker
Nykøbing Mors
Års
Hadsu
Mariager
Nissum Bredning
Hobro
Fyrkat
Skive
Lemvig
Kleitrup Sø
Struer
Hjerl Hedes Frilandsmuseum
Mønsted
Viborg
Randers
North Sea
Nissum Fjord
Holstebro
Kongenshus Mindepark
Gudenå
Tangesø
Ulfborg
Storå
Skive Å
Silkeborg
Herning
Julsø
Ringkøbing
Videbæk
Jutland
Mossø
Skanderborg
Ringkøbing Fjord
Skjern
Omme Å
Brædstrup
Hou
Horsens
Givskud
Grinsted
LEGOLAND®
Jelling
Henne
Billund
Vejle
Juelsmin
Varde
Fredericia
Boge
Esbjerg
Kolding
Harwich
Bramming
Vejen
Middelfart
Nørre Aaby
Fanø
Vissenbjerg
Ribe
Flads
Fanø Bugt
Glamsbjerg
Assens
Gram
Haderslev
Key
Motorway
Motorway under construction
Major road
Other road
International airport
Ferry terminal
Skærbæk
Toftlund
Helnæs
Rømø
Åbenrå
Als
Tønder
Ærøs
Sønderborg
Flensburg
0 kilometres 30
0 miles 30
GERMANY
Schleswig